Crichton, Robert
The Camerons.

THE CAMERONS

a novel by

ROBERT CRICHTON

Alfred A. Knopf   New York   1972

THIS IS A BORZOI BOOK
PUBLISHED BY ALFRED A. KNOPF, INC.

Portions of this book originally appeared in *Playboy* Magazine
and in *The Ladies' Home Journal*.

Library of Congress Cataloging in Publication Data

Crichton, Robert.
  The Camerons.

  I. Title.
PZ4.C92cam   [PS3553.R49]   813'.5'4   72-2249
ISBN 0-394-46582-2

Manufactured in the United States of America

Published November 9, 1972
First and Second Printings before Publication

For KYLE CRICHTON,
who helped inspire this story,
and ROBERT GOTTLIEB,
whose hand helped shape it.

A man must eat, musn't he not?

And a man's children must eat, musn't they didn't?

One   MAGGIE DRUM   1

Two   GILLON CAMERON   117

Three   THE CAMERONS   337

ONE

MAGGIE DRUM

1 SHE WAS AWAKE.

Sound asleep one moment, her eyes wide open the next, staring up into the blackness of the ceiling. She didn't like the night, but she had forced her mind to wake her in the deepest part of it. In control, that was the main thing. It pleased her.

She lay in her nest of quilts and studied the ceiling for any flickerings of light that would mean some coals were still alive in the fireplace across the room.

"Selfish gowk," she said aloud.

She meant to be heard. The fire was dead and the room was dead with còld. Her mother had broken the rule of the house and stirred the fire to steal the last of the good heat before she had gone to bed.

"Never think of the morning."

"What?" her father said from the other room. "What is it?"

"Nothing. Go back to sleep, Faither, it's still the night."

That would have to be gotten rid of when she got back. *Faither.*

She lay in her bed, a little warm ball in the cold black box, and practiced the word. Father. Father. It wasn't an easy word to say, but it was the correct word, and Father it was going to be from now on even though he didn't like it.

"Look," he had said to her the week before, "I am a Scotchman, not a goddamn Englishman. Call me Faither, which is right for a Scottish man." But she hadn't done it.

There was no sound inside the house or outside it. No cock crowing, no clogs clacking down the cobblestones, no stirrings from the town or the mines down below it, the whole world—her world, Pitmungo world—bundled up and muffled in sleep, and she sat up in terror. It could only mean snow. It was never silent in Pitmungo unless the town was buried beneath a blanket of snow.

It wasn't fair, she thought, it wasn't right. It had no right to snow that way in April, not on her day. She felt around for her clogs and couldn't find them, her feet were going to freeze on the stones of the floor. Then she heard the *tump, tump* of pit ponies nudging about in the garden to get out of the wind. The hollow sounds of the hoofs meant the ground was frozen.

And there was wind now, she could hear it whacking at the back windows so it was out of the north, down from the Highlands, unfair, she thought, unfair. Snow all over West Fife, certainly, the Cairngorms buried in it, the passes usually open by now clogged with it. A lot of spring lambkins would be dying today. She'd never be able to walk out to Cowdenbeath now to get the railroad to the north. She would have to hire Mr. Japp to take her in his wagon, a shilling wasted, two if he was a bastard about it. She felt tears start up in her eyes, which wasn't like her. There was no sense in getting up now.

When she woke again the wind had died and shafts of moonlight stretched across the room. By sitting up she could see it through the side window—a frost moon, pale and flat, but with no snow coursing across its face. The ponies had come around to the front of the house and from the ring of their hoofs on the cobblestones she knew there couldn't be much snow on the ground, and she got up. The stones were so cold they made her feet burn.

Fool, she thought, wasting that time, crying in bed at something that hadn't happened. She had an urge to use the chamber pot, but

4

the touch of the ice-cold crockery was too terrible to think about. The fire was crowned with a cone of ash, brittle to the touch.

"Selfish bitch," she said.

"What is it the now?" her father said. She hadn't realized she had said it aloud.

"Nothing, go back to sleep."

"I heard you. Pit-girl talk. I won't have it in this house."

"Yes, Father."

"Faither."

She shoveled the ashes to one side and was startled to see three large chunks suddenly come alive and flare up when the cold air reached them. The fire would be easy, and she felt a twinge of guilt about her mother. It was one good thing you could say about Pitmungo: Pitmungo coal was crammed with carbon and would see you through if you nursed it right. She began to add chunk after chunk to the already burning coals.

"Easy with coal out there, Miss," her father called in. "I can hear you laying them on like you're loading a hutch."

"All done now, Faither."

Calm the man just this day. She laid the rest of the coals on as delicately as if she were decorating a cake. When the heat began to well out of the fireplace she took her father's pit clothes and hung them near the fire. The jacket was frozen and when it thawed it hissed and began to smell of sweat and the mine. That was going to change, too, when she got back. In some houses the work clothes were washed every day; in the Drum house it was a once-a-week affair.

She went out to the washhouse in her bare feet and when she came back through the light snow with the hare and the fish she had hidden there, the flagstones seemed warm. Both frozen overnight, they clumped like stones when she dropped them on the table.

"Now what?"

"A lump of coal. Go back to sleep."

"I told you, go easy on the coal."

"Aye, Faither."

Calm the man.

The hare would take time to thaw, that had been a mistake, and now she would have to dress in her go-away clothes and risk a stain because there wouldn't be time to cook the breakfast and dress after it. She stripped down naked and washed herself with water from the cooking pot, what they didn't know wouldn't hurt them once the water came to a boil, and a cloud of steam wrapped itself around her body, making her feel soft and clean. She put on her undercoat and a little linen sark she had made the week before, and then put on the new tweed traveling suit that the Jew, Mr. Lansburgh, had had made for her in Dunfermline.

"You gave the Jew the siller? You put it in his hand and sent him off with it?" her father had said.

"I did."

"And you seriously expect to ever see it or him again?"

"I do."

"Then you're a good deal more daft than I had taken you for."

She didn't have to see the suit on her to know that she looked well in it—that she looked beautiful in it. When she was dressed she took the jacket off and worked in her linen shirt. For a small girl she had large breasts and the shirt was tight and made the breasts stand out, and she kept the jacket near at hand because she didn't want to embarrass her father if he came into the room. She had only recently become that way and both she and her father weren't quite sure how to act about it.

She skinned the hare swiftly and was thankful the animal had been frozen, because its flesh was firm and the skin was easy to remove. She cut it into ten pieces and put them into the pot with the leeks and tatties and while they were cooking toasted the oatmeal that would lend the nutty body to the broth.

When the hare was done she went to work on the haddock, a golden Findon haddie, the flanks a delicate buttercup yellow. She boiled it first, to bring out the fishness of it, and then covered it with thick cream and put it near the fire until it began going plop, plop in its bed of cream and butter. After that she laid out the oatmeal cakes, the bannock that would be heated to the steaming point just before serving, and the slabs of Dunlop cheese that the thieves at the Pitmungo Miners' Cooperative Store, better known as the Pluck Me, had charged a shilling for, and she put on the tea to boil and went to wake her father.

"With roasted oats. Och, you're going to spoil your daddie." He laughed aloud again. "No one will ever believe me down pit. Bawd bree for breakfast."

"Don't call good hare soup 'bawd bree,'" she said.

"It's what it is; I'll call it that."

It was a thing she liked about him. He didn't enjoy spending money but once it was spent he knew how to enjoy it. Most of the miners on the row wasted their money and never had any left or long ago had lost the nerve to spend and the heart to enjoy.

He watched while she added more browned oats to the soup pot, turning the thin broth thick and bodiful. The room was filled with the smell of roasting nuts.

"All right, then, Maggie, what is all this?"

But she got down two earthenware bowls—they called them pigs in Pitmungo—and filled them with broth. They ate in silence, out of respect for the broth, and on his third bowl she answered him.

"For one thing, it's my birthday."

"Ah, you should have told us; we might have bought you something."

"You never have yet."

"Aye, but you never can tell. A little more bree, please." When the bowl was empty he asked her how old she was going to be.

"Sixteen."

"Oh, that's a fine age for a girl."

"Aye, the age when I no longer need consent."

"Consent for what?"

"To get married."

He showed no surprise. He had put a bannock in his mouth, the butter from it dripping onto his pit jacket, and he kept eating. No one shows surprise in Pitmungo, because surprise might indicate some weakness somewhere.

"No, they're not going to believe it, bawd bree and hot bannocks for breakfast. They think you're a pawky little bitch, you know. Stuck-oop, they think. I try to tell them different."

"Why should you? It's true."

He knew it was true and so he was forced to laugh. They heard the whistle from Lady Jane No. 2 and he got up quickly from the table, habit driving him.

"It's only the wake-up whistle, not the work whistle. Sit down. And shouldn't we wake my mother?"

"If she's not awake by now, God never intended her to wake," her father said. "Give me another bannock."

She knew he would ask in his own time, on his own ground, in the Pitmungo way. She slid the clay baking dish from the ashes of the fireplace and when she took off the lid the cream was still bubbling and the smell of the haddock stung their nostrils.

"Findon?"

She nodded her head.

"All my life I knew I would recognize a Findon haddie when I met one. All my life I have wanted a Findon haddie in my mouth. Now I can die. Where did you get it?" She told him.

"You went all the way down to Cowdenbeath to get me a finnan haddie?"

"For *me*, Daddie. For *me*. This is my wedding breakfast, can you understand that, now?"

He went on with his eating, savoring the morsels of fish, even going so far as to take off his pit jacket in deference to it.

"All right," he finally said. "What is this? Who's the boy?"

"There is no man, but there will be. I'm sixteen."

"Sixteen is a girl, a lass. Sixteen is a bairn."

"No, sixteen is a woman. Sixteen makes her own decisions." His head was down, spooning the fish and cream into his mouth, and he looked up at her. There was light in the front room then. She had forgotten to put on her tweed jacket and both of them became conscious of her at the same time and even beneath his darkness a flush showed.

"And does the boy know yet?" She shook her head. "Where does he live, then?"

"I don't know. All I know is that when I find him he won't come from here."

The lane was getting noisy with the sound of hobnailed boots and wooden clogs on the stones of the row.

"What's the matter with here? I come from here."

"Come to the window," his daughter said. She opened the steamed glass and pointed down at lower Pitmungo, over the roofs of Rotten Row and Wet Row, down to the pits and the coal-black river beyond them.

"Be honest. Is that enough for you if you could live some other way?"

Although the day shift had just begun, the purity of the snow had already been violated and soon the row would be streaming with melting blackness.

"It's my living. It's the way I put salt on the table."

"Yes, but is it enough for a *life*?"

"A man must eat and this is a good way for a man to eat. Miners make money."

He was proud of being a good miner.

"Ah, that's it, you see, Daddie. Miners make money, but then they're trapped where they live because they're *miners*. I'm going to marry a man who can make the money and then get out."

He began getting ready to go. He picked up his piece bucket with his bread and miner's butter and flask of cold tea and put on his cap with the tallow lamp hanging from it.

"Well, you'd better marry a tough one. We Drums are hard."

"Yes, I know."

"Drums are lasters. Drums don't quit."

"I know, I know."

She only needed to look at him, short and dark and strong, his hair still dark and his body powerful, as crude as a chunk of coal, handsome in a rough-hewn way, and crippled by the mine. Not forty and already twenty-nine years in the pit, his back bent, his shoulders sloped, his legs bowed, his face tattooed with blue scars from cuts clotted with coal dust. A collier, a pit jock, destined to die in the mine as surely as any slave or bound miner in the past.

"Tough people."

"I know. That's why I can go and get someone—"

"Better than us, is it? You're too good for us, is it? And just what is the matter with us?"

She crossed the room swiftly and pulled him back to the window. The last of the colliers were going down the row.

"Look at them." She was angry with him.

"What's the matter with them?"

"Dark stubby little people brought into the world to howk coal. I don't want one. Swarty little people born to grub in the ground like moudieworts. Like moles."

"Your people."

"Coal miner written all over their faces. Coal miner branded on their tongues. Can't even speak the language of their Queen. I don't want one."

"They speak the language of their own country!" her father shouted at her. "Better than going around imitating outsiders like some I know."

"Their own country." She made a derisive laugh. "Can't even be understood in the streets of Edinburgh. No, I don't want one of them. I'm going to have a man that can be understood in London."

"Och, isn't *that* grand?" he said, and shut the window. He would have to run now to make it on the last cage down. He began collecting the rest of his mine equipment, but he didn't want to leave this way.

"What's the point of this?" he said. He had calmed down. It was another thing she liked about him; he couldn't bear to be angry or hold a grudge if it could be avoided. He might have put his arm around her if she had been wearing something more than her shirt. "Why are we shouting after you make me a feast like that? So you're going away, then?"

"Yes."

"You won't even say 'aye' no more, will you?"

"Not if I catch myself."

He wanted to go because they docked for being late—an hour's work for every ten minutes late—but he needed to know.

"Meg? Maggie?"

"Yes?"

"What is it, what pushes you that way, Meg?"

"I don't know. I just want something better than this. Is that so bad?"

She had hurt him again. He was proud of his hardships, proud of coming up a man in a mine town, and now his only child was looking down on the experience of his life.

"Look, Daddie, look." She took his hard black hand in both of hers, something she could not remember doing before. "Do you remember when you told me about those fish that must go home, that nothing can stop when they go, home to the one right place to make their young?"

"The eels?"

"No, not the eels. The others."

"The saumont?"

"Aye, the salmon. *Salmon*, Daddie."

"Saumont to me. Always will be saumont to me."

"Anyway." She rubbed the hairs on the back of his hand; they were like bristles on a brush. "That's me, Daddie. I'm like them. It's in me, Daddie. I must go, you see?"

He got up from the table. There were still the little black powder tamps he had made the night before to be packed in his powder box and then he was ready to go.

"What if I didn't give you my permission to go?"

She went across the room and kissed her father on the lips, which surprised both of them.

"You know I'd go anyway."

He was embarrassed then and pulled away from her. It was as much a display of sentiment as the spirit was trained to tolerate in Pitmungo.

"Good luck, then, but you never forget this one thing," her father said. "You may marry outside but never deny your own. In the end it's all you got. Don't *never* forget that, Maggie. Never deny your own."

He went out the door without looking back and began to run. She watched him all the way down the raw, as they call it in Pitmungo, and until he reached Colliers Walk and headed downhill toward the pit. The whole town was gray by then.

She put on her jacket and went to the keeking-glass near the window. The cut of the jacket was excellent and she wasn't displeased with the face looking back at her. It was too brown for her taste, and small, but the chin was firm and her lips were fine, something uncommon in Pitmungo, and her eyes well placed, very dark eyes but bright at the same time, and her hair was thick and glossy. She was well-favored, a simple fact. No one had ever told her so, but she knew. Her mother was in the glass looking at her from her doorway.

"What I don't understand," her mother said, "is who do you think you are?"

There was no way to answer it. She didn't know herself. Some of the half-blind pit ponies were standing out in the row waiting for a boy to come and lead them up onto the moor.

"You know," she said to her mother. "There are pit ponies and race horses in the world and I plan to be a race horse."

One of the Hope children was playing in the row, trying to make a snowman before the snow turned black, and she called him and gave him a ha'penny to run and get Mr. Japp and his wagon.

"What you don't know is that you are what you are," her mother said. "You're a Drum and a Hope, and what I don't understand is why a race horse would want to spoil his bloodline with yours."

She was clever, her mother. Fat and careless, but clever.

"Any woman can get any man she wants if she knows how to go about it," Maggie said. "Look at you."

"Your grandfather was a slave with a metal collar around his neck, don't forget that. I'm sure no one else will let you."

Her mother was smiling at her. Maggie smiled back.

"Yes, your blood and my blood. But not my *husband's* blood. Not my *children's* blood."

She went about putting the last of her things in the Gladstone. She hated it, the Gladstone, the feel of it, the look of it, the smell of it. It smelled of coal dust and the mines. It was the one weakness to her outfitting. If she could sever herself from the bag then she would have cut it all, all ties to the town, but she had lacked the last pound to do it, and now there was a piece of Pitmungo trailing her wherever she was to go. She could hear Mr. Japp shouting at his horse, forcing it up the slippery hill from lower Pitmungo. It was almost time to go.

"And what are they going to do about the school?" her mother asked. "Who are they getting to teach?"

"I don't know."

"You just upped and left the little children without a teacher? Without so much as a word? The great, dedicated teacher."

"Listen, Mother, I gave those children more teaching in two years than they got in five before. They're taught out."

"I suppose you drove them, like you do everything else?"

"Isn't that what you're supposed to do? They *learned* from Miss Drum."

"No wonder they didn't like you."

"It's all right; I didn't like them. I only taught school to get what I wanted, and I got it."

The Gladstone was full and she carried it to the door.

"I saved you some breakfast, anyway," Maggie said. "I saved you the good Crowdie cheese because of your teeth."

"Och, well, that was nice of you."

"I'm sorry we had to snash with one another that way. Will you wish me a little luck along the way?"

"Aye," her mother said, "I do," but neither one was able to move toward the other.

"And where are you going to get this marvelous man?"

"In the north somewhere, the Highlands somewhere, where the people have never been beaten."

"Oh, nonsense, Maggie. All Scotchmen have been beat. Ask your daddie. It's the story of the country," her mother said, but Maggie was shaking her head.

"No, not true. Scotland may have lost but not all Scotsmen."

There was a squeak of brakes on wheels and a sliding of metal and Mr. Japp was at the door.

"Well, good-bye, Mother." Still they couldn't move. "When you see me next, I'll be Mrs. Something-or-Other. Mrs. Highland Something-or-Other."

"I hope you'll speak to us."

"Speak to you? I plan to live with you."

Mr. Japp didn't bother to knock but simply threw the door open, coal-town style.

"Well, who's to Cowdenbeath, the Missus or the Miss?"

"I should think your eyes could tell you," Maggie said. He looked her up and down.

"Oh, aye, aye, I should say so." He had never seen her as a woman before. He pointed at the Gladstone. "Is this it, then?" He lifted the bag and took it to the wagon and came back in. "I had a load of fish but it isn't going to bother *that* bag. Let's go, then. Give us your hand, Meggie."

She wouldn't give him her hand.

"Miss Drum to you."

"Ooh?"

"I'm sixteen today, the age of consent."

"Ooh?"

"I earn my way teaching school and I'll be Miss Drum to you from now on."

"Aye. If that's the way you want it, that's the way it will be."

"It's the way I want it."

They went up the high way, up from Doonietoon across the Sportin Moor into Uppietoon because the Low Road was flooded, and from Uppie onto the High Moor. Before they crossed over the crest she turned to take a look back. The town looked small from where they were, and black. That was it, *black*, a stain on the moors and snow surrounding it, but a place to make money in. She was glad to be gone.

They didn't talk. She had offended him. Coming down from the High Moor she could see the train sitting in Cowdenbeath station, breathing heavily in the early morning frost.

"Well, you have managed to make me miss my train, Mr. Japp."

"Your arse, Miss Drum, will be on that train when it leaves Cowdenbeath station. And as far as that goes, the snow and the extra time makes the cost an extra shilling."

She gave him the look she had for students in her class who came unprepared and gave stupid answers.

"Because God chooses to bring down the snow, I'm supposed to pay for it?"

He whipped the horse on its rump in anger and it trotted the rest of the way to Cowdenbeath. At the station his anger couldn't overcome his curiosity and he asked her what she was doing on the Aberdeen train.

"Going to find a husband."

He nodded his head as if that was a perfectly valid thing for a sixteen-year-old Pitmungo girl to be doing.

"Aye, I see. Well, I'll say this. You'll get one and that's for certain."

"What makes you so certain?"

"You always do get what you want, don't you?"

"Isn't that what we all try to do?"

He thought about it carefully.

"No," Mr. Japp said, finally, "most of us learn to settle."

"Then that is why, Mr. Japp, I'm not like most of us."

She had him carry the Gladstone on board the train and put it away, so that on the long journey north she wouldn't have to be associated with it. It was her last recognizable link to Pitmungo.

2   SHE HAD NO IDEA WHAT THE TOWN SHE NEEDED would look like, only that she would recognize it when she saw it. When the train reached Strathnairn, she brushed the steam from the window and asked the conductor to see that her Gladstone was put off.

"Your ticket reads Inverness, Miss."

"Yes, but I want my bag down, please."

"Aye, Miss, and have a good holiday. It's a lovely town for a stay."

It was all working, the soft tweed suit and the little velvet tam slanted downward on one side of her pile of brown hair—a Highland hat, the tailor had assured her in Dunfermline, classless and timeless, in the classic tradition of some clan and some section of the Highlands that she didn't quite catch. Her shoes were new and unsoiled. There was no snow in Strathnairn.

From the station, which lies back up from the sea, it is possible to see the whole sweep of Strathnairn, the longest, as they never tire telling you, town or city in Scotland. Because of the abrupt rise of the hills behind it, the entire town hugs the narrow strip of land between the hills and the water of Moray Firth which it faces; for all the length of the town, there is only one street and everything faces or backs on it.

"Which one is it to be, Miss?"

A porter had taken her bag and without asking had put it up on the roof of the coach that serviced the resorts.

"Highland Lodge, Fiddich House, Ashton Burn, Royal Golf, Royal Marine, Glenriddle Inn, The Links?"

He took her for gentry on holiday, even with the coal-stained Gladstone.

"In point of fact, I've come to stay with my aunt in . . . what is the name of your main street?"

"Lovatt."

"Yes, in Lovatt Street."

"We only *have* the one street. What's her name?"

"In point of fact, I've forgotten her name since she's been married but I can recognize the house when I see it."

She handed the man a shilling, and although he was supposed to go out only to the resorts, he helped her up into the carriage, the first she had ever been in, and they started down the serpentine road from the station to the town.

The guttural thickness of his accent depressed her. This wasn't the way it was supposed to be. It went beyond an accent into distinct dialect.

"Does everyone speak the way you speak?"

He looked back at her, his face ruddy with anger.

"What's the matter with the way I speak?"

"Nothing is the matter with it. It is a very pleasant way to speak. What do you call it?"

The man was affronted.

"English!" he shouted back at her. "King's English, I speak." He switched his horse with a stinging blow.

She could see the lamps being lit on the glass-enclosed porches

17

of the resorts, one after another, as if it were a ritual. A resort town was a good town, she thought, an ideal town for her needs although she had never been in one. Something of the style and class and manner of the visitors would have to rub off on the workers. Who in Pitmungo would know how to behave in a restaurant? Lord Fyffe and Lady Jane and Mr. Brothcock, the mine superintendent, and a few of the others up on Brumbie Hill. No one else. No one else had probably ever been in a restaurant or sat at a table with a cloth on it. Probably hundreds of people in Strathnairn, some of them poor as field mice, would know. It was a matter of logic that the people who catered to the whims of the rich would be a cut above the people from the hard-work and heavy-duty towns.

"Well, Scotch-English, at least, as good as anyone else I know." He was less angry. "Scotch, in fact." He thought about that. "Aye, *Scotch*. What's the matter with a man speaking his own tongue, I ask?"

"Nothing, it's very becoming on you. I only asked did everyone here speak it."

"Nooo," he said, in disgust, "only the people in Herringtoon. All the rest of them go around trying to ape the Southroners, the Sassenachs, you see. They won't let you work in the resorts if you speak Scotch, can you imagine that? We're happy being ourselves, you see. Honest Scotchmen."

It was pleasant news she was learning.

"Then there's the Highlanders. They come down when they're starving or cold or can't stand one another; I don't know why they come. Lazy bastards for the most part. Excuse me, Miss."

"And how do they talk?"

"Some speak the Gaelic, but not many. But they don't speak Scotch, I know. Look, you can see the Highlands now."

He pointed to the west across the green Moray Firth waters. She could see the dark walls of the mountains there, rising from the sea. The crests of the higher hills were masked by banks of dark swollen clouds.

"It will be snowing up there," the coachman said. "Two worlds, you see; winter there and spring here. I don't like them. They think they're better than other people."

They were down the hill and into Lovatt Street and even in the carriage she could feel the chill in the wind driving across the narrow beach from the water. It was a hard wind but not unlike the wind on the High Moor, and all at once she had the feeling that things were going to be all right here, that she could handle herself in Strathnairn.

"Say when, Miss."

"I don't know yet but I'm looking."

She knew what she needed. She had seen them in Dunfermline —one of the merchants' houses fallen on lean times where they put discreet signs in the window inviting lodgers as if they didn't really care to take anyone in. She would ask for a small room and off-season rates, because there was, after all, still winter in the air. With a few rolls for breakfast and a few bannocks for lunch and a tea in the house, she could hold out indefinitely. They had no idea, Maggie felt sure, how little a girl from a mine town could get by with. With luck, she might be able to exchange a few hours of gentle lady's work for a part payment of her room.

"This is what we call the Toon," the driver said. "Out there is Herringtoon, where the fishing folk live. My people. Every bastard there—excuse me, Miss—is named MacAdams. And then out to the west there, where the resorts and golf courses are, is Poshtoon."

As they neared the business district, more and more large old houses displayed lodger's notices, some in the windows, some almost apologetically hidden among the salt-stained daffodils on the tight little lawns.

"This would be it," Maggie said.

"Then your aunt's name would be Bel Geddes."

"Yes, of course."

"Mrs. Alexander Bel Geddes."

"So she is."

"And she would have died, oh, eight or nine years ago." He smiled at her, stumps of teeth showing through the redness of wind-whipped lips and face. Gleed-eyed bastard, she thought. It was the Gladstone. He maneuvered his carriage into the narrow carriageway off Lovatt Street and to the front of the Bel Geddes house. The house was larger than the rest of the houses around it, gray stone, parapets, dark wood, gloomy but reassuring and respectable.

He was standing with the bag, keeping the carriage between the bag and the house.

"Do you ken the words *poor boire,* Miss?"

"Certainly."

"Weel, for a little one of those—say a shilling, Miss—I might just be able to get this up the back stairs without Mr. Bel Geddes ever setting eye on it. Whatever happened to it?"

"Fell off the train."

"Aye, and dragged all the way from Aberdeen."

It was a game and she could play it.

"Aye," she said, "all the way," and handed him a shilling.

"Tell him your bags are being sent from the station. When you get to your room open the window and I'll know where to go. And Miss?"

"Yes, Mr. MacAdams."

"If you ever need anything done, I don't know what, you can trust Mr. Cherry MacAdams to help you do it."

"Jerry?"

"Cherry. And it would make me blush to tell you why."

"Aye, I'm very sure it would."

They recognized one another from the start.

Looking back on it, when she was far enough away from it to look back on it, she always relished two little pliskies she managed to play on young Rodney Bel Geddes, who was manning the desk.

"Is it Miss Drum? Miss *Drum*, is it? As in bass drum!"

"As in snare drum."

Young snot, she had thought, lank dark hair plastered down on head with Macassar so that it looked like patent leather, so English-speaking that the words could barely reed their way through his nostrils.

"And what, if I may ask . . ."

"You may."

"Brings you here? Fishin', the waters, golf?"

"Huntin'."

He never knew he had been lanced.

"Home?"

"Carnegie Terrace. Dunfermline. Fife."

"Ooh." There was a show, a flicker it was, of interest. "And do you know the great man?"

"I would like to but our family doesn't bow to theirs. They were weavers, you see."

"I didn't know."

"Had a loom right in the house. Used to take dinner on it." Mr. Bel Geddes looked perplexed. "On the loom."

"Oh."

"And speaking of that, what time do we eat here?"

"We don't eat here. We dine."

"Ooh." And Maggie knew she had been lanced.

That first evening she had not been able to wait to eat or even to dine and she had walked down Lovatt Street to a shop she had seen and bought two little plump hot mutton pies, tuppenny each, and brought them back to her room. She liked the looks of the people she saw in the street. What she wanted was there.

She had gotten her off-season rates, and the room, despite the gray-stone gloom of the house, was airy and bright and there was a duck-down mattress on her bed, the first she had ever felt. The room was above the rest of the house, isolated from it, a garret with a winding private stairway leading to it, and she felt cut off from the rest of the world. After Pitmungo she liked that.

She lay on her bed and thought about the man she must have. Tall, that was essential, and fair. Speak clear English, essential, and have, if possible, one of the fine historic Scottish names. While she was lying there the light came in, the extraordinary light of late afternoon in the north of the country, golden light flooding in the room, the gloamin tide they called it in Pitmungo, and she knew, she was sure of it then, that she would find the Gael she required.

There was a tap at the door.

"Miss Drum?"

"Aye. Yes."

"We're dining."

"Thank you."

It was no help to her at all to find that every man at the table was thirty years old or more, and weak.

Her heart was set on an eligible Gael, but the problem, she discovered, was finding one. The Highland boys either went to sea and were gone for long periods of time or worked in the great resorts and never seemed to come out of them. If these were the Gaels so famed for their boldness in battle, they had left it all on the battlegrounds. They were the shyest men she had ever met. If she caught their eyes they turned away like deer surprised on the browse.

And the weather was no help. For days the wind came smacking off the firth, coating the stones with salt. When the wind wasn't blowing, the fog clubbed in, filling the long crescent harbor with damp. The cleaning men came around then to scrape the mildew off the walls, and the bonging of the buoys out beyond the harbor became more real to Maggie than the beating of her heart.

.   .   .

It was boring then, those days, lying in her room, waiting for the fogs to lift and the skies to clear. But any minetown girl soon learned the art of making time pass in a place where time seemed to stand still and nothing ever seemed to happen beyond work.

When the winds were right she walked through Lovatt Street and then out through Poshtoon and beyond. The winds and occasional sun had given her skin a glow she had never known in Pitmungo and her close diet had given her a lean delicacy that soon, unless she could do something about it, would send her over the line into looking wasted. There was nothing like a good work stoppage to get the pithead girls in Pitmungo looking lithe again, but if it went on too long the newly fine faces began to look like death's-heads.

And then the winds would shift, the fogs return, the rains come down, and she would be alone in her room again. Time became a problem then, not because of boredom but because it came to represent something else. Time became money in the most immediate way. Her money was running out.

Every day she felt the siller slipping away, a shilling or two at a time, draining from her purse with the regularity of the tides in Herringtoon harbor.

She loved that word "siller." That was the Scotch word it was going to be hardest to part with, because siller *was* siller and nothing could ever truly take its place for her. Some afternoons, when the rains and the winds and fogs locked her away in her room, she would lie on her bed after counting her coins, and then she could hear it, half awake and half asleep, the clinking of the coins into her metal box at home, each week a little more siller, the *chink, chink, chink* of the coins slipping down to the bottom of the box, hard and soft at the same time, something silken, something soothing: her marrying money. She always thought of silver as being warm.

What sustained her was that every day she saw the kind of man she wanted, tall and always leaner than the men in Pitmungo, blond with long white faces or sometimes with hair as dark as crows' wings, a kind of angular and easy bearing about them, a grace to their movements that was unknown to the pitmen, a *style* about them that told the world they were something other than objects to be hired out for work. When they talked she liked the quiet way they spoke, spare and lean, the accent clean and as tidy as their words, with only a trace of a lilt that she supposed was their Celtic or Gaelic—she wasn't sure of the distinction —Highland heritage. She wanted one of them.

When the weather was right, she went out every afternoon through Poshtoon, trying to appear at home there as if she had a reason to be on the grounds of the resorts. Those were the saddest times. No one noticed her but the caddies on the links, and she had made up her mind that she was never going to have anything to do with a man who·would carry another man's bag of clubs while he went after a little white ball.

There were nights after days like that when she lay on her bed and watched the reflections of the lanterns from the herring boats bob their wild patterns over her black ceiling and wondered why she didn't go down to Herringtoon and do whatever it was that a young woman was expected to do with a man and for doing it get paid a little pile of siller.

Who was it said that it could be a sin on Thursday and the same act be God's blessed will on Friday, with the same two people in the same rumpled bed doing it?

"Houghmagandie!"

She said it aloud in the darkness of her lonely room.

"Sculduddery."

"Fewkin." What was so terrible about that?

It was Mr. MacCurry, deacon of the Free Kirk in Pitmungo, who said that marriage was an institution designed to keep young men from sin. Thereby admitting, Maggie thought, that the institution was sinful or the act wasn't, because you couldn't have it both ways; that's one thing her father had taught her.

Sin was sin or it was nothing.

So she lay there and her mind drifted downstairs to Mr. Pomeroy, the elegant Mr. Pomeroy, traveling man for Plymouth Cordage, dealers in naval rope and twine, who could not, could *not* keep his hands to himself in hallways and away from her knees at dinner. Mr. Pomeroy, in and out of Strathnairn all the time, who more than once—at least eight or nine times to be more precise—let it be known, when Mr. Bel Geddes was entertaining his guests with piano playing after dinner, that if there was ever any difficulty in her keeping her room in the Bel Geddes house, that he was available—more than available, eager—to help her find some amenable way to meet the cost of her rent.

There was more than one sound to the clink of siller, Maggie thought, when one was driven to listen for it.

3   By being canny with her money, ca' canny to the brink of eccentricity, by nursing the last of her pennies with the care of a mother for her firstborn, she judged, when it was all over, that she had two weeks left to her when she found him.

It had been a dismal day for her. She had walked out to Fiddich House, the farthest out of all the resorts, and when no one was to be seen there she had crossed the croquet grounds, holding her hat against the wind, and gone on, since she had never tried it, to the edge of Rothesay golf course and down to the sands along the firth. The beach, as she feared it would be, was deserted.

It wasn't working, it wasn't working at all. Each day a little earlier in the day she was forced to admit that to herself. She was tired, which she recognized as a consequence of hunger, and her tiredness made her despondent. She was—she was very conscious of it—becoming demoralized. The thought of walking all the way back to the Bel Geddes house filled her with despair. Nothing was working.

And then there was the Strathnairn wind, endlessly blowing in from the sea, blowing against her, blowing at her, chilling her bones and her hopes and her heart. She found a high dune in the links, the flank of which mercifully curved away from the wind, a pocket of sand shielded from the wind and yet in view of the sea where some young yachtsmen were tacking about in the run of wind in the inlet, shouting to each other in those high English voices. They always sounded to Maggie as if they were meeting each other for the first time in their lives although she had often seen them together before.

"Hallooo!"

"Oh, hallooo."

Great surprise and animation in the voices. Silly nonsense, she thought, wasting their lives in those little boats like that when they had the money to do things. It never ceased to astonish her that people like them, the *halloos,* had managed to overcome the Scots.

When the wind slackened, she had—for the first time since she had been in Strathnairn and not in her bed—the sensation of being warm. She opened her tweed coat and let the sun play on her and then closed her eyes and listened to the water hissing up the shore, a rushing of water and grinding of pebbles as it washed its way back to the sea. When she woke he was there, down at the edge of the water, doing something curious to the sides of a large rock standing several yards out in the sea. She watched him without moving at first, wondering what he was doing. One decisive movement, as if he were turning a large screw and then putting something into a creel, an odd movement, and she knew without any doubt, while watching him, that this was the man she had come for.

He was wearing a kilt, and it made her smile because she had never seen a man in a kilt before, not a man doing natural things. Several soldiers once, lost on their way somewhere, drinking in the Coaledge Tavern, but those were costumes. And Lord Fyffe from time to time, trotting up Colliers Walk to the High Moor to pot a few moorcocks and grouse, looking self-conscious and as though someone were going to take a shot at his kilt or, worse, snicker at it. But this man was wearing a kilt.

She sat up, very slowly so as not to alarm him, the way a good bird dog moves in the field, and when she had arranged herself and felt ready, she started across the sand to the stone. He never noticed her. He was tall, by Pitmungo standards very tall, an inch or two over six feet, she thought, although it was hard for a person her size to tell, and lean. Even by Highland standards lean, but there was a heavy-boned quality to the leanness, a wind-burnished hardness to it, that made it different from being thin. He was down to sinew. The man could work, she could see that much.

He was fair in what she felt was the classic Highland way, his hair reddish gold and at times, in the sun, almost pure gold, and long, in the Highland fashion, to save on the need for haircuts, she thought. His skin was white, although around the cheeks he was red, as if he had been slapped, the kind of fair skin that didn't burn from the sun or mottle after drinking. Clear fair skin, she had felt since she was little, was the feature of the natural aristocrat. Everyone in Pitmungo had skins like weathered brick or as gray as badly done wash, or faces like fat plums, over-blooded and ripe for early death.

When he finally looked up he was startled by her, head flying up, eyes wide, like a deer caught in a clearing, and then very quickly, without seeming to move at all, he slipped around to the far side of the rock. In his haste he was forced to leave his creel behind and that, Maggie understood at once, would be the tool she would have to work with.

She waited for him to come around the rock again. She was not a patient person, but she felt now a kind of endless patience, as if she had a lifetime to wait and was prepared to wait it. The water where he was standing was deep, up to the hem of his kilt, and the wind was up again, waves slapping hard against the rock, and he was getting wet. It was a question of time and tide. Time was passing and the tide was flooding in.

"What are these horrible-looking things?" she called to him, but he didn't answer.

"I say, what are these beasts in your basket?"

No answer. It wasn't a matter of pride; there was no room for that now. She had to pretend he hadn't heard her and try again.

"I said, you behind the rock, what are these sea things you're collecting here?"

She was surprised to feel her heart beating quite rapidly in her throat.

"You know what they are," he called to her. He sounded angry and she was surprised by that, too, because she thought it would be softly shy.

"I don't. I've never seen such things before."

He came a little of the way around the rock for a fleeting glimpse of her.

"Barnacles," he said. "Now you know."

"They're unco ugly. What do you do with them?"

"What do I do with them?" His voice was sarcastic. He came fully around the rock and was studying her. He *was* angry with her, she could see that, and she didn't understand why.

"I *eat* them. Now do you understand?"

He went behind the rock again and she waited. He had no choice in the matter unless he chose to drown, and she didn't think shyness could carry that far. When the wind slacked off, she told him that she didn't come from near the sea. She spoke in a very unconcerned voice, as if she hadn't known or sensed his anger.

"Where are you from, then?" he finally said.

"South of here."

"A Sassenach, then? English?"

She pretended to be insulted.

"I'm a good Scottish girl, I am." She gave it a little burr, the faintest touch of the soul. "From near Edinburgh."

He was at once suspicious of her again.

"That's near the sea."

"West Fife, then. I've never been to the sea before."

He came fully around the stone but stayed in the water. He seemed embarrassed by his bare legs but she knew he would come out. The water was freezing cold.

"And how do you like it?"

"Very much, but I've never been in it."

"I love the sea," he said, and she noticed his face color at his outburst of emotion. She had never heard a man say "love" that way before.

And then there was nothing to say. He stood in the water, having revealed himself to a stranger, and she had nothing to say that sounded genuine. The water washed in and washed back around his knees, occasionally wetting the kilt. She could appreciate the fine lean features of his face, the hawkness of it, with a large sharp nose the way a lord's nose should look.

"Why don't you come out of there?" she said suddenly. "You must be freezing to death."

It was good. It broke the silence in a genuine way. The simple fact was that he *was* freezing.

"Aye, I'll come out. There's no more barnacles anyway."

She was surprised at how much taller he seemed when standing near her. Once again, the silence fell between them. He wanted to put on his socks but he was shy about doing it in front of her, and they stood by the basket of barnacles. He nudged the creel with his foot.

"Goose barnacles, to be exact."

"Ah."

"In olden times, they used to believe that geese came from these."

"It's strange to think what people used to believe."

Then there was nothing more to look at in the basket and

Maggie could think of nothing genuine to ask about barnacles. She pointed across the Moray Firth.

"And what are those?"

He looked at her again, to see if she was serious.

"Why, the Highlands."

The hills were beautiful then. Great flubbs of clouds were floating down over them, turning the tweed and heather colors of the lower slopes to a soft dark velvet.

"The Cromarty Hills, to be exact," he said, with a great deal of heat. He caught her look. "My family were driven from there like cattle out of a field. The Highland Clearances."

An occasional splash of bright spring green leaped from one of the hillsides where some surviving crofter had kept his farm and put in a crop.

"And came here and died. Froze to death." His face reddened again from revealing so much of himself to a stranger. "I suppose a man can get himself dressed?"

"Oh, excuse me."

She went around behind the dune and waited. In Pitmungo, the men took their tubs in the living room in front of the fire and here was a man who needed privacy to put on his knee socks. She waited and waited and when she came back around the dune she saw he had started down the shore away from Strathnairn. She had been dismissed.

The dunes ran parallel to the sea for at least a quarter of a mile. He was on the sea side of the dunes. If she ran on the landward side it would be possible to be waiting for him where the shoreline curved and the dunes ended. She ran. She stumbled in the sand and over the stones, but she ran, trying not to gasp so that he wouldn't hear her on the other side of the dunes, knowing that she'd have to arrive well enough ahead of him so that she wasn't gasping for air when he came around the last of the dunes.

He was far more startled to see her the second time than he had been the first. He looked at her and could not account for it.

Several times he opened his mouth to say something, and then closed it again. Surely, Maggie thought, he has got to be able to hear the pounding of her heart in her chest.

"You want the other way," he said, at last.

"Other way?"

"Strathnairn is the other way, Miss."

"But I could have sworn . . ."

"No."

He balanced the creel on one shoulder and then the other, on his head and then on one knee and the other knee, conscious of appearing ridiculous, and it angered him.

"I've never seen a man wear a kilt before."

That angered him too.

"All sorts of men wear them," he said, as if she were arguing with him. "Up there." He nodded toward Cromarty and beyond. "Army," he said. She didn't understand.

She began walking along the shore, away from Strathnairn as naturally as walking home along Lovatt Street, and he came along.

"Army?"

"I was in the army, the Cameron Highlanders"—he seemed bitter about that—"and they let me out and sent me home in this."

"At least it didn't cost."

"It's all I have, do you understand?" He reddened from embarrassment but he was angry, also. He made it very plain then. "I have never been able to earn enough to buy anything else; now do you understand?"

"Where I come from the men have one suit and it's meant to last them for their life. They're put in the dead box in it."

He looked at her with disbelief. An old stone wall blocked the passage down the shore. He stepped over it and when he was on the other side and about to say good-bye, she held out her hand to him and he looked at it and at her and took it and helped her up over the stones. As he did, some of the barnacles spilled from the creel onto the sand. She knelt at once to help pick them up.

"Stop it," he said. "Ladies don't do that."

They were on their knees, their faces almost touching. She noticed his hands in the sand, long and white, slender but strong, not like the chunky brown stubs of Pitmungo. Her own, she knew, were harder. It was her turn then, and she made it as plain as she knew how.

"I am not a lady."

He looked up at her suddenly, in that open, suspicious way, doubtful and yet believing at the same moment. He didn't know how to hide things, she realized, he never was taught. In the mine towns you learned very soon in life.

"I earn my way. I'm a working woman."

He looked at her clothes, the fine tweed suit and Highland tam, her tiny leather boots and the ruffles of her linen shirt, and bit his lip. She got up then.

"How do you prepare these?"

"You don't want to know, it's disgusting."

"I'm not easy to disgust."

"All right." He decided to shock her. He took out a knife from the top of his kilt and slashed through the stalk of a barnacle and peeled away the tough rind-like skin until the meat in the fleshy stalk was revealed.

"We boil them in sea water and eat them because we are hungry."

"I see."

"Because we are starving to death."

She knew better now than to say anything.

"The beggar's lobster they're called." He snapped the knife shut and started down the shoreline and she came after him. When she heard her feet on the pebbles, he turned around to face her.

"And that makes me a beggar."

He had to be faced up to now or it was over.

32

"Hunger is a good master," Maggie said. He looked at her in a different way and she was conscious of it. "Poortith is no crime. Poortith is no shame, just so a man tries."

He saw the dark brightness of her eyes. He liked the foreign darkness of her hair and skin.

"And poortith is no excuse."

He picked up the creel and started down the shore, and when she followed he let her come this time. Ahead of them, sheltered at the base of a pine-studded headland, a stone house stood.

"That's it," he said. "That's where poortith puts you."

She was disappointed. She had thought of a little house somewhere but this was a cave, a cairn, a pile of stones craftily put together, but a pile of stones nevertheless. It looked like illustrations she had seen in the school books of Pictish houses from a thousand years before.

"Did you do that yourself?"

"With my father. We had to. They died here."

They both knew the next step, to go to the cairn or not. He didn't move and Maggie wouldn't move, and suddenly he put the tip of his thumb in his mouth and bit it, hard—a strange thing to do, she thought—and said, "All right, come, then."

The cairn was clean. The floor was earth but hard and smooth from a generation of bare feet and he had sprinkled fresh sand on it. There was a smell of fish to the place but also of pine and peat.

"Knock the wet sand off," he ordered. "Here, I'll help you."

She lifted her boot, small and laced to the middle of her calf, and all at once the intimacy of what he was doing, holding a woman's foot in his hand in the semi-dark privacy of his own house, overwhelmed him. He dropped her foot and looked away.

"Excuse me," he said.

"For what?"

But he couldn't look at her after that.

His clothes were hung on pegs, and on a shelf fashioned from driftwood, indecently out of place, was a hat.

33

"Ah, you wear a hat."

"Why not?"

"Where I come from, only the earl and his sons wear hats. Miners don't have hats."

"Well, I have a hat," he said, his face turned away from her. It was a beautiful brown hat, soft and yet able to hold its shape, an arrogant slouch to it, with a band of grouse feathers around the crown and a silver medallion on one side with the tip of a red deer's tail bristling from it.

He could not get over the sensation of touching her leg, so small and compact and so strangely heavy.

"One day I heard that a guest of Lord Monboddo fell from his boat shooting geese and the next day this came in with the tide."

"And did he drown? Would you wear a dead man's hat?"

"Poortith can't be picky," he said, and they looked at one another and laughed. It was easier after that.

For a tall man he moved with a deceptive swiftness. He was not conscious of being watched doing the things he had done for years. He lit shark-oil lamps and with a blanched white branch he stirred the pot simmering over the fire. The pot smelled of the sea, of tidal flats at low tide, and of iodine.

"Kelp soup." He lifted several fronds of the seaweed out of the pot. They looked like strips of translucent boiled rubber. "Mixed with Irish moss, that's the cunning trick."

There was no other word for it, Maggie thought; it stank.

"I think you'll like it," he said.

"I think I shall."

He went out and came back a few minutes later with a handful of greens and bay leaves, which he put in the pot.

"Sea spinach and seaside salad," he said. "You'll like it."

"Aye."

He sprinkled the soup with dried sea lettuce that would serve as salt and herbs and then handed her a large whelk shell that would serve as a soup bowl the way the poor used gourds in Pitmungo.

34

"No spoons," he said. "You sip it from the buckie shell. Ah, you should have what comes in these," he said, tapping the shell. "That's a true treat."

The smell was very strong, totally of the sea, like being inside something from the sea. He watched her and she drank. She wanted to say something but she couldn't manage her mouth. She was glad that it was dark enough so that he couldn't see the tears come to her eyes.

"Very tasty," she managed to say.

"An old recipe. Handed down, you know."

Hunger was, indeed, a good master, Maggie thought, and was surprised to find her brow wet with little beads of sweat.

"Don't let it cool," he said. "It's no good cool. All the oils come up. Lots of fish oil in there, you see."

She took another sip of the soup and another after that, and finally the shell was empty.

"Och, good," he said, and poured her shell full again. "Do you know there's people along the coast won't touch the stuff? Wait until you try the kelp."

The sweat on her brow was very serious now, running in rivulets down her face and wetting her linen collar. She wanted very much to go outside. She wanted to walk in the wind. She felt the sweat running down her arms and between her breasts. She hadn't intended to get up but she did and went toward the door.

"Don't open that," he said.

"Why not?" She almost shouted it at him.

"Can't you hear it?"

Rain was lashing against the walls of the cairn and the surf was pounding, and she had never noticed it. She came back and sat down again and took off her tweed jacket. The sweat outlined her breasts against the linen and she didn't care. She tried to study her feet and concentrate on them, count the number of eyelets in her boots, and then he was holding a plate of something under her nose.

"I'm sorry there are no eels," he said. "A mess of eels in hot kelp soup is the thing for a day like this," and then his eyes saw her breasts and rested on them for that one moment, and her eyes met his and he reddened and turned away again.

"You don't have to be afraid," he said.

What a thing to say to a woman, she thought; he would really have to learn.

"Of the storm?"

"Aye, of the storm."

The rain had passed as suddenly as it had come, and the silence it brought with it made him uneasy. The responsibility of having her in his house, trying to keep his eyes and thoughts where they belonged, was too much for him.

"You can go now," he said. It was clumsy of him but he knew no other way. She put on her tweed jacket and saw that he was watching, although somehow managing to make it clear that he was not actually watching. He opened the door and the fresh wind was a blessing to her. At the door he didn't know what to say or exactly what to do. What did one do when a lady left one's house? He had no idea at all. He put out his hand and she took it, and she could see by his eyes that he was astonished by the hardness of it.

"Thank you for my tea," Maggie said.

"Och, the tea." He slapped his forehead. "I have the water on."

"Next time then." That was it, the opening she had been looking for. "That's a promise then."

He seemed bewildered.

"Tea next time."

"Aye," he said finally.

"I'll bring out a tea cake."

He nodded.

"Good-bye then. Until next time."

"Next time," he said.

He watched her go down the path to the sea. "Wait," he called, and ran back inside the house. He came back and handed her a sea thing.

"A sweet for your walk back."

It was a frond of dried dulse, green and black as the bottom of a tide pool, and crusty with salt.

"You have to keep chewing to bring out the full flavor," he said, and she nodded and they smiled.

"Do you know something? I don't know your name. I've eaten in your house and don't know my host's name."

"Cameron."

She kept looking at him. "Is that all?" she finally said. "Just Cameron?"

"Gillon Cameron. Gillon Forbes Cameron if you want it all."

She felt her heart leap pleasantly, just a tiny breaking of the beat and a dip back pleasantly into place. Yes, she thought, I want it all.

"A very famous name, a very fine name."

"Aye, a very fine family so I'm told. Warriors and nobles and scholars and the like."

"A clan, I guess."

"Oh, yes, a clan, of course. The Camerons of Loch Something-or-Other."

"And Forbes?"

"The same. My mother's name. She's a Rob Roy and a Sutherland, too. It's the Sutherlands drove us off the land, I think. They're very serious about that up there," he said. He motioned toward the Highlands. "Names."

And why shouldn't they be, she thought; names with a history and a meaning to them. Not like Pitmungo, where everyone was a Japp or a Cook or a Hogg. Hopp, Begg, Minto, Mengies, Pick. Pick was good for a coal miner. Pict was better. Ugly little clod-like names, as dull as coal, a race apart, the descendants of slaves. It didn't matter where he stood now; what mattered is that they were great once and that somewhere in the bloodline greatness was lying in wait to climb out. She was smiling at him without knowing it, her eyes not even seeing him, and he was taken by her, by her small even white teeth, little keen teeth like the moor fox, and her eyes, little hard brown ovals that glittered like the fox.

"Tell me something," she said. He nodded. "Are you a Gael?"

He thought about it. He looked to the mountains now lost from sight in the clouds.

"Well, they all are, aren't they? Then I am," he said, and wondered why she smiled that way. It was such a brilliant smile, he thought, those foxy teeth in that alien brown face.

He watched her go down the inlet and turn in the right direction for Strathnairn and then he slapped himself in the head for the second time in the day. He had never asked her name.

He began to run. When he reached the mouth of the inlet he turned down the beach and then he saw her and stopped. Something told him not to go on. Her back was to him, away from the wind. She had pulled a blade of dune grass from the sand and with great care and neatness, her back to the wind at the right angle, was sticking the grass down her throat and vomiting up his hot kelp soup, his seaweed, and his dulse.

4   SHE GAVE HIM THREE DAYS, MAKING HERSELF VISIBLE along the docks of the Toon where she knew he must come, walking the sidewalks of Lovatt Street until she felt her legs would collapse. The merchants thought she was a little asklent, just a wee bit off the line, standing outside staring at their boring little displays for hours and never coming in to buy.

Her problems were the same, time and money, and every day they were more acute. The leather of her boots was growing dangerously thin, and then in May the resorts began to fill with fishermen from England hoping to kill a big salmon in the leased salmon rivers that run in from the sea through the forests to the south. Mr. Bel Geddes told Miss Drum that he soon would be forced to raise the price of her room now that the fish-killing season was upon them.

"But I don't see any fishermen staying here," Maggie said. "You have no rights on any streams."

"They stay here just to say they've been in Strathnairn for the spring salmon run."

"You really expect me to believe that? You Italians are all alike, not to be trusted."

"Bel Geddes happens to be a *noble* Scottish name, Miss Droom. Standard bearers of the noble Gordon clan. And I expect you to believe that as much as I believe you came here to hunt."

"But I did, though. I have spotted my noble stag."

She infuriated him. He couldn't stand the way she used her body when she was around him, as if he didn't exist or couldn't see her. He watched her once put her hands on her breasts and adjust herself beneath her sark—she really should know better—not ten feet from his desk. "Outrageous," he said, loud enough so he hoped she could hear it. He let her stay on another week at half rates.

On the morning of the fourth day she walked out through Poshtoon, over the wind-raddled links, and down to the sea and the dunes toward the stone house. The wind from the firth was cold, everything about Strathnairn was cold. The people on the glassed-in porches were breathing smoke as they talked. It was a high price to pay, she thought, to kill a salmon, and then she thought of the price she was paying to hook her own prize. All trophies worth winning come dear, her father had always said, not that he ever won one. She found herself yearning for the coal-filled fireplaces of Pitmungo.

The stone house was empty. And cold, as cold as the tomb it was. Peat still smoldered in the fireplace; she must have missed him by less than an hour and she was angry with him. He should have come for her, he should have stumbled across her, he should be here waiting for her. She put straw on the peat and when it caught she burned what was left of his driftwood. When the fire went out she would have cried except that the tears wouldn't come for her. Pitmungo people never had found it easy to cry.

The shadows thrown by the dunes were long and deeply blue, and it was much later than Maggie thought it was when she saw him standing on the seaward side of a dune staring savagely at the sea. The anger in his face excited her, because the man she needed would have to be capable of anger. She went up the dune and stood beside him. She didn't know if he was aware of her or not, his intensity was so great, but he finally looked down at her.

"I came for my tea," she said. He tried not to show his surprise, but that was beyond him. He went back to staring out at the sea.

"What is it? What do you see there?"

She knew she was interrupting some kind of ritual being carried on between Gillon and the sea.

"The salmon," he said. "I can see them out there."

He looked at her to see if she believed him.

"I can smell them. You think that's crazy, don't you?" She shook her head that she didn't and he believed her. "I can smell water that spawning salmon have been in. I know them, the way they are and the things they do. I know where they sleep at night."

They went down the dune and near the bottom Gillon gave her his hand to help her across a rough spot and when she didn't withdraw it he held it, surprised at himself, looking down at her from the corner of his eye to see if she objected in any way.

"Then you must catch a lot of them," Maggie said.

"I've never killed one. The lairds own the salmon streams, the lairds own the fish in the sea."

"No one owns the fish."

"The lairds own the salmon—I like 'saumont' better—and the Englishmen kill them. The rubber-gum waders with their twenty-foot rods and their gillies running up and down with hot meat pies and flasks of whisky, looking down their noses at you because they're certain you're out to try and steal one of their sacred fish."

"God put the fish in the sea. It isn't fair."

"Aye, well. I suggest you go tell that to the water bailiffs."

He gave up too easily, too quickly for Maggie's taste. There was not enough passion in his submission.

"What would they do to you if you took one and they caught you?"

He looked at her and smiled.

"You're not from here, are you? Three months in jail, a little thrashing sometimes when the bailiff closes the door on you, and worst of all a five-pound fine."

The wind was bad again. Scud from the waves blew across the inlet and the shoreline was lacquered with froth. It was becoming plain to Maggie that what was known as a storm in Pitmungo merely meant wind in Strathnairn. She hated it.

"I would do it," Maggie said. He didn't hear her.

"What?"

"I would get me one. I don't care what the risk," she shouted. They didn't talk the rest of the way but she knew where his mind was. At the house he walked out into the water to secure his little boat that was tied to a stone in the inlet and came back to the door.

"What is your name?"

"Meg Drum."

"MacDrum?"

"Maggie Drum."

"That's it? Maggie Drum?"

"Aye. Meg Drum."

He thought about that.

"A very fine name," he said after a pause. "There used to be a man in my regiment named Drum, Willie Drum. He looked after the horses."

"Of course."

Gillon was embarrassed. He hadn't meant it to sound that way.

"He was hanged for something or other."

"I can imagine."

"What I meant by bringing that up was, what I meant by it, you see, was that he was very brave when he was dropped."

She said nothing to that.

"Little short, dark man."

"Naturally."

He decided to close his mouth. They went into the cairn.

"Someone's been here," he said. "I can smell pine and I used no pine."

She wondered if she should tell him and decided against it. Silence is sometimes better than honesty. She hoped she hadn't left anything behind her. He had eyes like some of the fishing birds she had noticed on the shore. They missed nothing.

"They used it all up," he said. "Can you imagine the selfishness of it? Every stick of it." He prowled around the edges of the cairn.

"We descend from a long line of Pictish moudieworts," Maggie said. He didn't know the word but he would learn. He hadn't really heard her.

"They didn't take my food." He was lighting the shark-oil lamps. "Why are you smiling?"

"You sound like the papa bear coming home."

"But they must have been here for hours."

"They was me, silly."

And there it was, exposed to him if he understood what she was saying, that she had sat there in darkness for hours waiting for him to come. All he noticed were those little teeth and knew that he had missed them. And her, in this house. She made him nervous but he was happy she was here. He had been dreaming about her in exactly the situation he was now in, alone with her again, and the dreams excited him and frightened him. In the morning when the sun was up, he managed to put them aside but they came again in the night. It was almost dark outside and time to go, but this time she knew she would be back.

. . .

It became an afternoon ritual with them, the tea and the search for field salad to go with the loaf of bread she brought out from the town each day. She liked to hunt for the greens—the Pitmungo in her, she realized, getting something for nothing. Every time she filled her basket with watercress from one of the golf courses, it was like finding money in the brook.

And he was hooked, her fish, but he was such a shy one, swimming about at the bottom of the pool, not really knowing the gaff was out for him, that she despaired of ever landing him before Rodney Bel Geddes put her out of her room. There were things she could do, she knew, and all of them dangerous. She could invite Rodney up the narrow stairs in exchange for her room; that she was certain of now. He wet his lips every time she passed him, not knowing that he did it.

Or she could go down to Herringtoon and pay a call on Mr. Cherry MacAdams, who, her Pitmungo instincts told her, would know some way a pretty, canny young girl might earn her salt without losing her soul in the bargain.

Or she could ask Mr. Gillon Forbes Cameron to marry her straight out, but that, she knew, would never do. Even with the hook in his mouth he'd break the line and run.

They were picking fiddleheads, the beggars' asparagus, the little tight-rolled, fuzzy heads of the bracken ferns, for their tea.

"Pick every other one, so there'll be ferns when I come back next year," Gillon said.

"Aye," Maggie said, but she didn't bother, because there wasn't going to be any next year in Strathnairn.

"Gillon?"

"Yes?"

He looked up, surprised and a little pleased. It was the first time she had called him by name.

"If you were to catch a very big salmon or two, would you be able to sell them?"

43

"It isn't the selling, it's the killing. All my life I have wanted a saumont for my own."

"But if you got it, could you sell it?"

She snapped the heads off the little burgeoning ferns. She liked that, neat and precise and final.

"Oh, there are those in Herringtoon that deal in that, I think. They pay the water bailiff, I think. But it's very dangerous work."

"And does it pay well?"

He stood up and studied her.

"If they're big enough, yes. Very well."

"How well?"

"I don't know, but very well. They want them for their tables back there." He nodded south, meaning England. "But it's bad business."

"Aye, I see that, but at least the saumont wouldn't go to *them*." She pointed to the Fiddich House and the Royal Golf and the others across the links. She let that settle with him for a while.

"Gillon?"

"Aye."

"If I *were* to arrange some way so you could get your salmon— your *saumont*—and sell it, too, would you do it?"

He didn't answer her for a long time.

"You arrange it?"

"Yes, me."

They went on with their work. The creel was almost full.

"You know where the biggest saumont in all of Scotland hide, don't you?"

"Aye." He stood up and looked out at the sea. There was no telling by his face.

"Would you, Gillon?"

The lamps were being lit all across the windswept links. It was her favorite time of day here; the wind died down in the early evening before picking up again and the sky never seemed so high and stretched out, and the lamps were the world being turned on.

44

"Yes," he said, "I would."

It was time to go back to the cairn. He came to help her hoist her basket.

"But look what you've done," he said. He was shocked at her.

"What have I done?"

"You've killed the whole patch."

She wanted to say, What does it matter, what in the world does it matter now? but she didn't. She bowed her head and said, "I'm sorry, Gillon, I am truly sorry," and he accepted it.

5   SHE WOKE HIM AS THE SUN WAS RISING. SHE EN-tered the cairn and looked down at him. He never stirred, although his face looked troubled. The fishing lines were spread all across the floor, and she realized he must have been up for most of the night, just as she had been. She was sorry to wake him. She ran her hand through his hair—it was finer and silkier than she had thought it would be—and he drew away from her but then allowed the hand to stay.

"What did Mr. Drysdale say?" Gillon asked. He didn't open his eyes.

"He said you were a capable fellow with a propensity for steal-ing a few shellfish now and then, but a good seaman and someone I could trust."

"Propensity." But Gillon smiled.

"A Highland beach beggar, I believe he said."

"Why, the bastard!" He sat up then. "Where the hell does he think he came from?"

"Oxford? St. Andrews?"

"Mr. Angus Drysdale, the high and mighty water bailiff. I've seen the croft where he comes from. The family used to share the privy with the cattle." He got up. "Turn around, please."

He didn't like to have her see him arrange his dress and wash his face, it was too personal a thing. "Oxford," he mumbled. "Oxford, indeed." It was so easy to get his goat, she thought.

He picked up a bobbin of fishing line and headed with it for the door of the cairn. "You can put water on for tea; we have time for that." And then, "Well, the line's all greased and set," rather sadly, she thought. At the door, he turned back toward her. "I don't like this, Meg."

"Ooh," she said softly, almost breathed it, "the unco guid Mr. Cameron. Put on your Free Kirk face, so the world will know how good you are."

He knew he had on the face his mother used to wear when she pretended to put money in the collection plate and only rattled the coins. Maggie was on to him and it made him smile.

"When the 'sportsmen' want a fish, they get a fish even if they have to get the torches out at night; didn't you tell me that?" she said. Gillon nodded. "Then today we're 'sportsmen.'"

She wondered if she was always going to have to provide the finishing force for whatever it was they started. It wasn't too high a price to pay, she thought.

He had beached the boat, and once in it Maggie began to wrap the greased line around her legs. What astonished him was that she had gone right at it, not asking him to turn away, and it was hard for him not to look. He had seen those legs once before, helping her over a stile, and he had not been able to forget them. Gillon felt ashamed of himself; she so trusting, his mind so rampant with thoughts.

"And what did Mr. Drysdale say?"

"He believed it all. He wanted to take me over himself."

"He would. The man is a notorious lecher, you understand."

"Aye, I know that," Maggie said. What did she mean by that, he wondered, but said nothing.

It was an acceptable story, they both felt, a credible cover for the day's work. She was a student of Gaelic-Celtic heritage and had gone to Mr. Drysdale, the senior water bailiff in Strathnairn, for advice about Holydeen Island, which she was led to believe was a treasure house of Celtic lore and artifacts, much of it not even catalogued. He bent her ear over a half-dozen shandygaffs. The Druidical circle of standing stones at Stornish, not to be missed, the bailiff said. Then the celebrated broch at Dugg. Pictish, of course, which Maggie promised herself not to see, the chambered burial cairn, and, of course, the Witches' Rock, on which the last witches burned alive in Scotland had blazed.

"And would a Mr. Gillon Cameron be an acceptable boatman to take me across?" she had said. The bailiff was startled.

"Why him? Why *that* Highland beach beggar?"

"I'm on a tight budget, Mr. Drysdale."

"But let me take you over. For nothing."

"I have given my word to Mr. Cameron and my word with me is my word," Maggie said. Mr. Drysdale respected that. Now when they were seen together in the salmon waters not only did they have a story, they had the bailiff's blessing. It was, indeed, acceptable.

"You'll have to help me with this," Maggie said. The net had to be wound around the upper part of her body and then hidden beneath a blouse and jacket. Gillon wrapped the knotted twine softly around her and despite every effort on his part he felt the weight of her breasts and found that his hands were trembling. His lips were nearly touching her neck. Once around again, he went as fast as he could safely go, and once again he touched her and experienced a shock of pleasure that became an embarrassment so profound he could barely force his arms to continue. What astonished him was the softness of the breasts, the sense of weight about them, and the fact that they felt exactly as he knew they would feel.

"The question is . . . " He had nothing to say. "The question is . . . "

"How long it will take."

Gillon was spared. "Four hours out and four hours back if the wind is right and the tides are right and if we don't—don't—"

"Drown."

In half an hour they were out of the inlet and in the open sea. The fetch between the swells was deep and long, a product of the weeks of wind, and the rise and dip of the boat was pleasurable for her. With the small sail up and Gillon hard at the oars they made very good time. At the top of every swell she could see Holydeen off to her right and then hear the rushing, hissing of the swells running under them. From the sea, the Highlands seemed enormous. For all of Gillon's slenderness, Maggie could feel the boat leap each time he pulled on the oars, and she was impressed with his wiry strength.

"Shouldn't you pace yourself, Gillon?"

"I can do this from sunup to sundown and never stop," Gillon said, and she was impressed again. He would do; he would do very well. After an hour, despite the wind off the water, he was sweating but he didn't stop.

"Oh, God," he suddenly said. Maggie was alarmed.

"What is it?"

"Drysdale. His boat's at sea and he's coming our way."

She relaxed then. It was the sea she worried about.

"Let him come."

"You don't understand," Gillon said. "On the water, Mr. Drysdale is God."

The cutter was bobbing above them a few minutes later. The crew leaned over the side to check the contents of Gillon's boat. There was nothing to see but a gaff, which was allowable landing equipment.

"Boy taking good care of you?" Mr. Drysdale called.

"The boy is doing well."

"Cameron?"

"Sir?" He hadn't meant to say that.

"See that you look after Miss Drum, Cameron, the way you would your own mother."

He nodded. Mr. Drysdale wanted a "Yes, sir," out of him.

"Did you hear that?"

He nodded again and when he did, he saw with cold horror

that part of the line wound around one of Maggie's legs had become unwound and was trailing from beneath her dress along the bottom of the boat.

"Yes, sir!" he shouted.

"Miss Drum?" Maggie smiled up at him. "I came out to tell you something I neglected last night. Cameron?"

"Sir." He shouted again.

"Make sure she sees the wonderful statue to wee Bobbie Bartle. The lad was lost in the forest, you see, when a wee white birdie flew down and showed him the way to safety. Very moving, very touching. You know it, Cameron."

"Aye, sir."

"I'm *sure* you do," he said archly. It was an accusation of poaching for grouse on the island and all the seamen were smiling.

"Miss Drum, if you will look behind you, you will see Hardmuir rising from the sea. Where Macbeth and Banquo met with the witches, of course."

"Oh, indeed."

"Don't stand up," Gillon whispered.

"I didn't think the boy would know," Mr. Drysdale said.

"No, I doubt the boy would know."

The line had unraveled further, and Gillon knew there was nothing to do now, as absurd as it was going to look, but to pick up his oars and row away from the cutter while they were still talking.

"Don't forget our drink, Miss Drum. Pretty manners, Cameron, pretty."

When they were several hundred feet away, Maggie turned on him.

"That was childish of you," she said. "An old man makes a few little winks and nods at a girl and you pull up your oars in a sulk. . . ." He had been pointing at her feet and she finally looked down.

"Oh, dear God."

"Aye, dear God."

49

He rowed in a kind of sullen silence, taking his anger out on the oars and the sea.

"The boy. The boy wouldn't know," he said. She let him mumble. He looked her in the face at last. "What is this Macbeth and Banquo I'm not supposed to know about?"

"I don't know."

Then he was furious. "And you sat there and let him think you knew and I didn't, just as cool as that?"

"Yes."

And, finally, he began to smile because the laugh was on Mr. Drysdale.

"What is all this about a drink?"

"He wants me to have a drink with him at Highland Lodge and tell him all the secrets I found on Holydeen Island."

"But, my God, the man must be forty."

"Aye."

She felt the boat leap out from beneath her again.

"Are you going?" he asked.

"Aye. Is there any reason you should care?"

Her words fell like a dry fly on fast deep water, as light and dangerous as that.

He didn't rise to the bait. A mile or so from the island, the sea becomes unprotected and rough. Gillon rowed until the veins stood out in his forehead, and he was happy for the work. The wind shifted and the canvas moved around, hiding her from him for a moment. He was happy for the privacy, he needed to be alone with himself, but when the sail slapped back he was startled to see that her face was greenish yellow.

"My God," Gillon said. He felt his heart thump. "You're the color of sea lettuce."

"Well, turn away, then."

He felt helpless watching her narrow shoulders rise and fall with the effort of vomiting. She was so brave about it, he thought, and it was all done so swiftly and neatly. She leaned over the side and washed her mouth with cold sea water and it was all over.

"Any other woman—" he began, but she held up her hand to stop him. It had been very easy. She had merely thought of the words "hot kelp soup" several times and the deed was done.

Gillon was on his feet. "They're all around us now!" he shouted. "This is their nest before they go into the streams."

She thought she could almost feel them nudge the bottom of the boat. She was afraid of the water but she looked over the side of the boat and when she did, she saw them, enormous shadows, gliding, magnified by the sea, sudden dark shadows that seemed as large as the boat itself, the largest fish she had ever seen, fish large enough to feed a village, and she let out a cry of fear and excitement when one shadow broke the surface of the water in front of them, and for an astonishing moment she witnessed the arched silver thrust of sprung muscle.

"Hurry, give me the line!" Gillon shouted. He stood up in the boat, the gaff already at hand. "Give me the line," but she knew better. It was too early in the day for fish. When she wouldn't move, he sat down and looked at her bright brown knowing face and wondered how she had gotten so wise at her age.

Because she had been right. Mr. Drysdale had done his advance work well. They beached the boat down from Holydeen harbor so that Maggie could unwind the fishing lines from her legs and Gillon could hide the gear in the brush up from the beach, and when they walked down the shore to the town, a cluster of three or four squat stone houses topped with grass-sprouting thatched roofs, a man in a gig was waiting for them.

"You would be Miss Drum and this would be your caddie, Cameron," he said. "I am Mr. Comyn, your guide, compliments of Mr. Drysdale."

"I am no caddie," Gillon said. The old man had eyes cut from gray granite.

"Were you hired to row this young lady across from Strath-nairn?"

"Aye."

"Then you are her caddie."

Gillon was furious when he saw the foxy teeth flash in a quick grin. She had no right to do that.

"There is only room for one besides me in the gig," Mr. Comyn said, helping Maggie up into it, "but we'll go slow and your boy can trot along behind," and cracked his whip over the pony's ears. Maggie didn't dare to look back into Gillon's face.

They covered all of it that morning, the famous vitrified fort, the Pictish broch, a cunning piece of stonework that looked to Maggie like nothing more than a stone roof pack for a mine, fitting monument to a race of miners, then along a trout stream in which Gillon could see trout lolling in their pools, and down through a pine-studded glen to Bothwell Cross, a Celtic shrine in the middle of a small clearing. She could hear him, all that time, choking for air, his feet pounding the rough path, kicking loose stones, hanging on.

"You will be especially interested in the runic inscriptions on the base," Mr. Comyn said.

"That I shall."

Gillon whispered something in her ear when she was handed down from the gig, which it was just as well Mr. Comyn did not quite hear. It was, "Liar."

"And aren't you glad of it?" Maggie said.

"What was that?" Mr. Comyn said.

"Nothing, it was meant for the boy." The foxy teeth again.

The cross was an impressive piece of stone, beautifully carved, at once rough and delicate, a curious combination of the qualities of the people who made it.

"This I would say is one of the triumphs of the Celtic race, a great tribute to your people," Mr. Comyn said to Gillon.

"I am not a Celt, I am Scotch Gaelic," Gillon said. He was very sullen about it.

"Do you see what has happened," Mr. Comyn said to Maggie, "the degeneration? They don't even know who they are any longer."

He turned to Gillon with icy contempt, as if he were talking to some kind of mentally injured person. "You do not have to be a Scots Gael to be Celtic, but in order to be Scots Gael you *must* be Celtic."

Gillon reddened, and when Mr. Comyn turned away she whispered something in his ear it was also just as well Mr. Comyn didn't hear. It was, "Gowk."

After that they trotted down through a dim, deep glen past a rushing cascade and came to a stop near the sea in a stand of towering Scotch pines, last descendants of the ancient Caledonian Forest, where Mr. Comyn stopped to water his horse. Gillon lay down among the fallen needles on the forest floor and slept. He slept for only five or six minutes and when he woke he seemed completely refreshed. He would make a remarkable miner if he could do that in the pit, Maggie thought, and then Gillon got up and brushed the needles from his kilt.

"This is where I would like to live," he said.

"What would you do here?"

"Live."

He felt her eyes on him before he looked down into them.

"Just live? Is that enough for a man to do?"

"If he's happy." He couldn't understand why her eyes seemed so angry. "I could be happy here."

"Why do you think no one else is here?"

"I'm not anyone else. I know this much. I could be happy here."

She got up and left him and pretended to examine the thick red spongy bark of the pine.

"Oh, I don't know," she said, very low and very coolly. "I know I wouldn't want to spend my life in a little stone house sneaking things from the sea."

Mr. Comyn was bringing the gig back up the slope and she started down toward him.

"In my wee kiltie," she said, and didn't turn back to see the way he took it.

They were invited to lunch at Mr. Comyn's place, where the caddie was given his soup and bread in a pot outside the house on the lawn, and when they were done they went down by the shore and followed an old road that ran parallel to it until they came to a bog, which in time, a little further inland, became a swamp. Somewhere in the cool darkness of the swamp they found the stone. It was black and smooth with age and use. Gillon had never seen one like it.

"On this stone were burned more witches than were burned in all the rest of Great Britain together," Mr. Comyn said. Maggie ran her hand along the cool smooth stone.

"Don't touch it," the guide said to her, "bad luck. It is the worst luck in Scotland. They would stretch them out and stake them here and here and here—do you see the little holes in the stone where the iron stakes were locked? They would be, of course, naked. Excuse me, Miss Drum, but history is history, and all their parts shaved because the hair of the witch, especially from certain parts, excuse me again, was said to contain very strong and valuable properties." His eyes were glittering and she didn't like the way he licked his lips, like Rodney Bel Geddes when he passed her. "And when they were staked they put a fire on their bellies, just a wee one, a few little twiggies, and if they screamed, for each scream—proof that the devil inside them was being burned out of his hiding place—they added another stick, bigger each time, until the screaming was steady and they were consumed in flames."

Gillon had wandered away. The stories of witches did not interest him. He was, he felt, a believer in the rational explanation of life, but he turned around when he heard Mr. Comyn shouting, "Oh, Miss, please don't do that! No one has ever done that before," and was as stunned as Mr. Comyn to see Maggie lying on the Witches' Rock, spread-eagled on its cool blackness, her arms and legs stretched wide in order to touch the holes in the stone. It made Gillon feel strangely indecent and, for some reason, afraid, watching her lie on the black stone.

"Get off," he shouted at her, "get off the stone," and she sat up and looked at him in a very queer way and did. Even Mr. Comyn didn't think it odd that the caddie had yelled at his mistress.

"Never," Mr. Comyn was saying. "Never before. No one ever did that to me before."

They made the rest of the trip in silence, Mr. Comyn breaking in by cluck-clucking several times and shaking his head. He left them where he had found them and they started back up the beach. The wind was up, scud was flipping from the tops of the waves, and the water had turned to a hard blue from the soft milky green of the morning.

"Why did you do that?" Gillon asked.

"I don't know. I only know that if I had lived then, they would have burned me there."

Gillon didn't know what to say. Part of him suspected that she might be right.

"But I wouldn't have made a sound when they put the twigs on," Maggie said. "I wouldn't have given them the satisfaction. They wouldn't have gotten a whisper out of me."

He never forgot that.

6   THEY WAITED FOR A FAMILY OF SEAWEED GLEANERS to pass up the beach in their raggedy duds before carrying the hooks and net and lines across the beach to the boat.

"Yeer noo goon oot ter new?" the man asked.

"Aye, we're going," Gillon said, and the man shook his head. Maggie liked the determined way Gillon said it.

The gleaners watched them until they were far out at sea. The wind was whipping them hard.

55

"What's the matter with them; haven't they ever seen a boat go out before?"

Gillon smiled at her.

"They were hoping to get a beautiful tweed suit or at least an old kilt when the tide came washing in."

It left her with a cold feeling.

"Would you like to start tying the hooks on the lines now," Gillon said.

"Yes, yes, please." It would give her work to do while the water hissed under the floorboard.

It would be a hard trip, Gillon explained to her, but not a dangerous one if a man knew what he was about.

"Just go by the rules," Gillon told her. "Never test the sea. You must be humble before her."

It was what her father said about the mines. One more good sign, Maggie thought.

Their goal was to get a mile or so out beyond the spilling mouth of the Buckhorn River by twilight—the gloamin tide when the sun would be low in the water and they would be swallowed in its golden blindingness, hidden in that troubling light and by the high chop of the sea—and still be left with light enough to fish by.

It was a belief of Gillon's that somewhere out at the far mouth of the salmon rivers, somewhere between the full salt of the sea and the full fresh of the rivers, was a compromise point in the sea, a holding station for salmon, where the fish readied themselves for the fresh water after their long run from the open seas. Since the river water, fed from melting snowfields, was colder than the sea water, and colder water sinks, vast unseen kettles of salmon lay down in the black, almost brineless water outside the rivers, far deeper than men usually hunted them.

When they left the cover of Holydeen, the swell suddenly hit them broadside and the boat began to roll. Gillon saw Maggie look up suddenly.

"Frightened?"

"Are you?"

"No."

"Then why should I be?"

As suddenly as the swell had hit them, he felt he loved her for that.

"Excuse me," she said and, using part of the sail as a shield, she vomited her lunch, careful as always about the wind, and washed her mouth with brine. "That ends that," Maggie said, and he loved her for that. He decided to dare it right then.

"Now would you put these on the hooks?"

It was asking a lot of her. While he rowed, with his foot he pushed down to her a little metal tobacco box filled with crawling prawns. Some were dead and some smelled and some squirmed and thrashed for their lives. She studied the little shrimp and, without asking him a question, began hooking them on the barbs. He watched her spearing the prawns one after another, her no-nonsense head with that heavy rich brown hair bent to the job, never looking up from it when the boat heeled far over to one side. He loved her for that.

"I couldn't have come this far without you," he called to her, the wind was that strong.

"There's a long way to go," she said back to him.

Let him ponder on that one for a while, she thought.

He had read his winds and tides well. When he dropped his sea anchor in the water outside the estuary mouth and looked from the front of the boat back toward Maggie, he could see nothing but the fragment of a silhouette. He was blinded, and they were masked in the sun's slanting glow. And when the sun finally slipped under, they would then be veiled in dusk. So far, so good, he thought, better than he could have hoped. If the sun had been hidden by clouds, there was no way they could risk what he was planning to do. Gillon was very excited.

"They're here, I know that," he told her, and she believed him.

There was a way he went about it—looking over the sides of the boat, sniffing at the water, reaching down to feel its temperature, tasting it for salt—that made her think of fish, of salmon.

He had told her about that, about his affinity for fish, especially the salmon; how each spring he would go miles up from Strathnairn to see the great ones trying to leap Doigh Falls and how he always knew, at first look, the ones who were going to make it, the ones with the spring and the heart, and the ones who would drop back and never complete the mission some force had driven them thousands of miles to complete. He could often tell the fish apart from one another, something no one else could do. At night he would think about an individual fish he had seen fighting all that day to best the falls, and early in the morning he would walk miles back to see if it had made it over or failed.

"Now it's my turn," Gillon said. "Give me a line. This is the place."

The line was in the water no more than a few minutes when the fish struck. They felt the shock of it, a thump through the boards of the boat, and then the line began to strip out of the boat.

"He's running now," Gillon shouted. "He has the hook. Hold on."

His face burned with excitement, his eyes were wild with it. When the fish had run as far as the line would allow, there was a second shock; the hook had held, the fish had stopped, and the bow of the boat was pulled down toward the water.

"I have got my giant," Gillon shouted.

An angler along one of the streams, if he could have held such a fish on his line, might have spent an afternoon bringing such a fish to shore. With Gillon using the handlines, it was a matter of strength, his against the salmon's, and of the hook holding fast. Pull, hold, secure the line that had been retrieved, and pull again. It was hard work; this was a fish determined not to die before reaching its natural home in the fresh-water river.

It wasn't the way Gillon wanted to do it but the way he was forced to do it.

"I'm sorry," he said aloud.

"What are you sorry about?"

"It isn't sporting, it just isn't fair."

"And what is?"

When the salmon was brought to the side of the boat and felt the wood against its flanks, it leaped, the fine hard silver of its body showering them with sparks of lights and sea spray, and with that leap it was spent. It had uncoiled its life. It lay in the water alongside the boat, moving its fins to maintain its balance in the sea from some old memory, alive but actually dead.

"I'm sorry," Gillon said to the fish. "Forgive me." He turned to Maggie.

"I don't think I can get it in the boat."

The fish was as long as Gillon, well over six feet and all dead weight on the hook of his gaff. With a sudden tremendous effort that came close to causing the boat to tip and spill them into the sea along with their salmon, Gillon got the head and upper part of the fish up over the sideboard and was holding it there, resting, when once again it thumped hard against the side of the boat, one more compression of muscle left, one last spring of life.

"I can't hold him," Gillon cried out. "Oh, God, I'm going to lose my fish," and was conscious of something swishing dangerously close to his ear—the tail of the salmon, he thought—and heard a *thwack*, a hard wet smack of wood and fish, and the struggle was over as suddenly as it had begun. He put both feet against the gunnels and slid his salmon the rest of the way into the boat and then he saw her putting the oar back into the oarlock.

"Is that what you did?"

She nodded.

"You came close to hitting me." He smiled at her.

"It had to be done."

"I was nearly your salmon."

"It had to be done."

"Aye, it had to be done."

They looked down at the fish in the bottom of the boat. It was by far the biggest salmon Gillon had ever seen. It was a cock salmon, and old. Gillon knelt in the boat and ran his hand down the sleekit silver side of the fish.

"I feel sorry for you, old cock," Gillon said, "coming all this way and dying in the doorway."

He looked up at her.

"But it had to be done," and he smiled such a sudden sweet smile at her that she smiled back and thought, You sweet fool, you sweet romantic man.

"Better *us* to get him than *them*," she said.

Gillon turned his back to her so that she wouldn't have to witness the gory business of working the hook out of the fish's mouth.

"What makes you so angry with *them*?" he asked. His own anger was like a line squall, blowing up and blowing out as fast as it rose, but her anger was a cold and steady one, a season of anger.

"I don't like the way they look at me."

"And how is that?"

"They don't see me when they look."

"Aye, I understand."

"But one day I'll make them see me."

"Och, who cares? Who cares at all?"

"I care. All."

The hook was out and he began to reorganize his line as he talked.

"One day they closed the mussel beds at the Kyle of Tongue and we were living on mussels then. No one would say why. So one night when we were hungry enough and it was dark enough, sleet and snow, my mother went out to the beds at low tide and filled her creel with mussels. On the way home, a water factor, one of the bailiff's boys, crept up behind and cut the straps on her creel. The loss of weight was so sudden she fell backwards in the water."

He looked up at her. The line was ready. There was no anger in his face, which she found disappointing.

"By the time she got home, she was frozen. She died the next week."

"And what did you do about it?"

He lowered his head. "Nothing."

"Then you know what to do about it? Let's kill another of their salmon now." Gillon smiled at her again.

"Saumont."

"Saumont," Maggie said.

Gillon's theory proved to be right. The mouth of the river was deserted of fish except for the few who would run the river the next day, but farther out, where the brine and fresh water mingled with each other, dark shadows slid around their boat and then dropped away into the darkness below. In the next quarter of an hour or half an hour—there was no telling the time in the excitement—they killed three more salmon, hens and cocks, all of them big, the smallest bigger than Maggie.

It had been exciting, a rage of killing, and then it was over. All his life he had dreamed of killing one great salmon for himself and now he had done it four times over, and he suddenly felt terribly empty inside, quiet and a little puzzled at himself, and sad.

"We can go now," he said to Maggie. "Are you ready to go?"

"Yes. I'm set."

"Because this is the hard time, see. Are you prepared for it?"

"Yes."

He put the sail up and got his oars.

"Can you swim?"

"No."

"Nor can I."

They were very quiet then. He didn't tell her that he was testing the sea, but she knew. The boat was riding terribly low in the water. The good thing, which Gillon had counted on, was that the wind had died. The sun by then was sitting on the water. The dangerous time would be when the sun had set and evening not yet come, and they could be seen from shore. Gillon picked up the oars and began to row. It was heavy going.

The problem was light. Gillon wanted darkness now; the sun had set but darkness wouldn't come fast enough. He could still see the shoreline. Each pull of the oars was one more pull toward safety, but true safety lay in calm seas and darkness.

"How do you feel?" Maggie said. She was puzzled by the look on his face.

"I don't know. I never know how I feel," Gillon said. "Sad, I think. I don't know why."

"I know how I feel. Very happy. I know why you feel sad."

"Why?"

He was glad to be rowing, to have the feel of the oars in his hands, to be doing something.

"You had your dream of catching the great fish, and now you've done it and nothing lives up to the dream, does it?"

Gillon said he didn't know, he had so few dreams.

"No, nothing does," Maggie said, "and as soon as you learn that the better off you'll be."

"Don't move," Gillon ordered. "Bend down and sit still."

A circle of cold whiteness bloomed on the water ahead of their boat and began to slide and dip across the tops of the waves toward them.

"He has us," Gillon said, and put down his head, and then the brightness seemed to explode in the boat, a stunning white coldness of light; they were ringed in it, and then it passed on.

"He has us," Gillon said.

"They have *nothing*," Maggie said. She could hear shouting far off on the shore.

He began to row but there was no leap to it.

"Row," Maggie said.

"He *knows*," Gillon said. He was in despair. "Drysdale knows, he knew all along."

"No one knows," Maggie said, and her voice was very hard

and cold. "If they had us, the light would be on us now. Now take that sail down and row."

He felt foolish about the sail, and leaped up to pull it down. She was right, he knew, and he began to pull with fresh strength. Everything was running against them, the wind and the currents, the weight of the boat, the lack of a sail, but they moved out into the firth away from shore, fighting to get out beyond the sweep of the light.

"Oh, God," Gillon said, and put down the oars.

"What now?" She was angry with him.

"Don't you hear it?" She didn't. She didn't know the sounds of the sea the way he did. "Drysdale's cutter is in the water."

"He can't find us out here."

"He can if he has the light. The joke of it is, he's coming out to save you."

"Well, he can't save me if he can't find me. Go on now, Gillon, *row*."

But he didn't pick up the oars.

"We've got to get rid of the fish," Gillon said. "We've got to get the evidence out of the boat."

He stood up and came down the boat to where Maggie was sitting to seize the tail of the topmost salmon. He started to pull and she held him by the arms with a grip that amazed him.

"You don't throw those fish out. Those fish are as much my fish as your fish."

He would not let go of the salmon.

"If those fish go over the side," she said, very slowly and quietly in his ear, "I go with them."

He dropped the tail of the fish and went back to his oars.

"It's me who'll spend the time in jail," Gillon finally said.

"And it's me who'll wait for you to get out."

What did she mean by that? Gillon thought, but he rowed on, and soon, he knew, if everything continued right, they would begin making their turn for Herringtoon, picking up the favoring winds and currents. Maybe, he allowed himself to think, just maybe . . . And that was a mistake, as he knew it must be, because as soon as he thought it he heard the thumping pistons of Drysdale's engine pushing the cutter into the waves. There was no searchlight, only a large sea lantern on the bow, and when the ship was perhaps a hundred yards away, Gillon reached out and pulled Maggie forward on top of the salmon.

"Och, Gillon," she said.

"Quiet," Gillon ordered, "don't move," and she lay there groaning to herself, very quietly, while they rocked in the darkness, her face flat against the flank of the topmost fish, the stink of death and the sea overwhelming in her nose and mouth. She could hear members of the crew talking and calling to one another and then the voices were gone, but he wouldn't let her sit up until the lantern was nearly gone too.

"He'll be back," Gillon said; "we've got to get going." He took the oars and began to row as hard as he had at any time of the day. "They're making a search pattern in the water. With luck we'll be outside it when they come back down."

She didn't want to ask him, he was rowing so hard, but she did at last.

"Why did you do that to me?"

"To hide the reflection of the fish scales from the lantern. They shine like fireflies."

"Yes, good, but you've ruined my lovely tweed suit."

"It had to be."

"Aye, it had to be," Maggie said.

He wondered if he should tell her what he planned to do and decided she deserved it. The wind was rising and now was the time to risk it.

"I want to hoist the sail again but if I do we could swamp. We can be spotted by the sail but we also can run before the wind."

He waited. She didn't realize at first that it was a question.

"Well?"

"Put up the sail," she said. It was brave of her, he thought, and again was aware of his love for her. He went to work swiftly and skillfully until the sail was rigged and the wind hit the canvas with a slap and the boat began to plow through water. There was a moment when it heeled over and water began running over the gunnels and Gillon was certain he was wrong, that he had tested the sea and lost. He felt he should prepare her for drowning, there was no way, he thought, for the boat to right itself, but it did, agonizingly slow, inching its way up out of the water and then it was up, that suddenly, and the boat driving through the chop, almost skidding through the scud-flecked sea. Gillon was exuberant.

"Do you believe in God?" he called to her.

"Sometimes."

"Well, you should. You should offer a prayer."

"It was that close, then?"

"Aye, that close," he said, and saw that she was crying. He didn't blame her. Sailors would have cried; he might have cried if the work hadn't demanded all his thought and energy.

"Don't cry," he said, "don't cry, now; we're over the worst of it."

"It's not that." The tears wouldn't stop. He wanted to go back and hold her like a child.

"What is it, then?"

"My lovely tweed suit. It'll never be right again."

Far to his stern he could see the light from Mr. Drysdale's boat working over the choppy water. They would have beach parties out before long, scouring the coast, looking for washed-up bodies. And up ahead he could see the first of the little blinking lights from the herring fleet anchored outside Herringtoon harbor.

"We're safe," he said, and his head fell on his chest. He slept that way for several minutes. When he woke, he felt revived. They had won a tremendous victory, she would never know how great.

"Do you know what you and I should do?" Gillon said. He felt bold and very much at ease.

"What should we do?"

"We should . . . well. Perhaps I shouldn't have . . ." and he stopped. It was absurd, of course, a kiltie boy and a woman such as she. A man who never earned as much as a pound in a week—not fifteen shillings, usually.

"Yes?"

"I was speaking out of turn," Gillon said, and put his feet up on the salmon and let the sea carry him.

He looked back down the boat at her and then at the fish and suddenly began laughing. It was all so mad. What was this woman doing in his boat stealing these fish with him?

"What are you laughing at?"

"Us." He wanted to ask her how it had happened. He wanted to tell her what a victory they had won, but only a sailor would understand that. He was filled with the sadness of having done something memorable, surviving some tremendous storm and sailing into harbor safely, with no one to tell it to. They were coming into the first of the boats and Gillon got up to take down the sail and cover the salmon with the canvas. There was no need to flaunt the catch, not even in Herringtoon, where they despised Mr. Drysdale and his water factors.

She said very quietly, "I know a place where a man can earn forty-eight shillings a week."

It was a great deal of money. She could see his head nodding. It was incredible, he was thinking, how she knew what was in his mind.

"What do you think of that?"

"I think a lot of it."

He was back at the oars and glad to be rowing, since it gave him time to think.

"And in two years' time, he can be making sixty shillings in a week."

They were coming through the first of the boats, and he was pleased that no one seemed to pay any attention to them.

"Where?" he asked at last.

"Where I live."

The idea of it excited and puzzled him. What was she after?

"And what kind of thief do I have to become?"

"The kind my father is."

It was getting closer and closer, a kind of game they were playing, but he didn't know the rules, only that he was in a box and didn't want to get out of it.

"Which is what?"

"A collier."

"A what?"

"A collier."

He let go of the oars. "One of those who go down to mine the coals and all? That?"

He could see her nod.

"A coal miner?"

She nodded again. He slapped the water with an oar.

"He couldn't be," he nearly shouted at her. Some men in a boat looked at them and went back to their nets. He could see the teeth, her bright little moor-fox teeth, by the dim lights from the herring-boat masts.

"I couldn't be one of those—oh, no, never, down under the earth all day in the dark. I'd die down there. Oh, no, out of the question. How could I do it, anyway?"

"If you came with me."

She said it so offhandedly he couldn't let himself believe he heard it at first.

"I've heard about those people, anyway. Read about them. The dregs of the earth, scum of the earth. They used to be slaves in this country, you know."

"I know."

"No different than the blacks."

"I know."

"Then why would I want to be one?"

"Miners make money."

It was slow going through the herring fleet. The salmon-heavy boat was almost unmaneuverable but Gillon poled it through the crowded harbor until they were near the shadows of the wharves. They were not due to come in until the fleet had gone out and he dropped his anchor in the shallow water, hiding in the shadows, and waited.

"Is it cold down there, or hot? I would guess hot because it's nearer to hell."

"It's cool in the summer and warm in the winter."

He didn't know whether to believe her or not.

"And what about the black? Does it ever come off?"

"I would wash it off for you."

He felt his heart constrict as if it had been squeezed. The thought of her small brown hands running over his sweaty back, her hands pouring warm water over his head, the water flowing over his chest and back while she laved his body with rich creamy soap, made his hands tremble. He was afraid to talk because of the quaver he knew would be in his throat. He could see her smiling at him.

"They're beginning to go out now," she said to him.

"Oh, yes." He was glad for any movement but then he didn't move.

"You said, 'If you come with me.' "

"Aye."

Gillon lifted an edge of the canvas and pretended to be studying the fish.

"And what does that mean?" he asked, after a wait.

"Ah, Gillon," she said. She was laughing and yet there was a kind of anger in her laugh. He couldn't stop thinking of warm water and brown hands and the tub and the soap. "I am asking you to marry me."

He dropped the canvas back on the fish and looked across the water.

"Aye, I thought you were."

He did nothing. All the boats were leaving the harbor; the noise of oars and creak of rope and wind hitting canvas covered his silence.

"Which is the last wharf?" Maggie said.

"Why, this one."

"We want the fourth one in."

He pulled the anchor and poled the boat along the line of wharves. At the fourth one he ducked his head and began moving among the blackness of timbers and pilings. There were some stairs and then someone seized the boat and said, "Is that you, Miss Drum?" in the heavy Herringtoon accent.

"We gave you up for dead. How did you do?"

"Five. Five big ones."

"Four," Gillon said.

"No, I think five," Maggie said. Gillon never understood.

There was a dim light in the loft overhead and gradually they could see. A line was dropped and fixed to the tail of a salmon and the first of the first was winched away.

"Och, they'rt *beeeg*," Maggie heard.

"Hoosh, hoosh," someone said, and she determined to ask for more than was agreed on. These fish—all of them, she knew then—were special. She felt for the steps and went up the stairs and into the loft.

"No women here," someone said.

"But I *am* here," Maggie said.

Gillon could hear the argument, the tone of it but not the words, and he never asked about it later on. When the last of the fish had been hoisted into the loft he heard the sounds of ice and then the sound of money, coins being poured from a box to a purse.

"All right, fair is fair," someone said. "I knew something would come of this, from that first day. You can call me Cherry now. Partners in crime and all. Anytime you have another plan you know where to find me," and then Gillon heard her footsteps on the wooden stairs and she was back with him in the boat. She handed him three notes and a bag of silver and copper coins. The notes felt soft and warm and used in his hands.

"I never had one of these pound notes before," Gillon said, "and now I have three."

He poled out from under the wharf and headed down Herring-toon shore, along the wharves, for the dock at the Toon. Without the dead weight of the salmon, the boat leaped ahead in the protected water. He tried the words over and over, and they would not come right no matter what combination he arranged. In a few minutes he could see the light from the dock. Mr. Drysdale's cutter was tied alongside.

"We'll have to beach it here," Gillon said, and jumped easily over the side and began to pull the boat up on shore so Maggie wouldn't get wet.

"You'll have to walk to Lovatt Street and get around behind him that way."

"Yes."

"And, Maggie."

"Yes?"

"I'll do it."

"Do what?"

"What you said before."

"What? I said a lot."

"What you *said*."

"Marry me?"

"Aye."

He didn't know what to do then. Just because he had said he would marry her didn't seem to give him the right to embrace her. He had helped her out of the boat and they were standing along the shore, Gillon a little way out in the water, the way they had first met.

"Yes, well, that will be all right by me," Maggie said. He started toward her, feeling some kind of gesture was called for, but he wasn't sure what it should be and so he stopped. He wasn't much for standing on ritual.

"It will be very good," Maggie said.

"Yes, I think so," Gillon said, and then was amazed to see her turn around and start across the beach toward the alleyways that led into Lovatt Street.

"Where are you going?" he called out.

"Why, my drink with Mr. Drysdale."

He watched her all the way across the beach until she reached the alleyway and was gone. She wasn't much for standing on ritual either, he decided, although perhaps a little kiss or something like that might have been in order. But it didn't really matter too much, Gillon thought, and suddenly felt how very tired he was and got in his boat and began the long row home.

7   THEY NEVER TALKED ABOUT THE WEDDING LATER on. It had been a disappointment for Gillon and he never knew how Maggie felt about it.

He had hoped, in a clannish sentimental moment, to be married in the family kirk, but the deacon in Strathnairn would have no part of it unless they posted a month of banns and agreed to sit on the cutty stool the Sunday before the wedding in prepayment for the sins he knew they were about to commit.

"Further," he had said, stones of eyes through iced glasses, "I will not marry a child. How old are you, child?"

"Twenty-three," Maggie had said.

"Are you really twenty-three?" Gillon asked later.

"If you are going to tell a lie, tell a substantial lie," Maggie said, and he had learned something. But he never learned her exact age. Having never been a child, she was, in her way, ageless. Age was never a concern; it didn't seem to matter with Maggie the way it did with other people.

They were married, instead, in an O'er Boggie, a marriage conducted without a minister and arranged for them by Cherry MacAdams, who would know how to do that, in a fish house in Herringtoon by the Reverend Archibald Bothwell, unordained minister of the Reform Kirk of Nova Scotia for Returned Highlanders whose congregation consisted, as far as Gillon ever found

out, of one person, Mrs. Bothwell, who was not a returned Highlander.

It wasn't that Mr. Bothwell didn't try. Some of the service was
in Gaelic and some in English and some in Scotch. There were
songs sung by both the Bothwells, and the Reverend Bothwell
did a ponderous Highland dance that Gillon thought he remembered seeing danced before the bull was sent into the byre to mate
with the cows, and poems were read, most of them written by
Bothwell himself and a few by Burns. Before the service there was
an intermission and Mrs. Bothwell went downstairs for wedding
refreshments, which turned out to be pints of ale and drams of
whisky. It was a *very* reformed kirk. When the Reverend felt
strong enough the service was continued.

"Now, before I pronounce you man and wife, I will have my
closing words," Bothwell said.

"Gillon Cameron, from this hour forward, I want you to be the
master of the union I am now joining. Just as children are unhappy deprived of the guiding hand of a father, so is a wife
without a master in the house. It is a very sad house where the
rooster clucks and the hen crows.

"It is the way of life, the order of nature, the command of God.

"Will you do that for me, Gillon Cameron?"

"I will."

"And you, Margaret Drum. If your master does something
that you disapprove of, will you be understanding and not stamp
your foot and make pawky faces but know your proper place
in the order of the house? Because this is a good man. He may
at times be wrong—indeed, none of us are perfect—but he will
be right more often than he is wrong.

"So I say to you, for a happy nest, learn to close your mouth
and open your heart. And remember, Margaret Drum, as a
woman your silent submission is your beauty."

"Amen," Mrs. Bothwell said. Gillon was surprised to see that
she was crying, her eyes milky blue with warm tears. Margaret's
eyes were as dry as little brown pebbles on the sand.

"In your submission is your strength, in your submission is your key to freedom and to glory—the glory that God, not man, understands—and in your submission is your duty, which is the meaning of all life.

"Margaret Drum, will you do these things for me?"

She stared at the floor, in which Mr. Bothwell read humility. The floor was so rich in fish oil that bubbles came out of the boards.

"She will, she will," Mrs. Bothwell cried, and she embraced Maggie and stained the bride's bottle-green velveteen dress that Maggie had bought in a second-hand shop on Lovatt Street.

"In that event, I now utilize my authority as your agent of God here on earth to pronounce you man and wife. The ring."

Gillon was stunned. "You didn't tell me to get a ring," he said to Maggie.

"You're the master, you should have known."

Mr. Bothwell produced a tinny kind of ring that could not have cost a ha'penny to make. With the aid of a dab of fish oil, it was slid onto her finger.

"Mr. Cameron, you may now kiss Mrs. Cameron."

It was then that it reached him, the whole of the experience. How had it happened, how had it come this far and this fast? And why was he standing next to this little dark girl who he was supposed to kiss in public and live with for the rest of his natural life? He found he was trembling.

"In a kirk?" Gillon finally said.

"Oh, go on, give her a smooch," Mrs. Bothwell said, and she turned Maggie's little brown face toward him, and he kissed her on her cheek.

The cost of the service was ten shillings. It was more than Gillon had intended to pay, but when one considered the sermon and the songs, the dance and the poems and the ring, it was not that far out of line. Men of God must eat like everyone else, Gillon thought, and felt better about the ten shillings. When they went down the stairs of the fish house, Mr. Bothwell played them out onto Lovatt Street on his pipes with "The Liltin'," a very moving lament that Gillon only long afterward discovered was written for the dead at Flodden.

It was strange being out on the street in the morning, the fog cleared away and the sun shining, daundering along with no work to do. They walked along the harbor's edge, Gillon closely studying the boats in harbor, wondering if he should take her hand and deciding that it wouldn't look right at that hour of the morning, even if they were just married. In the week before the wedding, he had not had any trouble in talking to her, but now he had nothing at all to say.

"Well, how does it feel to be Mrs. Gillon Cameron?" he said. He knew it was lame.

"I don't know, I haven't tried it yet."

Gillon turned brick red.

"I didn't mean it *that* way."

"I did," Meg said.

"Ah, come look," he called.

It was his old boat, which he had sold the week before. The new owner had beached it and was at work caulking the bottom. They watched him work and Maggie took Gillon's hand.

"Our boat," Meg said.

The "our" was another shock to him, the way "Mrs. Cameron" had been. What was his was hers for the rest of his life.

"I'll miss her," Gillon said, and took his hand away. It was too much for a Strathnairn morning. The wind from the firth caused the brim of his hat to flare up on one side and it gave him a jaunty, even arrogant look.

"You look like *them*, Gillon."

"Och."

"It's why I married you."

"If you married a kiltie lad to get one of *them*, then you made a bad bargain." Maggie merely smiled.

With the salmon money Maggie had bought him a Shetland-tweed suit the color of peat-bog water, like the ones the painters who came to Strathnairn wore, all russets and rusts and reds, and a white linen shirt with a long soft collar and a wide tie, the color of heather, loomed from coarse soft wool.

"How does she seem?" Gillon asked. The man looked up from his caulking pot and stared at them. He didn't recognize Gillon in his hat and new suit.

"For a man who's starving, good enough."

They went on.

Over the tops of the gray-stone houses lined along Lovatt he could see the upper floors of the Bel Geddes house and her window, her room, and the intimacy of it alarmed him. He wasn't prepared to go there.

"I'll tell you what. Since I'm one of *them*, let's walk out to Fiddich House and have ourselves a proper toff's lunch."

He was surprised when she agreed. He thought she would object to the money.

"We'll have champagne," he said, and she nodded. "I'll snap my fingers and shout 'Champagne.'" Maggie nodded.

He was excited by the idea. A person should do that once in his life. Ever since the days when his family had been driven from their croft in Cromarty, he had wanted for one day to sit on a glassed-in terrace and have some bobbing Scottish girl, especially one he knew, serve him his tea.

"You know how to order it, of course?" She said it very quietly.

"You shout, I've heard them."

"What about fish? Do you just shout 'Fish,' and let it go at that?"

"I guess not."

"They ask you what kind of fish and how you want it done."

He was beginning to feel a little flattened.

"And they order champagne by the size. And by something called the vintage. And the color."

"I see."

He was flat. It was such a childish dream. He was ashamed of himself for even thinking of subjecting her to it.

"And do you know how to read a menu in French?"

"No, God, no, this is Scotland."

"The menus are all in French."

The worst of it, he understood then, just as he had been understanding things all that morning, was that he was never going to sit in one of those glassed-in terraces and have someone bring him his tea, not in all his life ahead. That was always going to be for someone else.

"Let's go back," Gillon said, and she agreed in the same voice she had used when she agreed to go out to Poshtoon. They cut across a lot where a great house had stood and into the area of old decaying houses where the lawns needed cutting and the hedges were overgrown. It was a sad place and felt chilly in the shadows. They walked along the backside of Lovatt Street until they came to the gate outside of the Bel Geddes house.

"Why are you turning in?" he asked her.

"We belong here."

"I don't."

"If I do, you do."

"And what will we do?"

"What people who are just married do."

He hesitated at the gate.

"With him in the house?"

"Yes."

She started down the path to the side door of the house but he wouldn't follow her.

"I won't do it," Gillon said. "I order you not to go."

Maggie looked at Gillon so hard that he was forced eventually to look down at the graveled path.

"Now you listen to me. I am Mrs. Gillon Cameron and you are Mr. Gillon Cameron and we are husband and wife under the laws of Scotland and the eyes of God, and we are entitled to share the same room and the same bed and I intend to do both." She took his hand. "Now come on with me, we belong here." He took his hand away but he followed her up the path. Before going up the steps he heard a tinkle on the white pebbles and looked down to see the tin ring bounce on the pebbles and roll into the weeds that edged the path. The ring will be there until I die, Gillon thought, and realized what a peculiar thing it was to think. Rodney Bel Geddes was at the desk, doing his ledgers.

"Congratulations," he said. He stood up, which he had never bothered to do before. "And, Cameron, congratulations." Gillon didn't even know he knew his name. He took Gillon's hand in that special way men have when something extraordinary has happened to one of their own kind.

"How did you know?" Maggie said.

"How did I know? This is Strathnairn, Miss Drum. Mrs. Cameron. One street, Mrs. Cameron, perhaps you noticed. What happens at one end gets down to the other end and what happens at the other end gets down to this end and nothing goes un-noticed. 'Did you hear about your little Miss Drum?' they said to me. 'Married a kiltie lad named Cameron.'"

"The key, Mr. Bel Geddes," Maggie said.

"Ah, yes, the key."

He put it in her hand, large, glinting dully of brass, and for the final time that morning, Gillon was faced with the truth that whatever paths life had intended for him, this was the most important one he would ever take. He thought of the sea just then, the openness of the water and his life in the boat with the winds and waves, the sun and the rain; and there was the key and up ahead were the stairs, dimly to be seen, and there was Maggie next to him, the key in her hand, and he knew there were no longer any choices left to him at all.

8 HE WISHED HE COULDN'T SEE THE SEA FROM THE window of the room but the glass was filled with the blueness of it and the sky, a sun-burning blueness so rare for Strathnairn, and

when he turned away from all the brightness he could almost not make her out, sitting on the foot of the bed.

"I don't think we should stay here," Gillon said. "Everyone must know. Everyone in the dining room must know."

"And I should be left alone on my wedding day, is that what you think is proper?"

He sat down on the one chair in the room as far from the bed as it was possible to get and twirled his hat in his hand as if it were an important occupation. He knew he looked foolish doing it. When he looked up at her, she was slipping out of her green dress and he quickly turned back to the window and the blueness out there. He wished it were darker outside; it would seem more natural that way. There was so much light in the room.

"All right," Maggie said, "you can look if you want. You might as well see what you have bargained for."

"Och, Maggie."

He wouldn't look. The word "bargained" bothered him. It was strange: she was there, something very solid and calm poised on the edge of a bed, but he didn't seem to be in the same room with her. He was standing and yet he could see himself sitting in the chair looking away. He wanted to leave and he wanted to stay, to become a part of the room the way she seemed to be, and all the while he had a dangerous sense of doing something wild and unpredictable.

"All right," he said, "what exactly am I supposed to do?" It had taken all his courage to say it, but as soon as he said it, he was glad.

"Make love to me."

He felt a numbness possess his limbs. He had once come out of the water that way, close to drowning, all numbness and a dying heavy slowness to his limbs.

"And what does that mean?"

"I can't describe it, Gillon," Maggie told him. "It's the natural thing to do."

He could not bring himself to look up from his hat.

"If it's so natural, why don't I know it?"

"You do know it."

"I don't."

"I don't believe you, Gillon. Come over here to me."

"But it's true."

"You were in the army."

"But I never listened. I turned away when they talked. I didn't like it, they made it seem so—I don't know—clarty. Saint Gillon they called me."

That had taken as much courage as all the rest. He felt that if he could keep track of the several boats clearing Herringtoon harbor, follow the raising of their sails and the lowering of their nets, then he could eventually place himself in life properly and get things in the room in order. And all at once she was beside him. She was in her robe but without moving his head he could see part of her brown leg and her thigh. He had been alone with her in the cairn but not this way: in a civilized room, in the real world, with a real bed and her, a real woman in a robe.

"Gillon." It was a kind of order. "Put down your hat." He dropped it on the floor.

"Do you know the word 'houghmagandie'?"

"Yes, they all said it."

"Well, say it."

He said it, his lips almost touching the window glass.

"There, is there anything so terrible about that? I said it and I'm still here and you said it and you're still here. Do you feel so terrible, so clarty?"

He felt a little better.

"And daffin, do you know it?" He didn't. "Daffin is different, daffin is like us, daffin is when a husband and wife make love. Luve, we call it in Pitmungo; it sounds more like what it is that way."

"Yes." He liked that, luve.

"In daffin there is fun and nice and that is all there is to it."

"How would you know?"

"Girls in coal towns know everything sooner or later."

He could see her toes, little lean brown toes keeking out from under her robe, playing with the floor and the soft clothing, and without his knowing why, perhaps because it was so personal and so inoffensive at the same time, they excited him.

"I know the words," he admitted, "but I don't know how to go about it."

She said nothing.

"And, besides, the bed will creak." And she began to laugh, not at him, he knew that, not very loud, but at the situation he was in and they were in and what he had revealed.

"So, Gillon, you know all about it."

"I do *not*."

"Sit on the bed with me." It was an order and she led him across the room to the bed before he could find a way to resist. When they sat on the bed, holding hands, his hand very cold and wet in her hard little dry warm hand, he was suddenly enormously conscious of how loosely tied the robe was, how open to him, and that underneath it were only her few underclothes and that although this was his wife it was also fairly outrageous. She found his eyes looking at her and he reddened.

"Do you know why you turn red all the time?"

He pulled away from her. He didn't like to talk about himself and he told her that; it made him restless and uneasy.

"You don't?"

"I don't."

"Because your mind is so filled with everything about it, you think the whole world can read it."

"Och."

"It's true, though. You're worse than Rodney downstairs and worse than Mr. Drysdale."

"Och." It was absurd. "He goes after all the girls."

"And so would you."

"Och."

She took his hand again and he allowed it.

"You are a romantic, you see, Gillon. Do you understand the word?"

"Aye, I know the word."

"You've thought about the day and dreamed about the day so much you almost can't do anything about it now it's here."

"Och, that is your absolute pile of . . . well, nonsense," but he knew the moment she said it that it was true, and once it was there it wasn't so painful.

"But you'll get over it, Gillon, I will guarantee you that. I've seen them before, shy little boots in kirk, little angels in their pews, and then they go into pit and get their lass and the little boots are prancing goats. Doup skelpers."

"Doup skelpers?"

"Bottom pinchers, bottom smackers."

"Och."

"You will."

Absurd, he thought, a man who had never dared run his hand down the arm of a woman and he should be a carouser, one of the world's lovers, absurd, and yet it made him smile a little bit.

"Because you have luve-glint in your eyes, Gillon, and nothing you can do will put it out. Anyone can see that. Now, this is what we are going to do. I am going to get undressed and get into our bed."

His pulse began to pound as if he were rowing into a headwind.

"And when I am there you will get undressed and come to bed." Orders again, it was better that way.

"And after that nature will tell us what to do."

"I see."

"God will reveal it to us."

"I see."

"Because that is the way that must be natural. The original ones, they didn't have anyone to tell them, they didn't have guidebooks about it."

"No, I see that."

"They just . . . *knew*."

. . .

He lay there looking at the ceiling, conscious of the heat coming from her body, trembling a little bit but not as much as he had feared he would. It is enough, he thought, for a start, just to lie there and watch the sun shots from the water far out glister in patterns across the ceiling. Nothing is being revealed so far, he thought. It was just as well, the slow way. When he finally dared to turn and glance at her he was surprised to find she had fallen asleep. He had a mind to get out of bed. It was certainly insulting to him, as a man, as a doup skelper of the world—but then he lay still and watched her the way he had the night of the salmon, smelling the essence of her the way he did with the salmon, breathing her, knowing all of her presence, knowing everything about her.

It became clear, each minute a little clearer, what was demanded of him, some force in him now running stronger than his own nature. He was the salmon and she was his goal. All his life he had spent getting here and now, he knew, he must have her, because it was right and nature's way. So he struck.

She never said a word but once.

"I told you," she said, right into his ear; "didn't I tell you?"

He knew everything that had to be done and was aware that he always had. He was only surprised by the force of the climax and at the fact that such a little person could accept it so totally without being damaged. He didn't know if she experienced the same thing he did and he was never able to bring himself to ask her. He hoped she did.

They moved apart from each other and lay in bed, looking upward, trying to understand the meaning of what they had just experienced.

"I don't believe other people have ever done it just this way or else we would have heard a lot more about it," Gillon finally said.

She had liked it, which had not surprised her. All the pithead girls liked it, and she could see no reason why she wouldn't like it when her time came. It didn't really matter whether she liked it or not; it was the way it was and the main business was to begin getting her family as soon as possible. The fact that there was some strange kind of animal fun in it besides was just so much added butter to the oatcakes.

But it was also, looking back on what they had just been through, thinking of the wild things she had wanted to say in Gillon's ear, all the hungry biting of the body that had gone on, a little bit absurd. If this was the only way that He could find to reproduce his kind on earth, Maggie thought, then God's imagination was more than a little childish.

Gillon rolled over on his side. God is truly wise, he thought, and fell asleep.

She woke him once that afternoon.

"Gillon?"

He opened his eyes but didn't move.

"I want you to promise me one thing."

"Yes?"

"When we go, and when we get there, I want you to promise me to wear your hat."

"Is that it?"

"That's it."

It was so silly it made him laugh aloud. It was amazing, he felt, how at ease he was in the bed.

"And if I do, one promise from you."

"Oh, no."

"Oh, aye, a promise for a promise," and he reached over and although she was trying to move out on her side of the bed he caught her.

"It's unhealthy. I know it is. Excessive."

"It's natural. Nature told me to do it and could nature be wrong? God must know what is correct. God is always correct."

"God is a gowk sometimes," Maggie said but decided that since this was what had to be done, she might as well do it as well as she knew how.

When he woke again, it was early evening, he could tell from the light in the window, and she was dressed and four little hot meat pies were steaming on a chair by the bed.

"Come on now. Two and a half for you and one and a half for me. Eat them while you dress. We have to go."

"Go?"

"I have booked for the evening train so we don't lose a day."

He got out of bed forgetting where he was. Naked in front of her, he bit into a pie. He had been starving.

"Oh, these are good," Gillon said, crossed the room to where his tweed suit was laid out for him, and caught sight of himself in the window.

"Good God, I must be mad," he said, making an effort to cover himself with the meat pie.

"Oh, what's the difference, in the bed or out of it."

"There is one, there is one," Gillon said.

He turned his back and put down the pie and dressed as quickly as possible. All his things were in the box that his suit had come in and Maggie's were in the Gladstone.

"What happened to your bag?" Gillon said.

"Nothing happened to it; that's the way things are in Pitmungo."

She smiled at him and he didn't believe her.

"Isn't there a back way?" Gillon said. "He'll be there."

"That's why I want to go down the front way."

He was at the desk and he gave Gillon a man-for-man wink that Maggie was intended to see. She winked back at him.

"So the huntin' was good, then," Bel Geddes said.

"I bagged the prize buck."

Gillon didn't know what they were talking about.

"And one more thing," she said. "About your coal."

"My coal?"

She gave it the full Pitmungo treatment. "Weel, they're no selling you coal at all, Jock, they're selling you blackslate and charging you for cannel. Plenty of ash and very little heat."

She nodded to Gillon and he picked up the box and the Gladstone, and they went down the walk and out the gate and into Lovatt Street.

At the station, she left him on the loading platform and went down to the ticket office and wrote out a wire to her father. It was the first wire ever received by a Pitmungo miner, and they had to call Tom Drum out of the pit when it came: "I HAVE GOT MY GAEL AND AM BRINGING HIM HOME." Ten words, not one more.

9 THEY WERE BARELY ON THE TRAIN AND OUT OF Strathnairn when they passed the loch, very deep by the blueness of it, steep walled by pine-covered hills, and an island in the middle on which stood the ruins of a sprawling, time-battered building. Maggie was surprised that she hadn't seen it coming in.

"What is that?" she asked, and Gillon was forced to turn away from his examination of the train. He had never been on a railroad train before.

"I had forgotten you could see it from here. It's the castle."

" 'The castle'!" She mimicked him. "What castle?"

"Cameron Castle."

"Oh."

She was struck by the enormity of the possibilities. It was much more than she had bargained for. A castle in the family. She loved that word castle exactly as she loved the word siller, sibilant, hissing off the tongue like water sliding beneath the bottom of a boat.

My castle. Our castle. Cameron Castle.

"Do we have a claim to it?"

He didn't notice the "we." "All Camerons have a claim to it.

My family own a brick or two in the dungeon." She was silent until the castle was gone from sight and the train was in the darkness of the tunnel. Although there was another traveler in the carriage with them Gillon dared to kiss her.

"That was a clarty trick," Maggie whispered.

"It was meant to be."

He even held her in his arms for part of the night.

In the morning they were in the Cairngorms, which were deep in snow although it was almost June. As the sun came up, the night-blue peaks turned red and then, as day came on, back to white again. They ate oatcakes and drank cold tea Gillon had bought at a stop the night before. The other passenger was asleep.

"What is a moudiewort?" Gillon said.

"A mole."

"You said you came from a long line of them."

"It was a joke, you see. Moudieworts. Moles. Miners. Miners moil underground."

It had bothered Gillon for days. He didn't see anything funny about it and she caught that in his face. He was worried about the work ahead.

"Being a miner isn't as bad as people think," Maggie said.

He didn't want to talk about it. He wanted to see this country he had never seen. Far below them he could see a soft green river, fed from melting snow, running in a glen. On the side of a hill there was a croft like the one he had grown up on, all brown mulch and bright greens. There were still flinders of snow in the cow yard, and for some reason he felt sad and thought of his father and mother and sisters.

"Mining is a way of thinking. Are you listening?" Gillon nodded. "You can mine coal and not be a coal miner."

He nodded.

"If you let yourself act like a miner, you become one, but the Camerons will *not* be miners."

He wanted to point out a pasture filled with shag-haired High-land cattle, but when he turned to her he saw that she was not focusing on anything, that she was far away from him or the train, in her own world.

"We're going to mine coal, oh, yes, and when we have enough siller put away, we're going to become something else."

"Aye."

"Something better."

The man in the carriage was awake now and was staring at Maggie with his mouth slightly open.

"What locks the miners in will spring *us* free." She said it triumphantly.

"Yes."

"Because we're a going-on people."

He wasn't listening at all any more. They were passing through good farm country, better by far than any he had ever seen, winter wheat already high and green and the cherry and apple trees in bloom. The land looked fat and rich and the barns beside the whitewashed houses were enormous and clean. God could sleep in one of those barns, Gillon thought.

"Is this what Pitmungo is like? Anything like this?"

It took a true effort on Maggie's part to bring her mind back to the train and to look at the farmland outside.

"Well, no," she said, "not like this."

She saw the man smile when she said it.

"Do you know it?" she asked him.

"I know what it's like," the man said, and got up and went out into the passageway.

The train chuffed into a small dark mill town where they made linoleum, and the stench of jute and linseed oil made Gillon cough. He could see men and women and children in the mill working with cloth tied over their mouths. They were covered with oil and looked black.

"How do people stand it there?" Gillon said.

"They get used to it."

"I wouldn't."

"You will, you'll see."

The traveler was getting off.

"That's a very nice dream you have, Missus. I hope it comes true for you."

"It will, I'll see to that."

"Aye, because it never has for no one else before."

"We're not no one else."

"Aye. Time will tell. Good-bye, then."

She nodded at him coolly.

"What was that all about?" Gillon asked.

"A mean little man with a mean little mind."

Gillon went back to looking at Scotland.

They rode all that morning into early afternoon and the countryside became more rugged and dotted with more of the little dark mill towns, and then Maggie asked Gillon a strange thing.

"Are you a good fighter?" He looked at her in a puzzled way. "I mean fight *very* hard, where a man wants to break your bones?"

He thought about it and said he didn't know.

"Take a real beating and still stick it out?"

"I'd have to see. Why?"

She looked at the fine bones of his face, those sharp vulnerable cheeks and that fine lean nose, and felt a little ashamed of herself.

"I'm fast and can last a long time," Gillon said. "The way I did when I was in the army was stay away from the man—hold him off; I've got the long arms, you see, and when he got tired, crack him good."

It didn't sound reassuring to Maggie. They passed through Upper Kinglassie and she let Gillon know that Cowdenbeath was next and it was time to start getting their things together.

There was no one there to meet them.

"What do we do now?" Gillon asked. "Can't we hire a carriage or something?"

"We walk."

They went down the Kinglassie Road leading out to the river and on to the Pitmungo Road.

"Why are all the houses in rows that way, all staring into each other's face?"

"That's the way they're built. It's cheaper that way."

"I wouldn't like it."

"You get used to it."

Outside Cowdenbeath, the countryside was pleasant enough and Gillon's fears were calmed, except by the river.

"Why is the water all black?" he asked.

"From the mines."

"Where are the mines?"

"You'll see."

He followed her and could not take his eyes off the rising and falling of the muscles of her leg, like ripples in brown water, the compact shock of muscle at the calf, a ball of muscle, and then a rippling away, an actual flowing of the flesh. Compact was the word for her, Gillon realized, watching her, every part in the right place, and yet despite the compactness, a suppleness to her compact body that made his mouth dry with desire.

To the right of the road, up on the moor, was a stand of weeping beeches. It would be dark in there, and quiet, Gillon thought.

"I want to go up and see those trees," Gillon said. His voice was high-pitched. "I've never seen anything like them before."

She knew what he was after but she went. She had read somewhere that on the eve of battle, Indians or Africans, some people like that, indulged themselves and that it drained them of their fear. In the little wood the leaves were damp but it was dark and still.

"You didn't come here to see the trees," Maggie said.

"I swear to you I did," Gillon said, but he seized her, almost without knowing what he was doing, and she let him.

When it was over she looked at the brilliance of the sky through little openings in the dark copper-colored leaves.

"You are out of hand and need to be controlled," she said. She wasn't angry; it was a statement. Her skirt, which buttoned down the side, was open and some sheep had come to edge of the copse and were looking at them.

"Did they see us?" Gillon said, and made a move to close her skirt.

"Och, Gillon, in the name of God," Maggie said, but he tried to close the dress again because he didn't like the idea of the animals seeing her. "You don't notice anything when you're carrying on, do you?" She pointed at the sheep. "Notice something lacking?"

Gillon studied their long sensitive stupid faces and finally admitted that he didn't.

"No ram. You know why?" Gillon didn't. "He's tied up. Tethered out there somewhere, because if they let him go you know what he would do?" Gillon said no.

"He would do himself to death," she said, and swung her skirt closed. Gillon turned red. "And that is the way of all rams." She put a ribbon from her hat around his throat and pulled, one little quick jerk of the ribbon, and laughed and got to her feet to go.

They went on across the High Moor, upward all the way, until Gillon felt they were walking to the sky. Near the crest of the moor, the Firth of Forth suddenly spread out below them.

"You have the sea here? Why didn't you ever say so?" It made Gillon feel better.

"No one goes down to it. You won't either."

But I will, Gillon thought, I will; and then they went up over the crest, and down below them stood the town.

Squatted the town. Blackly in the bottom of the black valley by the black river. Gillon knew what it was but he didn't want to believe it.

"And what is that?"

"That's it. We're home. Pitmungo."

He sat in the thick moor grass and looked down into the valley.

"I don't want to live in a place like that."

"But that's where we live."

She was sorry the day on the moor was so beautiful, making

Pitmungo look blacker by the contrast. He looked down at the mine tipples and black little rows of houses.

"I won't go down. We can find some other way to make a living."

"You will for me," Maggie said. "You know that. You promised me."

He looked down at the town for a long time and went back up to the crest and looked down at the Firth of Forth and saw Maggie standing alone on the moor and knew that it was true: he had promised her and, more important than that, he wanted to be with her and he wanted to have a child by her. That astonished him. Because he had known this woman, this girl, she was even now possibly carrying the beginning of his child. He trotted back down the moor.

"How long will we have to live here?"

"Until we make enough to make a new life."

"All right. Let's go down."

He shouldered her bag and took her hand—the moor was very rough there—and they started down.

I will go as a miner, he promised himself, and be the best coal miner I can, and when the debt to her was paid they would go away and leave all this blackness behind them. Because he also promised himself that he would not surrender his entire life to dirt and darkness merely in order to earn some silver.

10 WHEN THEY CAME DOWN THROUGH THE WHITE Coo plantation, out from under the budding trees in the orchard, they could see the crowd in front of Gaffer's Gate, sitting on the gate and along the wall.

"What's that about?"

"Don't stop, Gillon, just keep walking as you are."

They could hear them shouting. The crowd had seen them.

"No matter how loud they get, don't show them any fear."

The wind over the moor had tilted the brim of Gillon's hat up and the tail of the deer shivered, and to Maggie he looked gallant. Perhaps they would respect that. One thing was certain, she thought, they had never had one like him before in Pitmungo. Mrs. Gillon Forbes Cameron returning home with her gentleman husband. Perhaps they would respect that.

"What is it?" Gillon asked. He started to slow down.

"Don't break stride, don't show them any hesitation. Walk through them as if you were Lord Fyffe's nephew."

Her heart was beating like a bird in her throat. The first of the little pit boys, the more daring of them, all gray and shite-faced, were leaving the gate and coming up the footpath toward them. She had timed it wrong. The shift was out and the miners were up from the pit. But it didn't matter. If they didn't get him at the gate, they'd get him at the shaft head, where they caught the eight men from Glenrothes the year before and beat them into pulp. The Coal and Iron Company had brought them in at night, hoping passion would die in the brightness of morning, but the Company had been wrong. The shouting—that boisterous roar of a mob that has no fear in it, only the expectation of blood— had grown louder. Despite her, Gillon stopped.

"What in Christ's name is this, Maggie?"

She had never seen him angry this way before. Perhaps it was for the best.

"They don't want outsiders to come and mine their coal."

"But how did they know I was coming?"

"They know, they always know." She was sorry for her wire now.

"But you said there was work, lots of work."

"There is. The Company wants to fill the jobs but the men send them away."

"Send them away?"

"They make it so the men don't want to stay," Maggie said. She took his hand.

"You stand by me, Gillon, and I'll stand by you." He knew she would do that.

"What do they do? Just tell me." He seized her by the arms.

"Not in front of them," she ordered. "Ding you, smash you so you can't work."

It was ironic, Gillon thought. He had made his peace with this town and with its work, and then it turned out that the town was determined that he not work even if they had to break his bones to make sure of it.

"You should have told me, Meg. You should have let me know." He looked at her in a way that disturbed her. With her silence, she had lied to him. "All right," he said, "let's go down."

They were on them soon after that, the pit boys, dancing just out of reach, shouting obscenities.

"Don't look at them," Maggie said. "Don't give them an opening. Don't see them. They're only the mouthers."

Slee, shite-faced pit boys, clarty with their pit dirt. To Gillon they were horrible-looking ugly little gnomes in black masks, bony little hungry faces, fierce little eyes like weasels in the dark and gaps between the stumps of their teeth.

"Weer gunta flype yerr Hieland arse," one screamed.

"What is flype?"

"Turn inside out," Maggie said.

"An't he gruund, a fewkin toff come t'howk coal wi' t'peepule?" another shouted, and darted in and laid a wet black hand on the back of Gillon's tweed jacket. Another tried for his face and touched his lips. It was his first taste of coal dust. Gillon lifted a hand but Maggie stopped him.

"You've got to stand above them."

It was the hat that bothered them the most.

"The hat," they shouted, "get the hat," and the shout was taken up down at the gate. "Knock the bloody hat off the man's bloody head." The pit boys tried but Gillon was too tall for them.

When they were perhaps fifty yards from the gate the people grew quiet, watching them come on, hand in hand, looking straight ahead of them, looking through and over what was waiting for them. When they neared the gate the people began to back away from them, a response to a man who seemed strange and alien to them, not another miner from another mine whom they could understand but a man who seemed to be from another class entirely, and Gillon and Maggie were doing it, actually going through when a miner stepped in front of them, blocking the way.

"That's far enough."

"Oh, God," Maggie said. She hadn't meant to, but she knew him: Pitmungo's self-appointed enforcer. She pulled back on Gillon's hand, but he kept walking until the two men almost touched.

"I said far enough. No going through the gate."

"I have a job promised here," Gillon said, but the man shook his head.

"Pitmungo coal is for Pitmungo people. No incomers through the gate."

"And who's to stop me?" It was a formality. Gillon felt his heart begin to thump rapidly. The man was built like a young bull and his pit dirt only made him more menacing.

"Andro Begg."

"With that pick?"

"With these." He showed Gillon his hands. They were chunks of black rock.

Begg took his pick from his belt and threw it on the cobblestones. Gillon didn't know that in coal town this was the gauntlet being thrown. When the pick head hit the cobbles the miner swung and hit Gillon in the chest with a smashing blow that knocked the wind out of his lungs. Gillon held up his hand in trust that the man wouldn't hit him again and began taking his coat and tie off, slowly, buying himself time.

"That was not a personal blow," Andro Begg said; "that was a civic duty."

Gillon then decided to take off his linen shirt, and the crowd hooted at his lean whiteness. "It's a chicken fighting an ox," someone shouted.

"If I was you," the miner said, "I would take that fancy hat off your head before I have to knock it off." Gillon put the hat neatly on the pile of clothes.

The blow had hurt but it had also knocked some of the fear from Gillon. The anticipation was as bad in its way as the blow and a man can hurt so much and it doesn't matter after that. He was sizing the miner up. His neck was almost as thick as Gillon's narrow chest and his arms were like oak piles, but they were also stubby, as were his legs. He had just worked a ten-hour shift underground and his thick pit clothes and woolen underwear were heavy with sweat and mine water. The man's hobnailed boots were clumsy and the nails slid on the cobblestones. If he didn't get hit too hard too soon, Gillon reasoned, if a bone didn't get broken, if he could hold him off with his long reach, there was a chance of surviving, not of beating the man but of wearing him out until the fight became some kind of stand-off. When Begg knocked him down a second time, he helped Gillon to his feet and appeared sorry for him when Gillon said no, he hadn't had enough.

After that, he began sparring with the miner, staying away from him, stalling for time, afraid of him but not too afraid to move, letting the smaller man come at him, swinging, swinging, spending his energy, listening to Begg's breath come increasingly in gasps, until he stung him once, a hard quick jab to the cheek that knocked some of the pit dirt off the miner's face and caused a puffing under one eye. It frightened Gillon—he hadn't wanted to arouse the bull too much—but when Begg came at him again to make him pay for the insult, Gillon found he could move back—back away, circle around, keeping his long left arm out— and make the man miss and miss again.

Few men not in training can fight more than several minutes

at a time. The miner was fighting and Gillon was holding him off, and the kind of work the miner did may not have prepared his arms for a fight the way Gillon's work at sea had done. It was almost with fear that Gillon realized the man in front of him could no longer hold up his powerful arms. With each futile swing they dropped a little, the effort to hold them up and swing once more becoming unbearable. Like a fish that has struggled unwisely, Begg had played himself out and was ripe for the gaff, his mouth open, gasping for air, his tongue showing like a dog's at the end of a chase. Gillon took his hand away from the man's head, where he had been holding him off, and danced around him, wondering if he dared. His arms down by his side, the miner turned and turned to face him, the way wounded bulls turn toward matadors, and suddenly Gillon smacked him full in the face, a terrible blow he could feel all the way up his arm before he danced away.

Begg stood there, staring at Gillon, his jaw hanging open, and Gillon realized he had broken it. The bull rushed him, crying in rage, and swung just once, and Gillon hit him an open full blow to the kidneys that made the miner cry out against his will.

"In the gut, Gillon," he heard Maggie shouting, "you'll break your hand on his head. Go after the baggie, Gillon, you've got him, you've got him. Hit him in the gut and his head will die."

The crowd had changed, in the manner of crowds. They wanted Begg down now. They had come for blood, and now that they smelled it, they wanted it no matter whose it was. They weren't going home without it. Gillon looked at Maggie.

"Hit him," she said.

He pounded the man in the belly and the miner simply stood there. There were lumps the size of grouse eggs under each eye, and with a high blow Gillon ruptured one and it bled like a lanced tumor and covered them both with blood. Gillon dropped his hands again. "You can't leave the man that way," someone said to him, "he's entitled to the ground," and Gillon decided to knock him down before the man died. He pummeled him in the stomach until the miner slid down on his knees and knelt there on the wet stones in front of the gate like an ox that had received the killing blow.

"Go down, Mr. Begg, for Christ's sake fall down," Gillon said, and when the moon-faced ruin of a man looked up and said nothing but shook his head, tears coursing out of sightless eyes, Gillon kicked the man in the shoulder and he went over, all at once, the way boats at times go down, keel up and over, and with a plash landed on his face on the stones.

Some man had his hand in Gillon's hand.

"That was a brulzie, lad, that was a *brulzie*. Never one like that in Pitmungo before."

"Take your hand out of mine," Gillon said.

"But I'm your faither, lad. Tom Drum."

Gillon was too tired and too sick to look at him. Mr. Drum wasn't offended.

"I've always wanted a boy and now I've got a man," he shouted to the crowd.

Gillon put on his shirt and his tie and his coat, and then went over to the fallen man and knelt down by him.

"Mr. Begg?" He was afraid the man might die in his own gore, but his face was sideways on the stones and he was breathing heavily but regularly. Gillon watched the fall and rise of the powerful shoulders and felt proud and ashamed and sad all together.

"Let him lie there," Mr. Drum said. "He'll want to come to on his own. It's the way here."

Then it's a rotten way, Gillon thought.

One of the boys who had been the most obscene on the path down to the gate came running with his hat.

"Your hat, Mister. We was goin' to keep it," the boy said. Gillon pushed back his long hair—they wore it much shorter here, he could see—and put on the hat, and the people shouted at that.

97

"What is it about the hat?" Gillon said.

"We don't wear them," Mr. Drum said. "The coal masters wear hats. We wear caps. Hats is for the gentry."

"I wear hats," Gillon said.

He wanted to get away from that body on the stones and the noise and all these small, dark, hard-looking people.

"Are you ready to go down, Gillon?" Maggie asked, and she took his hand. It hurt, he noticed. They stepped around the body of Andy Begg, which was still guarding the gate.

"Look at that," Tom Drum said. "The great Andy Begg lying on the ground and bleeding like a stuck grumphie," and then they passed through the Gaffer's Gate, the first incomer to win the right to dig coal there in the history of Pitmungo.

"You were brave, Gillon," Maggie said.

"I won't forgive myself soon for doing that to a man."

"Meaning you won't forgive me."

Going along Colliers Walk down to the Drum house on Miners Row, Gillon found he could no longer hold his head up and they half carried him the rest of the way. Later, when he was lying in bed, he could remember almost nothing of the walk down except one impression that had come to him over and over. It was the dirtiest place he had ever seen.

11

HE HAD NO IDEA HOW LONG HE STAYED IN BED—A week or more, he thought. (He wondered who the dark woman was who watched him from the door of the room, never speaking to him, but watching always. Maggie's mother, probably.) When he got up he had to hold on to the walls and the furniture in the house. There was a buzzing in his head that caused him to lose his balance and he took several falls.

"Sometimes I have to wonder who won the fight, after all," he said to his father-in-law.

"Oh, no, lad, you would have to see Andy Begg. He'll never look the same again. He tried to show up for the shift today and Mr. Brothcock sent him home. He didn't want a dead man in the pit. Make you sick to look at him, lad. Beautiful."

They poured powsowdie into him, broth made from the head of the sheep with chunks of oatmeal bread dunked in it, and stuffed him with hotchpotch from the garden, the first of the greens, and he felt his strength come back. It was his bones that bothered him, still bruised and cracked and healing slowly. And the house itself. He learned about the miners' houses, the classic but and ben, two rooms in all, the but holding the fireplace and what passed for a kitchen, where the tubs were taken and the pit duds washed and hung and the food prepared and eaten, and the back room, the ben, where the parents slept and visitors, if one had any, could be entertained. Gillon and Maggie slept out in the but and it was the privacy he missed the most. There was none of that that Gillon could see in all of Pitmungo. Life moved in and out of their room the way life existed for rabbits in a hutch.

One afternoon he could stand it no longer and when Tom Drum came home from the pit, Gillon got up and determined to see the town he had fought his way into. He put on his suit, in considerable pain, and Maggie put on his shoes. He put on his hat and the three of them went down Miners Row and up Colliers Walk, across a stretch of moor, and up to two long rows of houses high above the moor.

"This is Uppietoon," Mr. Drum told him. Tosh-Mungo Terrace was on top and just below it Moncrieff Lane, pronounced "Loan."

"Strivers' row," Maggie said, "where anyone with any ambition wants to go. We'll be up here."

"We will?" Gillon said. "I'm not that ambitious."

"You'll see," she said.

They sat down on a bench at the edge of an overlook and Mr. Drum was pointing out Easter Mungo and Wester Mungo when a group of old men, with bony faces and hard eyes, descended on them.

"Off the bench," one of them said. "Uppies only."

But Tom Drum told them this was the man who had smashed Andy Begg and they were cordial after that; it was only that they were very jealous of those privileges they had spent their lives underground winning. The houses were bigger, the air was cleaner, and the water was purer in Uppietoon.

"Now, down there are the Doonies. They're no good down there," an old man said, ignoring the presence of the Drums. "Wet Row, right in the river, Rotten Row, falling down, and Miners Row, that's the best of them."

"The drinkers, the agitators, the ones who never learned to get along."

The Uppies and the Doonies even sat in separate parts of Pitmungo Free Kirk, Gillon learned.

"We don't bow to them and they don't talk to us," an old miner said. "They don't have the gall."

Down below Uppietoon and above Doonietoon, between them, was an enormous expanse of bright green open moor known officially as Lady Jane Tosh-Mungo Miners' Recreation Park, and unofficially, for more than a century, as the Sportin Moor. On one part of the moor, a colony of Gypsies, the Pitmungo Gypsies, lived in their ark-like wagons and Gillon could see weavers at work at their lint holes.

"That's where they have the fair and the markets and the circus and the races," Tom Drum said, "and see, there's still room for football and rugby and cricket."

"And quoits. Quoits is best after a day down the pit."

They all agreed quoits was best.

It was plain to Gillon that the Sportin Moor was what made some kind of decent life possible in Pitmungo, a clean place for children to grow in, a place for the young men to get rid of their extra energy if they had any after a turn in the pit, but his eyes were below the Sportin Moor and below Doonietoon, where he could see the Pitmungo River snaking its way through the valley and the first of the mine mouths gaping beneath the great bull wheels spinning over the tipples. Behind it all, a mountain of waste from the mines, the slag heap, was burning and smoke drifted down its black sides and clouded the work areas with its gassy breath.

"What are the wheels spinning above those dark sheds?" Gillon asked. The men couldn't believe he didn't know.

"Why, the winding wheels," Mr. Drum said. "They bring the coal tubs up and take the men doon."

Doon. Doom. The words were too close and made his stomach feel odd.

"I don't think I want to go doon," Gillon said. "I'm a seaman and seamen don't go down except to die."

They laughed at him. They didn't believe that, either.

"Everyone goes doon the pit. That's what a man *does*," an old miner said. Gillon could not help noticing that parts of both his hands were missing.

"You'll get used to it" was all he heard, over and over, so often he began to doubt it. It was a litany they said to each other in hope that they would come to believe it. No one could ever get used to being three thousand feet down into the innards of the earth. It wasn't natural. God, if there was one—and, he promised himself, he was going to finally decide on that soon—never intended man to go there, violating the rules of nature, testing the earth that way.

"Is it true men work out under the sea?" Gillon asked.

"Oh, aye, miles out, some of them. In the great storms you can feel the whole mine move."

"You can feel the surge of the sea in the coal seams," Tom Drum said.

"One thing is, the gas squeezes out of the stone, that's a fact."

"It's the roof props crying out; that's what used to bother me, squealing like hurt animals."

I'm going to die down there, Gillon saw very clearly. I will be drowned as I always knew I would be, but it will be in a black hole in the heart of the earth.

They went down after that and crossed the moor and when they were halfway across Maggie stopped and they looked back up at Tosh-Mungo Terrace.

"That's where our children are going to live someday."

"Och, Maggie, keep your head about you," her father said. "Doonies don't become Uppies."

"Some will," Maggie said.

The rugby and football players had stopped their games to watch them pass.

"That's him, the one with the hat," Gillon heard.

"He don't look like he could do it, man."

"He did it, man."

Tom Drum was very proud. The young miners went back to their game, smashing into one another. Several had bloodied heads and noses. Gillon didn't understand these people, working in the pit all day and coming out in the evening to crash into each other. They were, he thought, a breed apart.

When they reached the Doonie raws all the women were in the doorway; word had come down. Some of the men from the day shift were still coming up from their after-pit drinks, and the sight of them, so tired and filthy, depressed Gillon. But worse, through the doors of the houses he saw the children in the tin tubs in the middle of the rooms, sad and angry-looking, too small for the work they had to do.

"Children shouldn't look that way," Gillon suddenly said.

"A good tub will put them right, you'll see," Mr. Drum said. He was a rough, ready man, but he was not, as they say in Pitmungo, a bluntie. He knew what was in Gillon's head.

"It's the way things are, Gillon, and the sooner you come to accept them, the easier it is to bear. You'll get used to it."

In the middle of the Doonie rows, in what passed for the business section in Pitmungo, they came to the Coaledge Tavern, as the sign on the two-story gray-stone building read.

"Here it is, son," Mr. Drum said. "The College, and well named, too. You'll learn more about the pit and life in here, lad," and he winked at Gillon, "than in any buke you'll ever read."

The smell of sweat and wet and pit dirt was so dense that Gillon didn't want to go in for a pint. They were lined several deep along the bar and walls, black hands wrapped around fruit jars filled with ale, almost frantic in their need to put back in their bodies the quarts of liquid they had lost underground that day. Mr. Drum was terribly disappointed.

They filed through the line of men outside the College who were drinking their ale outside, squatting on their hunkers. Several of them raised their jars ever so slightly as a tribute to the man who had bashed Andy Begg, but mostly they were silent and watched.

"Yes, a *very* nice hat," a miner said, in an affected accent. "Fit for a toff, that one."

They went a little farther down where it was possible to see the pitheads, and beyond the mines, hidden behind lines of oak and tall privet hedge, Brumbie Hill on which Lord Fyffe and his wife, Lady Jane Tosh-Mungo lived with a few of the officials of the mines, their homes huddling behind Brumbie Hall like sheep behind the shepherd when a fox is about.

"You may get to Tosh-Mungo Terrace, which I very much doubt," Mr. Drum was saying, "but you will never—and this I guarantee you—get on Brumbie Hill," when they realized Maggie had gone back up toward the men.

"I heard the remark about the hat," Gillon heard her say. "Which one of you cares to step out into the Walk and try to knock it off my man's head?"

No man moved.

"Come on, come out and put up your hands like Andy Begg."

She knew that Begg was inside the tavern and that the sight of him had sobered every man.

"I thought as much," she said, and came running back down the Walk to them.

"What did you do that for?" Gillon said to her, humiliated.

"You wouldn't understand."

They went down by the breaker room where the women were sorting coal from the last shift, and they were forced to shout.

"These people," she said, "you have to rub their noses in it. Now you've challenged them all, you see."

He didn't understand; not her, not them.

"Look, you!" She was shouting. "It isn't enough to win. You have to make the losers admit defeat."

No, I will never understand, Gillon thought, but he also thought he had never seen his wife look happier or more beautiful than when she had come running down the Walk toward him.

12 HE DID GET USED TO IT, WHICH LATER HE WOULD see as a crime against humanity and reason. Man accepts too much too easily, and he learns to accept the unacceptable.

Gillon went down the pit and to prove he was a man went to work like a beast. Because he was a new man and an outsider, he was given the lowest seam of coal in Lady Jane No. 2 to howk, although he was by far the tallest miner in Pitmungo. He worked on his side all day, lying down in water four and five inches deep, and at night he came home too exhausted to take his tub until after he had slept, and too tired to take his tea, his muscles endlessly sore from heat and cold water and the postures he was forced to work in.

Then the whistle in the morning, as black as any time at night, his clothes still wet although Maggie tried her best to get them dry for him, her mother watching him in the doorway of the ben, never saying a word, just watching, dark as a miner and shameless about her staring.

"You'll get used to it, lad, you'll get used to it," his father-in-law kept saying.

The piece bucket in his hand, strips of bacon in it, slabs of bread smeared with miner's butter, which he learned was oleomargarine, as thick and white as lard, and a flask of hot tea that would be cold when he came to drink it. In the row and along the Colliers Walk, the men coming together in twos and threes, like streams emptying into a river, until there was a river of men heading toward the bridge and the pithead, coming together as if to reassure one another that they weren't alone in this blackness. Sometimes a man would shout, often something meaningless, a cry in darkness that would chill something in Gillon's soul, but mostly they were silent, the men coming off the night shift not even looking at the men going in, as if they were ashamed of something they had done down below. Mostly it was the sound of equipment, water and tea flasks clanking against pick heads and gas lamps, wooden clogs and iron-toed rubber boots. Some of the men, the old ones, to save on leather, which rots so rapidly from the acids in the water of the mine, went barefoot. Gillon couldn't stand to look at their feet.

The men did not speak to him.

"Are you scared, lad?" a miner had asked him once, early in his work.

"No."

"You ought to be; I am every day in my life." But they must have told the man not to talk to the outsider. Gillon convinced himself he didn't mind the silence. So he worked on, learning his craft, learning to handle his tools, lying in the glush, the awkward Highlander—"gloafish glumyieman," in their dialect—learning to kerf the coal, undercutting the seam so that it would be easy to howk or blow it off the coal face, learning to use his pick in clean hard thrusts even when lying on his side, and, finally, because of his reach, being able to go in deeper than the others and come out with more coal even though he was working the lowest seam.

Shouted at by Archie Japp, the deputy, for too much slate in his coal, and by Walter Bone, the overman, for continuing to work in a stall where you could hear the methane gas hissing its way out of the coal.

"I know you're brave, Cameron—oh, everyone knows that much, Cameron—but not a goddamn fool. *You* may be brave but *I* don't want to die for it. What I can't understand is why you didn't pass out first."

Because my face is on the goddamned floor and the gas is on the roof, Gillon wanted to shout back, but he kept his mouth shut and they ventilated the mine before it could explode and the Firth of Forth drown them and their coal.

Sometimes Tom Drum duck-walked almost a mile in from the stall where he was working, and while it was good to talk to someone they never had much to say.

"How are you making it, lad?"

"Fine, fine, Dad."

Mr. Drum liked that.

"Did you put up those props?"

"Aye, I did."

"But the base is too narrow, you see. It needs more assurance than that," and he would show him how to pack gob (slate and stones) and make stone roof pillars and how to prop the roof correctly with the wooden pitprops so there would be no danger of a roof fall or of a slab of slate dropping out of the roof and burying them, the miner's greatest danger.

The strange fact, Gillon began to realize, was that he had some of the same kind of feeling for coal as he had had for the sea and the fish. He had a sense of the roof and the pressures, a feel for the direction of the coal seams, and when he put up his props they never broke, even in those times when the barometer shot up and the atmospheric pressure rose and the pitprops began to groan and sometimes shatter in splinters under the new weight imposed on the world above.

And then the time came that no matter what Archie Japp felt about him, or what Walter Bone might wish, they both had their quotas of coal to get out and when a productive miner was hurt in a seam of high coal they had no choice but to move Gillon into the new workings and turn his low coal seam over to a child who could properly work it. The boy could not have been five feet tall.

"How old are you?" Gillon asked. The boy was flattered to be talking to the man that had dinged Andy Begg.

"Fourteen, but I told them sixteen."

"You're too young altogether for this."

"Aye, but my daddie's hurt; he's lost his foot under the slate and now I must be the man in the hoose."

That shouldn't be; that's no system at all, Gillon thought, but he moved on to the high coal. It was Lochgelly Splint, a fine hard coal, and great chunks of the gleaming stuff crashed down out of the walls at times like a flood of black stony water. The seam was five feet high and that first week Gillon almost tripled his coal production. Within the month, he was mining as much coal as any collier in Lady Jane No. 2.

What Gillon liked was coming up out of the under-ground. He loved to savor his re-emergence into the world. In the morning he would study the coming day, and then all through his shift in the depths of the mine he imagined the day unfolding overhead. When they came up on the little cages, rushing three thousand feet up from below, he never ceased being thrilled to find the sun shining or the ground blanketed in snow, or even to find it was raining and cold. The effect was that of stealing another day, having a second chance at life. It made the pit bearable.

And then there was the tub. He came to love his afternoon tub. From the first day, Maggie had been true to her promise about the tub. Although she had gotten her job back at the Pitmungo Coal and Iron Company School, because no one else wanted to take it and live in Pitmungo, she found a way to come home and have the water boiling and have his tub ready for him. Most of the men had their beer and ale at the College and then had their tea in their pit filth—Mr. Drum was one of those—but not Gillon. After freedom from the pit, freedom from pit filth was his delight.

"Where do I take the pit clothes off?" he had asked her that first day.

"Here, right here, where you're standing, silly."

"But your mother is in the house."

"And what does that matter?"

"Well, close the door at least, then."

"It doesn't *matter*."

And it didn't—not in Pitmungo; only to Gillon, who wasn't bred to the blindness. He didn't know then about Turnabout Time. From 5:00 p.m. to 5:30 p.m., no woman in Pitmungo was permitted to look out her window or into another person's house or to go out in the street. This allowed the men in the crowded houses to take their tubs in the wynds between the rows of houses or in front of the open doorways and windows or out in the kail yards if the weather was right. The other concession to decency, learned in the cradle, was a blindness to the naked body, where pit dirt was concerned. Men who in other circumstances would be shy to be seen with bare arms walked around their houses naked in their pit filth and were not seen. With pit dirt there was no such thing as sex; sex came later, when clothes were on. Sisters bathed brothers and wives washed husbands and grown sons. Meg was right; in Pitmungo, it didn't matter. But still he didn't like her mother standing in the doorway, invisible as he was or wasn't, studying the unusual whiteness of his body.

"I told you how white he was," Maggie said proudly.

"Like royalty," her mother said.

"Not like the brass-colored baboons here."

"Not like your father."

She slid her hands along his back and around his neck, and Gillon, not raised on the rules of the tub, feeling her hands slippery and silky and warm in the fresh strong soap, found that he was disgracing himself.

"Stand up," Meg said.

"I can't," he whispered.

"Oh, get up. I have to work on the back of your thighs."

"I—can*not*."

"Stand up, Gillon."

"Get her out of the *doorway*."

"Get out, then, Mother."

She very reluctantly went back inside her room. "Maybe he has something to hide," he heard her say, and there was a timed pause. "And maybe he has nothing to hide," and then a burst of uncontrollable laughter.

She was, Gillon was forced to realize, something of a slut. But she never, as far as he knew, watched again.

It was the tubs that aroused his passion. He knew how she felt about it, the act itself—what an absurd invention it was; she never forgot to mention that—and yet what astonished him was the excess of their passion once they were committed to it. He knew they were a scandal on the row, making love after the tub and before tea, before Tom Drum could work his way up from the College—unheard of, but he couldn't help himself. No matter how bad the day had been in the mine, it was all bearable when the work was done and the new day still lay ahead, warm and safe in the tub, feeling those hands on his tired limbs, thinking of the promise of her in the evening and the night to come. And then the evening came when she said "No, no more," as flat as that, with no explanation. He was too hurt to ask at first.

"What do you mean, no, no more?" he finally asked that night.

"It's over the now."

"It's not over the now."

"I'm going to bear a child."

He looked at her in such an odd way, surprise and joy mixed with disappointment, that she nearly laughed in his face.

"Haven't you felt my wame? What did you think I was doing, putting on weight?"

He was still bewildered. He knew he should feel happy but all he felt at the moment was disappointment.

"Then you mean you can't—?"

She shook her head. He didn't know about any of those things and how to ask or whom to ask or what to ask. And so he chose to believe her.

That was the way it went after that. The moment Maggie found she was pregnant their sexual life was over. It wasn't that the act disgusted her; it merely seemed a little ridiculous, all the postures and tanglings of limbs and sighs and groans and whisperings—she was a very audible groaner, as anyone on Miners Row could testify to—and, above all, so useless and impractical. There was no need for it, and if there was no need, the effort involved was a waste of time.

After that day, although Gillon never tied the two together, he became a student of coal. He found a book titled *A Manual of Coal and Its Topography in the West Fife Coal Region*, and he read it several times over until he began to see coal as something very beautiful and even mysterious. Here in front of him, in every black stone he chunked out of the face before him, the sun of five million years was locked. When working a hard-coal seam he would bring a specific coal home, put it on the fire, and then watch the sun climb out of it, sprung from its prison by him, licking blue and yellow flame.

"I don't think you know how fantastic this is," he said once to Maggie and to Tom Drum. "I don't think you understand what it means."

"It means a waste of good coal," Maggie had said. "Put something on top of it, for God's sake."

There were two kinds of coal to Gillon, but he never told that to anyone. Soft coal was female to him, stubborn but ultimately yielding. He loved to slide his hands along the soft silken sheen of the coal. And the hard coal, the flanks of stones hard and cold and dry, sheer and glistening under his pick, was masculine. It gave in hard, but when it broke it shattered.

Before the baby was born, Gillon found that his only real satisfaction in a day came in sinking his coal pick into the virgin seam he was working. He loved to feel the chunking of his pick in the soft retreating wall, until sometimes there were so many silky pieces of coal piled on the floor of his stall that there weren't enough ponies and coal tubs to carry them away.

"Slow down, Gillon," Tom Drum shouted at him one shift; "what the hell has got into you?"

Gillon didn't even answer him, just the thud of his pick sinking deeper into the untouched coal.

And then there was siller. Even Gillon got to call it that, finally; it *was* a better word, soft on the tongue, soft in the pocket. He came to like that, too, going down to the pay shed every fortnight and getting his pay packet from Archie Japp, who liked the ritual of passing out the money when Mr. Brothcock wasn't doing it.

"Cameron, G."

"Aye."

Push through the crowd of men drinking their pints outside the shed.

"Sixty-two shillin's fourpence." There would always be a commotion after that.

"Highest in the fewkin pit," Japp would say, never directly to Gillon. "Outsider," and shake his head in disbelief. Pitmungo miners found it hard to believe that anyone not born in Pitmungo could ever learn to howk coal.

He liked walking back through the men with his packet in his hand, and then walking up Colliers Walk, the money warm and solid and secure in his pocket, pound notes, ten-shilling notes, and the siller—crowns and half crowns and shillings rubbing against each other in his pocket. He always exchanged his notes for coins with the men who wanted to tuck a little drinking money away from their wives.

One Saturday night when he came up from the College, there was a large solid steel box with a sturdy tempered steel lock on the floor of the but, next to the table.

"What in the name of God is that?" Gillon had asked. There was little enough room in the house as it was.

"The kist."

He had never heard the word before.

"Our strongbox. What's going to take us out of here."

She held out her hand for the pay packet and began to drop the crowns and shillings through a slot in the top of the box, and they dropped with a solid metallic *chink*, the good chime of siller striking siller and cold pressed steel.

"What's going to take you out of the pit." *Chink, chink.* "What's going to put us up on Tosh-Mungo Terrace." *Chink, chink.*

"Och, what pushes you; what drives you that way?" her father had once asked. She remembered that, and the answer was still the same. She had only to open the curtains and look down on Rotten Row and the pits again and there was answer enough for her. The chinking went on.

It became the fortnightly ritual after that: putting the siller in the kist.

Close the door, shut the blinds, move the dining table, bring the box up from the hole where it was buried, like a coffin for a child, and drop the siller in the kist.

It was almost a religious exercise, Gillon realized, there in the dark room under the guttering light of the tallow lamp. For a time they counted it all in a little ledger, but after a while they let it mount up on its own, the total unknown even to them, a quarter of Maggie's pay as a teacher in the Coal and Iron Company school, and a quarter of Gillon's pay from the mine. They came to call it the Cameron Pot and nothing after that was ever allowed to interfere with the ritual of the Pot. "The kist comes first" was the watchword of their house.

13

THE FIRST BABY WAS A BOY, WHICH WAS THE WAY Maggie had planned it. It never occurred to Gillon that it could be a girl, since Maggie wanted a boy so much. He was long and thin and fair—a proper Cameron, everyone agreed—and they named him Rob Roy, after one of Gillon's uncles.

From the start he was a sweet child, and docile, and Maggie was good with him, which surprised most of the women living down the row. But after a while she gave him only the attention he needed, because she knew what the others didn't know—that this wasn't one of the children that could lead the family to where they were going. He lacked the mix Maggie had gone in search of—Gillon's style and Drum guts. After that, she took only the care of the boy she was required to, so that when he came of mining age he would be ready to take his place in the pit.

After the birth it was the way it had been before: she wanted Gillon again, and she was shameless about it. The second child, as planned, was a girl, who could help around the house when her brothers came up from the pit. One girl for the clothes and the cleaning, another for the food and the house and "the messages," which is what they call shopping in Pitmungo. It was another Cameron baby, blond and friendly, as docile as Rob Roy and as fair and smiling. They named her Sarah and the women on the row were jealous at her get.

"It doesn't follow nature," Mrs. Hodge, in the adjoining but-and-ben, complained. "How can you get sugar from acid?"

He knew he was being used, and there was nothing he could do about it. It was his own weakness. His pride was damaged daily but he didn't care. When her rutting season, as Gillon came to think of it, was upon her, it was impossible for him to resist her. Once he tried for more than a week to salvage his pride and assert some semblance of masculine control over the sexual act, but she would find him in the tub after his work, the house quiet and dim, her mother still working down at the mine mouth and her father good for another hour at least in the College before coming up the hill, and the struggle was decided with the first move of her hands.

What astonished him always and what eventually always won him over, even if she was using him as a breeding machine, was the genuine nature of her passion and of her rediscovery of the act and art of love. It still embarrassed him some mornings, alone in the darkness of his stall with his memories, to think about the things they had done the night before, and it still excited him. What angered him, so deeply that she never imagined the depth of it, was the way she could forget the truth of her passion the moment she found she was pregnant and had gotten, once again, what she wanted from him.

The third child was born on November Thirtieth, the day of Saint Andrew, the patron saint of Scotland, during the first snowstorm of the year. He was aggressive from the start, pushing into the world with a howl that could be heard in the next but-and-ben.

He didn't go after his milk the way the others had done; there was an impatience about this baby, a gasping for air while continuing to suck. Gillon wanted to give him Snow for a middle name, in honor of the storm and because Gillon had always been partial to the name.

"We'll name this one Andrew Drum Cameron," Maggie said, with such finality that no one wanted to argue with her. She knew what the others didn't understand, that she had the first of her mixes.

The child angered Gillon a little.

"Can't he wait at all?" he had asked.

"And why should he?" Maggie said.

When the baby was hungry it woke at once, and when it woke it cried out for what it wanted.

"Doesn't he ever get enough?" Gillon said one night.

"This one knows what he wants." Gillon had made some kind of sound at that.

"Gillon?"

"Aye," he had said.

"I think you're jealous of the bairn."

"Och, blether!" he had shouted, but later in the night, as he watched the child, he realized that he was jealous. Not a great deal, but jealous, because at birth it already seemed to have mastered the one thing he had never been able to do. It knew how to get exactly what it wanted from her.

TWO

GILLON CAMERON

1 THE YEARS PASS MORE SWIFTLY IN COAL TOWNS
than they do in other places because there are no true seasons to
measure the passing of time in the coalfields. The life of the town
exists in the mine, and it is always the same season underground.
In the summer, for a few minutes each day, there is an illusion of
coolness when the miners first drop down the shaft, and in the
winter it seems warmer than usual, but soon it's the same. Winter
or summer the men sweat the same amount of sweat and drink
the same number of pints in the public house and spill the same
amount of blood.

Sometimes men coming up from the pit are astonished to find
snow on the ground or summer heat, because they have forgotten
the season they're in. The only real season is in the pit, and days
slide into one another.

If it hadn't been for Gillon's children, who continued to come
and continued to grow, incontestable pieces of evidence of time
passing in the cramped confines of their house, he would have
found it hard to believe his life was passing away as swiftly as it
was, that although he had only come to serve an apprenticeship
and a short sentence before moving on, almost half of his life
had been spent buried in Pitmungo.

After Andrew, Sam had come—another mix, but this more on

the Drum side, Cameron fair and Drum darkness, physically precocious and mentally easygoing.

Then James—Jemmie, totally Drum, short and dark and tough, slope-shouldered as a child, in his cradle already cut out for the pit. When he began to speak, he spoke Pitmungo, not the language he heard at home but in the rows and lanes. No amount of laundry soap in the mouth had been able to cure him. He was as Pitmungo as the coal dust on the cobbles in the lane or his grandfather Tom.

And after Jemmie the twins, Ian and Emily, not a mixture but strange from the start, born during a thunder and lightning and snow-shower storm, out of place, star-crossed; Gypsies, people said, the old dark strain emerging out of Maggie's mother's bloodline.

"Oh, aye," they said so knowingly in Pitmungo, "and what Hope slept with what Gyppo in what haystack at the end of the moor," nodding and nodding, because it was well understood that there was Gypsy blood running wild somewhere in the line.

"How else could you account for her?" they sometimes said, meaning Maggie.

Gillon hadn't aged the way most of the Pitmungo miners aged. There are two ways a man's body can take working underground and still survive. One is to "bull up": for the neck and shoulders to thicken, for the entire body to slope forward from the pressure of the work and the weight of the muscle, which was the usual way. The other was to go to "wire," as they said, which was the way Gillon went, the flesh drawn down to the bone, tense and lean. Most of the wiry breed were small men who looked pinched and aged before their time, but because of the angular planes of his face, Gillon avoided the pinched look. His fine-boned face was harder but still fine and even more hawklike. Had he had more ease about him, a little of the softness that freedom from hard work can bring, he would have been considered handsome, but it took a good eye to see it. Yet even with

all the mines can do to a man, the work hadn't taken too hard
a toll on Gillon, since he hadn't been hurt.

What bothered him most was the silence of the others, their
stubborn insistence on not speaking to the outlander unless forced
to. Now that he had his boys with him the pit was more bearable
but he was unhappy his loneliness had to be solved that way. He
was sorry to take the boys down with him after only six years in
the Coal and Iron Company School, it was too much and too soon
for boys of that age, Gillon thought. But they wanted to go down
and become men and it was the way of the town, and they went
down. Rob was helping Gillon break the coal off the face, an
apprentice face miner, and soon he and Andrew would be quali-
fied to have a stall of their own and bring home man's money.
Sam was a filler, loading the coals into the tubs and hutches and
Jemmie was a putter, seeing that the tubs were pulled or driven
to the shaft head and taken to the surface.

The girls worked above ground, Sarah around the pithead,
hauling pitprops and mine equipment like a man until Maggie
decided she was more needed at home, and Emily, the quickest of
them all, would soon be working in the breaker room where the
coals were sorted and sized and chunks of slate and stone picked
out of the coal. The trick in the breaker room was to avoid going
deaf from the noise of the huge shifting screens sorting the coals
and avoid losing at least a few fingers when a hand was mashed in
the picking and sorting.

But despite Camerons in the pit and above it Gillon still missed
the approval of his fellow miners. He wanted, finally, to belong
with them. One of the things he had come to value in mining
was the need of each man for the next man down the roadway,
a dependency closer and stronger than in other kinds of work
because of the helplessness of their situation, a mile down and
miles in; because of the depth and the darkness and the dangers
the men faced each day, and the need of each collier to protect
the next collier in the next room, if only to save his own life.

He appreciated the look in the men's eyes up and down the

roadway when the roof began to "work," some pressure above causing the pitprops to groan in anguish, occasionally causing them to shatter under the force—a crack like the recoil of an artillery piece—sending splinters and chips of coal and wood splattering down the gangways.

It will be all right, man, don't worry, the eyes said—even to him then—although the men stood rooted where they were, picks poised, listening, unable to go on with their jobs until the working in the roof stopped.

But they wouldn't talk to him and take him into their lives. Sometimes a miner working in a stall nearby would go so far as to mention that Gillon understood how it was—he was an outsider, after all—and Gillon would always nod. And then on the day before his eighteenth Christmas in Pitmungo that came to an end.

2   THE SHIFT WAS OVER AND THE MEN WERE GAY AND noisy coming down the gangways to the shaft bottom, even though they had worked two extra hours to load some of the coal that wouldn't be loaded the next day. They were going home to a day on which they could sleep the whole morning away, and to the traditional Christmas dinners of steaming-hot kidney pies and black buns and slabs of Selkirk bannock drowned in melting butter, when a section of the roof in Lady Jane No. 2, a slab of slate the size of a miner's room, dropped onto the back of a young collier from Tosh-Mungo Terrace. Only the edge of the slab hit the man, but the force of the blow threw him forward, face down in the water and pit glaur, so that the upper part of his body was spared but both his legs were trapped under several tons of slate.

"Sandy Bone is under the slate" went down through the rooms, and the men came back down the haulage roads quickly and quietly, fearful of creating any new disturbance in the roof but wanting to help. They stood at a distance from their fellow miner. He was in terrible pain but conscious. Above him, suspended just over his head, was a second piece of the roof, an immense triangular slab of slate, its hold so fragile that when a ventilation door somewhere down the roadway was opened and closed the segment of stone actually moved like a banner in a light wind.

"Let it drop!" Sandy Bone screamed. The men stared at their feet.

"Please, let it drop, make it drop on me." He tried to lift his head to touch the stone and loosen it enough to fall down on him. "Have you no guts to put me out? Please. Please!"

He tried it again but the effort caused him to cry aloud. It was more than many of the men could stand and they went away, against the code of the mines. There was nothing they could do.

"You don't have to come near me. Throw a pick at it." They had never heard anything like it before, this begging to die. Now he was begging for a pick to be put through his head. It wasn't that he was a coward; it was that he was denied the natural blessing of unconsciousness, of blackness and relief from pain.

"Cut off my legs, then. Mr. Japp, you. Archie Japp, take off my legs if you have any courage at all in you."

The horror of it was that he was still able to single out a face in the guttering light of the miner's lamps.

"You have that peat knife, you know you do," the young man shouted. His breath was coming in rushes, as if he were struggling against drowning, and the words came the same way, in out-bursts that seemed to batter the men physically. He wasn't much more than a boy, eighteen at most, and he began to cry after that, great swallows of crying, from the pain and from the knowledge of his broken body, his broken young life, his death. The men could not look at him.

"Christ, I'll do it, then," Archie Japp shouted, but the others held him and he made no real effort to pull away and go to the boy. They stood near him, away from the overhanging sheet of slate, wanting to give him the reassurance of the presence of their bodies, staring at the roof, wanting it to fall on the boy, terrified of its falling, waiting for the doctor to come, as if he could do something they couldn't do.

Gillon couldn't bear to be near him any longer and yet he couldn't leave him as long as he was suffering that way—the pain had to be shared among all of them—and he went down the roadway to be a little out of the sound of the boy's crying. He was sitting in a pool of pit water when Andrew found him.

"What about the Telford jack, Daddie?"

He knew it was right at once, a daring idea but dangerous. Terribly dangerous, the kind of thing a father might want to forget he had heard.

"Can you get it? Do you need me?"

"I have Rob Roy."

"Get it," Gillon said and got up and began stripping down his pit gear for what would lie ahead. The jack was new to the pit. Most of the men didn't understand how to use it yet, and they didn't like it because it was new and new could be dangerous. "Stick with what you know and don't go outside it" was the rule of the pit. Miners, Gillon had found, were more conservative than kings and more superstitious than peasants. But Andrew, not yet fifteen, was different. He had seen the jack in the mine workshop, and in his prodding, curious way he had had to know what it was for and how it worked.

It was not, Gillon realized, going to be as dangerous as it was going to look to the men. And it could work. The jack was a low, mechanical device with an extremely long handle that one turned as if cranking an engine. It was designed to be worked under overturned or broken coal tubs. If a hole was scooped under an edge of the fallen slab, they could work the jack in under the slab, and then, because of the length of the jack handle, at a distance safe from the hanging slate, raise the slab the few inches that would be needed to pull the boy out from under. The dangerous time would come, Gillon knew, in placing the jack.

Andrew and Rob Roy came back with the jack and they put it on the pit floor and inserted the handle and it worked easily and well, the lifting surface rising an eighth of an inch or so with each turn. They would need a hole seven or eight inches deep in which to place the jack. Gillon took a deep breath—he felt the exhilaration of fear and excitement, of the expectation of success and the possibility of death, and started pushing his way through the men.

"The doctor's here. The doctor," they said, and then, when Gillon pushed through followed by Andrew, there was disappointment.

There were two choices, Gillon could see at once. To work under the hanging slab or to slip by it and work behind the direction it would fall. He decided that in the long run it was safer to squeeze by the hanging slab, although for a moment it would be more dangerous.

"Where are you going?" Archie Japp said. Being the deputy in the mine, he was as much in charge as any mate on a boat in the absence of his captain.

"I'm going to go by the rock and place this jack under the slab."

"The hell you are," Japp said. "I'm not going to lose two lives to try to save one that's already lost. You don't go by that hanging slab and that's an order, Cameron." He stood in the way of Gillon and blocked him. He was a hard man, strong—hard as coal but small. Someone suddenly seized him from behind and pulled his arm up behind his back, the police hold, so that if he moved his arm or body too much he would break it.

"Don't move, old man," the miner said.

There were several inches between Gillon's chest and the wall of the roadway. If it had been a doorway, there would have been little trouble squeezing by, but danger exaggerates. The Bone boy was barely breathing. Gillon inched his way past the rock. And then he was through and Andrew after him.

The digging was not as hard as Gillon had feared. The floor there was a generation deep in coal dust. The hollow to take the jack was picked loose and scooped out in several minutes and the jack lowered into it beneath the slab and then Gillon was able to back away from the hanging slab and begin to work the handle. The release of the pressure on Sandy Bone's legs caused him to scream aloud again.

"Oh, Jesus, stop it, Cameron," someone shouted, "let the boy be," but Gillon kept turning and the stone kept rising. Someone crawled up then and placed a haulage rope around and underneath the boy's shoulders, risking his life doing it, and when the slab was high enough they began to inch Sandy Bone out from under it.

"Pull him!" Gillon shouted to them. "The jack won't hold forever," and they did, they yanked him out from under the stone, and the jack snapped, the slate thudding back onto the floor again with a jarring thump that made the hanging slab go down after it, barely missing the men who were trying to put the boy together again, enough at least to carry him down the haulage road to the shaft where the cage was waiting to take him up.

It didn't seem like Christmas Eve when Gillon came up. There had been winds from the south for several days and rain had melted the snow. Green was showing on the Sportin Moor. The boy was on a coal cart, planks of coal-blackened timber over a springless frame, with iron wheels that took every pothole in the road as if a sledgehammer were ringing the rim.

"He can't go down that way," Gillon said, "not all the way to Cowdenbeath."

"They always have," someone said, and Gillon looked at it, never having seen it before, the Pitmungo miner's ambulance, a rolling death cart. How many must have died going down that way, he thought, and how many might have lived. One hour's worth of coal from the mine would pay for a well-sprung, enclosed, rubber-tired ambulance, but somehow that hour's coal was never forthcoming.

"Oh, God, no, he can't go down in that," Rob Roy said, and began running. He came back several minutes later with Mr. Japp and his well-sprung van.

"Who's going to pay?" Mr. Japp, the van man said. "I've been down *this* road before. If they die the family never pays."

"I'll pay, I'll pay from my own day's darg," Rob Roy said. "I'll pay double rates but get going."

They moved young Bone from the ambulance to the van and still the van didn't start, and then one of the boy's cousins got down from the wagon and came running for Gillon.

"He wants you," he said; "he wants you to go down with him." Gillon thought of his own family and then climbed up on the van and in the back. He was certain the boy would die on the way down and he didn't want to be with him when he did, but he had no choice in the matter now. Those who save are responsible for what they save.

"Don't tell my father and mother. It will spoil the Christmas," the Bone boy said.

"Aye. Yes."

"Tell them I got overtime. Tell them I broke an arm or some such."

"Aye, I will."

"Tell me a story, then. Any kind. Tell me about the Highlands away from here," so Gillon knelt by the boy and held his hand, a thing he never did with his own boys, and began whispering any kind of thing that came into his head. He told him about his boyhood on the Cromarty croft and about the clearances, how the land was cleared to make way for the red deer and game birds, and then about the sea and his salmon. From time to time, the boy broke into tears and Gillon didn't know if it was for pain or because of the sadness of his stories. They were all sad, he realized, except the saumont killing.

"I'm going to die, aren't I?" the boy suddenly said.

"No," Gillon said, "absolutely not. You beat death this time."

"But they're going to take them off, are they no'?"

"That's for the doctors to say. They're doing wonderful things these days."

"Oh, aye," Sandy Bone said, "with a saw."

Gillon stayed with him at Cowdenbeath until it was over. They took off the boy's legs and buried them in a graveyard for limbs outside the hospital. Gillon couldn't help noticing how large the graveyard was as he headed homeward.

It was gloamin tide then, and not for long. The warm day began to take on a chill, and his pit clothes, which everyone had stared at in Cowdenbeath as if he were part of a Christmas mummer's show, were still wet. He took the Low Road back along the river and when he got too cold, as tired as he was, he forced himself to run a hundred steps and walk a hundred until he began to sweat again. It was black when he came through the brickworks and the foundry in the lower part of the town. Up on Brumbie Hill the houses were all lit and looked warm and cheery. Someone must have had a window open despite the evening, someone who could afford a lot of coal, because he could hear a family singing some old Scotch Christmas song. He went past the pit he had come up out of so long ago and up Colliers Walk. He thought of going into the Coaledge for a dram to see him up the hill but decided not to. He had come this far without it. Once off the Walk into Miners Row he stopped to collect his feelings before facing the family. He knew she would be angry with him. They had not waited for him, as he had expected, but had eaten their Christmas Eve dinner—beef-and-kidney pies, by the look of it—and now they were all in different parts of the but reading and playing cards and the girls cleaning up after dinner.

He was right about it; she was deeply angry with him.

"Don't tell me about it. I heard it all," Maggie said. "That was an irresponsible thing for a man to do. Worse than that, it was *dumb*."

"The boy was trapped under the stone. He was dying."

"Aye, he begged to die, I hear."

Gillon nodded yes.

"But Gillon Forbes Cameron steps to the front. Step aside for the vaunty Highland lad, only seven children of his own to support."

"He was under the stone." It sounded weak.

"Does he have a wife? Does she have any bairn? No, but what he had is brothers and cousins and uncles in the pit. Where in the name of God were they?"

Gillon didn't know. He had never thought of it.

"They say he'll never walk again."

"No, he'll never walk."

"Then tell me this. What sense did it make to risk your life for damaged goods?"

She didn't really expect an answer.

"And tell me this. The boy begged to be left to die . . ."

He was astonished to look and find that she was crying, not much, but actual tears. If it was from concern for him, she had an odd way of showing it, but even at that the tears made him feel a little better about the day.

". . . then who the hell are you to play the Savior?"

There was little beef-and-kidney pie left, but there was water for the tub. He felt foolish, having his wash in a room smelling of pies and black pudding, but the tub was good, as it always was for him, and despite everything he began to feel better. Thank God for the restoring virtues of good hot water, Gillon thought; it, at least, never failed him. The house smelled of beef and fresh soap and scones, and they were satisfying smells—even the pit duds when you got used to them. Maggie took her load of wash out of the kettle, steaming and dripping water, and went out the back way of the but-and-ben up to the washhouse to rinse them before hanging them by the fire. When she left, the house was totally silent.

"I don't care what she says," Jemmie finally said, "that was a braw thing you done in pit, Daddie."

"Och, it's what you have to do," Gillon said.

"No, you dared it and you did it, Dad," Sam said.

"I'm proud of my dad," Jem said, and the door swung open and there she was, the clothes still steaming in her hands.

"Aye, proud," their mother said. "It might be brave, but remember this. Smart comes before brave. *Smairt,* can you ken that, Jemmie? Your father could well be in the pit right now and you digging for him with your picks. Very brave. Very dead. Very *dumb.*"

And she slammed the door. They were silent again. That was the word in the house. Dumb. Do anything but don't be dumb about it. Gillon got out of the tub and dried and dressed. He felt foolish when he thought of it. Bravery, if that is what it was—and the more he thought of it, the more he thought that maybe Maggie was right—it was only a vaunty thing, a middle-aged man showing off to get the approval of his fellows. Bravery belonged to the young and to those with nothing to lose. It *had* been a dumb thing to do. He didn't feel like any warmed-over kidney pie and thought that maybe the Coaledge Tavern would be the place to be on Christmas Eve. He stood in the doorway, not sure what he wanted to do.

"Where are you off to, then, Daddie?" Sarah said. He shrugged his shoulders and went for his hat. The fine hat, the soft brown gentleman's hat that he didn't wear often any more but which still got attention when he wore it.

"The Coaledge." He wouldn't dignify it with the name College. "I thought I would treat myself to a dram or two."

"Aye, I understand," his daughter said. "Go on, then," she said. but he heard the unhappiness in her voice.

"What is it?"

"Oh, I was hoping we might have . . . you know, Father, a wee bit of singing and music the night."

She was shy with her father; she was shy with everyone, although beneath the shyness she was stubborn, which led her into troublesome contradictions at times, Gillon had begun to notice. But she played the flute well and there were times when she played and he sang—"My Heart's in the Highlands," "The Collier's Bonnie Lassie," "Green Grow the Rashes"—when even Maggie was touched by the sweetness of it and didn't resent the money they had spent for the flute.

"Christmas Eve and all."

There it was, the shy persistence.

"I'm going *down*," he said, with an anger that surprised him. She made him feel guilty, and he decided he wanted the Coaledge more than ever.

"I understand, Daddie."

He slammed the door on her. It was cold going down the row. He could hear a family singing in one of the houses, several young boys and girls, very clear and simple, and it made him sad. He thought of the young Bone boy lying legless in Cowdenbeath. That was a hansel for Christmas. If there was a God, God was unfair, he thought, and then felt ashamed of his thoughts. He started down Colliers Walk toward the Coaledge but turned back up toward the Sportin Moor and walked out on it. It was very cold on the moor; the wind had been coming down from the north since his return from Cowdenbeath. The grass was stiff; winter was back. He could see the little orange lights from the Gypsies' caravans far across the moor. The lights seemed miles away and warm, earth stars in comparison with the cold stars overhead. They reminded Gillon of something he couldn't at first place, and when he turned away from them, he realized it was the lights of the herring fleet out at sea, and that made him feel sad also. He decided to go down to the Coaledge for his whisky.

The windows of the tavern were fogged from the heat of the bodies inside. He could hear them inside, boisterous and loud, some singing the old old songs that surface from the past on nights like this one, some joking in that sly way of the Fife miner, always a barb and a challenge to the fun, some already glazed with drink. He would like to be like that, Gillon thought, just an edge beyond feeling.

He put his hand on the door handle—the metal was warm despite the cold outside—and took it away. They should be home with their families, he thought, and felt guilty once more. Sarah sitting there with her flute, no one to sing with her because they always waited for him. She had been practicing for days. She understood, she said.

The men would only ridicule him for the heroics of the day. That sly—slee; that was better—cutting wit. They'd give him their hail-the-Highland-hero routine, the mock toast, the mock raising of glasses; he didn't want any of that. The light was still on outside the new room next to the Pitmungo Coal and Iron Company School. Probably a mistake, Gillon thought, but he went down to look at it and make up his mind about going into the tavern because he wanted some whisky inside him. He read the sign over the door:

THE INDUSTRIAL WORKERS' READING ROOM.

ESTABLISHED WITH A GRANT FROM

THE ANDREW CARNEGIE WORKINGMAN'S EDUCATIONAL FOUNDATION,
DUNFERMLINE, FIFE, SCOTLAND.

Books on mine engineering and mine equipment so the colliers could learn the latest ways to bring up more coal at less cost to the master, Gillon thought. The door was open. There was a lighted stairway leading up a flight of stairs. Gillon hesitated and then went up. The light at the top blinded him so that he couldn't make the man out clearly, but he could hear him, because the voice was like metal being scraped across metal.

"Well? What do you want?"

Gillon didn't know what he wanted.

"Certainly not to read."

Silence was best, Gillon decided.

"Hundreds of books here, not one taken out yet."

Gillon could see him then. Short and heavy, going bald, with a face as red as the exit lamp in the pit. His eyes were blue and cold, but watery. He smelled of whisky.

"It's Christmas Evening," Gillon said. "They don't know you're open."

"They never have." He swept his arm around the room. "My virgin. She's never been *touched*."

"People are shy, sir. The men are shy when it comes to men of books."

"Because they're stupid and they're stupid because they know nothing. They're afraid of everything they can't hit with a pick."

The disgust in the man's voice, the quality of despising, was so strong and sour in his mouth that it made Gillon afraid of him and angry with him at the same time.

"Well, which comes first? Perhaps if people like you would help . . ."

The man held up his hand for Gillon to stop.

"I've heard all that," he said flatly. "Well-meaning blether. You can't teach a man who doesn't come to be taught, and it doesn't do any good if you do. Now, what is it you want?"

I want to be home with my family, enjoying what's left of my Christmas, Gillon thought, but something held him. There were hundreds of books on the shelves, more than he had ever seen anywhere together before.

"Well, come on, what is it?"

It was the thing that had bothered him ever since the day on the sea with Mr. Drysdale.

"Macbeth," Gillon said, and reddened. The man didn't seem to notice. "I want to know about a man named Macbeth."

"Macbeth." The man fixed Gillon with a look that made him want to turn away or run down the stairs. "There are thousands of Macbeths. The Highlands are crammed with them. You can't part a bush without finding a Macbeth there."

It was odd, Gillon thought, he had never met one there, but then he had probably grown up in the wrong place.

"This Macbeth is more famous than your ordinary Macbeth, I think," Gillon said.

"Oh, you think. You *think*." Gillon blushed. The librarian looked at the miner for a long, sardonic moment. "Was this Macbeth a *king* by any wild chance?"

"I don't know."

"You don't know. You come in here asking about a man and you don't even know if he was a king of Scotland?" Gillon lowered his head and mumbled no.

"Not know if he was a *king*?" Gillon could not raise his head. "What is your name?"

For a moment, he thought of lying. "Cameron," he said, finally. "G. Cameron."

"Well, Cameron. Turn around so I can see you." Gillon turned in to the light of the coal-oil lamp. "When you were talking, I thought, Here is a man I might be able to converse with, not a beast from the pit. Then you ask about a man and don't even know if he was a king or not. You make me sad."

"Aye. I'm sorry to have bothered you." There was nothing to do but go. He went downstairs and into the safe cold darkness of Colliers Walk. Chuffie-faced bastard, Gillon thought, watery blue eyes, and realized that his hat was still upstairs in the Reading Room.

The hell with the hat, he can have the hat, Gillon told himself, and as he said it, he knew he would have to go back and face the wet-eyed man and get his hat. The Coaledge seemed easy to face, compared to the library man. When he went back into the library, the man was sitting at his desk, staring at the doorway drinking from a small brown bottle.

"My hat."

"The man you are talking about is Lord Macbeth, who is the central figure of a great play by a man called Shakespeare. *The Tragedy of Macbeth.* What do you want with it?"

"To read it."

The librarian looked at him closely. "Who put this in your head?"

"Something. A long time ago. When I used to catch fish and not mine coal."

The little man got up and went across the room to the row of books. Gillon read his name on a cardboard sign on the desk. "Mr. Henry Selkirk: Librarian." He came back with a large, dusty book. The print was very small.

"You'll not read it," Mr. Selkirk said. He took out a card for Gillon to sign. "It will murder sleep," he said, and began to chuckle in a way that made Gillon angry.

"I'll read it."

"Oh, aye. In the but-and-ben, with the bairn all about and the childer shouting for food, you will read it."

The card was numbered ONE. He was the first in Pitmungo to take out a book. That was something, anyway. He put his hat on his head and went to the stairway.

"Cameron?"

"Sir?"

"I was a wee bit hard on you. Screw your courage to the sticking point and you might make it." He laughed again for reasons Gillon couldn't understand.

As he left, the librarian was uncapping the brown bottle and staring across the desk. For all his wisdom, the enormous sum of his knowledge, he must be very lonely, Gillon thought, even lonelier than me.

3 WHEN HE CAME THROUGH THE DOOR OF HIS HOUSE, it was the same thing again: the eyes couldn't adjust to the light and he was blinded for several minutes. He was developing some form of miner's eye and it worried him. Everyone was there, they were all about him, talking in his ear, and finally he could see her, sitting on the cutty by the fire, handsome in a full-length shawl that was bright and yet subtle at the same moment, looking beautiful in a way she hadn't looked in a long time.

"Where were you? We looked all over Pitmungo for you," Maggie said. She didn't sound unhappy.

"On the moor, walking."

He held the book behind him and put it on a table in the dark part of the room.

"I ran down to the College for you, Daddie," Sam said. "They wanted to stand you a drink."

"Who wanted?"

"The men in the College," Sam said. "All of them."

"The Bones. The Bone family, Gillon," Tom Drum said. "Och, you should have seen that, Gillon." His voice was proud, although Gillon still couldn't make out his face. "The whole bunch of them, brothers and sisters, his mother and dad, of course, coming down over the moor on a night like this. Never such a thing as *that* before."

He was beginning to put all the pieces in the room in place. Some of the neighbors on the row were in the house, the first time ever, the Hodges from next door, some of the Beggs, Willie Hope on his way to getting drunk, Tom Mengies and his young wife and his concertina. Tom Drum had come up from his house down the row. The Drums had been moved out long ago, so long that they had forgotten this was their house. It was the Cameron house now.

It made Gillon smile. This had been a long time coming.

"Get this, now," Tom Drum said. "The Uppies coming doon —*doon*, mind you—to pay homage to a Doonie." He was shaking his head. "No, never such a thing as that before."

At the edge of the fireplace, being kept warm, a roasted turkey —bubbly-jock, as they called it in Pitmungo—sat steaming, its fat legs pointing toward the ceiling, one of the gifts from the Bone family. Gillon had never had a piece of turkey.

"What did they say, then?" Gillon asked.

"Say? Christ, man, you should have been *here*. 'Thank God for Gillon Cameron and his good sense and courage' is what they said—something like that."

In the middle of the table stood a brown earthenware jug of whisky. While the boys got tassies, Tom Drum worked on the cork.

"None of your blended shit, you'll note—excuse the pit talk, Meg, but sometimes pit talk is the only way, so no blended shit," her father said, "but the true, single malt, eight-year-old Glendoon, from your own part of the world, Gillon."

It was a benediction, a moment of reverence before summoning a great spirit, and the cork was popped. Gillon would have his Christmas drink after all.

"To our dad," Sam said, and they drank. "To my son," Tom Drum said, and they drank. There were several more toasts and the whiskies went off in Gillon's empty stomach like little warm flares. Eventually they linked arms and the Mengies boy played a tune and they drank in the old Scottish way. Gillon crossed the room to Meg.

"Come and share a drop." She nodded and put down her sewing. They linked arms and drank from their cups.

"It's a very beautiful shawl," Gillon said.

"It's a Paisley," Maggie said. "A genuine Paisley. I always

wanted one and now you got it for me." She seemed to want to kiss him or for him to kiss her—it had been a long time with that, too—but it seemed too much in front of all the rest of them, and the moment passed and Andrew was there pointing down at his Wellingtons, heavy rubber boots with heavy rubber knobs on the soles, the desire of every miner in Pitmungo.

"Look what you won me," Andrew said.

"You won those," Gillon said. He slid his arm out of Maggie's arm. The moment was over. When most of the whisky was drunk and people were tipper-taipering around the room, they cut the turkey and it was as glorious as Gillon heard it would be— white meat, clean and gusty, washed down with swills of Glendoon.

"It puts hot kelp soup in its proper place," Maggie said.

"Och, I wouldn't want to go *that* far. No, this *is* the way man was intended to live," Gillon said. "This *is* the way Christmas should be."

He looked around the but rather defiantly.

"Will be."

"Aye," everyone agreed, "aye, aye."

And then the whisky was gone; they had sung the Scotch songs, most of them sad ones because those were the best late at night. Gillon had sung and Sarah had played her flute and then everyone had gone home, the children to their beds built into the boxes along the walls of the but and Gillon and Maggie to their bed in the ben. Cocks were crowing, the first crack of day-daw showing over Easter Mungo, and it had been, Gillon thought, the longest day of his life.

He thought he was asleep but he wasn't. That was the way to bring in Christmas, he thought, but it was a high price to pay for it. He thought of Sandy Bone and "the price of coal," as they called it. The acceptance of the price by the men and even the women—the shrug of the shoulders, the age-old wisdom of learning to accept what can't be changed.

The price paid in bones and bodies and blood, in amputations and disease and death that came in a startling number of ways, by fire and flood, cave-ins and explosions—the cost of coal, always in terms of a body brought up from the pit or a body sitting in the corner of a cold dark room too destroyed to work. Miner's eye that caused the world to flash and dim and even spin about. Miner's knee, making old men out of young ones; miner's asthma that first choked you with coal dust and, when the lungs were properly coated, drowned you in your bed with your own lung fluid. Miner's mascara, the little coal-dust filaments that ingrained themselves around the eyelids, so that if you ever did get out of the pit the eyes still told their story to the *other* world—pit yakker, coal jock, coal miner—classless social leper in the eyes of "the decent world." And finally the miner's tattoo, the blue scars left on the bodies and faces of the miners where coal dust had closed their wounds for them, the miner's stigmata.

But the price was always paid and always accepted. Why did it have to be accepted, Gillon wondered? And why did it have to be paid?

"Gillon?"

"Aye."

"You were right. If one of ours was under the rock, I'd want a Gillon Cameron to do what you did."

It made him feel good and warm, the whisky in his stomach, the sound of the cold wind outside, the warm bed, and now her words, so few and far between but when she said them—he had to admit it—worth it because they didn't come easy; they always were earned. He even had the faintest feeling of, the dare of, desire for her. If any time was a good time, this was a time to try. She sat upright in bed.

"The money. I forgot the money."

She got out of bed despite the cold.

"I left it right out. God knows anyone could take it. I couldn't blame them. Oh, God."

He heard her feeling along the shelves of the dresser and finally heard her breathe a sigh of relief.

"Oh, thank God," Maggie said, and got back into bed. He could feel the coldness of her feet from where he was. "Four pounds."

"Four pounds? From who?"

"The Bones."

"You shouldn't have taken it." He was upset. "The turkey, yes. The whisky, yes. But money?"

"Not for you. For the jack." Gillon couldn't grasp what she was saying.

"You broke the jack. Mr. Brothcock sent a boy up here with a bill for damages while you were on your way to Cowdenbeath."

That was it for Gillon then, the death of desire, the death of anything except the mixture of anger and foolishness that seemed to seize him more and more often. He woke once after that, dreaming or daydreaming, he couldn't tell which, about the iron collar with the wording on it that had been dredged up from the quarry when they had drained it the previous week, still riveted around the neck bone of a skeleton:

> Alex Hope found guilty of death in Perth for stealing meat the 5th of December and gifted as perpetual collier to Thomas Tosh of Pitmungo. If wearer found on road, ample reward for return will be made.

"All we lack are the collars," he said, and found that he was talking aloud again when Maggie stirred and said, "What?"

"It's Christmas," Gillon said. "The Christ Child is born."

"Aye, well, go back to sleep, then, will you?"

It was becoming clearer to Gillon—here was a fresh example of it—that if there was a God of justice and mercy, Thomas Tosh would have been the one to end his days in a flash of flame and exploding coal dust in the pit. But everyone knew Mr. Thomas Tosh married into the Mungo family and died on Brumbie Hill, and that Alex Hope, once of Perth, was thrown or jumped, which was more likely, into the collier quarry.

4 HE STRUGGLED WITH THE BOOK IN THE EVENING after the pit, and sometimes in the afternoon when work was slow and the shifts were cut short. For the first time since he had been in Pitmungo there was a shortage of work. Several times in the past month, and still deep into winter, the work whistle had shrilled out its doleful message, three long blasts in the blackness at dawn—*Nooooo Wooooork Tooooodayyyyy*. They went back to bed, but it wasn't any good there. Maggie was so nervous seeing them lying around the house that they soon all found some place to go. Gillon usually went down to the Reading Room.

The book was so difficult and so boring he wondered why he was torturing himself this way. For one thing, he didn't believe in witches, unlike most of Pitmungo, and the whole story—what he could make of it—seemed to turn on the prophecies of three swill-drinking, swine-killing hags. But he went on, determined to learn something Maggie didn't know and unwilling to return the book to Selkirk unfinished. He read the play through, page by painful page, and when he was finished he forced himself to go back to page 1 and read it again, and he was gratified the second time that little by little it began to make more sense. The third time he read it, it was as if he had never read it at all. The words were all different in their meaning, and clear in a way they weren't before. In the pit, he found he was saying some of the lines to himself, sometimes aloud, afraid of being heard, but wanting to hear them. One line in particular had caught him, when Duncan, the King of Scotland, says:

Whence camest thou, worthy thane?

and a nobleman named Ross answers:

> *From Fife, great king;*
> *Where Norweyan banners flout the sky*
> *And fan our people cold.*

And all at once, several thousand feet down in the pit, out under the ocean, in darkness so complete the grave can get no darker, he found that it was beautiful.

After that, words and sentences from all parts of the play, usually for no reason he could understand, floated into his mind and onto his lips like fish coming up to break the surface of the water. Sometimes, when he was alone in his stall, he shouted them out. And from then on he read all his spare time, by the light of his lamp in the pit when there were no tubs to be filled and right through teatime after work.

If one could call it teatime. Because of the shortage in work, the pay packets were slimmer than before. When the money got tight, most families just shifted to food some of the money they might have spent on such things as football matches down at Cowdenbeath and went on as before, but in the Cameron house, at the first cutback, they went on hard-time rations. Because despite the cutting down of the pay packets, there would be no cutting down on the kist. Nor would there be any dipping into it for food. The kist would get its due; the kist came first.

They called it in Pitmungo "tattie and dabs at the stool," bowls of boiled potatoes and a smidge of butter and a bowl of salt to dip the tattie in after a bite, the whole family seated in a circle around the tattie stool.

"This isn't enough for a coal miner," Sam said one night, throwing his fork onto the floor. "Christ, Mother, it's enough for an old man or a ribbon clerk but miners need meat on their bones."

"Bosh," Maggie said. "People eat too much as it is."

"Not in this house they don't."

"It's good to go without."

She really believed that, they knew. It was a hopeless battle.

"The Irish people eat nothing but tatties and they seem to do all right."

"Oh, aye, yes, fine, Mither," Rob Roy said. "You ought to see them filling the gutters down in Cowdenbeath. A fine spectacle of tattie eaters. A glorious example of the virtues of the lowly spud in improving the human being."

"There, now," Maggie said. "Did you hear him? What he said?" She tapped Gillon's arm and he looked up from his book. "Do you see what I mean? He's become so . . . so sanshauch he can't see straight."

"And what, pray tell," Rob said, in his imitation British accent, "would sanshauch be? *Mither*?"

"A smairt-arse, sinny boy," Maggie said, and Rob had the grace to flush. "You can't talk to him any more; it's all this Selkirk."

It was true, Gillon realized, they were always after one another; and went back to his reading. He was reading *King Lear* now and it was better than *Macbeth*, Gillon thought, but perhaps that was because he was more ready to take it; he didn't know.

"Deny yourself, that's the trait to master," he heard his wife saying. "When you deny yourself, you free yourself." It was true, he thought, with her at least, that sometimes at Sunday breakfast when she denied herself a second kipper, he noticed a look of satisfaction on her face. "If you can learn to say no, you will be able to say yes when the time comes." He never knew where she got these sayings, these slogans. Despite having been a teacher she didn't read, and didn't talk with her neighbors from one month to the next. His only conclusion was that she made them up.

"How sharper than a serpent's tooth it is to have a thankless child."

He looked up then and around the room. It was amazing how often, he thought, he read a line in Shakespeare and it applied to him, a collier in Pitmungo. But then he realized the exaggeration. There were no thankless children in this room. Rebellious, yes, honed and primed to be that way by the person they were rebelling against, almost as if it were planned that way, but loyal, and a loyal child couldn't be called a thankless child.

But he made you think. That very morning, for instance, loading a coal tub, it had struck him that even in a coal town he would never be a Macbeth, fired by ambition to make some mark in his world, however small that world might be; but it *was* within the range of the possible for his wife to be a Lady Macbeth. *That* was worth knowing, worth understanding . . .

They were arguing again—discussing, they called it, no matter how heated it became. They thrived on it, the Cameron Sunday afternoon and evening ritual. Gillon had never had anything like it in his house, nor had Maggie Drum, he knew that, and yet something between the two of them had bred this restless, relentless examination of everything and every idea that came down the lane and into their cluttered house.

Sometimes he looked up at them and wondered who they were, where they had come from, not knowing them, not even recognizing their physical bodies.

"The simple fact is that most people are bad," Rob Roy was saying.

"Ah." Andrew had him. "There you go, you see. You admit most people are bad and then you would turn over to them the control of all the means of production? Do you see the inevitable disaster that lies there? You admit it?"

"And *you* walked right into it," Rob answered. "People aren't bad by *nature*. Left to their own devices people are good. Society *forces* them to be bad."

"I don't think most people are bad," Sarah said from the ben. "If you ever bothered to go to kirk, you'd see an awful lot of good people."

"Being seen in kirk isn't proof a man is good, for God's sake," Sam said. "My God, Sarah, Mr. Brothcock goes to kirk."

"A man's neighbor isn't his brother's helper, you see," Rob said. "He becomes, in *this* society, his competitor."

"Who's playing tomorrow night?" Jemmie asked.

"Hearts of Cowdenbeath against Kirkcaldy Celtics."

"That's nonsense and you know it," Andrew said. "If man was good by nature, then there'd be no need of all the laws we have to govern him."

"Och, Jesus, the *reasoning*!"

"I wish you wouldn't let them use those words in the house, Mother."

"Because a corrupt society creates corrupt laws to hold men down, you then deduce—have the gall to deduce—that man, *made* bad, *must* be bad. Don't you *see* it, for Christ's sake, man? The flaw, man?"

"Rob is right, though," Sarah said. "Man is good because he is made in God's image and therefore he must be good."

There was silence. No one wanted to hurt Sarah's feelings, yet almost against their wills they groaned, even the football boys. It made her, as they knew it would, furious. It was the only time they ever saw her angry, when her Savior, as she thought of Him, was attacked.

"It's true and you know it's true." She came out of the ben and she was crying, as they knew she would be.

"Look, Sarah . . ." Andrew began.

"Man is good and the temptations of life rotten him," she said. They were silent. "And if you don't believe it, you go and ask Mr. MacCurry, if you have the nerve."

"You had to add that," Rob Roy said sadly.

"Which is like asking the thief whether he did it or not," Sam said.

"Thief?" She crossed the steaming, clothes-clogged room, pit clothes hanging everywhere from hooks near the fireplace, a maze, a jungle of sweat-wet mine duds, and faced her father.

"How can you let them talk that way? You make them take that back, Daddie."

He didn't know what to say. His weakness was that he couldn't act like a proper Christian parent because he believed with the boys. She turned away from him.

"Where has God gone to in this family?"

To Gillon's surprise, it was Maggie who was gentle with her about it.

"Don't worry about it," she said. She put an arm around her daughter. "He may not be here now but I'll tell you where you'll find Him." She looked at her sons and her husband. "Down in the mine when the roof begins to work and the props to pop. Oh, you'll find him then. 'Don't let it happen now, please, God, not just now, not on *my* head.' Och, you ought to hear the prayers come floating up the shaft. I can hear them all the way up here at the house."

It quieted them by the simple device of being true. Even Gillon, often against his conscious will, found himself turning toward God for a little protection when there was the smell of danger in the mine, standing there, listening, listening, heart knocking ribs, "Dear God, I promise you," and then going back to work again, the smell of death having passed as mysteriously as it had come. Fire insurance, Rob called it. He was the only one who would deny he found himself spinning Godward when there was trouble in the pit.

"So will you be going down to the match, then?" Jemmie said.

"Are you mad, man? Ask her for the siller?" Sam said. There would be no football until the work shortage ceased.

"Don't you worry about your God," Maggie said to Sarah. "It's all talk; it's all so much Selkirk blether."

Selkirk. There was no getting around it, things had changed for the Camerons since the Reading Room had opened. Gillon went into the ben, out of the way of the steaming clothes and all those faces and tongues and lay down on the bed, a thing he rarely did before night, and tried to recall the night he felt ready enough to go down the hill and take *Macbeth* back to Mr. Selkirk. The room had been filled with old men, the human slag heap, Selkirk called them, the inevitable human residue of the capitalist mining community, come not to read but for heat, sitting nodding on benches and chairs. Gillon stood before the librarian, holding the book out as a form of identification, waiting until the man would look up and take notice of him.

"I've come back, sir," Gillon said.

"Isn't that fine? And why did you ever go?"

Gillon saw he had been drinking and was, in fact, a little drunk. Miners never got a little drunk.

"You gave me this to read."

Mr. Selkirk took the book from Gillon and looked at the front of it and the back, until he had pulled his remembrances together.

"And you're going," he said, the sarcasm heavy on his tongue, as heavy as the whisky he had been drinking, "you're going to stand there and tell me you read it."

Gillon nodded. "Aye, I read it," he said, and all at once Selkirk was on his feet, staring at his hand, his blotchy red face contorted.

" 'Is this a dagger which I see before me,' " he cried out— several of the gaffers woke in alarm, as if they had just heard a danger cry in the pit— " 'the handle toward my hand? Come, let me clutch you.' "

" 'Thee,' " Gillon said, without intending to. The librarian stopped his acting and stared at Gillon.

"What do you mean 'thee'?"

"It is 'clutch thee.' "

"Do you know what I say to you, coal jock, bloody coal jock, do you know what I say?" The blotches were gone from his face, because the entire face was bright red. "I say bullshit. How does that sound? Tushloch! How does *that* sound? Give me the book."

Gillon stood there, his own face scarlet now.

"The buke."

"In your hand, sir." Gillon was sorry he had ever opened his mouth. Drunk or not, the librarian flipped the book open to the right scene. Gillon could see his lips moving, playing back the role, and then he was silent and looked up at Gillon and back down at the book and slammed it shut.

"I'll be goddamned," he said. "I will have God personally damn me." He opened the book again. "Fewkin coal miner," he mumbled, but Gillon heard him.

"Here we are." Very loud once more. " 'Who can be wise, amazed, temperate and furious, loyal and neutral in a moment?' "

Gillon didn't know what he wanted of him.

"Well?"

" 'No man,' " Gillon said, and Mr. Selkirk laughed from pure joy.

"That is, of course, also tushloch. Henry Selkirk can." That pleased him and he chuckled. He tried Gillon after that on several of the more famous lines and Gillon was up to them.

"Well, well," Selkirk had finally said, and then to Gillon's amazement—that wasn't it, Gillon thought, lying on the bed, his shame, embarrassment bordering on fear—he found Mr. Selkirk holding his hand in his soft little white hand, whimpering.

" 'I am a very foolish fond old man, fourscore and upward, not an hour more nor less; and, to deal plainly . . .' "

He waited for Gillon to give him the closing line, which Gillon, not having read *King Lear*, didn't know. The librarian looked mildly disappointed in his newfound protégé. "Tripped you there," he said, and took out a pair of harsh-looking steel-rimmed spectacles. All business.

"Now, then, what to do with you?"

"I thought another book by the same man."

"Oh, no, not yet. I fed you strong meat and now you deserve your pudding."

He flurried across the room, hustling old men out of the way like geese in a barnyard, until he reached the shelf of books.

"Here we are. You'll read this next. Your librarian's orders. Must have orders or we have intellectual disorder, can you understand that?"

Gillon nodded that he did. It sounded like one of Maggie's lines.

"I'll want a report on this one. Now, when shall we two meet again, 'In thunder, lightning, or in rain?'"

"'When the hurlyburly's done, when the battle's lost and won,'" Gillon said, and Mr. Selkirk had let out a whimper of delight. He had finally found the makings of a colleague in this black, backward, bookless wilderness. He crooked a finger at Gillon to have him come closer.

"Just remember this, now," the librarian said. "'Ripeness is all.'"

Gillon had been puzzled.

"That's it? That's all? I don't understand."

"You don't have to now," the librarian had said, "but you will, you'll see, you will," and that had been the end of it, or the start of it.

The book had been *Hard Times,* by Charles Dickens, and it had disappointed Gillon because it was all about the kind of people who lived on Brumbie Hill and so, Gillon reasoned, it couldn't have taken much work. But he came to like it anyway, despite the material, and after that he began going down to the Reading Room and taking Rob Roy with him. His son and Mr. Selkirk had gotten along well from the start, and Gillon was pleased to have a second reader in the house even though he thought *The Communist Manifesto* was a strange choice of book to send the boy home with.

Lying in bed, he could hear Rob quoting part of the book right then. Rob had read it through ten or eleven times the first month it was in the house, although Gillon himself could never get much beyond Marx and Engels's proposals for the abolition of the family. He felt guilty about the idea, even reading about it, and disloyal. He wished Rob Roy would learn to shut his mouth about that in front of his mother, because in Maggie's manifesto the family, like ripeness, was all.

5   HE HEARD THE THREE LONG BLASTS ON THE WORK whistle—no work again that day—and rolled over, happy to hear them, and when he finally woke for good he was conscious that for the first time he could remember he was alone in his own house. The luxury of lying in his bed with the sun well up and the house silent gave him a sense of stealing something from life. Stolen sweets *are* best, Gillon thought—that was one thing Marx had never understood—and then decided he had better start reading the latest book Mr. Selkirk had assigned him.

It was *The Martyrdom of Man*, by Winwood Reade, and Selkirk wanted Gillon to understand the mind of "the opposition," of *them*, the owning class, the Entirely Comfortable.

It was hard going for Gillon. The argument was that all mankind had suffered to bring the world to the present state of prosperity it was in, and so it was only fair that mankind should continue to suffer in order to improve the lot of those coming after, just as others had suffered for us. Mr. Selkirk had written some comments in the margins, one-word ones, that Gillon had heard down pit but had never before seen on paper.

Deny today in order to have tomorrow—that was the heart o' the nut. Maggie should have it on a sampler over her bed, Gillon thought, and he thought of the "discussion" the night before.

"Oh, aye, fine, but *I* have only one life to live," Rob Roy had shouted. There was too much shouting in the family, Gillon realized. It had gotten out of control. "I'm not going to be around tomorrow to live it all over again. I have to take what I can from it now."

"Yes, take. Take. That's all you think about," Maggie had said.

"It's the trouble with you Socialists. You want it all now. You can't see beyond your next pint."

And Rob was drinking too much, Gillon thought. She was right about that.

"He who drinks a little too much drinks much too much," his father used to say. He went back to his reading and gradually became aware of someone in the house or just outside it at the doorway, and he put down the book to listen.

"Why are you wasting time kicking a football all morning?" Maggie said.

"A lad should have some fun sometimes." Andrew's voice.

"Nonsense. Children don't need fun."

It was a game he had heard them play before. What struck him was the easy way they played it with each other. Andrew was the only one who could talk that way with his mother, because there was an understanding between them and always had been. Gillon heard the football bouncing in the row outside the house.

"The business of the parent is to beat the frolic out of the boy and put the responsibility back in."

"Nonsense. All work and no play makes Jock a dull boy."

"Aye, a dull *rich* boy."

She had him. Gillon heard Andrew laugh, which he didn't often do. It bothered him to find that he was faintly annoyed by the closeness between the two of them. He thought he was above that. If he was a good father he should welcome it. Andrew must have been showing his mother some trick he had mastered with the football.

"You must have wasted a lot of time to learn that one."

"I did."

"Have you finished the *Overman's Hand Book* yet?" She was —that suddenly—deadly serious. He hadn't, he said, because it was too hard.

"Dumb," his mother said. "If Archie Japp can be an overman, you can be one."

"He was appointed, he didn't earn his certificate."

"Well, you'll earn yours. You know what your Granddaddie Tom said. 'Play today or pay today, which one do you want? You can't have it both ways.'"

"Oh, I don't know about that. I want to pay people to work for me so *I* can play."

It was what she wanted to hear, Gillon knew that. She was baking scones and she told Andrew to come in and have one.

"I don't know," Andrew said. "I'm not that hungry." They never were allowed hot scones except on special occasions, because they tended to go wild over them and eat more than they should.

"Come in the house," she ordered.

He ate the scone quickly, because he felt guilty about it, the others not sharing it. Gillon remained totally quiet, knowing he had let his presence go unknown too long. Maggie buttered the scone, unheard of in hard times, and then put a dab of honey on the melting butter. And after that she gave him a cup of milk. He drank it down and ran for the door.

"The others needn't know," she called to him when he was at the door.

"Aye."

"*Yes.*"

"Yes."

The door slammed. They were alone. He didn't know what to do with her, how to face her. But he didn't want her to find him first, back in the ben as if he had been hiding there all along. He brushed his hair because he wanted to look as presentable as possible, and went to the door of the ben and stood there, waiting for her to discover him. When she did, she did so with a start, a look of surprise on her face, her mouth making an O, and then went back to herself.

"I would have thought you'd have been gone long ago," she said.

"Where?"

"I don't know. Where you go. Your lovely Reading Room with your lovely Mr. Selkirk."

It was so much like her to seize the initiative that despite his anger with her he found he was smiling.

"As long as you're home, the least you can do is go and get us some water."

"Aye, some water."

He got the buckets and the yoke and started down the row to the well. It would do her good to stew alone, Gillon thought, and him some good to have time to figure out what price she was going to pay. At the well, waiting in line with the women and children who hauled all the water in Pitmungo, he looked at the back of the Gillespie girl in front of him. He liked her straight back and noticed her hair. It was beautiful hair and it excited him. He had never thought of her as beautiful before, as a desirable woman, but he could see her beauty now, hidden—as all beauty was in Pitmungo—hidden by a water bucket on her back. The waste of beauty and youth in this place, Gillon thought. He went back up the row, the water spilling all the way because he was too tall for the balance of the yoke.

"I'll have a scone for breakfast," he said. She brought him a hot scone.

"With butter and honey."

So then she knew.

"And milk."

She paused before telling him that there was no more milk.

"No more?"

"No."

"Not a drop. That's too bad, then."

The scone tasted like sawdust in his mouth but he ate it. It was strange being all alone in the house with her.

"Why do you wear your hair that way?"

"Pitmungo way. All the others do."

"Untie it. Take it down."

"I'll have to take the snood off."

"Take it off then. Terrible word, 'snood.' Beautiful hair trapped in snood."

She took out the pins and took off the knitted snood, and her dark hair fell to her waist. He had almost forgotten she could look that way. She turned to him and saw his face.

"All right, what do you want with me?"

"To go to the High Moor."

Her sullen reluctance to do his bidding, but doing it, excited him.

"Will you go?" That was wrong. He never should ask.

"Yes, I'll go."

Because, as he well knew, she was guilty, and now she had to pay her price. She was guilty of the second worst crime in the Cameron family, next to denying the kist: she had played favorites in the family.

"I can't go like this," Maggie said. "I'll put it up under a bonnet first."

"And let it loose on the moor."

"Yes, I'll do that." She knew what Gillon didn't realize, that he would never be able to forgive her without some payment on her part. Now she wanted to go.

They went down the row and everyone looked at them. A husband and wife simply daundering—daundering down the row—didn't happen very often.

"You should have worn your hat," Maggie said.

Most of the children were on the Sportin Moor and the women were in the houses, but the men were sitting in clusters of twos and threes in the doorways facing the sun, taking their ease. It was a strange, rare day for late March, warm and clear and hardly any wind, and they sat out in their knitted underwear tops, drinking in the sun, their powerful arms looking ineffectual because of their codfishy whiteness, although here and there some blue streak or gash, wound stripe from some old accident, caused the muscle to leap out from the whiteness. Some of the men nodded to Gillon and some of them made the cracks, the give-and-take, the old banter, about being tall and thin (the corbie, the hawk, the stork), about the hat, whether he was wearing it or not, about being an outsider—an incomer, as they called it—and the Hielands, all the old cracks about the place and the people who come from there.

"Don't they ever get tired of saying the same things?" Maggie asked.

"Not as of yet," Gillon said.

At the end of Miners Row, where it enters Colliers Walk, a miner came out of his doorway and signaled Gillon away from Maggie.

"I thought you ought to know you're on Brothcock's victimization list," he said. "Don't say I told you."

"What do you mean?"

"His suspect list. His shite list. Agitators, troublemakers, the like."

"How the hell do you know? Why would he do that?"

"Look, man, don't ask me how I know. You're on it. You and that son of yours."

"Rob Roy?"

"Aye, that one."

Gillon was angry at the man and upset by what he had heard but he realized the man meant no harm and went back to thank him.

"I didn't expect you to be happy about it," the miner said.

They turned up the Walk and came out on the Sportin Moor.

"What was that all about?" Maggie asked.

"Oh, that? Pit talk."

She knew he was lying but she let it go. A boy came running down from the moor holding a hand over his nose and mouth, which were running with blood, and Gillon stopped him. The nose was bleeding and a tooth was loose but otherwise he was all right.

"What happened?"

"Fewkin Cameron," the boy said. He hadn't seen Maggie. "Smashes everybody."

"Was it fair? A fair shot?"

"Oh, aye, fair all right," the boy said, and continued down the moor for home.

They stopped and watched the rugby players. The game belonged to Sam. Sam Cameron all over the field, in every scrum, almost every breakaway, it seemed, almost every tackle. When someone didn't get up very fast, or get up at all, usually Sam was involved. There was nothing intentional about it; it was Sam. He had the bones of the Drums, as heavy as old oak, and Gillon's grace and speed. He moved with deceptive swiftness. He had once caught a trout in a moor stream with his bare hand, Gillon recalled, grabbing it and flinging it out of the water the way a bear would do.

Jemmie was in the game, chunky and dark and low to the ground, a defensive player who went right into the runners, bare head into their gut, hitting them low and hard, making up in nerve what he lacked in style. Andrew, Gillon noticed, was on the sidelines watching. He broke more easily than his brothers.

"What a *waste*," Maggie said.

"They say that Sam could play for Hearts of Cowdenbeath right now. A scout came all the way up to see him play."

"Isn't that fine?" She was sarcastic.

"Professional, Maggie."

"Oh?"

"Two pounds a week, three pounds a week."

"For that? For running around on the moor?"

"And they can keep working besides, if it doesn't drain them too much. He'd be the youngest in all of Scotland."

She turned around and looked back down at the game. It didn't seem quite so wasteful to her then. "Where is this man?" she asked, with genuine interest, and it made Gillon want to laugh.

"He'll be back. You have to be sixteen to play."

They walked up through Uppietoon, past Moncrieff Lane and the Tosh-Mungo Terrace, the miners there—overmen and deputies and shot-firers, a notch above the face miners—lolling in their doorways exactly like the moudieworts down below them.

"Something has to be done about it," Maggie said. "This waste, this waste of time and men."

She didn't mean it in the social sense, Gillon knew, but in the Cameron sense: one more day lost to them forever, one more *earning* day, seven more daily wages gone and no way in the world to ever recover them—money stolen from the kist as surely, if you looked at it that way, as if someone put his hand down in it and came away with a clutch of siller.

If only they knew in advance that the mines would be closed, there would be something they could do with their day; that was her complaint and her dream. There had to be some way of telling in advance, some reason that would guide them, but she had never found it. Some miners believed the shutdowns were dictated by the number of filled coal tubs on hand, some by the size of the coal bing, the rate of future orders, but none of the factors ever held true in the end. The mines shut down with empty tubs in the yards; with orders for hundreds of tons of good hard coal on the books, the mines were closed and the men sent home.

"Why don't they tell you, Gillon; why won't they *ever* tell you in advance?"

He didn't want to get off on that. Her mind belonged to him this day at least.

"I've told you and told you," Gillon said. "They want the men to be dependent on them. They *like* to keep them dangling that way."

So the men got up late and puttered around the house. No wonder miners were so good at fixing things around the house, at whittling and making furniture, cutting hair, fixing shoes, repairing anything that broke, at flower gardens, kail yards, and quoits. They had so many open days to work at it.

. . .

They went up through the White Coo plantation and Maggie took Gillon's hand. He was pleased by that but he had to let her understand that it wasn't enough. He wanted to go all the way up to the top of the High Moor and see the fresh spring blue of the firth before having her—one of his whims, he knew—but decided it was too dangerous, too long a walk during which too many things could come between them. There was a suggestion of buds in the apple and pear trees, and when they came out onto the moor, Gillon was happy to find it deserted.

"Now's the time to take your bonnet off." She did as she was told, in a compliant, submissive fashion, which again excited him, and her hair flowed down the back of her jacket and the light winds on the moor lifted it and dropped it lightly back again like wind on water.

"Who would know you were the mother of seven children?" Gillon said. "You don't know how young you look. You don't look your age at all."

"You don't act yours at all."

They went up the moor. He was as excited for her as he was the day they had first come across the same moor toward Pitmungo and he had found the little dark copse of beeches. He wanted to say all kinds of things like that to her but nothing seemed right. He was afraid of breaking something he knew they had established. She stopped in a little culvert out of the wind, a sun catch on the moor already floored with small ferns and the first shoots of spring grass and moor moss, and she took off her jacket and unbuttoned the first and second buttons on her linen sark. Despite the sun, it was chill in the wind on the moor though warm in the hollow. It reminded Maggie of the sand nest she had been warming in the day she had found Gillon.

"You were my kiltie boy," Maggie said. "I knew it the minute I saw you in the water."

He heard but didn't really hear her. He kept saying aye, aye in a low soothing voice, conscious that he was being overly hasty about it, but fumbling with her buttons, and finally he was able to make love to her while she lay back and watched hawks soar and skid along above the moor in search of moles and mice.

When he was spent, she didn't push him away from her, as she usually did, but allowed him to go on, and he grew more selfish and more violent now that there wasn't a problem of spending himself so soon.

"Moothlie, Gillon," she murmured; "there's plenty of time, Gillon, plenty of time," and she gave herself to him totally because this was her payment, and Maggie respected debts, and because she had also made up her mind that this was her farewell to the carnal act and she might as well enjoy it while it went. Gillon felt he had never been more pleased and satisfied. When he finally went to get up he was dizzy and had to lie down again and she let him sleep for a few minutes next to her in the sun.

When he woke, she was standing in the moor grass in her bright clean white underwear, the little sleeveless linen sark and her short petticoat. She was very dark against the whiteness of her clothes, and he was able to appreciate how firm her body still was. So many of the women—most of them in Pitmungo, no matter how hard they worked—went to dumpiness and the others went to dry sticks, used up and almost always dead by the time forty came around. She was holding up her skirt.

"Well, you've done it, Gillon Cameron. We don't dare go down now until dark. At my age, you've turned me into a green gown."

He didn't know what she meant. It had to do, she informed him, with coming down from the moor with innocence on one's face and grass stains on one's rear. Half the pithead girls in Pitmungo entered maturity as green gowns. Gillon got up. He felt tired but pleasantly tired. When he was dressed he began going around the moor as if he were looking for lost money.

"This is something *you* don't know about."

He was looking for stones and when he found enough of them he fashioned a neat little pile, a cairn of a sort, quickly and expertly, the way a miner learns to build a stone pack to support the roof of the mine he's working in. When he was through, he stood back from it with Maggie.

"And what in the name of God is that?"

"A tryst stane," Gillon said. He felt he loved her then and that so many things were forgiven, they were on new ground. "It's an old Highland thing. When a man and a woman have had a very special time, the man leaves behind a memorial of it, you see, a piece of Scotland covered with stones so that the land always belongs to them."

Maggie was moved by it. "I thought you didn't know about things like that. Oh, you lied to me in Strathnairn."

She surprised him. She stood on her toes and kissed him on the lips and started to run toward the crest of the moor. He started to run after her and couldn't keep up. He ran slower and slower until finally he had to walk doubled over. He knew what it was: the coal dust had gotten to him. He couldn't get enough air into his lungs. Compared to Maggie, he was an old man.

"Too much houghmagandie, Gillon Cameron," she called down to him, but he couldn't even smile back up at her; he felt too old and sorry for himself. She waited for him at the crest of the moor.

"What's the matter with you?"

"I don't know; I'm getting old, I think."

"You didn't act that way before," she said, and Gillon smiled. They rarely joked about that. And then there was the sea down below them, as vast and empty as the moor. It was always so surprising to Gillon that the sea was here—one never thought of the sea in Pitmungo and what went on there was a world apart to them—and it was heart-lifting to discover it shining so cleanly below them. In the whole expanse of sea there was not a ship to be seen. They sat on the soft spring grass and looked down on St. Andrew's harbor where the Pitmungo coal was sent to be shipped.

The wharf was empty of men but filled to the breaking point with coal. Coal covered the wharf itself and the loading areas behind, and coal filled all the two-ton tubs that lined the wooden tracks leading to the wharf.

"I think I have the black lung," Gillon said.

"Och, Gillon, every man in pit gets some coal dust in his lungs but it doesn't mean he has black lung. They can't even walk up a flight of stairs, Gillon."

"Aye, I guess." He lay back on the moor, on the sunny side of the crest, and looked at the sky. The big clouds were starting— the great flubbers, they called them—early for March.

"That was nice," Gillon said. "I've missed that. It's good to spend a day that way once in a while."

"Not a working day."

"One day, three days, Maggie, what's so terrible about that?"

"You add it up in shillings and tell me." She wasn't being harsh or mean about it, just very sensible.

Gillon suddenly sat upright. She had paid well, she had fulfilled her contract, but he felt she still owed him something else.

"What's so important about it? Why won't you ever answer that? How long do we keep putting money in the box and never knowing what for? I'm tired of it, Meg, and the children are tired of it. There's going to come a time, you know, when they're not going to put another penny in your kist and you won't be able to do much about it."

It was difficult for her—it was, more than that, almost impossible for her—to talk about it. The dream had been her dream for so long that it seemed to have become inseparable from her. It was as if to talk about it was to sully it in some way, and so the family let it alone, literally, from one year to the next. It was a question of wanting. She wanted what she wanted more than they wanted to resist her, and so they surrendered to her.

"We were going to use the mines to get out of the mines and here I am—Goddamnit, now, face the truth, Meg—almost twenty years a miner, half my life a miner, me, a seaman in his heart, and now, and I am not joking, thinking I have the start of black lung. Sure there's enough in the kist to get us out of here."

She pulled blades of grass and started several times to talk, her mouth opening and struggling to begin and then shutting hard, as if she were never intending to speak again.

"To get out, yes, but not to get out the right way."

"The right way?"

"Aye, the *right* way. When we go, Gillon"—and there was that look again; he knew it would be on her face well before he looked up at it—"we're going to go big. No sweetie shop for us, Gillon, we could do that now. No livery stable, no little ten-shilling-a-day greengrocer for us. We could have our hands white at the end of the day and be like those poor sniveling clerks in the Pluck Me, soft and fat and poor as mine mice."

She stood up, which is what she always did when she got on the subject, and Gillon could not help seeing what an unconscious effect she was making, the grass to her waist at the crest of the moor, the whole reach of sky spread almost limitlessly behind her, her thick brown hair being fondled by the wind, her breasts rising and falling with her emotion. He wanted her again.

"We're going to get into a situation, Gillon—into a business, Gillon, a real business—where all of us can work and earn a living, a *real* living, Gillon, and a business that grows, where one thing leads up to another and out to another, everything going on to the next—if we work, if we work it right." She sat down very suddenly, as if a spasm had passed. "And we will. We will."

He waited awhile before asking.

"Is that what the letters from Cowdenbeath are all about?"

And she waited her time, because it was her secret and she was jealous of it.

"Yes."

He let it go; he was generous about things like that. There were things people should have to themselves, even at the expense of others. The way it was with his reading.

. . .

The ship had managed to come up the firth without their seeing it; one minute the firth empty and then the ship was well into it, as if it had been placed there by some supernatural hand. It was an old four-master schooner, once a proud ship, Gillon knew, refitted now as a coal bottom, high in the water, barely luffing its way toward St. Andrews although it was empty.

"It's very beautiful," Maggie said; and Gillon said yes even though it wasn't beautiful, it was sad. People who didn't know the sea always said that when they saw the sea and sails; it seemed to be required. They got up and went down the hill a little way, out of the wind, to see the ship enter the harbor, and when they did they were surprised to see a file of men going down the road toward the dock with shovels and coal creels over their shoulders, a ragged army of dark little coal-dusted men.

"Wester Mungo miners come to load the coal."

"How do you know?"

"I don't know; I just know," Gillon said.

There was a primitive crane lifting up the coal hutches and emptying them in a forward hold but most of the coal was being loaded by miners shoveling the coals onto a metal chute that ran into the bottom of the boat. Clouds of coal dust were rising from the wharf and the sea around the schooner was turning black.

"Talk about your black lung," Gillon said, but Maggie hadn't heard him. She was starting down the moor as if drawn by some force she couldn't resist, and Gillon got up and trotted down the slope after her.

"What's the matter with you?"

"There it is," she said, "your answer."

She was so detached from him then, so in the grip of what she was seeing, that he said nothing. She turned on him and pulled at the lapels of his jacket.

"Look, Gillon. You mine coal sometimes when there are no coal tubs ready to take your coal out." Gillon nodded. "And sometimes they shut you down when there are tubs standing empty all around."

He nodded.

"And you mine coal when the coal bing in the yard is a mile high, and they close the mine when the bing is half its usual height."

She was triumphant.

"Because it's all *here*. It doesn't matter what goes on in the mines. When the wharf is loaded with coal and there are no boats, they shut the mines. When the wharf is empty, they mine coal until the wharf is full and then they shut the pits until a boat comes in. And if three or four boats come in they mine around the clock, overtime and extra shifts and Sunday work against the law."

"Aye."

"It's all *here*."

It was true, Gillon saw; it was the only way to account for what took place back in Pitmungo. Maggie pointed down at St. Andrews.

"The mines will open tomorrow."

"Aye, it's true."

They started back up the long rise to the crest. Gillon was tired but Maggie was full of excitement.

And when they got to the top they looked back down and saw a second coal bottom on the horizon coming in from Norway or Denmark, where Lord Fyffe sold his coal. She grew even more excited.

"And now we'll see how long two boats keep the mines open."

It was wise of her. They would have some sort of crude measuring stick to go by.

"But there's something else, you know," Maggie said. "They don't tell you because they don't know themselves. Until that boat comes into the harbor, they can't be sure it's coming in; they have no way of knowing."

That, too, rang true. There was no way for a coal bottom starting out from Norway to tell when it would make its way to the Firth of Forth and Fife. Any strong headwind could hold the lumbering ships up for days at a time, granted even that you knew the day they were starting.

"But *we* will know," Maggie said. "We will know as soon as they know."

He didn't ask her how. It would be revealed. He felt tired now and envied her energy. They went down the other side of the moor, and there sat Pitmungo, blackly defacing the green world around it. He hated to go back down. And Maggie looked so young and keyed up then that he felt an almost uncontainable desire for his wife despite his tiredness.

Energy creates energy, he had read somewhere, and appetite creates appetite. Going without doesn't create hunger, not after a while; it creates a system of accommodation to going without. He wanted her while she was this way. They passed the tryst stone that shepherds would look strangely at the next day or so, and he thought of trying her once more, because he had a feeling that it might be a long time coming again. But he could see that her mind had long ago forgotten the early afternoon and that he would only be an intruder in her life now.

She took his hand, though.

"Gillon?" He squeezed her hand. "It's going to do it for us. Put us out ahead of all the rest. A march on all the rest."

He yearned to have her on the little fresh ferns.

"When the rest have nothing to do, the Camerons will have work. When the rest are flat broke, the Camerons will be putting siller in their kist."

Gillon didn't know if he should approve of that. What was it Rob Roy had been saying only the night before? About the system that destroyed us as people. Instead of helping our brothers, we were driven to compete with them. He wasn't sure what was right.

She held his hand all the way down across the moor and through the White Coo plantation, the orchard almost smoky then with budding leaves from the warmth of the day, and held it all the way until they came to the back of the houses on Tosh-Mungo Terrace, when she slipped her hand from his and swept up her hair and hid it, to Gillon's sadness, beneath her snood again.

The day for Gillon was over.

That was the birth of it, of the Cameron Watch, the High Moor Watch, the St. Andrew's Watch—everyone in the family had another name for it—that began to separate the Camerons from the rest of Pitmungo even more than they had been separated before. It was to be their secret, as precious to them, as sacred to the family, as the kist. The next time the whistle blew in the morning—the three long dreaded blasts—when the rest of the men in Pitmungo would crawl back into their beds, the Camerons would be up and gone.

6

" 'IT WAS THE BEST OF TIMES, IT WAS THE WORST OF times,' " Gillon read aloud, and slapped the book shut so hard that water leaped from the tub onto the floor.

"No, I won't go along with that," he said.

"Read the next line," Andrew said.

"It's a writer's trick," Gillon said. "The best of times, the worst of times. It seems to make sense but when you analyze it, it makes no sense."

"He must have thought he was awful clever when he thought that up," Rob Roy said.

"Read the next line; maybe it clarifies it," Andrew said.

"Clarifies! Jesus," Jemmie said.

"It doesn't matter," Gillon said. "I'm talking about this line. It's simply a clever trick. You can't have it both ways."

"Good and bad times, yes," Rob Roy said, "but not the best

and the worst. They're both superlatives, you see. The one rules
out the other."

"Oh, Christ, we're getting deep around here," Sam said.

"Language," his mother said. "I won't have that. It's vulgar."

"Yes, but look at *us*," Andrew was saying. He got very excited.

"All right, look at us," Rob said.

"That's exactly the situation here. It's the worst of times for
them," he said, waving his hand to the outside, meaning the
other people in Pitmungo, "and the best of times for us."

None of them had an answer to that.

"I don't know how the sentence is grammatically," Andrew said,
pressing the point home while he had the chance—he always
seemed to be defending the wrong view by their standards, the
conservative one, and not very well—"but I know how it is
actually. It's right!"

And for a change he had them.

All that spring and summer, the mines had been closing, which was unwelcome but not unexpected, but then it
had carried into the fall, which had never happened before,
shutting down for a day or two at a time, opening suddenly in the
afternoons and working through the night, and then closing
midway through a shift with no warning. No one knew why, not
even the mine superintendent, Mr. Brothcock.

But the Camerons knew. Every morning and afternoon, one of
them would be sent up to the High Moor to take the harbor count
with the little counter Andy had invented for the watch. For
every ten coal tubs waiting to be unloaded on the spur line leading
to the wharf, a white peg in the board was pushed down; for
every ten white pegs pushed down, one red one; and start over
again. Each night Maggie and the others, too, would make the
count.

"Three hundred and twenty tubs with coal on the track."

"And the wharf?"

"Covered with coal. A mountain of it there."

"And coal ships?"

"None in the harbor, none in the firth."

Then by the "equation," as they came to call it, they would know there would be no work in the morning, and unless a coal bottom luffed into harbor in the afternoon, there would be no work the day after.

Armed with their knowledge, secure in their secret, the Camerons began to find work and make work. While the rest of the Pitmungo miners dabbled their days away wandering up and down the rows and lanes, playing quoits on the Sportin Moor, the Camerons were gone. While the siller slowed to a trickle in the rest of the valley, the siller kept flowing into the Cameron kist.

"He that tholes, overcomes," was the title of one of Mr. Mac-Curry's sermons, and for the first time in anyone's memory, people laughed in the kirk. There was nothing to thole at. Except for the Cameron family.

Their first major venture was in the herring trade. In coal towns, in the heart of winter and at the end of it, there comes a craving for something fresh—something that hasn't been salted down or smoked, something that was alive the day before, walking on the moor or swashing about in cold salty water—that becomes a craze. Some men were smitten with it, were sometimes driven, even when the pits were open, to fake illness and sneak up into the Lomond Hills north of Pitmungo to try and snare a rabbit or a bird on the moors. The chickens and doves in Pitmungo were always gone well before the winter neared its end. Maggie was determined to profit from the craze. On a Friday morning in February, when the equation said that the mines would be closed, long before the whistle blew with the sad news, Gillon and Rob Roy, Andrew and Sam were on the road heading south for the Firth of Forth and the little gray fishing towns that edge the north shore to buy a barrel or two of fresh herring. They had rented Mr. Japp's wagon and horse at eight shillings a day, about what a miner might earn in a shift then, a horse being considered the equal of a man.

They were in West Wemyss after six hours of walking, at eight o'clock in the morning, meaning that by pushing it hard, they would be able to get back to Pitmungo before night fell in order to sell their fish before darkness.

"You're sure they'll have fish to sell?" Maggie had asked. "I don't want to be renting the wagon for naught."

"Not to mention walking our arses off for naught," Sam said.

Gillon was in his element. "The herring have no season," he said, with easy confidence. "The herring are always now."

"And you're sure," Andrew said to his mother, "that when we bring the fish back, the people will buy them? There's not much money in this town."

"If the fish are kicking in the barrel," Maggie had answered, "the money will be found."

"They'll be fresh," Gillon promised. The cold of the road would see to that.

There was no problem buying the fish in Wemyss. The problem was holding the fishwives back. Fish they had, siller they needed. Gillon got a good price.

"I think we should risk a second barrel," Andrew said. They looked at him with surprise.

"Try one first and if they sell we can always come back," Gillon said.

"If one is going to sell, then two will sell."

"You take the risk with your mother?"

"Aye, I'll take the risk," Andrew said.

Four hundred pounds of herring. Gillon paid the money out and they headed home. It was harder then: the horse was tired and they were tired, and the road from the sea back to the mining areas was uphill all the way. By the time they reached Kinglassie, they were forced to beat the horse with sticks and get behind the wagon and help it along.

> *"I had a little pony*
> *His name was Dapple Gray;*
> *I lent him to a laddie*
> *To ride a mile away.*
> *He whipped him, he slashed him,*
> *He drove him through the mire;*
> *I would not lend my pony now*
> *For all the laddie's hire."*

Rob Roy sang that. It made Gillon uneasy.

"I only hope the poor dobbin don't die," Sam said. You could always count on Sam to say the unmentionable.

They reached the bottom of Colliers Walk an hour before sundown. They had planned on setting up somewhere outside the College, where the drinkers might be enticed to take home a fish after a day spent in the tavern, but before they managed to get there a crowd had forced them to stop and open the first of the barrels. The word went through the town as if there had been a disaster in the pit. Men and women came running down the walk with baskets to take their fish home in, children streaming around their legs in fear of being left out, the whole scene, Gillon thought, like a run of herring themselves, headless, heedless, simply rushing on to the goal they were being driven to. They scraped the bottom of the second barrel, stick and stowe, before seeing the lights of the College. Some of the drinkers came down and took bites of the herring raw.

That night the sound of siller sliding its way home in the kist was like a run of silver herring in the sea. It was a happy place in the house that night. No tubs to take, no filthy coal dust and water making black glaur on the floor, no sweaty pit clothes crowding the room steaming their smelly way dry, and still—

money in the pot. She gave them fresh butter on their bannocks and real cream on their porritch.

"You saved none for us," Jemmie said. He was outraged. He had an end of winter frenzy for fresh fish like any Pitmungo lad.

"Not a fin, not a bony fewkin fin," Sam said.

"I would have liked a herring for my dinner," Sarah said, which was rebellious for her.

The twins, as they so often did, had handled it best. They managed to get themselves invited for dinner at the Hodges house next door and came home wiping their lips like the cat that got into the goldfish bowl.

"For spring herring I would have to say, not bad, not bad at all," Ian said.

"A little too much butter in the sauce I would say," Emily said, and went to her place in the but to write in her diary.

"Fish is for others," Maggie said, "and siller for us."

Rob Roy got out his *Manifesto* and began to read.

"We have started down the road to petit-bourgeois hell," he said and no one paid any attention at all.

"With the blood of our brothers, we shall manure our fortune. They feed us their gold, we throw them our fish."

Ah, well, the prophet in his native land, Rob Roy thought. They'd find out. But he would have liked a fish, too.

She always had an idea; she always knew where to go. Because they were able to show up at sunrise, when the farmers hired their help, they got work setting out seed potatoes on one farm and thinning sugar beets on another. At the start, farmers were doubtful about hiring miners; they were afraid they would steal things or hit the overseer or say insulting things to the women in the fields, but they needed help at planting and harvest time, and when they saw the work the Camerons did, the word about them went the rounds of the farming district north of Pitmungo. Maggie worked in the fields with them and they always let her do the talking.

"D'ye ken aboot strawberries?" a farmer would ask.

"I'd like a penny for every ton of *them* we've picked in our day," she would say.

It was a rule with her always to lie about farm work because there was nothing on a farm to be done by field hands that couldn't be learned in two and a half minutes. They would watch the others and in a few minutes would have mastered all there was to the job except the broken back from bending. They picked berries along the valley where the river was no longer acidy from the mines, and cherries on the hillsides, bruising their insteps on the ladders. It was better in the autumn when the big harvests came in, the wheat and oats and barley, swinging the long-handled scythes, out in the sun and air on the high hillsides, drinking cold milk from the farm, so that it was painful for them to go back underground.

In exchange for their work, since unlike other farm workers they didn't require the cash, they began to take their pay in farm produce, beets and spuds and turnips, barrels of oats and barley, at the price the farmer would get from a wholesaler. It was one of Andrew's ideas. To get the food back to Pitmungo, they leased Mr. Japp's wagon and horse, and finally they bought the wagon and horse and leased it back to Mr. Japp on days when they were down the pit. Andrew was smart about things like that. From that time on they could sleep on the wagon going out to the fields, while the tough little Highland garron did the work, and sleep under the stars on the way in, instead of trudging the roads in the dark of night. For a small share of the crop, they milled the wheat and oats in Wester Mungo and then sold good oats and flour from behind their house for a penny less a pound than could be bought in the Pluck Me.

There was always the possibility that Mr. Brothcock might find out, but not much. When a woman could get freshly milled oats and new potatoes at a price cheaper than she could get stale oats and old potatoes, there would be no idle clish-ma-clash going up and down the lanes about what was going on behind the Cameron house. They even came down from Tosh-Mungo Terrace to buy. When it came to a bargain, there were no informers in Pitmungo.

It had been a bad year for Pitmungo but a good one for the Camerons, when Sam came trotting down from the High Moor one day with news that the dock was covered with coal and no ships were in sight. The mines would be closed the latest into the year they had ever shut down, and Gillon announced that night, based on his knowledge of the sea, that the delectable whitefish would be running somewhere between Fife Ness and Largo Bay and that the price by barrel should be cheap. The people, he said, would be willing to pay because there had been a period of steady work the weeks before and it would be their last chance for good fish before winter came and locked them in the valley. For Gillon it was quite a speech. He wasn't much on selling.

"Stick to herring," Maggie said. "Herring you know, herring you can trust."

But he was beyond listening to her; his mind was at sea with the whitefish.

"No, it's autumn and they'll be running from the open sea for cover," Gillon said. "Besides, the people deserve a treat and we can make money giving it to them." It sounded sensible.

"Aye, it's time we gave the workingman a break for a change, instead of milking the blood out of him," Rob Roy said.

"How can you milk blood?" Sam asked.

"Time to stop feeding him the tushloch the coal masters have been feeding him all his life," Rob said. He always talked as if he weren't one of them.

"Those who get tushloch deserve tushloch," his mother said. It was odd about that word in the family. Just so it was said in the dialect, it was allowed, as if then it wasn't really a word. " 'It's the nature of society.' " She was imitating him. "You earn from it what you put into it."

"Some people aren't able to earn."

"Some don't care to and some are too *dumb*. Am I to worry about that?" Maggie said. "That's your nature of society again. In the end, the fittest must win out; you say that yourself."

Rob was confused. He was a Darwinite. He feasted on the idea that man was descended from the ape. He was constantly talking about inviting an international committee of scientists to come and visit Pitmungo to prove conclusively the missing-link theory. And now his mother was using his argument against him.

It was decided that the three oldest men—Gillon, Rob Roy, and Andrew—would take the wagon down to the sea the next morning, and the rest would walk out to St. Boswell's farm to dig and mash neeps. They hated the turnips, all of them, ugly clumps of fibrous meat plucked out of the chilled muck for cows to muzzle; it always seemed to rain the days they were in the turnip fields. So it was almost festive for the older ones, their escape from the turnip patches, even though they had to be out on the road before midnight, before the next day had even begun. There was a moon, and although it was cold they slept on the wagon off and on, waking to see if the little garron was staying to the road, and sleeping again until they were waked for good by the sun. It was going to be one of those beautiful fall days, the shadows clean and everything sharply defined and then, as the day warmed, things becoming hazy and suffused in gold, softly smothered in it, until evening, when they would be coming back under the stretched-out blue of the early evening sky and the first stars. Pittenweem and Anstruther and St.

Buxton-by-the-Sea, off Fife Ness, where Gillon expected to find the whitefish, were a long way from Pitmungo.

It was so beautiful it made Gillon think about God. Could there be such beauty, such a rightness to things, without a God? And if there wasn't a God, and no hereafter, would this alone be enough? He finally decided to put the question to his sons.

"Is this enough? If this was all there was to life, if there was no God, could I say, 'This is enough'?"

"It's not a true question," Andrew said. "You take God away and there's no reason left to anything. There'd be anarchy; people would go around stealing and taking things because there would be no fear. But they don't, because they *know*."

"I don't believe in God and I don't go around stealing things and beating people," Rob said. "People use God as a crutch and then hope to hobble through life leaning on him. No wonder there's so many pathetic people around."

But what was so wrong with giving people a crutch? Gillon thought. Why did he, sometimes, and Rob Roy and Mr. Selkirk always, want to take that crutch away from the people? And put what in its place? It bothered him endlessly; he would never really be at peace with himself, he knew, until he could decide on that.

And did he respect God from fear or from love? He had seen a man on fire in the pit a few weeks before and had found himself praying at night again. The man had held his lamp up to the roof to test for gas, and a ball of fire had wrapped him in its flame. There were dreams of mortality and hell for many nights after that. To burn like that for eternity? To scream the way the man had screamed until infinity because he had been too proud to say yes to God?

Ahead on the road they saw an old caird, a Scottish tinker, limping his way along with a pole of pots and pans.

"Here's your chance to play God," Rob Roy said. He was needlessly sacrilegious, Gillon thought. They offered the old man a ride and he didn't seem pleased or displeased but took it as his due. They could barely understand him when he talked, and he smelled.

"Religion is the opium of the people," Rob Roy said. It was said so often at home that it was clearly meant for the ears of the caird. The day was getting warm and they took off their jackets and let the autumn sun warm them.

"Instead of going out and fighting for their rights, people sit back and wait for paradise to come. They're going to be sadly fooled."

"Implying there *is* life after death," Andrew said. "You can't fool a corpse unless there's something else afterward."

"You'll find out," Rob said, as if he had already been there. "You have exactly one life to live . . . *one* . . . count them, friends, and you had goddamn well better start getting around to living it *now*."

The fields going to the sea were fenced with stone and the little plots, all different crops and color, autumn-sered or still golden green, were like an enormous beautiful patchwork quilt spread over the ground. They passed through Crossgates where the East-West roads come through and the caird signaled he wanted to get off. He didn't thank them but walked alongside the wagon until he got next to Rob Roy.

"You," he said, "you're full of shit," and clattered off down Crossgates West Road. No one said anything for a long time.

"So much for the people's revolution," Andrew said, a few miles down the road, more as a way to soften things.

"Well, this is what we face," Rob Roy said. "The great stubborn stone face of the mass. Until they learn, until they can be taught, the whole of Scotland is one great smelling caird."

Soon after was the surprise of the sea, and God and Rob Roy's insult were forgotten with it. Gillon's spirits soared, as they always did at the sight of it.

Near nine o'clock, they came around a bend and out onto a headland that hovered above St. Buxton-by-the-Sea. Gray stones, a rough breakwater, a little sunny square out of the wind, the walls of the houses draped with nets. It made Gillon homesick.

They started down, and as they did they saw a remarkable sight. The women of the town were carrying the boats down to the sea and walking them out in the breakers until the water was waist high. While one woman held the boat, the second went in, put her husband or her friend's husband on her back—and in some cases her shoulders—and carried the man out into the water so that he wouldn't get wet. It was still a mile to the town, and when they got to the narrow winding street leading down to the square the women were back from the shore, sitting outside their gray-stone and whitewashed houses, putting fish on racks to be smoked or wind-dried and mending the extra nets that weren't in the boats. They were the strongest-looking women Gillon had ever seen. Their skirts, which they wore high in the first place, were tucked up under their belts, and none of them made any attempt at all to put them down when they saw Gillon and his sons. Some of them were smoking pipes.

The Camerons rode the wagon down the steep narrow street into the sunny square where most of the women were gathered. None of them said a word and only one or two even looked up from their work.

"My name is Cameron and I've come to buy some fish." He was met by silence.

"The whitefish are running, I know. Are there any whitefish or bass to be bought?" They wouldn't look up from their nets.

"You're fishing folk, aren't you? Well, we've come down here to buy fish." He was embarrassed in front of his sons. He took out a roll of ten-shilling notes and fanned them, like a deck of cards.

"Don't do that, Daddie," Andrew said. The money didn't move them, nothing drew a response from them. Gillon stood on the back of the wagon and waited.

"What's the matter with everyone here?" he finally said. Rob

Roy, embarrassed, had gone down from the square to the beach to be away from the sullen-looking women. A race of Amazons gone sour. Och, well, treat people like dogs, as they were undoubtedly treated, and they respond like dogs. And all those bare legs bothered him. At last a middle-aged woman in black, clearly a widow, came over to the wagon.

"When the men are in the boats, the women speak to no men," she said.

"Down for a little tanty-ranty, are they?" an old lady called to the widow. "Think they can flirdoch with our women because the men are in the boats; you tell them they have another think coming."

Now that the women were talking, however, the others felt free to come around and examine the strangers. They crowded around Gillon.

"Look at the black eyes on them," a woman said. They didn't know where the blackness came from and Gillon was glad of that. The women were what they call "gawsie" in Pitmungo, buxom and full-blown. The older women were too red from the weather but the young ones had clear, wind-washed faces. The town costumes were madder-red skirts and white linen shirts, laced all the way down the waists, and the breasts of many of the women seemed to be trying to break through the lacing. Where the lacing was loose on several of them, Gillon thought he could actually see their breasts but he was afraid to be caught looking. They wore no bonnets and their hair was worn in buns or in tails or simply loose, falling freely over their shoulders. They didn't seem Scottish. Several of the younger girls were beautiful in a shy, wild, seaside way that made Gillon think of other times. He had always found it difficult to express himself in the presence of beautiful women.

"I don't think they have any fish to sell," Andrew said.

"You can't tell," Gillon said. He didn't want to leave then.

"Well, ask them, Daddie." Andy was getting impatient. Time was becoming important.

Rob Roy came up from the beach with several large shells in his hands.

"What are these?"

"Whelks," Gillon told him. "Very good, too. In stews and soups. You can even bake them if you want. One's enough to make a meal for a family."

"Horse buckies is what they are," a woman said. Some of the women were laughing at Gillon and he didn't know why, and then he saw a woman striding down from the upper part of the town like a queen coming to reclaim her throne. When she reached the square, the other women parted to let her through, the way they would do for royalty, Gillon felt, and then she was at the foot of the wagon.

"What do you want here?" she asked. There was the tone of command in her voice. She was the tallest woman Gillon had ever met and, he thought then, the most beautiful. Everything about her was excessive and dramatic and somehow foreign, from another time or place—a Nordic princess, a Viking goddess, Gillon thought. He had never been close to anyone like her before.

"I came to buy some fish," Gillon said, and his voice sounded thinner than hers. Every time she moved her body, no matter how—just a hand up to sweep away her mass of golden hair—there was something defiant about it, or dangerous, challenging; he didn't know what. It was certainly sexual, but unconsciously so; a kind of seductive innocence—the arrogance of innocence—and she seemed to glitter as she moved, incredibly clean-looking, utterly unlike the gray and sooty people, the over-ripe plums and copper pots, of Pitmungo. He realized his mouth was open.

"We have no fish, just these lampreys for salting; no one has any fish all the way down the coast, but I see you have the buckies. We have the buckies for sale. We'll give you a price on them you'll be thankful for."

She smiled at him and her teeth were as white as Maggie's teeth, but not small teeth, foxy teeth. They glittered, too.

"That would be good," he heard himself saying.

She paused and looked at the whelks in his hand and tapped them and looked at the other women.

"Tuppenny each would be more than fair," she said.

"Daddie," Andrew said. "Daddie, no. Don't."

Several of the women made a sucking-in sound, and Gillon, blinded as he was, knew the price was high.

"Is that your son?" the woman said. Gillon nodded. "You don't look old enough to have a lad that age." Gillon smiled.

"Don't do it, Daddie. No one in Pitmungo will touch those things."

"I tell you what we will do, then. You look like men we can do other business with."

"Aye," Gillon said.

"We're going to let you have a dozen for tenpence; that's a seaman's dozen, you understand?"

"Aye," he said. He had never heard of it.

"That's *thirteen* prime fresh whelk for the price of twelve, a seaman's dozen for the price of only ten pennies."

Afterward he told himself it was the words "seaman's dozen" that dazzled him so, but later still he realized it was the idea of doing other business with this golden woman, coming leisurely down in future days to conduct business with her at St Buxton-by-the-Sea.

"Please, Daddie," Andy said. "I beg you, Dad. Don't do this."

"I think he's right, Daddie," Rob Roy said.

Gillon never remembered hearing his sons say anything.

"That sounds about right to me," Gillon said. The woman turned to the others in the square.

"Get the man his buckies, then," she ordered.

It was a sight the three of them never forgot: the women running for pots and pans, using their skirts for carrying, showing up above their knees and higher if it helped them hold one or two more whelks, totally losing their dignity, fighting one another, the young snapping shells away from the old, even the princess joining in, although she walked to the shore, loading her creel full with a sweeping grace. And then the paying time. Gillon, like the laird of the estate after harvest, paying off his anonymous field hands, dispensing his largesse, smiling on the line of women who were practically crawling to him for their pennies. They filled a barrel and the second barrel, and when that was full the woman produced several broken lobster traps to hold more whelks. Gillon didn't know how to stop her; it seemed to be out of control. Things were all reversed; he wasn't buying, they were selling. And they sold until the whelks were gone and Gillon had no more than two shillings left of all the money he had come down to St. Buxton with.

The women walked them up the steep hill out of St. Buxton, helping the pony with the load, asking them to come back again, to come soon, because this was manna for them, picking pennies off the shore. Gillon knew it was improper but he had to know the answer.

"What is your name?" he finally asked, just before they parted at the headland.

"Beth." He didn't dare ask if she was married. There was no sign that she was.

"And your last name?" She looked at him so clearly and levelly, eyes the color of the firth. Everything was correct about her: Beth of St. Buxom, so perfect.

"Axtholm."

And there it was, the old Viking blood, stuff of legends and sagas, the myth of the blood reborn into reality before him. He was dazzled; he was, as they said in Pitmungo, beglammered. He was in love, Gillon felt, for the second time in his life.

"You made the worst mistake of your life, Daddie," Andrew said, but Gillon only shook his head and smiled.

"No, no," he said, and he believed it as much as he had believed anything; "it will be a triumph, you will see. A triumph!"

7 SOMEWHERE SHORT OF CROSSGATES, THE LITTLE GAR-
ron gave out. There was no warning of it. He just suddenly
stopped. It wasn't stubbornness; the horse had exhausted itself.

"Like a good little loyal miner," Rob Roy said. "He should
have stopped miles back, but he goes on until he breaks himself
apart."

They found a place to water the horse and then they brought
him back and tied him to the back of the wagon.

"And now what do we do?" Rob said.

"We pick up the shafts and become horses," his father said.

"Och, Christ, the dignity of *man*," Rob said. "I'll push but I
won't pull."

They had oatmeal cakes and water—Rob gave part of his to
the pony—and then they picked up the traces and pulled. It
wasn't too hard at first. Some people hooted at them in Crossgates but they were too tired to be bothered then. It was coming
into evening and cooling fast but they sweated like horses.

"I don't know," Gillon said, "I don't know," but when they
saw the Pitmungo hills ahead he knew they'd make it, even
if one of them had to go on and bring down the rest of the
family to pull. They stopped for water then, a little burn coursing
its way across the foot of a moor.

"How do we know it's good to drink?" Andrew asked.

"Oh, it's good, all right," Rob said.

"How do you know?"

"Because it *has* to be," Rob said, and knelt down and began
cupping water to his mouth and pouring it over his head and
neck.

"If I die, I blame it on you," Andy said.

"Who cares? I will have died a few minutes before you." Rob lay back on the turf. "And you will go to bourgeois heaven and I will go to workingman's heaven, and once a year, on Miners' Freedom Day, I'll be having my workingman's beer and you'll be having your tea, and we shall wave at one another."

What bothered Gillon was the smell beginning to come from the cart.

"There is no beer in heaven," Andrew said.

"Beer *is* heaven."

They got up then, and the short rest had stiffened them. Gillon was sorry they had stopped. The cart seemed much heavier than before. They had packed the whelks in seaweed and kelp, which Gillon planned to cook and use as fertilizer in the kail yard, and he hoped the smell he was noticing was simply the kelp drying with the day.

"And, Andy," Rob said, "when God floats by, make sure to have your pinkie up."

It was much harder after that, because the road begins to rise more steeply up near the first of the mines. Dust from the road had pluffered up, and the barrels and the lobster traps, the seaweed and the whelks were coated with it, as the three men were.

"It's hard to believe we've been down to the sea and back today," Gillon said.

"Not if you have a nose it isn't," Rob said. Gillon felt a nervous flick run down his face. So it wasn't just him; they had all noticed.

"We look like we came out of a brown mine," Andrew said and then they saved their breath for pulling. Gillon had hoped they could avoid another stop but they couldn't. By some unspoken agreement, when they reached the top of a rise where a huge old oak stood, they all stopped without a word and fell on the ground beneath the tree and stared up through the deep red leaves of the tree at the last of the sunlight.

"I would say, thrupenny each," Andrew said.

"What did you say?"

"Three pennies a whelk, at least. That's the price we're going to have to ask."

Rob Roy sat upright.

"Have to ask? *Have?* Christ, man, we got them less than a penny each and you want to charge three? Why don't you just go and get a gun and put it in your fellow man's ribs?" Rob Roy was shouting.

"They don't *have* to buy them. No one is demanding they pay," Andrew said.

"Aye, but the point is to treat your own kind right. We can still make some money and treat them right."

"Daddie?" Andrew wanted his father to be judge. "We found the place, we risked our money—which, by the way, *we* saved. We dragged them home, we gave our time and sweat. Three pennies is not too much for a risk like that."

Gillon didn't know what to say. In a way, he agreed with both sides.

"Three hundred percent profit is not too much?" Rob was on his feet.

"A man is entitled to get what he can for the things he sells. That's the law of life," Andrew said.

"That's the law of the jungle that has kept us all down."

"A man is entitled to get what people are willing to pay. That's the true value of anything, and you know it."

Rob slapped himself on the side of his head, a trait Gillon himself had. "Are you going to lie there and let him say things like that?" he shouted at his father.

Once again, Gillon wasn't sure of himself or whether he should even intervene. "He's got a right to his opinion, Rob."

"Opinion? I'm not talking about opinion. What I'm talking about is fact! There's two kinds of people in this world, the exploited and the exploiters. That's *all!* Two kinds, two classes, two people. You have to be one or the other; you can't have it both ways." Gillon recognized his own words when he heard them.

"I don't want to exploit anyone," Andrew said. "But I'd rather not be exploited."

"Och, Christ, what a way around it," Rob said. "I'll tell you this. There'll be no justice in this world until there's one class. And there *will* be one class." Rob advanced on his brother as if he were preparing to hit him. "Someday, someday the exploited are going to come together and when they do they're going to drive the exploiters off the face of the earth, into the sea, and drown them there like the rats they are."

Now Gillon was up.

"Ah, Rob."

"I mean that, drown them like rats. Two sides, that's all. As simple as *that!*" He slapped his hands together and dust sprang into the air. He turned on his father. "And which side are you on?"

It was unfair. It was hopeless.

"I'm on the side of getting these whelks to Pitmungo," he said, and knew he had failed both his sons. Rob Roy turned away from his father and sat down with his back against the oak, out of their sight. Gillon waited for him and finally went around the base of the tree.

"Time to go, son. We need you."

Rob shook his head. "I've made my mind up. I can't be part of this."

"We can't make it without you."

"I can't help that, Daddie. That's your business now. There comes a time when a man has to make a choice."

"You're not a man, Rob."

"Aye, but I am. You become a man when you make the choice."

Gillon looked down at his son shading his eyes against the weak autumn sun, and realized that Rob's young eyes were going, like his own. He never should have let his boy go into the pit before his body had had a chance to mature in the sun and air. It was too much to steal from a boy. He knelt by Rob.

"There is sometimes a loyalty to something higher than yourself," Gillon said, not sure that he was right, and Rob just shook his head no, *no*. Gillon looked at his wiry neck and remembered his son during those first days underground, so thin, willing but afraid. Always afraid but still he went down; that was the main thing. He was not a bad miner and not a good miner; he simply was never meant to be a miner. The wagon stood there.

"Rob?" The boy tried to look up. "Until there is that other society, as long as we're forced to live in this one, your best chance is to live in the family. It's all we have holding us together against *them*."

"No, I can't go on doing this any more. I gave my word to myself. If a man breaks his promises to himself, what good is he to anyone?"

Gillon stood up. It was, he told himself, for the boy's good.

"I ask you now, I *order* you now, to stand up and take your place at the wagon."

Rob sat.

"You know what it means, Rob." Gillon felt tears in his eyes but he kept his voice strong. "Don't expect to find a place at tea tonight."

"I know."

"Don't expect to come and share the salt."

"Aye, I know, Daddie, I *know*. Good-bye, Daddie."

"Good-bye."

It had gone too far but neither of them knew a way to turn it around again.

Jemmie found them on the road and after that it was easy again, fresh legs and arms, and Jem was stronger than Rob. Sam met them at the foot of Colliers Walk and when he saw his father's face he trotted back up to the College and brought down two quarts of ale and several drams of whisky.

"This will bring you back from the dead," Sam said. "By God, the fish stink."

"That's the seaweed keeping them fresh."

"Then throw the seaweed out before going up the Walk."

"No, the seaweed's for the garden. It will make the melons grow like velvet moons."

He liked that. He was a little drunk; it happened that way to him in a minute or two after the first drink, and then it gradually went away.

"What are those ugly-looking shells?"

"Ah, you'll see."

"Where's Rob Roy?"

Gillon couldn't answer. The younger ones were pulling the wagon, and Gillon was feeling very light-headed, relieved of the burden, home at last, downing his ale in gulps while walking up the Walk.

"What if the people don't like them?"

"Then we will educate them. Educating the people is one of the noblest duties of man."

"Thank you, Mr. Henry Selkirk," Sam said. He had, his father thought, so little respect.

When they reached Lady Jane No. 2, some men were clearing pipes outside the mine pump house.

"What have you got for us now?" one shouted to them.

"New treat from the sea." That was more like it: loyal, expectant audience. That was a thing Rob chose to forget. The people, far from being jealous of the Camerons' success, were grateful to them for the things they brought the town. And that was a thing Mr. Karl Marx neglected to mention, the thrill of buying and selling. "Fruits from God's good firth," Gillon called back.

That was another good line he would have to remember, Gillon told himself. The whisky with the ale was especially good, new life in the veins. He told the boys about the whelks, how you broke the shell and cut the muscle connecting them to it, and how you prepared the beast for the pot, cutting off the heavy, elephant-like foot and pounding it with a mallet until it was pulpy.

"You can lead a miner to a whelk," Sam said, "but you can't make him eat one."

Gillon chose to ignore him and to ignore an old woman who, in passing by their cart, held her nose. He thought of Saint Beth of Buxton. Or was it Buxom of St. Beth? In any case, she was a kind of saint, actually, in a broad and earthy way. If she wasn't, and it occurred to him that he hoped she wasn't, she was the way saints should look. If God had sense, he'd make a lot more like her. It had been a good day all told, he thought, and then thought of Rob Roy and realized that only part of it had been good.

They were all there up ahead on the Walk, his customers, lined along the walls next to the College, the walls of the houses black where the men were squatting and leaning against them. A few of the men, in a good-natured way, Gillon thought, were already holding their noses, but then they had done that with the herring and the eels, if Gillon remembered clearly. He went beyond the College—men shouting at them as they went through the file, the usual miner's ribaldry, good wet senses of humor— up to where the Walk widens out into what passes in Pitmungo for the square, really just a bulge in the roadway. It was getting dark then, but people came out of their houses as always and the men came up from the tavern. When the people were quiet, Gillon took the top off the first barrel and began to strip the fronds of kelp off the top of the whelks. With the kelp to one side, Gillon hoped the smell would recede, but he was forced to admit it grew a little richer, more of the deep-inside-the-sea smell, like the bottom of a fishing boat coming back to port from a long haul. He piled the kelp neatly at the foot of the wagon and the first people, almost as if he were exhibiting snakes, came up to peek in the barrel. A man picked up a frond of the kelp and shuddered at the dead rubbery feel of it, but a second man grabbed another and began running about the edge of the crowd, whipping it back and forth, frightening even the men with it. When Gillon held up the first of the whelks, still wrapped in bright green sea lettuce, the way a jeweler holds up a stone for inspection, the man with the kelp stopped.

"What in the name of God is it, man?" someone shouted, and Gillon smiled.

"Whelk." He had to repeat it several times, and then turned to "horse buckies"; it was easier that way. Whelk was never designed for a Scotch tongue. There was a stillness at the sight of it.

"Looks horrible," someone finally said.

"So do eels, and you love *them*."

"What do you do with them?"

"Do with them, man? Eat them. Boil them, roast them, fry them, stew them. The poor man's steak of the sea."

That was good, too, Gillon thought. He was making a lot of good ones.

"They smell bad."

"Fresh as paint. Plucked from the sea at sunup this morning." The littlest of lies there.

"Crude, mon, they're rail crude."

"The thicker the shell, the sweeter the meat." Another good one. The whisky was working well.

"How do you get the bloody beasts out?" Gillon smiled the easy knowing smile of experience. It was going well. "Pot of boiling water and they march out like they're on parade. And then there's this way."

He picked a whelk from the barrel and, with a sudden shocking *swack*, he smashed the shell against the iron rim of a wheel. It shattered like broken china and the whelk was exposed, the gross fleshy foot dangling down from a shard of broken shell, whelk meat, the viscera hanging from the thick foot like a

189

drool of slime and the horny plate that covers the mouth of the shell pulsing with dying life.

Even that might have been overcome if a woman hadn't chosen that moment to scream. The first of the mollusks was being passed among the crowd and the woman was holding the shell when the operculum, like the lips of a rhinoceros, moved and either seized or tried to suck her hand.

"Get it awa'," she screamed, and dropped the whelk on the cobblestones where it split, all whelk and water, all foot and guts and stink. The people made a circle around the shellfish and stared at it, the way they would at the body of someone fatally injured. They were quiet.

"Why, it's a snail," someone finally said.

"Jesus, Cameron wouldn't *do* that," someone said.

"But he done it. Snail, right in front of your eyes. A bloody fewkin *snail*."

They looked up at Gillon on the wagon, more hurt than angry.

"A man could die eating those, you know. Rot your liver out of your body."

"What did you do it for, Cameron?" a man asked. "How could you do a thing like that to us?" He seemed bewildered.

"Jesus, man. We bought your fish, we paid your price and you come up here and try to poison us to gain a few pennies."

Gillon held both hands out, palms up, in the gesture of innocence.

"Ah, you knew; don't give us that, Cameron. You go down to get fish and you come back with shit. What do you think you're trying to pull?"

Gillon stood up then.

"When have we ever . . . have the Camerons ever, *ever* . . ."

"Man, don't *give* us that. You come up here and play with our lives, try to poison us for pennies, and you expect us to forgive?"

"I am telling you . . . Wait, now. Watch me. I'll eat one . . ."

They shouted him down. They wanted no part of Gillon or his snails.

"Don't try it again, man," someone shouted from the dark. "Just don't ever try anything like that on us again."

He tried to say something—all their reputation lost in one evening—but it was no use. The men were leaving him, they were going back down to the College, and the women and children were pushing their way out of the square to get away from the smell of the whelks and the sight of the Camerons.

8 GILLON SAT DOWN ON THE WAGON. THE WHISKY and ale had done their work well, disguising his fatigue, but they weren't working for him any more. He leaned against the side of one of the barrels feeling exhausted and ashamed. He was afraid to look at his sons, and they in turn couldn't bring themselves to watch the suffering of their father.

"We still have the seaweed for the garden," Andrew said.

"Aye, that's something, anyway," Sam said.

It was night by then, and getting cold.

"I think we had better go now, Daddie," Sam said.

"Go where?"

"Home. It's cold. I'm cold, the garron is cold, you must be cold."

He wasn't cold. He felt nothing, inside or outside. They sat on the wagon not knowing what to do, listening to the pony neighing for something, water or food, they didn't know which; they weren't very experienced with horses.

"The question is, what are we going to do with these buckies?" Andrew said.

"The question is," Sam said, "we might as well face it, how are we going to tell her?"

"No, *who's* going to tell her?" Jem said.

After that, silence again. The questions were too painful and too dangerous to talk about. Sooner or later, something would simply happen.

"Do we have any money among us?" Gillon suddenly said. Among them all they had eight shillings.

"Go down," Gillon said to Jemmie, "and get me a bottle of whisky. Not the good whisky, the cheap whisky."

"The cheap will leave you bad, Daddie; it will make you sick."

"Good."

"I wish you wouldn't do it, Daddie. It isn't going to do any good."

"Go down there and get me my whisky."

They sat on the wagon and waited out the drunkard's deathwatch. Occasionally they took a sip from the bottle but the whisky was too raw for them. It was illegal whisky, made for shebeens, desired by alcoholics and men like Gillon, determined to suffer for their sins.

It was Gillon's hope that somewhere along the passage to unconsciousness he would find the right moment and the courage to go and face his wife with the history of the day, but when he felt that the time was right, he found he couldn't talk. They carried him up the hill in the wagon, quiet and still—which was a blessing; the raw whisky made some of them wild—and when they reached the house their mother was at the door.

"Leave the man in the cart," she said, and as gently as possible they lifted him back over the guardrails and dropped him among the seaweed and whelks. Later that night it began to rain and someone must have heard him groaning, because in the morning he was covered with the patchwork quilt that Maggie had made from scraps of old mine clothes. By dawn both the quilt and the man under it were sopping, but smoke was still coming from his mouth when he breathed. The mines were opened that day but no one tried to wake him.

When they came back up from work he was still in the wagon. The rain had stopped and when her mother wasn't looking Sarah had covered him with her own blanket. Jemmie insisted on carrying his father into the house but Maggie wouldn't allow him to do it.

"I'm not going to stand here and let my father die in the wagon!" Jem shouted at her.

"He's not going to die. As long as the smoke is still coming from him, the whisky is still burning inside. When the smoke stops, you can cart him in."

But in the end it was Maggie herself who went out, late at night, to see him. He was awake and cold. He was trembling, but too weak to get up and make his way off the wagon and into the house. She knelt down by him; he knew she was there, and gradually he found the strength to open his eyes.

"I don't know which stinks worse, you or the snails you brought home."

"Water," Gillon said.

"When I'm through with you. Well, you disgraced yourself, is that what you wanted?" He mumbled aye. "All day the children and the women coming up and down the row to see the drunk man in the snail cart." Gillon groaned. "You've disgraced your family." She would wait until he said yes. "You have disgraced me. You have besmottered the name of Cameron."

He didn't know whether he was trembling from cold or weakness or simply from shame, perhaps all three. He couldn't stop himself.

"Hold up your head."

He couldn't. She lifted it for him and began to spoon hot beef broth between his cracked lips. It burned him.

"Oh, shut up," she told him, and continued spooning the broth. In a while it cooled or he grew used to the heat. There was even a little whisky in it, he realized. When the broth was finished she let his head drop back onto the seaweed and wet wood. It stank down there. He could see stars around her head.

The victor isn't victorious until the vanquished admits defeat. All right, he thought, he was prepared to admit.

"You ruined us, you know."

"Aye, I know."

"All the work we did this year, all the nights trudging home in the dark, all the money we risked and the money we made—all gone, Gillon, all waste, Gillon, all dust."

"Aye, gone. I know."

How can I pay for it? What can I do? ran through his mind. There was no way now. Any money he made would belong to the house anyway.

Her voice grew very intense. "Dempster Hogg fell down the shaft today."

"Oh, God, I'm sorry to hear that."

"One thousand feet before he hit a thing."

Why was she telling him this? He felt sick enough as it was.

"They're burying him in a slip coffin. Are you sober enough to understand what that means to us?"

He knew what the words meant; a burying box with a hinged bottom that allows the corpse to drop into the grave after the mourners have passed so the box can be used again. Paupers and the very poor leave the world via slip coffins. But he didn't understand why she was telling it to him.

"It means they don't have a bawbee to their name. Hogg drank it all away." The bitterness in her voice went to the marrow of him. "It means we could have had their house on Tosh-Mungo Terrace but now we can't because of you."

"Aye."

"Thanks to you."

All her dreams and hopes undone in one ridiculous day.

"Because by being dumb you stole siller from the kist. The siller for our house up there."

She got up and began to work her way back down the wagon. Even the little sound of her feet on the boards jarred him.

"Maggie? What can I ever do?"

"I don't know. You'll not lead another expedition, I know."

"No, I know."

"And tomorrow you can get rid of these. The stink, man, is tremendous."

"And what will I do with them?"

The question infuriated her.

"You ask me? You got them, you do away with them. Take them up to the graveyard and bury them there. You might as well. You've buried everything else. What are you, a baby? Have you become a baby?"

It stung the worst, of all the things it hurt the worst, because that's what he had become, lying there all curled up, barely able to crawl around in his own filth. He heard her feet on the cobblestones and the door open and slam shut. He thought he wanted to cry but tears wouldn't come. Cry like a baby, he thought, go all the way down to the bottom and when you're there long enough you might somehow be able to climb out again because there'd be no other way to go. The door opened and she was back.

"Someone left the horse out after the long walk."

"I didn't know."

"No, of course not. It was exhausted, you know. You broke it with your barrels of snails."

He felt a surge of sorrow for the pony.

"Standing all night in the rain."

"Och, I'm sorry. That was bad."

"Very bad," she said. "He died."

And then Gillon did cry. He cried for the poor dead pony that had never even been given a name and he cried for Dempster Hogg at the bottom of the shaft. He cried for the rotting whelks and the wreckage of his wife's dream, his tears mingling with the brine on the floor of the wagon. After that he just cried, for his life passing by him, for the disappearance of his youth, for simply being in the wagon where he lay sprawled. The crying was more than tears, although Gillon wasn't conscious of that. The children came down from the nearby houses, drawn by the sounds of his sobs, and the Camerons came out simply to be there and from fear that he might do something violent. He cried for the whisky he had drunk and the damage he had done himself and then he began to cry for his lost son. He cried on until there were no tears left in him, and he finally fell asleep.

"Put this over him," Maggie said, coming out of the house with the blanket from their bed. "He'll be all right in the morning."

Everyone who saw it agreed that probably no one had ever cried the way Gillon Cameron had cried—not in Pitmungo, no miner at least, not in all the history of the town.

9   WHEN THEY FOLLOWED THE DEAD-KIST ALONG THE path out to the burying ground on the lower part of the Sportin Moor, Maggie couldn't take her eyes off it: her house, high up there on Tosh-Mungo Terrace, waiting for her.

It was only a question of time now, whatever she had said to Gillon to punish him. She listened to Mr. MacCurry go on about what a gentle father and good provider Mr. Hogg had been —provider to the upkeep of the College, Maggie thought— and still her eyes were on the house. Not just a house on Tosh-Mungo Terrace, but an end house with windows facing the lane and side windows looking out beyond Pitmungo to Wester Mungo and farms and fields and the loch beyond them.

A question of time. One or two more missed rents to the Pitmungo Coal and Iron Company, and Mr. Brothcock would be sending someone up and Mrs. Dempster Hogg would be coming down to where she could afford the rent from the labor of one teen-aged son. And then the Camerons would go up, because despite the Horse-Buckie Fiasco, as they knew it in the family, and the cost of a new horse, the damage had not been that bad; there was still a great deal of siller in the kist. Of all the families among the Doonies, they were, in these lean times, the only ones able to rent a house up on the Terrace.

Then they would be the first true Doonies to rise up to Uppie-toon. Others had gone before them, but they had come from Uppie families and had always been booked to live on the Terrace or Moncrieff Lane, serving time when first married among the Doonies before a house on the hill opened up for them, a way station in limbo before entering Pitmungo paradise. The gates would not be opened wide to the Camerons but she was determined to breach them.

"Pay attention," Gillon whispered. "People are watching."

Mr. MacCurry, taken by her look, had in fact stopped his sermon to stare at her.

They walked alone back across the moor.

"What were you looking at?"

"The Hogg house. They'll be moving out soon, moving down."

"Och, the Hoggs will see the rent is paid."

"Not at those prices. And she isn't a Hogg by blood. You think they want to throw money to a Gillespie?"

Life was so harsh that way, Gillon thought. He didn't like what was going to happen, but he didn't have the will to stop it, not since the whelks. Maggie wanted things so much more than he did, and she knew what to do with them so much better than he did.

"And we'll be moving up," Maggie said. She heard him groan but said nothing, and Gillon was thankful for that.

The romantic she had begun to call him again, incapable of standing up to life. Face it, he told himself, Hogg was a drunk and a row brawler, never cut out to die a straw death in his own bed but made for falling down mine shafts. Gillon knew Hogg's brothers stole coal from other miners' tubs at the weighing room to cover for Dempster's half-filled tubs.

"We've worked for it, we've deprived ourselves for it," Maggie said. "We're not taking anything that doesn't belong to us."

They were playing rugby across the way and Gillon could see Sam suddenly burst through the reaching arms of the other side and break clear, going all the way. They'd never catch him now.

"The Camerons have earned their way onto that hill."

"I don't want to go there," Gillon said. It was the first time since the whelks that he had even remotely disagreed with her. "I don't want to go anywhere I'm not wanted any more."

"Well, we're going," Maggie said.

The first fortnight in September, Mrs. Dempster Hogg received her peace warning, the notice of eviction from the Pitmungo Coal and Iron Company. When no Hoggs came forward to pay her rent, there was nothing left for her, as Maggie well knew, but to prepare to move down. On the first Sunday after the notice, her son Ross came down Miners Row, his head held straight but his eyes scanning left and right, ashamed to be caught doing it, looking for a new home for his family. The disgrace of becoming a Doonie was enormous. He was a good boy, forced by his father's childishness to become a man too soon, and Maggie knew she could talk to him. She called to him from the doorway.

"I think you'd better take a good look at this house," Maggie said. The boy pretended to be astonished but he came to the door.

"It's sma'," he said.

"Aye, it's sma'. Exactly as every house in the Doonies is sma'. But there's none bigger and there's none more solid and none more clean and scrubbed and tended."

It was far cleaner than his own home; she knew that.

"The rent on this house is two pounds the year. The rent on your old one is six pounds and ten. I will take your house off your hands and you can have this house for your own. If your mother can come down, I think she had better get down before this house is gone, because there are families all up and down the row who want it."

"It's so mirky in here," the boy said sadly. "It's so bright up on the hill."

There was no sense lying to the boy.

"Aye. It's why we want to go."

He came in the house and looked into the corners and at the fireplace.

"My mother will be so sad. All for the difference of four pounds the year." He looked at Maggie. "It isn't easy to come down." He was like a very old man then, and she felt sorry for him because this was something she could understand in the inner part of herself. He held his hand out.

"What's that?" Maggie asked. The boy appeared to be flustered but he was stubborn.

"A contrack."

"Wait a minute," Maggie said, and went into the ben and came back and slipped a half crown into the boy's hand.

"And what's that?"

"Arles money, to seal the contract." He was reluctant to take it; it smelled of charity to him, but eventually he put the coin in his pocket.

"Now, you're sure you speak for your mother?" His face flamed at that.

"Aren't I the man in the house the now?"

"Yes," Maggie said, and felt sorrow again. It was a sad house that had a boy for a man.

"Done, and *done*," the boy said, and slapped his pocket where the coin was and started for the door.

"When can we move in?" Maggie asked. He had forgotten that part.

"As soon as we can get out," he said, sad again.

"Tomorrow after tea."

He thought for a moment. It was all going faster than he had dreamed. "You're the people own the wagon?" Maggie nodded. "If you give us loan of the wagon, tomorrow after tea, then."

"We'll be ready."

"Done, and *done*," the boy said, and shook hands once more and closed the door behind him. It was that simple.

10

SHE DIDN'T TELL HER FAMILY BECAUSE SHE wanted her surprise, she wanted to savor the sweetness of it before sharing it with others. When they came up from pit the next evening, the wagon was waiting for them, the new pony standing in the traces outside the door, the wagon filled with all but the few heavy pieces still in the house. They were dazed at the suddenness of the move. To get up as a Doonie and go to bed an Uppie—it took more time than that. To go from Miners Row to Tosh-Mungo Terrace should take weeks of getting used to, but they were going a half hour after getting out of the mine.

"I don't want to go. This is my home. I like it *here*," Jemmie said. "I was born *here*, I belong *here*."

Only Emily wanted to go. "I'll stand in my bedroom window and spit on the people down here," she said.

"I'm glad your brother Rob isn't around to hear that," Sam said. "He'd kick your ass for good. These are your people."

The mention of Rob Roy saddened Gillon, who saw the move to Tosh-Mungo not as a moving up but as another step in coming apart. He hadn't spoken to Rob since the day they parted and this would take them further apart. He walked through the house, which already looked so naked. What did they have to show for it all when you looked at it? A few bureaus, a sideboard, a few tin and wooden tubs in return for a hundred years in the mines. The rough-hewn table carved from a log, traditional wedding gift from the mineowners to their boys on their wedding day—how many hundreds of thousands of meals had been served on these rough boards? A few pots, a few plates, a few cups and glasses, a few pots of geraniums.

And the bed Maggie had been born in—in which most of Gillon's children had been fathered, and all of them born—that Maggie's father, dead now, had been born in.

"There's no value standing looking at things," Maggie said.

"Your father was born in that bed."

"And his before him. There's no good looking at it; we can't take it with us."

The bed, like the rest of them in the house, was built into the wall. Whoever built them had never thought of moving. People in Pitmungo rarely moved except out of the house to the graveyard at the end.

"We had some strange times in that bed," Gillon said, but Maggie didn't want to be reminded.

"That's all behind us. The past never matters. What's to come is the only thing that matters."

"All those days mean nothing? All those nights?"

"Nothing. Only the results." She motioned to the children in the but of the house, taking out the dresser and carrying out the heavy iron cooking pots. "Some good, some bad, some unknown yet."

She was probably right, he thought. He had come to accept it that she was almost always right.

"I wonder what your father would have thought if he knew where we were going."

"He would have been proud. He would have been so proud. He would have liked to come up the hill and visit."

Which made Gillon sad again. Tom Drum gone and not a trace of the man in his own house. Dead a few winters before, fifty years underground and one morning something had given in him, some spring in his soul or heart snapped. He couldn't get up and handle his pick, and so he lay in bed and died. And then she had died, his dark strange wife, the way good miners' wives go when there is no more need for them. Her work ticket punched, her time book shut at last, time to go, permission to leave granted. She knew when she was going awa', and Gillon remembered always the terrible thing she had said to him.

"It wouldn't be polite to say good-bye to you, because I don't know you that well. You never thought to name a bairn for me, did you?"

She had never called him by name, he had never used hers. That's all there was to it, to the silent dark woman and her silent dark passage through life. For what godly reason had she been put on this earth, Gillon wondered, and then Maggie came in the room and Sam and Andrew behind her, and there, for whatever end, stood the reason.

Because there was nothing else to account for any of it. A hundred years of Drums in this house on Miners Row, and not a thing to show for all that living except some wear on the stones on the floor and some layers of blackness on the walls from all the fires they had sat around.

There must be more than this, Gillon thought; there *must* be. They were taking out the dresser on which the little chipped china dogs and purleypigs stood. Someone must have cared about someone to have wasted their hard-earned siller on them. But there was no other sign of it. Maggie was right, Gillon thought; if this was all there was to living then there was nothing to do but get on with living.

"Andrew," Gillon shouted. "Come in and give me a hand with the chest of drawers."

"Aye," Andrew said, and when they leaned over to get a grip on the bottom Gillon could see there had been tears in his son's eyes. That was good, he thought; for all his business ways, Andrew had a sense of occasion about him the way Sam did.

When the house was empty and the wagon full they performed their last ritual. Andrew lifted up the stone for the last time and

Maggie took out the kist and carried it to the cart as if she had a chalice in her hands, and then Andrew slid the stone back.

"Someday they'll find it and they'll never be able to figure it out," Sam said; "they'll never be able to understand."

Maybe, Gillon thought, that's all there was to it, anyway, to all of it, an empty hole in the ground and no explanation for it.

The men were still down at the Coaledge or in their tubs and the women were inside preparing their tea when the Camerons went down the row. It was the way Maggie had wanted it: no handshakes, no waves, no false farewells for the Camerons.

At Colliers Walk, they started up and across the Sportin Moor, and although they pretended not to be looking up at it, they could see the sun slanting on their new home. It was shadowy on the moor but still daylight where the top of the hill caught the last of the sun. It was a dream they couldn't believe they were living through. At the top of the moor young Tom Hope came down to see their way up.

"Mr. Brothcock's heard about you," he told them.

"About what?" Sam said.

"Your moving up. He don't like it."

"And why don't he like it?"

"A miner should know his station and be content with it. I heard him."

"What else did you hear?" The boy was shy about talking to the best football player in Pitmungo.

"Oh, he don't like uppity coal jocks. He don't think Doonies should become Uppies."

"Go on, Tam," Sam said. The boy was embarrassed now.

"Said you think you're better than other people and give them ideas. He don't like Rob Roy and his big gob, he said."

The wagon creaked its way upward. It was strange to think

that others elsewhere were thinking about them, watching them, people in powerful positions.

"Maybe we should go back," Sarah said. "Maybe we should turn around and go back down to our old place."

Maggie swung so quickly that no one, later, could recall seeing the hand move, and she slapped her daughter hard enough in the face to knock her off balance and back against the wheel of the wagon.

"Go back?" her mother shouted at her. "There is no going back."

After that they went ahead in silence. There was no joy in it. Why was it that they always had to be out front, pushing in where no one wanted them, pushing in where they didn't belong? How was it Andrew had put it? A comin'-on people. The Camerons were a comin'-on clan, and Gillon didn't like it. It was so all alone out there.

"We ought to be going to America, not up there," he heard Jemmie saying. "America is the place for us."

"Yes, and miss the Dunfermline matches."

Sam could never take him seriously.

"America is where the money is, man. They treat a man like a man there."

"What do they treat a man like here?" Andrew said.

"Like that." Jemmie pointed at the new pony. "A beast of burden to do their bidding."

Now *he* had it, Gillon thought, he who never held a book in his hands if he could avoid it, as if free thinking were some disease you caught simply from drinking at the same well.

"In America, if you want some land, you go out and get your land. You want a tree, they say, 'Go on, cut down the tree' they have so many there."

"And how do you know all this?"

"I just know. I know it's good there. Look what happened to Andrew Carnegie."

"Yes, look. He came back, didn't he, back to bonnie Scotland," Sam said.

"Aye. To buy the place."

It was the first time Jemmie had ever beaten Sam with his wit.

Not so dumb, not so *dumb* at all, Gillon thought. I'll try and pay more attention to that one.

Regrets. He was getting sick of it. Everything was regrets.

When they reached Tosh-Mungo Terrace the men and women were in the lane and their doorways and at the windows, waiting to inspect the intruders, to welcome, in their fashion, the first invasion of Doonies into their realm.

"Heads up, now," they heard their mother say. "Don't answer them, don't hear them, keep walking." It was familiar to Gillon from so long ago.

"Look at your house at the end of the Terrace, not at them."

The Tosh-Mungo men had had their tubs and looked fresh and clean compared to the Camerons, still in their pit dirt. That had been a tactical error, to come up for the first time in their pit dirt.

"They do, too, wash," he heard a woman call across the Terrace to another. "Every Tuesday."

"Pots of flowers; fancy that, now, will you?"

"They put them on the window sills to hide the dirt inside."

Gillon was pleased to see that it wasn't getting to the children. Sam was even smiling.

"Well, and where's the great man's *hat*? How can a Doonie come to Tosh-Mungo without a *hat*?"

Over twenty years and the hat still held a fascination for the town. It was a commentary on the town's cultural level, Mr. Selkirk had said.

"And where's the one falls asleep on the floor of the College every night?"

"He's better off down there. At least they sweep him out every night."

Laughter and hoots. Gillon hadn't realized Rob Roy's drinking had become such public knowledge.

All this hate, this bitterness, this maliciousness. One of the troubles was that they were so skilled at it. The side way of putting things—"asklent," as they called it—talking to each other across the lane as if the person they were talking about wasn't there, knowing half-smiles on their faces. Gillon came up behind Maggie.

"We should walk together," he said. She was not unpleased.

"Och, they're only warming up. Did anyone throw anything yet?"

"No."

"Then consider ourselves blessed."

"It's so mean and ugly. I feel sorry for the children."

"They grew up here; they know it all. Don't worry, it isn't just us. They do it to themselves."

It was true. They were even worse than the people on the rows, a little more clever, a little more biting, a little more ice in the blue of the eyes.

Uppies!

The Hogg furniture, what little there was of it, was all out in the lane. Mrs. Hogg was trying not to cry, but the tears came. All her life had been spent on the Terrace and now she was going down.

"You'll be back oop, you'll be back on top," people said to her, but she knew, as they did, that she never would. Not with six children, four of them girls. They were going down forever.

The Camerons unloaded their cart, each piece observed by the people on the Terrace—sarcastic, overly praised.

"Isn't it *graaand*, isn't that just so *grannnd*, a chopping block that size?"

"That's no' a chopping block, you fool; that's the dining table."

"Oh. Sorry, Missus." And disbelief.

"Have you ever? So many little chipped purleypigs. Considering not one of them is more than a face miner? They must have spent ten shillings at least on the lot."

All the little verbal pliskies one learns in a lifetime in Pitmungo. They heard them all, and then the boys loaded the cart with the Hogg things and Jemmie grasped the bridle of the pony to take them down.

"I hope you're happy here," Mrs. Hogg said. She had stopped crying. "I wasn't." And, without looking around once, she followed the cart down Tosh-Mungo Terrace to Doonietown.

The house was filthy.

"And now we're going to show them how Camerons work," Maggie said. The boys took the tubs up to the pump—there was a pump on the Terrace, not a common well—and filled them with water, and the girls had already begun sweeping the four rooms. Gillon started a strong fire and the pot of water was soon boiling. It was growing dark and they lit every lamp and candle and miner's lamp they had and they kept working into the dark, scrubbing floors and scrubbing walls, scrubbing stairs—the first they had ever been on in a private house. They scrubbed the brick floor and when Jem came back up he started on the blackened walls, washing them with vitriol and cold water and, when they were dry, whitewashing them with white rock lime and a little painter's blue, so that even by the guttering lights the inside of the house could be seen by the people in the lane to glister. Long before that, some of the onlookers had begun to drift away; no matter how they tried to phrase it, there wasn't anything funny or cutting to be said about people working in a way they could only admire. Around midnight the last of their things were carried into the house and the boys went up into the garden and brought down the straw mattresses, which had been airing there, and took the pony to the moor to graze and sleep. The wind had come up, as it would every night off the High Moor, now just beyond them and the White Coo plantation— Gillon could smell rotting apples in the wind—and then they were finished.

The house was theirs; they were, like it or not, Tosh-Mungo Terrace people now.

It was almost too much to take in at once. Four rooms: two upstairs, one for the girls and one for the boys. Downstairs a ben large enough to be a bedroom for the father and mother and a sitting room for guests, if any ever came; and a but with room— now that the mattresses and boys' clothes and pit things were out of the way—to cook and wash, room for the daily tubs, and, best of all, room for the pit clothes to hang and dry by the fire without dripping onto the heads and mattresses of the boys.

Because it was the end house the wind thudded against the windows in the boys' room and the ben, both exposed to the full blast, but no one minded it. Just below the side of the house towered a dark, outstretching Scotch pine, the only one left in Pitmungo, out of place, a survivor from some other time and society. No one knew why it was that the people decided to let it stand, but it stood and was now, in a way, theirs. The heavy branches groaned and sorrowed in the wind—maybe that was what had driven Dempster Hogg out of his house— and when the wind was strong the branches whomped against the walls. No one minded. From the upper window, they could see the moon through the branches. One branch scraped against the window, and then they could see the moon through the needles and the wavery glass as if the moon were under water.

"Tea," Sarah called. Her eye was swollen. "Come down for our first tea."

The men hadn't eaten since having their piece down in the mine fourteen hours before, although it seemed even longer than that. The family was gathered around the table, crowding together because it was getting cold in the rest of the house. There was hot bread and butter, porritch with sugar or salt, depending on your bent, the pot of tea, and a little ceremonial whisky for those that wanted it. Before they ate Gillon held up his cup.

"I don't know the habits in this place but before we take our first meal in this house I think a grace would be in order."

There was a looking down. No one was prepared for it. Why should a man who didn't believe in God ask for a grace on his house? Gillon wasn't sure himself, and then he found he had nothing at all to say. There was an embarrassed silence. They were hungry, but no one wanted to eat before the grace. Jemmie got to his feet.

"I wish my brother Rob was here to share this house with us," and drank off his cup of whisky.

"That's no grace," Sam said.

"It's what I'm asking God."

Silence again and they could hear the wind moaning in their pine. Rob Roy was a subject that could no longer be handled in the family. Sam got up.

> *"Some hae meat and canna eat,*
> *And some wad eat that want it;*
> *But we hae meat, and we can eat,*
> *And sae the Lord be thankit."*

There was a cheer, they had their grace; Sam had done it and they could eat now. Sam, ready for the occasion, a quality Gillon found lacking in himself.

"Where did you get that one?" he asked his son.

"I don't know. I just learned it."

Like his mother, Gillon thought, mysteriously learning things without knowing where. And he—he couldn't even make an acceptable grace in the embrace of his own family.

It was almost one o'clock in the morning when they started upstairs to their rooms. Light in three hours, shriek o'day, time to get up and go back down in the pit. The boys spread their mattresses along the wall.

"Well, good night, Sam. That was a good grace."

"Good night, Andy."

"Good night, Jem."

No answer from Jemmie.

"Don't take it so hard. He doesn't *want* to be here. He wasn't sent away; he went on his own free will," Sam said. They were silent for a while and finally Jemmie said good night. It was over. The wind must have died down, because the tree was silent and there was only a slow shifting of shadows from the moonlight in the room. After a long time—Andrew had no idea how long—he whispered to his brother.

"Sam? Are you awake?"

"Aye."

"And me," Jem said. Only Ian, silent, sleekit Ian, ferret of the family, was asleep. Or was he? They never knew with Ian.

"I feel strange."

"Oh, we'll get used to it."

"I don't feel like I belong here."

"Nor me," Jemmie said. "They don't want us here. We don't belong."

"I feel funny here. I feel we ought to be creeping around the place," Ian said. He *was* awake.

"Doonies should stay with Doonies," Jemmie said. "They don't want us."

"We don't belong," Andy said.

They heard the light step on the stairway, quick, and then she was in the doorway, staring down at them. They couldn't see her face in the moonlight, but they could feel her anger matching the coldness in the room.

"You belong here, do you understand that? This *is* where you belong. Up here. Not down there with them."

They watched the white breath spurt from her mouth with each swift hard word.

"You listen to me now and you never forget what you hear.

"There are castles in our family; ask them about theirs.

"There are barons in our family, earls and chieftains and Lord Chancellors of Scotland; ask them about theirs.

"We're not scarred and tarred like them. Look at us and look at them."

Her voice had been angry at first, but now it sounded triumphant, moving upward in its excitement.

"Let me tell you something you had better understand. We bow to no one. NO ONE."

Breath puffs exploded from her mouth in the cold moonlight. In the next room Emily cried out in fright.

"Camerons take crap from no quarter."

She said it in a hushed voice, as if she were imparting a truth passed down for generations. They were embarrassed by her, but also in awe of her and afraid of her intensity. She hovered over them, there was no way to avoid the burning coals of her eyes.

"That would be good to put on a family banner," Sam said.

"Camerons take crap from no quarter," she said, defiantly this time, and they heard her go back down the steps. They lay on their backs and watched their breaths steal in and out of their mouths, as pale and cold and shivery as they felt inside.

"If only she didn't take it so hard," Sam finally said. Something had to be said before they could sleep. Being a Cameron, Andrew thought, was such a burden to bear.

11 WHAT WORRIED THEM, WHAT BECAME ALMOST AN obsession with the family, was who their first-footer would be. It was one of the few superstitions that seized them as a family, because they had several times before seen the truth of it borne out. In Pitmungo, and in other places in Scotland as well, to insure good

fortune and good health for the new life in the new house, it is vital that the first outsider to cross the threshold be a handsome, well-built, dark man, dark hair and dark complexion, and, if not a man, a comely fair woman. He must, furthermore, come with something in his hand, a gift or offering, or there would be hunger in the house and even death. Some people in Pitmungo who didn't have a friend handsome enough or dark enough to qualify for good fortune went so far as to hire men to walk through the door on the first day of the year or on moving and to hand them a bag of oranges or a bottle of whisky that they had bought themselves.

But no one came to their house on Tosh-Mungo Terrace. Every morning, after their bacon sandwiches—a new thing for them, a move upward—they filed out the door and got their piece buckets from Sarah and reminded the women staying behind to keep an eye out for a handsome dark man who would do, and down the Terrace they'd go, together because no one else would go down with them, a good-looking lot of men, even Maggie had to agree. Each night they asked first of all about the first-footer. When he finally came, it wasn't the way they had hoped.

Sarah was in the front room boiling clothes in the soup pot over the fire when the knock came at the door. He was a young man, fair and blond, tall and not handsome at all. He was well filled out by Pitmungo standards, well fed, sonsie, and even sleekit, in the better sense of the word, smooth-faced, clean, and almost glossy.

"Well?" he said. She didn't know what he meant. "What do you usually do when a person comes to your door?"

"I don't know," Sarah said; "people don't come to our house."

"You invite them in," he said.

"Aye, of course you do. Come in, then." She was embarrassed by her red hands and the damp strands of hair hanging down on both sides of her face, and while he made a move to cross the threshold she ran into the back room to pin her hair up.

When she came back he was still in the doorway and she realized, with horror, a fear that made it impossible for her to go near him, that this would be their first-footer if he came through the door. He wasn't right at all, large and blond, although he carried something in his hands. There would be bad luck for the family, perhaps serious luck, danger, an injury, death.

"You'll have to help me over the step," he said. "I can't quite make it over."

He held out his arms, and there was nothing for her to do then but go to the man and help him over the threshold. She felt terrible about it; not only was she inviting misfortune into the house, she was actually dragging it in. When she let go of his arms, too suddenly, he fell and she caught him, balancing his weight against her breast, off balance herself, and for an agonizing moment they embraced each other, both helpless to move apart, feeling the full length of each other, until she found her footing, stunned with embarrassment.

"Well, there's one advantage in being a cripple," he said. He walked well enough with the aid of two walking sticks, but when he sat down she saw by the two carved wooden legs above his boots that he had no real legs, and she realized it was Sandy Bone, older and changed from before his accident. At least he came with a gift, a bottle of good whisky.

"Your family already gave us one of those," Sarah said.

"That was for one leg. Would you open it?"

She uncorked the whisky and poured a good drink.

"Won't you take a drop with me?"

She didn't know if it was correct, but she went and poured whisky in her teacup. He knocked his glass against her cup.

"Bless this house," Bone said, and Sarah began to whimper, like an animal being punished. He was astounded. He reached out his arms to her again. He wanted to hold her like a child. She didn't know if she should tell him—why should he be burdened with the knowledge that he was the bringer of bad luck? —but she did.

"You're our first-footer," Sarah said, and looked away and was hurt a little when, instead of being appalled at himself or at least sorry, he began to laugh, almost as uncontrollably as she had whimpered.

"How the hell can I be your first-footer when I have no feet?" and the logic of it struck Sarah as ludicrous and yet correct, a first-footer surely was required to have feet, and she began to laugh too, at first in relief and then because he was laughing and in that crazy way of laughing that becomes something other than laughter, something that takes one up to the edge of something else. Finally they stopped.

"Oh, God, I haven't laughed like that since—oh, I don't know. Since never," Sandy Bone said and ticked her cup.

"Down the shaft. Not that I'll ever go down one again." It wasn't a bid for sympathy.

"When did you get out of hospital?"

"A long time ago. Two years. More, I suppose. But I didn't want to come home until I mastered getting about on these, you see. I wasn't going to have that."

"Oh, no."

She felt the drink and liked it. She suddenly didn't want to look into his eyes; she was afraid of them, of something in the clear blueness of them. There wasn't any hurt in them, none of the shame she saw in the eyes of other young men and boys who had been injured and abandoned as if it were somehow their fault.

"I'm crippled, you see, but not a cripple," and that made Sarah laugh. He was puzzled by her laugh and it was hard to explain to him.

"It's just that it's so like my mother, you see. We mine coal but we're not coal miners." He didn't understand but he didn't care. He looked around the house and Sarah was pleased it was in such good order.

"They told me your mother was a strushlach; can you believe that?"

She appeared to be puzzled. He thought it was the word.

"A slob, you know."

"I know."

"Being an incomer, you might not ken the word."

"Incomer? I was born here. Went to school here."

"Aye. I used to see you coming home sometimes. Long hair in pigtails."

"Och."

"You were the prettiest of them." She shook her head. "All right, the sweetest of them. That's *better*. Amy Hope was prettier, for a time. She's down in Dunfermline the now, selling herself on the street."

"No."

"That is a truth."

"Och."

"She tried to sell herself to me. Then she recognized me."

Sarah felt dizzy, unreal—from the whisky a little bit, but mostly from the conversation she was having with this man. She got up and began to move around to organize herself.

"And then I'll bet she ran in shame."

He let a shout burst from himself.

"You don't know Amy Hope," Sandy said. "She did not. She said any Pitmungo lad could have it free."

She turned scarlet and for a moment thought of running from the room. But then the idea of him, trapped in his chair—she didn't know if he could get out or not—kept her there. She turned back to her washing instead.

"Oh, God," she heard him say, "excuse me. What a stupid thing of me. It's just that I felt—feel—so much at home here. Do you understand?"

"Yes."

"That I forgot. Do you forgive me?"

She finished washing Jem's singlet and suddenly felt sorry for the man. He would never need a singlet again. To Sarah, going down in the mine was part of being a man.

"I forgive you."

But they didn't know how to begin again. He poured another splash of whisky.

"Strushlachs," he said. "What liars! I could eat my dinner off this floor. This is the cleanest house on Tosh-Mungo Terrace."

"Not when they come in from the pit."

"Och, what is clean, then?"

She saw his face, so ruddy and sonsie, turn serious. She shouldn't have brought that up.

"Do you miss it?" Sarah said.

"Oh, aye." He was glum and she let him drink. It was getting into afternoon and the slanting light was entering the house, turning the things it touched a dull gold, a dizzying time if you were in a chair and the light was on you.

"The clumphing into the College, I liked that, all sweaty and tired, but feeling hard, you know, that the work was done and you done it well; the good pints and then the tub and tea ahead and the evening spread out before you; oh, I liked that. I even liked it down there, you know, howking the coal out of the face, moving ahead into it, chunkin away, chunkin away, getting the best of it. Good men down there, I liked that, too."

The sun was resting on his sloping round shoulders—good miner's shoulders, Sarah recognized—and on his hair, blond and so red from the sun slanting through the glass that if you turned around suddenly you might think his hair was on fire.

"And what are you going to do now?"

It was a dangerous thing to ask of a man like this, but for reasons she didn't understand she found that she had to know.

"I want to be a winderman, and I will. I'm studying for it the now, taking lessons for it. The man that drops the men down the pit and brings the cages with the coal and men up, you know. Here, help me up."

She felt elated for him. She helped him from the chair and noticed the immense strength of his arms and hands, and remembered what they said when the accident had happened, that only a bull of a man could have survived the shock of it.

"And then I want to get married."

"Oh?"

"And I will."

"I know you will."

She felt happy for him again. All the sad-eyed cripples down in the Doonies, destroyed before they were men, given up before their twentieth year.

"So, then. Will you marry me?"

"Oh, yes."

It came out. Like that. She clapped her hand to her mouth in awe at what she had done. But there was no taking it back. It was the truth; she knew it and he knew it. It didn't matter about the tears on her face or the trembling hysteria she felt rushing through her; what mattered was that she knew and he knew, and they realized they had known when he sat down in the chair and they had begun to laugh.

"Then will you kiss me?" She pulled away from him, almost causing him for the second time to fall.

"Oh, no."

"Why? You'll marry me."

She went away from him where he couldn't reach her.

"I don't know. It's different." It was different, alone in the house, a man, their first visitor, the strange sun-sinking light. "I don't know you well enough for that yet."

He said nothing for such a long time that she was afraid she had hurt him or that, as suddenly as he had asked her, he had changed his mind.

"I understand that," Sandy said. He *could* get up from the chair and he crossed the room with the aid of his leaning sticks, as he called them, and to the door. She wanted him out then. She couldn't stand his being there another moment, the pressure of his being weighing on her; it was all too much for her to sort out. And she wanted him gone and out of there before her mother came back from the Pluck Me with the messages.

"Well . . . thank you," Sarah said.

"Thank you."

She hung the singlet by the fire and went to empty the water.

"For the whisky," Sarah said.

"Oh, yes, that. That was nothing."

Sarah colored slightly but he didn't notice.

"And for asking me to be your wife."

"Oh, that. Yes, that was something."

Please go now, her eyes said, but he didn't seem to read them. He wanted to leave with something more than that, as if she had delivered a loaf of bread and not her body and heart.

"When can I speak to your father?"

"Father? You speak to Mother here."

"No, no. You always ask the father."

"Oh, I didn't know. Soon."

"How soon?"

"Soon."

He suddenly reached out and seized her, wrapping his arm around both of hers, and kissed her on the lips until she felt they were burning.

"We've known each other long enough," he said, and laughed, and then managed this time to get over the threshold with his sticks, unhampered now by the bottle of whisky, and get down on the Terrace and head up it for his home, at the end where all the Bones lived. He didn't turn around, but he waved his stick just once and she knew.

"How long was he here?" her mother said.

Sarah had no idea at all. She tried to find the sun in the window to put herself back in time.

"Who?" she finally said.

"The man."

"My husband?" She felt her mother grip her arm.

"What's the matter with you?"

"Why, what is the matter with me?"

" 'My husband?' " she mimicked.

"I said that?" Her mother nodded. "I must have been dreaming." Her mother looked at her carefully.

"Aye, you must have been dreaming, because you remember this. We're not going to bring any hippety-hincher into this family. The man who comes in it for you will be a man who can work and put some siller in the kist."

"Aye, Momma."

They found out about the first-footer later, of course, the bottle on the dresser and whisky on her breath, and they were seriously upset. The blond man was an omen of trouble for a year at least to come.

"He's a nice man but how could you let him in?" Andrew demanded. Sarah merely smiled. "You could have talked to him at the door."

"He just came in."

"You don't seem very upset about it."

"No."

"Is that all you can say? 'No,' like that," Jemmie said. "Of course it's not your head the roof is going to come down on."

"How can you be a first-footer with no feet?"

And it worked with them the way it had worked with her. They were spared by a reasoning so simple and obvious that it made them laugh. They decided right then to end the first-foot nonsense. Sam trotted down to the Sportin Moor and came up with Black Willie Stuart, Pretty Wullie, short and chunky and considered by those with common taste to be the most handsome young man in Pitmungo. Sam led him over the threshold for a drink and, to the amazement of the family, Sarah kissed him.

12

Ian heard it first because in his uncanny way Ian always heard the bad news first. He caught Sam trotting up from the Sportin Moor where Pitmungo had just whipped Kinglassie.

"How'd you do?" He knew.

"Killed them," Sam said. "Ran them off the turf."

"Aye, that's good, because that might be the last time you ever do that," Ian said. Very casual, very coolly. Sam finally decided to go for the bait.

"What do you mean by that?"

"What's it worth to you if I tell you something that means a very great deal in your life?"

"Nothing. You have such a big gob you'll tell me sooner or later."

But later that night Sam took his brother by the arm and pulled him out of the house.

"All right, what is it?" He threw a threepence on the stones of the Terrace.

"I don't mind stooping, but not for that." Sam flipped a penny onto the ground. "It'll take another one of those."

"How about one of these?" Sam showed him his fist.

"Won't do any good."

Sam threw a second penny onto the cobblestones. Ian drew a deep breath.

"They're going to shut down the Sportin Moor." He seemed to delight in telling it. "They're going to close it down; they're going to take it away from us."

"They can't," Sam said. "It's ours."

"They're going to," Ian said.

Sam looked at Ian's pinched face. "You're a liar," he shouted at him. "Tell me you're a liar." He reached out and seized Ian. "You tell me you're a fuckin liar."

Ian made no move to escape or dodge, no move of any kind.

"Fuckin LIAR!" Sam screamed. Doors opened down the lane.

A man came out with a heavy gnarled walking stick. "You watch your mouth, you understand?" he said, and then put the stick down. "It's Sam Cameron," he called back into the house. "Can you imagine that? And I always thought he was a decent one."

Sam was ashamed of himself but he held on to Ian.

"All right, where did you get it?"

"Brothcock's office. Letter to Mr. Brothcock from Lady Jane's law agent."

It was believable enough. Brothcock hired pit boys to clean his office and it never occurred to him that a pit boy could read, especially after going to the Company school.

They were going to put a fence around the moor, Ian said, and sink a new mine shaft in the middle of it. The slag pile for the refuse would be where the cricket pitch now stood and the breaker house where the rugby field was. The tipple would be on the football field, Sam's personal field of glory, and the coal bing, where they stored the new-mined coal, where the quoiting was played. Sam let him go.

"You know where you're wrong?" He felt suddenly better about it. "That land is a common, and under English law the common land can't be taken away from the people, not even by the great Lady Jane Tosh-Mungo, or Countess Fyffe, or whatever the hell she calls herself now."

Ian shrugged.

"Don't shrug at me. She feus that land and we're the feuars, and just so we pay our fee—that's the tub of coal we give her every year on Miners' Freedom Day—she can't do a thing about it."

Ian shrugged. He believed in nothing. Sam smiled. He believed in law.

Sometimes at night after that, it bothered Sam, lying in bed thinking about it. He wouldn't put it past Brothcock and the Pitmungo Coal and Iron Company to try something like that. He would resolve then to go down and see Mr. Selkirk about the law, but in the morning, as he went down across the rich green moor grass on the way to the mine, the idea of taking the moor away from them grew ridiculous with the rising of the sun. Besides, he couldn't stand Selkirk and his swollen red face, filling his father full of ideas that only made him restless and unhappy, Red ideas, and he couldn't forgive him for taking Rob Roy away from them with his slick glib-gabbet. It would all come to nothing anyway, just like the Cameron name being on the Company's victimization list—families and people to watch. If they were on the list the Company had an odd way of showing it, because the Cameron men were making more money in the mines than in all their previous years. The coal bottoms were lined up along St. Andrew's wharf so steadily and in such numbers that Maggie Cameron no longer ordered her children up on the High Moor to take the Cameron count.

They must have been right about their first-footer. When the time neared for Miners' Freedom Day, the real New Year in coal towns, and the yearly parade—the paraude, in Pitmungo— no roof had fallen in, no fires or explosions had taken place, not one miner's body had been found sprawled in the pit dead from gas. And the siller kept chinking its way into the kist until the whelk loss had been made up and even Gillon's memory of it eased with the growing heaviness of the money chest.

From Maggie's point of view there were three things troubling the family and only one of them was serious. Rob Roy had given up all pretense of contributing his share to the Cameron Pot, but that had not been unexpected. The fear was that his drinking would soon cost him his job, and even though he had left them she knew the family would not allow him to go hungry. Rob Roy would become a drain on the family.

And then Sarah had several times been found behind the

houses on the Terrace holding hands with Sandy Bone. Sarah was always remorseful about it.

"Look, you," Maggie had said. "He's a nice lad from a good family but you must stay away from him. You only lead the man on. We're not going to have any cripple-dick in this family and that is the final word on that."

Sarah always said aye and that she knew and understood; she always cried in remorse and she always got caught again, like a drinker and his temperance pledge and his bottle.

And the trouble with Sam.

A month before Freedom Day, when it came his turn to put his share in the Pot, he had nothing to put in it.

"Where is it? What's happened to it?" Maggie had said.

"I can't tell you."

"You're committing a sin, you realize." It never occurred to any Cameron that he might not be.

"I know. All I can say is that the money will be made up."

There was shock in the room. Rob Roy at times had gone light with the kist but no one had ever flatly failed it.

"It's Rob Roy, isn't it?" Gillon said, finally. "He's gotten in trouble and you gave your pay packet to him."

Sam looked at the ground and only shook his head, and then Jemmie understood and crossed the room and put his arm around his brother.

"Look, man," Jem said. "Whoever it is, don't marry her. It's as much her fault as yours. She had as much fun doing it as you did; there's no sense you got to pay for it."

Sam kept trying to break in on him.

"Let her sit on the cutty stool a few weeks; that's not going to kill her. Won't be the first time that has happened; won't be the first time some pit jock has himself a merry begotten."

"Jem. Jemmie," Sam said. "There is no bairn, there is no merry begotten."

It took time for that to sink in, because the problem had been seen and solved.

"What happened to the money, then?"

"There is none."

"What kind of answer is that, man?"

"The only one there is."

He had never failed her before. He was bringing in as much siller as Gillon now. In his way Jemmie had helped; at least there was something to be thankful for—there wouldn't be a new baby in the house. She put a zero after Sam's name and said, "Let's get on with the rest," bitterly, because she needed it all now, every bawbee of it. The kist had been committed to something bigger, but only Maggie knew that then.

13

FOR YEARS, SHE HAD HAD HER EYES ON IT, RELISHing every little sign of disrepair and decay.

Douglas Ogilvie and Sons, Ltd.
Dealers in Mining Equipment
Back Street, Cowdenbeath

Poorly managed, poorly run, going down. No one ever about the place as far as Maggie could make out. The company once had dominated the mining supply business around Cowdenbeath and it still had a certain amount of business, the residue of habit and inertia. But Mr. Ogilvie, who had inherited the business, had no real interest in it or aptitude for it. Stockpiles were always disorganized, orders got lost, bills went uncollected, and major pieces of equipment were allowed to stand out in the rain and snow and would finally have to be sold at cost or less in order to get sold at all.

Then, when his son Malcom had died from drink or a fall from a horse or both, and his other son, Donald, decided he could no longer live in a place like Cowdenbeath and left Scotland for Canada, Maggie knew her moment had come. Within a month of Donald's going she wrote the first of her letters to the aging Mr. Ogilvie, signed "M. D. Cameron" and written in as manly a hand as she could manage.

No, he had written back, he had no interest in selling his business just because his sons were gone; he still had a living to make. Then she had written back that he must have misunderstood: the Cameron Group, as she called them, had no intention of trying to buy him out but merely to purchase an option to buy, at a price that was acceptable to both of them, in the highly unlikely event that anything happened to him. The option would be renewable each year at a fee that would be paid in cash to him. She was not surprised to be invited down to Cowdenbeath for a talk one Saturday with Mr. Ogilvie. He was very surprised to find that M. D. Cameron was a woman.

"A woman," he said. It struck him as enormously interesting, enormously odd, enormously amusing. "A woman in the mining equipment business." He smiled at her, shaking his head. Not a tooth in his head, she was pleased to note. "As likely as a woman running a bull farm."

She was also pleased to see that Mr. Ogilvie had gone downhill as swiftly as his business was going. One close look at him was enough to convince anyone that something serious was going to happen to him soon. He studied her closely, although he could barely make her out in the gloom—filth would be more accurate —of his office.

"Have you ever been down in a coal mine?"

"No. Does Mr. Westwater know how to write books in order to sell them?" It made him laugh.

"Clever," he said. "Damn clever reply. That calls for a drink, I'd say. Will you join me in some sherry?"

Ah, there it was, Maggie thought, the flaw, the fatal excess, drinking at noon on Saturday. Good. She had never had sherry but she agreed to have one, to encourage him onward. It was very nice. Mr. Ogilvie leaned back, his glass stirring dust on a pile of unopened orders or bills.

"Ah, ah, ah," he sighed. He seemed very content with himself and his situation. "If Mrs. Ogilvie could see me now, sharing a drink with a woman, a quite beautiful woman, in the confines of my office. She's keenly jealous."

Of what, Maggie thought, but she played the game.

"I'll say this much. If you do enter the mining equipment business you'll be the prettiest person in it."

Another excess, Maggie noted. He probably took laudanum or drank morphine cough syrups as well.

"Do you mind if I smoke?" he said. "A man likes a cigar with his glass of sherry." He poured another glass. He inhaled his cigar, she noted. The man is a mess, she thought. She was sure there was going to be some business about a little tanty-ranty in bed before any paper was signed and she found herself wondering just how far she was prepared to go.

They fenced and parried their way through the better part of the bottle, most of it drunk by Mr. Ogilvie, before getting down to business. The plan was unusual. The Cameron Group would agree to make Mr. Ogilvie a present of twenty pounds a year for as long as he lived or for as long as he wished to go on running his business, merely in return for a first option to buy the business at a price of three hundred pounds, to be paid to his estate or to him if he retired.

"You mean to sit there and tell me that if I continue to live another twenty years"—she knew he would pick that number—"you will have paid me the sum of *four* hundred pounds merely for the right to purchase my business for *three* hundred pounds?"

Maggie nodded and sipped her sherry. He would be lucky, she thought, to see the winter through. She poured him another glass.

"I can see now why women don't enter business," Mr. Ogilvie said. "There are those who would say you are out of your pretty little head. I have always said that a woman's place is in the bed —ah, *home*," he said. He would have blushed, Maggie realized, if he had had sufficient blood in his system to do so. As it was, he shuffled some papers about.

"I should like a little more time to think about it," Mr. Ogilvie said. He didn't need time, she knew, he wanted excuses to see her. It was the price she was going to have to pay, beyond the siller from the kist. It was certainly going to be easier than taking the money out.

He led her out through the front way. A window in which pumps for sale were piled was so thick with dust it was impossible to see inside. Maggie felt her lips grow wet with apprehension, with lust, at the thought of bringing the dying shop back to life. Even while he was kissing her hand and applying just a little too much meaningful pressure on it, she thought of the store on Front Street that could serve as the window display, for the equipment in the storage yard, and the second office that they were in, where the bookwork could be done. Outside in the raw light of the street the man looked terrible, there was something that reminded her of oysters about him, the great drooping wet eyes, the pouches under them, the deep-grained wrinkles on his face like the back of a mollusk shell. It was a risk, she knew, but, when she looked at Mr. Ogilvie in that light, not much of a one.

A few weeks after that he went too far, much too far, as she knew he must, his hands where they had no right to be, and she had him. Mr. Ogilvie signed the agreement and she gave him a payment of five pounds for the quarter of the year. His name was down with hers on the option and the paper was in the bosom of her dress. The kist was committed; the Camerons were committed, there was no going back now. However long it would take, the step up had been made. They were on their way out.

It was the reason she behaved the way she did the next time Sam failed to put his money in the kist. They were committed, and while no deviation from the ritual of the kist had ever been tolerated, now there was no room even to consider tolerance. The money *had* to come. She nearly drove her son out of his home until she realized that her loss in the end would be the greater and she regained control of herself.

Only Sandy Bone, who had gotten his job as winderman, had

any idea what Sam was doing. In the morning he would take him down with the other men in the cage and bring him up the shaft in the next cage. In the evening, just before the shift was due to come up, he would send Sam down to the shaft bottom again and bring him up a quarter of an hour later with the men who had worked the shift.

As far as the Company knew or cared—it was only his money he was losing—Sam was listed as being injured. The fact was that Sam had gone into training for the Games that were coming up. He began running the roads down below the work area, out of sight of the town. At first it wasn't much good; he was strong but his muscles were knotted in the way of miners, all of them tight and lumpy from the squatting and the endless bending and lifting of mine work. His aim was to uncramp his body and he forced himself to run in as easy and fluid a way as possible. For a week he felt it would never come back, but then one afternoon it began to come, the long easy strides he remembered as a boy before the mine had gotten him. It was pain all the way that week, because while the work was hard in the mine it didn't call for the sustained endurance that running called for. He ran until he began to achieve the runner's second wind, and then through that until he ran in a kind of nervelessness, running beyond any capacity he knew he possessed.

In the second week he worked on his jumping—the standing jump, the running broad jump, the steeplechase, the running high jump—and on the weight throws. That would be the dangerous one, because no matter how hard he practiced, there were men stronger than himself in Pitmungo, like old Andy Begg. He would have to make up with speed, with spin, with timing, with the swiftness of the lift, to match other men's superior natural strength. At the end of the second week he was throwing the thirty-six-pound stone twice the distance he had begun the week at, and, finally, five or six feet beyond any stone thrown in Pitmungo in his time.

At night, lying in bed, he went over the events, thinking each one of them through, knowing the opposition, planning what he would have to do, because it would in the end come down to a matter of pacing himself, of using his energy exactly right. There would be no sense in winning a race by fifteen yards when one yard would do, or taking three tries at the hop, step, and jump when his first try would win it.

Because he was going to do what no one had ever done before, not since the Games began in 1705, and no one had probably even dreamed of doing. He was going to win it all.

Everything!

He rolled over, kicking in bed, his covers off his bed again. "What's the matter with you, man?" Jemmie said to him. "What are you up to? You look as drawn as a race horse." It was what he wanted to hear. He decided to be as blunt as he could about it.

"Look," Sam said, "our mother has some kind of dream and no one asks her about it. Well, I have this dream and I don't want to be asked about it."

"You haven't spent a hell of a lot of time down in the pit."

"How do you know?"

"Och, come on, Sam. Do you think no one's seen you rubbing coal dust on your gob so you look like you did a day of work?"

Sam was embarrassed. That was the trouble in a place like this; there was always someone looking.

"All I can tell you now is that every cent will go back in the kist."

"I don't give a damn."

"I do."

Win it all. Every bottle of whisky, every ten-shilling note, every little silver cup donated by Lady Jane. Every ribbon, every honor, every prize awarded in Pitmungo. No matter where they went, when they left Pitmungo, the name of Cameron, of Sam Cameron, was never going to be forgotten.

14

SAM SAT UP SUDDENLY AND STARED AROUND HIM.
"What is it? We're late. We missed it."

Jemmie reached out an arm and pushed his brother back down onto his straw mattress.

"Easy, man, they're only warming up."

They lay in the dark room listening, and the sounds came again.

"Pitmungo Miners' Brass Band."

"The worst brass band in West Fife."

"In all Scotland."

"I don't see how you can afford to be so sarcastic," Andy said. "You could have joined, they asked you. You could have made it better."

"Did you see the hats they wear? Pillboxes or some such. The kind the monkeys wear."

"Blether is cheap, performance is high," Andy said.

There was a long sustained roll on the snare drum followed by a crash of cymbals at the end.

"Very timely," Sam said.

They heard Sarah's flute floating out above the drone of the drums.

"Sarah's good," one of them said.

"Sarah's the best."

They lay back relishing the comfort of bonus time on the straw.

"Do you think there is anything between her and Sandy Bone?" Andrew asked.

"Oh, aye, but what does it matter? *She* don't want her to marry him."

"Sarah's got a mind of her own," Andrew said.

"Yes, and it belongs to her mother."

Silence again. Her. It was always *her*. They could hear her bustling about in the but—swift steps, quick movements, a clicking of things—the plates were never put down, they were clicked down and zicked away, and her movements down below made her presence felt upstairs. A flatulent-sounding blast of air trying to force its way through the bell of someone's trombone bellowed in their room.

"Someone just put a knife to the throat of a grumphie," Jemmie said.

"Pig," Andy said.

"Grumphie is a better word."

"Don't let *her* hear you say it," Andrew said.

"Grumphie," said Sam.

"Grumphie," Jemmie said.

"Grumphie," Ian said. They looked at Andy.

"Grumphie," Andy said.

"Grumphie, grumphie, grumphie," they chanted all together, low but audible. "Grumphie, grumphie, grumphie."

"Oh, it's so exciting," Sam said. "It's so daring."

"Its so wicked," Andy said, and they laughed and took it up again.

Gillon lay in bed and listened. The sound came down the stairway into the ben as if it were a pipe. He should warn them about that. He was happy for the boys and envious of them, lying back in their beds, sharing all the things of their lives with each other. He had never had that. He didn't have it now. They didn't really listen to him any more; it was always her. His fault. He had abdicated, given up the fight. Andrew handling the money now. And what was one to say? He always got better prices. Andrew going down to Kirkcaldy to buy rolls of linoleum to sell in the town, talking to important men down at the factory gate, arguing with them, driving a hard bargain with them, because Gillon didn't know how to handle men like that. And he had heard them talking behind his back, in the pit and on the walk back home. "Aye, he's a John Thomson's man the now," which is Pitmungo for a man who has surrendered his masculine prerogatives to his wife's influence.

"Sad, the man that bashed Andy Begg." They always remembered that, to his detriment now. "Who would ever have believed that?"

Gillon got out of bed and by habit began getting into his pit clothes, and then took them off and got out his Sunday blacks. The black had faded and the back of the suit, he could see in this bright light, shined from rubbing against wood in the chapel for thousands upon thousands of hours. It wouldn't do much longer. He could see the light through the seat of his trousers.

It wasn't, Gillon thought, that he had surrendered so much as that she had taken; there was a difference. She wanted so much more than he did, she wanted so much harder, that in the balance with her he was unbalanced. If you didn't want a thing hard enough, it was so much easier to let the other person have it. That wasn't giving in; it was merely being sensible and making life livable.

He went upstairs to the boys' room. It was his second time there, which showed how little contact he had left with them. They were surprised to see him.

"Time to get up now," Gillon said. "Parade's due to begin in half an hour."

"Not going to parade, Dad," Sam said. "Going to rest up for the Games."

"Miners' Freedom Day," Gillon said. He looked around the room at the others. "No parade?"

"Rather rest, Dad. Just a paraude," Jem said. "With a very bad brass band."

"Aye, but you don't seem to understand. This is Miners' Freedom Day."

They didn't understand.

"Look," their father said. "I'm not from here but I know what took place here and it's something we should never forget, that much I know."

"It's over and done with, Dad," Andy said. Gillon turned and went back to the stairs. If they didn't know, he had failed them.

"Breakfast," their mother called. Gillon looked at her, almost not seeing her, and went out onto the Terrace and walked as fast as he could down toward the end of town. Selkirk, of course, was in bed but Gillon got him out.

"I want you to come up and tell my boys why they'd better be marching on Miners' Freedom Day. There's a half a bottle of Glenlivet in it for you."

"I could get Mr. Brothcock to march for that," the librarian said, and began getting dressed. When they got back up to Tosh-Mungo Terrace he was very red in the face and winded but awake.

"This is Mr. Selkirk you've heard me talk about," Gillon said.

"I couldn't have guessed," Maggie said.

"Where is the Glenlivet? Mr. Selkirk would welcome a drink."

"I couldn't have guessed that, either. Isn't it a little early, considering the paraude hasn't even stepped off?"

"Get the bottle doon," Mr. Selkirk said; "the man has kindly offered me a drink." She got it down.

They never had a chance, really, lying as they were on their beds against the wall, facing the door, no way out of the room.

"So you don't *choose* to walk out on Miners' Freedom Day, is that it? You don't elect to get up off your arses and march a little for the men who went before you, is that what I hear?"

When Mr. Selkirk chose to use his voice, there was a timbre to it that could make one's backbone shiver.

"You want to rest your poor worn bodies to do well at the Games? Hap, step, and loup, is it, and a fluttering blue ribbon at the end?

"Well, bravo for you, sporting lads, hurrah for the Cameron boys. No, don't get up, I wouldn't have that. Rest your worn-out limbs and forget those that made it this way for you, who died down pit not of noxious gases and explosions but of starvation in the middle of their shift.

"'Excuse me, lads, I think I'll sit doon the now,' and never get up again, dead from hunger, the pick still in their hands.

"I'm not talking ancient history; I'm talking about men rotting right now down on the Wet Row, stinking in the filth of their rat-infested rooms, too weak to do anything but shit on the floor in payment of sixty years in the bowels of the earth.

"But I'm not going to talk about them. I'm going to talk about your own blood, sporty boys, your own grandfather, dragged down the pit at six months in his mother's coal creel and left lying in the wet and glaur fourteen hours a day while his mother carried hundred weights of coal up the ladders and at the end of the day had climbed as high as the highest mountain in all Scotland with bloody hundredweights breaking her back."

He took a strong swig from his drink.

"Breakfast was water, and mid-meal in the mine was a drink of water and shave of bread the mine rats fought to get; and then dinner, dinner—ah, that was the treat that made it all worthwhile. Tatties mixed, if they were very lucky, with a spoonful of oatmeal.

"How do I know, do you want to know? It's in the bukes, it's in the records, all in the famous Royal Commission to Study the Employment of Children in Mines. All your family's names. The Drums. Mengies, Hopes, and Picks. All the good old slave names.

"And do you know, it was a very strange thing they found when the Commission came through Pitmungo. The little children didn't seem to have any bones in their bodies, and the few they had were bent. For no reason they could find, the little children were ill-informed and dejected.

"That was the word for them. Dejected. 'The children are dejected and need more teaching in the Bible and the value of good hard work.'

"And they got *that,* oh, yes, they did; the Company was good about the Commission's findings. They started the Bible School and the little children got more work. Are you ready for the Games, gentlemen?"

His glass was empty but he had his own bottle to give it a little boost.

"And chains—maybe you would like to know about chains; how your great-grandmother and great-granddaddie were chained to each other so when they pulled the sleds of coal to the ladders at the shaft, they would be forced to pull together. It was for their own good, you see.

"And when they didn't pull fast enough, what else do you think they did with the chains and were allowed by law to do? I'll bet you've guessed it. Ten across the face, sports, until their own brothers didn't recognize them. And slaves, that should be interesting, because no one in this village with the exception of your father is not the descendant of slaves. Odd how quick people are willing to forget. For you carry the blood of slaves, you should never forget that, as much as any slave from Africa, sold into the pit, sold with the pit, and their children condemned by law to enter the pit and die in the pit.

"But especially you'll want to know how your great-grandmother died. When your great-granddaddie was split apart by a stone, your great-grannie was left five children to keep from starvation. The masters were good about that. They let her go down the pit and dig the coals and drag them to the shaft and haul them several hundred feet up, and because she had so much to do and was slow, she had to be paid less, of course. Sir Gilbert Tosh-Mungo gave her eight pennies for sixteen hours of work, sporting boys, sixteen hours a day. So I say, 'Here's a cheer to Sir Gilbert on Miners' Freedom Day.' But to get back.

"One spud a day, lads, and all the foul water they could find, and at night cockcrow 'n' kail. You don't know it? We'll see it here again, if I know my coal masters. It's chicken soup with no chicken and no kail. Boiled moor grass with a stone for flavoring, sports.

"Aye, so you stay in your beds, boys, and rest your bodies for the fun and games ahead. And as you do, I want you to think of the way your great-grannie went. Because she was a woman, they gave her the wet places to work, and when her ankles were swollen to the size of her thighs, they gave her the gassy places to work. She worked where no light would burn, where candles were smothered and died, and where the foulest air the mineral world could breathe was blown out upon her.

"And when they found her she was face down in the glaur, trying to drink fresh air from the floor, but that wasn't the interesting thing. The whole sides of the stall were rimmed with rotting fish heads; she was mining her room by their little phosphorescent glow."

He let them think about that before going on. They had had enough; the lesson had been learned, but Mr. Selkirk didn't know or care.

"They didn't march either, sports, they never marched at all. When the coal masters came by, they put off their caps and they smiled until their face muscles froze.

"I'll tell you something time has taught me. It's bad to live in a place where you can't smile, but it's hell to live in one where you must."

They began to get up off of their mattresses, trying to get dressed and not have to look Mr. Selkirk in the face at the same time.

Mr. Selkirk took his glass and felt his way downstairs. His effort had exhausted him. In the but he saw the bottle on the dresser and he filled his glass and put the bottle in the pocket of his coat.

"I heard what you said," Maggie said, coming into the room. He was embarrassed at having been seen sliding the bottle into his pocket even though it had been promised him. "The lesson is that the tough survive," she said. "That baby in the gassy stall was my father."

"The lesson," the librarian said, and his voice was as hard as it had been upstairs, " is that if you had all got together and stuck together you needn't have been so tough to survive."

"It was hard but they made it," Maggie said. Selkirk turned on her.

"Aye, they made it. How many of your father's brothers and sisters died before they grew up?" Maggie was slow in answering.

"Four of the five," Mr. Selkirk said triumphantly. "I looked it up in Pitmungo Register. It's a wee bit of a price to pay to learn how to survive, I would say. Thank you for the drink, *Mrs. Drum*," and he slammed his glass down on the dresser.

The boys filed down the stairs in their Sunday black. They were quiet and subdued.

"Hot scones for breakfast," their mother said, but none of them felt like eating. They thought of their great-grandmother down in the pit, howking coal in the gas with the rotting shining fish heads all around her stall. Mr. Selkirk had taken all the fun out of the day.

15

IT WAS THE SAME AS ALWAYS, SAM SAW, BUT still he was glad he had come. A man has to show up and be counted. The Pitmungo Miners' Brass Band lined up on the top of the Sportin Moor, and then Wattie Chisholm, eighty years old and still doing his shift in the pit, lowered his beribboned miner's pick and the paraude was on. Five or six hundred miners with their sons and a few women and girls here and there, ones who still remembered their mothers or their childhood, stepping off to the thump of the drum. The brass would save their lungs until they got into the rows of Doonietoon.

It was a day of subtle defiance, a day when the miners made their unity felt, however amiably and however little came out of it. Still the threat was always there that someday they could mass together. Several black banners, commemorating the more memorable bad days in the Pitmungo mines, headed the march.

BLACK TUESDAY—1884
We Shall Never Forget You
36 Good Men Gone

Other banners, other slogans, the little ritual defiance fluttering overhead. Sam liked the "Stand Thegither" banner best, but decided not to offer to help carry it, to save his legs. The message was fairly plain.

Stand Thegither
Live Thegither
Die Thegither
Triumph Thegither

Some of the old miners were wearing the tall tile hats that spelled out "DIGNITY" and that had disappeared from most of Scotland years before. Behind the band came the coal tub with its two tons of hand-picked and washed coal that would be presented to Lady Jane Tosh-Mungo at Brumbie Hall, as the ancient accepted fee for the use of the Lady Jane Tosh-Mungo Miners' Recreation Park, and for the use of the wells and pumps.

The ritual had been perfected over the years. There would be the presentation of the coals and the gracious reception of the coals, and the canvas on the lawn at Brumbie Hall would be pulled back and there would be the hundred-gallon barrels of the best Scotch ale, festooned in ribbons, and piles of boxes of sweeties for the pithead girls and then the singing of the song by the miners on the lawn:

Hurray, hurray, for the Pitmungo Laird,
Lang in Pitmungo may she be spared
And the miners' bounty evenly shared
On Miners' Freedom Daaaaaaaaay,
                   Hurray!

The bungs would be pulled, the taps would be set, the first ale flow, and the day officially begin. It made Mr. Selkirk sick to his stomach, he said; it destroyed what little impact the defiance might have. Rob Roy wouldn't attend. But in the end the Laird knew best: the men wanted their ale.

After the ceremonial toast, the barrels were loaded in a second coal tub and pulled back up to the moor to get the men off the lawn and back where they belonged. Some of the men began to strip themselves of coats and ties before they were even off the lawn.

"You saw her accept the coals," Sam said to Ian. "Saw it with your own eyes. That, my friend, is a contract."

Ian didn't answer. If you didn't trust anyone in the first place, why trust the evidence of your eyes?

"No, one thing is sure. You can't take the coal and take the moor as well. That, my boy, is a fact of law. Oh, God," Sam said. "Look!"

Even from down on Colliers Walk, a quarter of a mile away, the embarrassment was evident. By long tradition, as they did in church, the Uppies tended to sit together in one part of the moor, with the Doonies in another. They would compete together later in the day, in the Games, but not sit and eat and talk together. Maggie Cameron had chosen a spot where the Uppies sat, and for a space of at least fifty feet around her no one had put down his blankets and lunch baskets. It was a public humiliation. She was alone on an island of green and the green was like an open green wound on the blanketed side of the moor.

"Spread your things out," Maggie ordered them.

"Don't you worry, they'll be all about us before this day's done," Sam said. "The world goes for winners."

She didn't know what he was talking about.

It was a lunch the like of which they had never had before. A cold roast chicken and a little plump grouse no one had seen her cook. Bottles of lemonade and limeade, the sun striking the bubbles in the bottles like sparks when they hoisted

them to their lips. They could see the other families eying them
with envy. If they were lucky and good, Pitmungo people got a
bottle of carbonated soda or a phosphate on New Year's Day.
Boxes of Kirkcaldy gingerbread—the best in the world, it was
said—and hot breads, steaming scones, and bannock smeared with
heather honey; lemon meringue pie, the meringue fluffy and
white, and then shortbread downed with bottles of orangeade.

"Who are you trying to impress, Mum?" Sam asked.

"Everybody. Is there anything wrong with that?"

"No," he said, not believing it, and then wondered who the hell
he was to be thinking that way after what he had planned for
the day.

Sarah came up, shy and out of place in her band uniform. She
was the only girl in the band.

"You were very good," her father said, "especially on 'The Blue
Bells of Scotland.' You stood out above them all, all alone, pure
and clear and true."

There it was again, Sam thought.

"The Walter Bones said why didn't we come and sit with
them," Sarah said.

"They did? Why don't they come and sit with us?" her mother
said. That was the end of that.

There was a cheer across the moor. The ale had been reopened
and Jemmie—you could always count on Jem for that—went
running with the two family pitchers to get in line. When he got
back the ale was warm but there was still a froth and the taste
was good. All around them the people drank and ate their potato
salad and cakes and pie and then they fell back on the cool moor
grass and studied the clouds and listened to the hum of life across
the moor; and one by one—except for Sam, who had had no ale
and just one piece of chicken and some scones and lemonade—
they fell asleep, even his mother, asleep beneath the sun.

At four o'clock, all across the moor the people woke up. There
was no special sound or signal; the people simply woke, as if they
had a Pitmungo clock in their blood. They got up and put their

things away in the baskets and creels to make way for the races, and Mr. Brothcock came trotting up from Brumbie on his horse, looking heavy and regal in his saddle, and behind him in a trap came the prizes from Brumbie Hall for the winners of the races. Although the prizes were donated by Lord and Lady Fyffe, one would never have known it with Brothcock in command. He dispensed the Earl's treasure with a personal hand.

It went the way it would have been expected to go if anyone had known about Sam. His weeks of training had left him lean and supple where the others were pit-cramped and chunk-muscled. Stones against water. They, full of food and good ale, getting their minds readied for the challenges; Sam's mind all set and his gut empty.

The hundred-yard dash was not unexpected. For several years now it had been Sam and Bobbie Begg cheek for chow, but the surprise was how easily Sam had won it, easing away from all of them at the end and barely breathing hard.

"Gude job running, boy. What's your name?" Sam told him.

"Cameron," Brothcock said to his wife. "Always into some goddamn thing; always doin' somethin', usually bad."

He held up the ten-shilling note. That drew applause from the crowd.

"Whole day's sweat in pit for that, lad. You're a lucky boy."

"Very conscious of that, sir."

"See hoo they speak?" he said to his wife. He imitated Sam while pinning the blue ribbon to his shirt.

"A hero of Pitmungo the now."

"Thank you, Mr. Brothcock, sir." Really pour it on him, Sam thought, fleech it up to him good.

There was the two-hundred, not often won by the same miner, because the winner of the first sprint was usually too tired to repeat, but Sam took it and then the call went out for the first of the big ones, the traditional Aince Aroon the Muir. A bottle of good Highland single-malt whisky and twenty shillings and, in some years, a ham for the winner. Many of the men stayed out of the sprints waiting for the Aince. It was not an easy run, the Once Around the Moor: clumps of grass, hidden peat holes filled with water, plashy plots of moor where one was suddenly ankle deep in mud.

"You're no' goin' to try this one, too, man?" someone called. "You're goin' to destroy yourself, man; you're goin' to run yourself into the moor."

Sam smiled.

There were two threats, little Alex McMillan, running barefoot because his father wouldn't let him waste shoe leather on a race, and Jemmie.

"Where the hell is Jem?" Sam called to the family. No one knew; no one had seen him.

"Can you hold the race until I find my brother, sir?" Sam asked. In case he lost, they might at least keep the title in the family. Jem would be fresh.

"You run your race and I'll run the races," Mr. Brothcock said, and ordered the runners to their marks.

It wasn't any contest. Little Alex had been drinking and so Sam glided, working slowly into his second wind until he passed him at the far end of the moor, sprawled in the shade of a Gypsy caravan, vomiting his Miners' Freedom Day picnic.

Mr. Brothcock handed him his whisky and his two ten-shilling notes and pinned another blue ribbon on his chest.

"Getting to be a bit of a habit," Brothcock said. "Getting to be a bit of a bore." The superintendent liked to spread his generosity to a larger audience. "I think it might be a good idea for you to sit out an event or two; you look a wee drawn to me."

"Oh, no, sir," Sam said, "I *love* the jumps."

Before the jumps Sam trotted down to the family blanket.

"Where's my brother Jem? It's no fun without my brother." He took off the blue ribbons and dropped them on the blanket. "Keep an eye on these," he said to his mother.

"You're making yourself kenspeckle," Maggie said.

"And *these*," Sam added, putting the four ten-shilling notes next to the ribbons and the bottle of Glenlivet. The children from the Uppie families had come from their family picnics and were crowding around the Cameron blanket, wanting to touch the blue ribbons and Sam.

"You get those, too, for running across the grass?" Maggie said.

"Just for running across the grass," Sam said.

"Where is Sarah is what we want to know," Gillon said. "She went away when we were napping and hasn't come back."

Sam had no idea, and then the call went out for the jumpers. The plan now was to save energy. Each contestant was allowed three tries, the best of three to count. Sam was going to risk it, take one, give it all he had—break their poor bloody hearts—and stay warm and loose for the next event. In the hap, stap an loup he broke the Pitmungo record.

The crowd was peculiar. The crowd is supposed to love a winner and up to a point it did, but then the feeling began to change, wanting something else, waiting for S. Cameron to become human and do something wrong; waiting for Sam to fall flat on his square brown face. The jumping events had never been the big ones, but now the crowd for each one grew, becoming unnaturally silent, grumpy in their silence but good-natured about it at the same time, because they considered themselves Scottish sportsmen, the fairest in the world. Still, all that blue on one man's chest! It was a little hard to take. Andrew grew very excited by it.

"Pour it on them, Sam! Lay it on them, man. No mercy, Sam. Up the Camerons!"

Sam had to jog over and put a hand on his mouth.

The high jump, the standing broad jump, the running broad jump. Mr. Brothcock ceased announcing the winner. He was direct enough about it, say that for Mr. Brothcock.

"I don't know if you've noticed," he said, "but you're making a royal pain in the ass of yourself."

"No, I hadn't noticed, sir."

"This is a civic celebration, not a one-man extravaganza."

"I was taught to do my best, sir. It's what we're taught in the pit, sir. To give your very best."

"He's right, you know," Mrs. Brothcock said. "Play the game to win or don't play the game at all."

"It's what my mother always says," Sam said, and they smiled at one another.

The call went out for the stane toss, the last event before the Pitmungo Marathon. The one for the big boys. Some of the miners had entered no other event, being too meaty and heavy-muscled for running and jumping. Some of them had been drinking to build up a head of steam for the toss. The area around the tossing pit smelled like the College on pay night. Andy Begg prodded Sam in the chest with his stubby finger.

"You dinged my boys in the races. And your daddie dinged me at the Gaffer's Gate." Sam nodded. "And now I put you on notice, boy. I will be goddamned if his bairn will ding me, too."

That drew a roar from the crowd. They wanted their kill; they needed their blood. For a bull of a man, Begg was graceful enough. He got in his spot, he anchored his feet to the moor, he tightened his thick black miner's belt to bind all his force together, he swung the thirty-six-pound stone back and forth on its steel chain, back and forth until he felt the rhythm of his body come together with the rise and fall of the stone, his face now as red as the moon at harvest time, and let fly. It was a good toss, a nice flight and a good rich plop onto the moor—into the plood, as they say.

A foot per pound usually was a safe margin for a Pitmungo victory. Fired-up, Andy Begg threw it further.

"A. Begg, thirty-eight feet three inches," Brothcock announced. That got the roar. The rest of the men took their turn and fell so far short they dropped out. The contest now was between Sam and Andy Begg.

Sam passed.

The boldness of it, the unprecedented arrogance of the man— the *boy*—silenced the crowd for the moment.

"Cheekie bastart," Begg said, not unkindly. He turned to the crowd. "Have you ever seen a crust like it?" The crowd let him know they hadn't. Sam could see his father coming across the moor to see what the commotion was about. Where in the name of God was Jem?

Begg's second toss was even better. Sam passed.

The moment Begg began his final toss, his rhythm a little finer now, up and back, up and back, in the sound traditional Pitmungo way, the people on the far end of the pit began to scatter. The toss was 39 feet 5 inches, a new Pitmungo record, which Mr. Brothcock, in a voice that could have been heard in Wester Mungo, let the crowd know about.

Sam picked up the stone and was surprised, as he always was when he first picked it up, to discover the complete deadness of the weight at the end of the chain. He had made his first mistake —he sensed it at once—passing his warm-up turns.

"Prideful chap," someone said.

"Aye, and pride goeth before the fall." It was the least they said about him.

He heard it all. He thought he had trained himself to put the crowd out of his mind, but he heard them and it bothered him. He swung the stone back and forth, feeling the weight becoming familiar to him, not so challenging now, and then he began to spin with it, not rock up and down, but twirl around and around, feeling the weight of the stone itself supply its own force, and when he felt all of it was right, neck and shoulders, thighs and butt fusing into one totally concerted effort, he let the stone go. No one had ever thrown the stone that way before.

Although it was a record that deserved being put down in the Freedom Day record books, no one bothered to place a little flag out on the moor to mark where it fell; it was that far beyond all the rest.

There wasn't a cheer and there wasn't a groan, only a numb silence. It was all out of proportion by then; it was no longer a sporting experience but something that had moved on into some other realm of experience: one man against a town and no one able to stop him. His father was beside him.

"What's left?" Gillon said.

"The Pitmungo Marathon."

"Can you win it?"

"Aye, I'm pretty certain of it."

"I'm going to ask you something. Don't you think you ought to give some other man a chance now?"

Sam looked down at his feet. The day had taken a hard toll on his only pair of light shoes. They were heavy with mud; he would have to scrape them before the run.

"I don't know; I suppose so," Sam said. He looked up at his father. "But I don't want to. Can you understand that, Dad? I want to take it all."

Gillon didn't mean to, but he shook his head.

"Isn't enough enough?"

"I don't know," Sam said, "I don't think any of us know when enough is enough." He looked at his father and they suddenly smiled at one another, one of those startled smiles of recognition that only close friends and close families ever know.

"So I'll win it, then," Sam said, and picked up his sweater and began making his way over the moor to where the men were gathering for the start of the Marathon.

"But God damn Mr. Selkirk, Daddie," he said. "He's taken all the fun out of the ribbons. Where's Jem?"

Gillon went back across the moor and sat down next to Maggie.

"He's going to run," he said. "No way to stop him."

"Why shouldn't he?" She patted the purse where a hundred shillings were already deposited. "That's what he came to do."

He should have known better, Gillon thought. The baskets

were packed, all the empty bottles and the food that was left, the pitchers and platters. Sarah should have been there to help.

"I'm worried about Sarah. She should be here."

"I'm not. Sarah will be home. We should go home." She got up to go but Gillon pulled her down.

"Oh, no. This is the end of it all. You'd better be here."

"What's the prize?"

"One gold guinea and a bottle of whisky."

"He'll be a drunk."

"He's going to sell the whisky."

"He'll be rich," Maggie said.

People kept coming up to pass the Cameron blanket where Sam's nine blue ribbons were pinned to the plaid, not in a boastful way but as a method of keeping them. Each ribbon had a circular crest, a cockade of blue with the name of the event printed in gold, and two streamers hanging out below. The bottles of Glenlivet were lined up in a row, and with several silver loving cups that could be kept and displayed by the winner in his house until the next year's Games. The people passed by but they didn't stop and sit, the Doonies perhaps feeling the Camerons would resent them now and the Uppies not prepared to make their separate peace. But they still came up and down to see the display, as Sam had said they would.

"What is that you keep reading?" Gillon finally asked Maggie. "You can't keep your hands away from it."

"Something personal to me."

"You'd think it was a love letter the way you keep stroking it."

"Aye, you would," she said.

At first it amused him but finally it began to worry him. All through the day, sometimes several times an hour, she had taken the paper out of her handbag and read it slowly, her lips moving because she was relishing the words, and when she put it back there was a look of peace on her face, a contentment he could almost not remember seeing before. He suddenly reached in and took the paper, only partly playful, and she seized his wrist before he could get it all the way out of the bag.

"You keep your hands off that, Gillon." There was no amusement in the voice at all. He let go of the paper and took his hand away.

"I saw it," he said. "The letterhead. Ogilvie and Sons. That old sad bastard."

"Yes, and be thankful he's old." Gillon made no effort to understand.

Andrew came trotting by. "Have you seen Jem?" he asked. "Last call for the runners." They hadn't.

"Poor Jem," Gillon said. "He must have gone off because Sam was winning it all."

"Och," Maggie said. "You don't understand them at *all*. If Jem went off it's to find some way to beat Sam."

16

MANY STARTED BUT NOT MANY FINISHED THE Marathon. In some years, when the weather was bad, no one finished. From the Sportin Moor down through Doonietoon, down past the tipples and pitheads, through the working areas and out the Low Road past Brumbie Hill to Easter Mungo in the twilight and then all the way home in the dark, uphill all the way. Home was the heartbreaker.

Part of the challenge was the run and part was the ancient challenge of the night and the dark and the moors. Some of the men still carried little lanterns carved out of turnips that they bought for a penny in Easter Mungo and some carried miner's lamps lodged in hollowed-out cabbage stalks, called custocks. Men had died of exhaustion on the run, some had died, it was said, of fear in the night and men had drowned when they had blindly stumbled into the Pitmungo River and been carried away in its current. There was no excitement at the start; the race was too long to worry about getting a lead position. For most of the men, it was an ordeal to be endured, a ritual of their fathers to be carried on. A man didn't expect to win, he only hoped to finish.

"I tried," he could say after that. "I gave it all I got, and by God that's all a man can be asked to do."

All he can do? He could win, Maggie would have said, and the thought of it forced Gillon to smile.

"Do you see my brother? Do you see Jem?" Sam asked his father. There were fifty or sixty runners spread out in the shadows behind the starting line, some with groups of friends and family. It was impossible to tell who anyone was. Gillon thought he saw Jemmie, way in back, but he wasn't certain of it.

"I don't know. I'm not sure, but I think he's in it," Gillon said, and then came the old cry:

"SAFE OOT! SAFE IN!" and the clump of runners were going, gone down into the gloaming, down the Sportin Moor to Colliers Walk, all hunched together, supporting each other at the start before the inevitable stringing out began and the men dropped off and got sick and crawled into the drainage ditches until they could get up and make it home.

Sam ran with the pack for several miles but the pace was too slow. At the rate they were going he would get leg-heavy and never break into the glide of the second wind that, once reached, made the running easier, although faster. No man should be so far above the others, his father had said, but he was doing it, stretching out his legs, stretching out his lead, leaving them all behind, running alone in the growing darkness, a little sad to be out there all alone again and happy about it at the same time.

There were a few men in Easter Mungo, keepers of the old traditions, waiting for the runners with sponges to cool their necks and spray cold water over their hair and pieces of orange for energy and good luck. The orange had something to do with the sun, Sam knew, but had never gotten the story right. There was whisky for those who felt the need of it.

"Good lad," a man said, squeezing the sponge of icy water over

Sam's head. It was good. "Where are all the others? You're all alone, lad."

Sam shook his head. He signed the Check Point Ledger, halfway now, and did the traditional tour of the town square, once around the fountain, up and down the kirk steps to shake the devil, down past the old men by their fires warding off the bad fairies and little people, keeping the customs, keeping the old ways.

"Safe in," they shouted to him. "Safe in, lad, God run with you. Watch yoursel' on the moor," and he was gone, back into his running trance, alone, alone, alone, and then he was startled to hear someone come upon him in the darkness and go by him.

"Who?" he called out, but the runner went on, *slap, slap, slap* into the blackness toward the fragile lights of Easter Mungo. He wasn't all that far ahead, Sam realized, and was surprised. Someone with guts. The uphill would get him. The rise began almost outside the town limits of Easter Mungo. An hour more to go now, almost all of it uphill. He began to pass the first of the men who had fallen out, sprawled along the edge of the road, a few sick, all exhausted, some just lying there in the dust.

"Safe in," they called to him. "Safe in, Cameron." After all he had done to them that day! Generous men. What was it his father had said, wasn't it time to let one of them have a share? and here they were, cheering him on. Finally he was through the fall-outs and felt better, out of their sight, alone in the darkness, when he heard the steps behind him. He didn't believe it at first. But someone was there, hanging behind him, matching him stride for stride, feet pounding the road, unlike his own. He was still on his toes the way a runner should run; the other man was running flat-footed and gasping for air. He went through the list of all the young men who could still be staying with him, the football players and rugby boys, and there were none. For a moment he was afraid, all the old stories of things that had happened in the blackness on the road.

Tam o' Shanter stuff, bogle-bo stuff, warlocks and witches, Sam told himself. Lies made up by men to account for their failure. Still, the steps kept coming. He looked behind him but couldn't see the runner.

"Who?" he called back. "Tell me who you are."

Only the steps pounding. He slowed his pace but when he did, the runner behind broke stride and slowed also. When he sped up, the runner came with him. To hell with him, Sam thought; run your own race and kill him on the hill. It was black but the stars were out. He could see the tipple, that was good, and suddenly the bonfire erupted on the moor. They were waiting for him. He hit the rise, the long long rise, Break Ass Hill, and started up. It was hard then.

"You're going to kill yourself," Sam shouted back. "You're going to crack your heart."

There was the river and the stream to ford and then the works, up past the brick kilns, the old tipple, and the new tipple, and he had lost him. Thank God for that, Sam thought, because no man who had not been in serious training should be doing what he was doing to his body. He felt a genuine sorrow for the man, someone who wanted to beat him so bad that he was pushing himself beyond where he should safely go. Men died.

He reached the cobblestones, the foot of Colliers Walk, and several times stumbled on the stones. His legs were heavier than he thought they would be. The day had taken a bigger toll than he had planned for, and then that bastard behind him had pushed him a little harder than he had wanted to be pushed. The first of the people were along the Walk now, lining the way. He could hear them and hear his name being shouted up the line ahead to the people on the moor, but he couldn't make out any faces. Too tired now to focus.

"Sam Cameron. It's the Cameron lad again," going up the Walk mouth from mouth. The lower town looked wild in the dancing shadows from the great bonfire on the moor. The sweet wages of victory, Sam thought sourly, his name fleeting through the town. He felt a strong desire to give in then; he had run enough. Many winners in the past had walked the last way in, and so he broke his pace trotting but not running the way he had been doing before, and then he heard the second cry, a new one, and it took him so much by surprise that he broke stride entirely and stumbled again on the stones.

"Someone else," he heard, "someone else. He's comin' on, he's comin' on."

He could hear him now, closer than ever, closing the gap on him. He turned but he still couldn't see him.

"Who?" he shouted at the people along the Walk. "Who is it? Who is it?"

They didn't know. He felt a new fear go through him, not of losing, but of a terrible price being paid because of him, someone wanted something so terribly that he was risking his life for it, tearing himself apart for it, he could hear him now, not his feet slapping the stones, the feet must be pulp, Sam thought, but the man's throat, gasping literally for the breath of life, sobbing from pain and what it was that was driving him.

He tried to pick up his pace, to re-establish his stride, and it wouldn't work for him. He had quit too soon; he had let down, and now the other man was getting him. But he couldn't be doing it, Sam knew, he could not be, he couldn't keep it up, his own legs like fleshed lead, his lungs on fire, his heart pounding so hard in his ears that he felt it was possible his head could split from the pressure of it.

Men had died on this hill, men had died, Sam thought. He was beginning to get his pace again, the muscles responding to a call he didn't know they still could answer. The other man was at his shoulder now, positioned in such a way that when Sam turned he couldn't see the smaller man hugging his shoulder blade.

"Stop it," he said, "don't do this." The man kept on. "Stop doing this to yourself." The man grunted something Sam couldn't make out. "You slow down and I'll slow down. You're going to hurt yourself." He was wasting his breath. For a moment he thought, I'll stop and let the bastard go past, and realized that he was never going to do that, that he would have to be beaten, because it wasn't a matter of winning now but of not knowing how to lose, and then the man was even with him, coming on, and, incredibly then, pulling ahead of him, pulling away from him, the people running alongside the runners, screaming at them, screaming at the dark little man pulling ahead, every stumbling step pulling ahead.

"Jem!" Sam shouted. "Christ, don't do this to me," and he put the kick on, four weeks of running mile after mile on the roads, feeling some kind of response in him again, up past Rotten Row and Wet Row, up to Miners Row and then the bottom of the moor. Three hundred yards upward to go now, deep grass, dark little holes in the moor, the young people of the town running along by Jemmie then, shouting at him to keep going, to go on, go on, go on, he was ahead, he was winning, some of them trying to hold Jemmie's elbows, propelling him upward toward the bonfire which must have been flaming liquid in his eyes. He's out of his mind, Sam thought, he's running on craziness now, because he had gone beyond human effort. And then he decided, I won't let him do it, I won't let him take it away, and he went into that land where he had driven himself several times before, beyond pain, beyond his own true limits, borrowing from sources never tapped before; and he moved, he was at Jem's heels and at his side and he looked down at his brother's stricken face, his distorted face, and he went by him as if he had never seen his brother before, running to the flame.

Gillon was there at the finish but almost no one else. The others had run down the moor to where Jemmie had fallen, fifty yards short of the line, and they carried him and put him down over the line so that he would get credit, at least, for the second-place finish; a little red ribbon and five shillings.

"You had to do that?" his father said to Sam.

"Aye, I had to."

At least Sam was crying, Gillon saw, for himself, he knew, and for what some force in him had driven him to do, and crying for his brother, too. He saw his son begin to run again, alone across the moor, looking as if he could run forever, run right up into the blackness of the sky, and then when the boy had punished himself enough he saw him come back down to where Jem was lying by the pump on the moor.

Sam thought Jem would be unconscious but he wasn't. His brother's body was burning but his hands were cold and that alarmed him. He put his hand under Jem's head and lifted it and cleaned his mouth.

"Why did you do that, Jem? *Why?*" His brother's eyes were vacant. My brother is going to die, Sam thought, and then the thought left him.

"One man can't have it *all*," Jem said. "You have to pass some of it around." He began to tremble and Sam told some of the football boys to go up to the house and get the cart and blankets for Jem.

"I nearly had you, you son of a bitch," Jem said. "I nearly got you."

"Had me? You nearly killed me, man."

"I'll get you, Sam, you know I will. I'll keep coming at you, Sam, and I'll get you."

"You should have won this year," Sam said. "You deserved to win."

As exhausted as he was, Jemmie sat upright. The idea amazed him. It angered him. It was Cameron heresy.

"How did I deserve to win if I didn't win?" Jem said.

It was enough for Gillon, enough of a display for one day. The brothers holding one another, that was good; and trying to hold back the tears that they couldn't explain, that was good. But that thing that drove them on beyond where others went, beyond where they very possibly were meant to go, there it was again, as full-blown as ever, nothing learned, only reinforced. Perhaps they would never learn.

. . .

When they went for the wagon they found it was gone. Both the wagon and the new little Highland garron, named Brothcock, were gone. Some Miners' Freedom Day lark, they said, a case of too much freedom and too much ale, but when Sarah didn't come home it was decided that Gillon should walk up the Terrace to the Walter Bone house to see if their son was home. Sandy Bone was gone.

"I can't believe it," Maggie said. "She wouldn't do that to me. I told her I won't have that cripple-dick hirpling around my house."

Gillon had never done anything like it before. He put a hand around her throat.

"A fine young man was buried under the slate, and I won't have him demeaned by you for it." She broke away from him, her dark face as flushed as his.

"Easy, Daddie," Andrew said.

"If my daughter has run away with him, if she's married him, she's married above herself."

"Marrying anyone from Pitmungo is to marry beneath your-self."

"Aye, I should laugh if it was funny," Gillon said. "If that man can make a life after what happened to him, he's entitled to it. If that means having my daughter, he can have her. If that means having him in this house, he can come."

"She promised me," Maggie said. That, Gillon could see, was the real insult. "How would she have the *gall* to do that?"

"Because she's in *love*," Gillon cried out. "Can you understand that? Or is it beyond you?"

Maggie got away from him, afraid of his hand again but un-willing not to say what she intended to say.

"She lied to me."

Gillon made an effort to control himself. He could see the red marks left by his fingers on her flesh.

"Love doesn't understand about lies," Gillon said.

"Love is all lies," Maggie said. "Love is promises that are always broken."

"Do you really believe that?"

"Aye, I do."

It had been cool coming up from the moor and Gillon looked for his jacket. He couldn't stay in here, he knew, not for a while at least.

"Jesus, I feel sorry for you," he said. "And, Jesus, I feel sorry for me," and he shut the door on his house.

17

To the surprise of Pitmungo and himself, because he was a Doonie and an incomer and a common face miner, Gillon was becoming a friend of Walter Bone. He had been shy about it. Mr. Bone was the pillar of Tosh-Mungo Terrace, the mainstay of the most solidly established family in Pitmungo, one of the deacons in the Free Kirk and an overman in the pit besides. Overmen didn't talk to face miners. But Gillon's need to know about Sarah broke his shyness down.

"How's my daughter doing in your house, Mr. Bone?" he asked one day, on his way down for their shift in the mine. Mr. Bone had looked at him in surprise and Gillon felt anger start but later understood that he had only startled Bone out of his early morning thoughts.

"Doing?"

"How is she getting along?"

"Your daughter," he said after a considerable pause, "is a blessing to my house."

"Then she's happy?"

"Happy? Let me see, I hadn't considered that." He was silent again. "I would have to say she's happy, whatever you mean by that. Her mother won't have her back in the house yet?"

"No, nor ever."

"Oh, she will," Mr. Bone said. "She'll come around. From what I hear Mrs. Cameron is a sensible woman."

Mr. Bone, Gillon thought, didn't know Mrs. Cameron well.

After that they met more often, going down to the pit and home from it, and found they had a great deal in common. In comparison to the other miners, they were serious and both of them were listeners and learners and, to some extent, readers. Like so many Scotchmen, they loved argument and disputation. For all his stiff-necked approach to life, one that John Knox himself would have approved, Mr. Bone was willing to question or defend any point of view for the sake of a good debate. They were arguing a point about the right of a workman to get compensation when they first saw the men—strangers to Pitmungo—with surveying equipment out on the moor. It was Bone's point that the workman must take on the risk in return for the opportunity to earn money in the employer's mill or mine.

"It's assumed the master doesn't want to wreck his equipment," Mr. Bone said. "It's assumed he doesn't want to hurt trained men."

"It's assumed the master doesn't really care," Gillon said. "And what do you think those men are doing?"

It was a touchy question. There had been rumors about the fate of the Sportin Moor and Walter Bone, who generally could be counted on to defend the established order of things, was one of those who denied that Lady Jane Tosh-Mungo, now the Countess of Fyffe, would allow such a thing. If they took away the moor Mr. Bone would be forced to admit that a part of his life had been based on a lie. He couldn't afford to believe the rumor.

"They could be doing any of a thousand things," Mr. Bone said. "They could be surveying for a new cricket green."

It was his belief, as it was with a great many workingmen, that there was a balance between the ruling class and the working class and that God had intended that balance. There were those to lead and those to follow, *them* and us, and it was to the mutual benefit of both classes to respect one another.

"When the balance gets out of kilter, one side asking or taking too much, nothing works right until the balance is restored. That's the order of society. It is ordained."

Gillon didn't choose to argue that one. And it seemed that Mr. Bone was right because nothing happened after that for a long time, until one afternoon they came up into the slant of a sharp September sun and found a gang of men, Irish road workers by the tattered despair of their looks, fencing in the moor. There was a desire not to see what was happening, but when enough men came to Walter Bone for reassurance that nothing was going to happen to the moor, Mr. Bone finally knew he had to face up to the issue with Mr. Brothcock.

"The men are a wee bit unsure, a wee bit upset, Mr. Brothcock."

"You tell them not to worry, Walter. The crossing rights to the moor will be secured. No man is going to have to walk around our moor."

Mr. Bone went outside the office but he knew it wasn't enough and went back in.

"What I mean is, will my grandchildren be playing football on that moor?"

Brothcock was annoyed.

"Look, you mine the coal and I'll mind the property. If we both tend to our own affairs I think you'll find it works out best for both of us."

When the men asked Walter Bone what the superintendent had said, he was forced to tell them he didn't know. Gillon wasn't the only one to see the hurt and puzzlement in his eyes.

The work went slowly. It was an ugly-looking fence, high wooden slats painted a heavy blackish green, none of the slats matching the next one. They were poor workers, demoralized men, forced to camp out at night by the Gypsy caravans because the people resented their presence. A few came down to the College one night but were asked to leave. It was the young men who bothered the laborers most, coming down hot from play, making comments on their work and asking them questions about the moor they couldn't answer. Finally Mr. Brothcock had to come up to the moor to put a stop to it.

"All right," he shouted to the football players, "all of you off the moor."

They stopped as they were, in the middle of play, the football still bouncing its way across the field.

"You heard me, everyone off this moor."

Jemmie trotted across the grass to the mine superintendent.

"We have a game, sir. We have a game this evening. Pitmungo against Kinglassie."

"I don't care a damn what you have. Get off the grass."

"They come a long way to play, sir."

The Kinglassie boys were across the field, stripping down to their shorts and undershirts. They had trotted five miles up from Kinglassie after a ten-hour shift in the pit.

"I wouldn't know how to tell them," Jem said.

"Oh, you'll find some way."

"It isn't going to hurt the grass none; we have to clip it all the time."

It was Jem's stance as much as anything else that annoyed the superintendent, his tough stocky legs spread wide apart, the lift to his dark chin, the hard bright nuts of eyes, just short of defiant.

"Look, you. I told you to get the hell off this grass and I mean what I say. Get your asses off this moor."

"You don't own this moor, sir. The people own this moor."

The issue, for the first time in Pitmungo, was joined. Mr. Brothcock walked up the moor until his belly was almost touching Jemmie.

"I know you. We know your name. You're the greedy pig who don't know when to stop."

Jemmie looked at Sam and then at the others who had come up around him. The odd thing to Jem was Sam's silence; there wasn't even anger in his eyes. There was nothing there.

"Aye. James Drum Cameron. The lads want to know what you'd do if we went on with our match."

Brothcock smiled.

"I'd see you never worked in these pits again. I'd see your brothers never worked again. I'd see your father never worked. And I'd see that all the coal masters in Fife saw you never set foot in their mines. That answer your question?"

He started back down the moor, the folds of his fat neck showing above his collar. He was stepping over a quoit bed when the rock stung by his ear, missing his skull by an inch or two. He must have heard it humming by his ear, but if he didn't, he saw it when it hit in front of him and went thumping down the moor. The superintendent had to be given credit for a kind of raw courage or style. He never stopped; he never gave the players the satisfaction of turning. But the fact remained for Brothcock and all Pitmungo to ponder. Someone had wanted the moor enough to try to kill Mr. Brothcock.

"Did you do that?" Jem said, turning to his brother. Sam didn't answer. There was no expression on his face at all.

Rob Roy was elated. After coming out of the pit and taking his tub in the boardinghouse wash room he skipped his pints in the College because he wanted to be clearheaded for the meeting with Mr. Selkirk.

"Well, we have it," Rob said. "We got our issue at last. They handed it to us." He was let down when Mr. Selkirk shook his head.

"I don't know, I don't think so," the librarian said. "It lacks the classic Marxian ingredients."

Rob was indignant. Here was the issue, on fire in front of them, and here was Mr. Selkirk trying to pour cold water on the blaze.

"Christ, they tried to kill Mr. Brothcock."

"They? One person. Probably one of your hardheaded brothers."

"I hope it was."

"Now, if all of them had joined together and mobbed Mr. Brothcock, then you would have something. One man throwing a rock is an act of violence, a group of men mobbing a mine superintendent is a revolutionary act."

"You just don't understand what that moor means to the people here, Henry." They were on a first-name basis now. "The moor is life and without it there is death. Do you know what it is? Without our moor we become Easter Mungo, we become Dirt Hill. We know it. They all know it."

"Bunch of quoit players. You want to form a revolution out of that?"

"Aye, that's just it. Damn good quoit players. The best quoit players in Fife. It's all part of it."

Mr. Selkirk pondered the problem for a while.

"No, Marx wouldn't approve. It has to be here"—he tapped his stomach—"in the gut. Everyone has to hurt. The rugby players are hurt, oh aye, I'll bet that one in your family is boiling . . ."

"Sam. Aye, he's not boiling, he's gone ice cold."

". . . but the women aren't hurt. If they sink a mine, there's going to be more work, more coal. The anger will go out when the pay packets come in."

Rob had turned his back on his teacher.

"I want your permission to write Keir Hardie." He waited. Selkirk said nothing. "I want to ask him to come down here and organize Pitmungo into the Scotch Miners' Union, so when we do something we'll have someone behind us."

"I can't stop you."

"I want you to write a covering letter so he knows I'm a serious man."

"Your letter will tell him that."

"So you won't do it?" Rob turned around and found Henry Selkirk studying him as if he were a herring for sale.

"Aye, I'll do it. And where are you going to put him if he comes?"

Rob's face dropped, the way his father's sometimes did. He hadn't considered that.

"I'm not asking him to come down here and get jailed or embarrassed or beaten by some Company police," Selkirk said.

It was a thing Rob would never forget about this odd angry man, that he had been jailed and beaten and blacklisted at every pit from Fife down to Durham and Wales. His fighting days were long done; he was all memories now and when he remembered, he drank, but Rob would always respect him for it. Rob looked down into Colliers Walk from the coal-grimed window of the Reading Room.

"I know a place where there's room and where we can get him into town without being seen."

"Where?"

"I can't tell you where right now. But it's there. I want you to take my word on it."

Selkirk was studying him again.

"Why can't you tell me?"

"Because it's personal. My pride is involved." Mr. Selkirk should understand what that meant.

"I wouldn't want to write the letter until I was sure," Selkirk said.

"I *am* sure," Rob said, in an outburst of enthusiasm. "Ah, this is going to be the start of it all. The first step on the path, Henry."

Such a romantic, Selkirk thought, so much like his father, so much like himself when he was young, so filled with the idea that when people finally heard the truth they would respond to the truth. That was the hardest thing to learn.

"You write your letter," Selkirk said. "I'll cover it."

Because where would one be without the dreamers, to make the first blazes on the trail that the practical ones would take later on? Rob Roy was going to suffer, he knew that, and that was the standard price for dreaming. He wished the boy would go away then because he felt a need for a little of the reassurance in the bottle at his hip.

18 Rob Roy wrote his letter and waited. No answer came.

"Keir Hardie will answer you," Henry Selkirk said. "He's a busy man, they're killing him with work and he's on the run from the law at the same time. But Keir Hardie will answer you."

There was nothing for Rob Roy to do but wait, but others in Pitmungo were moving in their own way. To everyone's surprise the leader was Walter Bone. Moving very quietly through Uppietoon and then down through Doonietoon, where people were flattered to have him in their but-and-bens, he raised a legal fund to explore the miners' rights in the matter of the moor and one Sunday, against his religious scruples, went down to Dunfermline to consult Mr. Murdoch Carnegie, of the eminent firm of Carnegie and Company, perhaps the first miner in Pitmungo ever to engage a law agent. Gillon was honored to be asked to go along.

What they learned from Mr. Carnegie, who never asked them to sit down—men from the pits stand—was not reassuring.

The fence was put up, in his opinion, to re-establish and reinforce the fact of possession of the moor by the Tosh-Mungo family. Allowing the miners to use the moor did not mean the owners had relinquished their rights to the ground.

"For three hundred years, sir?" Walter Bone said.

"For three hundred years, yes."

"What about the cart of coal, then?" Gillon found himself saying. "When she accepts the coal she admits our right to the moor."

The other miners with Mr. Bone nodded. It was to them a crucial point.

"No, no," Mr. Carnegie said. "Just the reverse. The fact that you pay her a cart of coal each year is proof that you recognize her ownership."

Gillon felt the taste of gall in his mouth. The thing they had felt established their right worked out instead to establish their debt.

There was, Mr. Carnegie said, one legal step they might take. They could file a claim of presumption in the Court of Session— that it was simply presumed by tradition, common law and local habit that the land, by their continued use of it for such a long time, had become theirs by right of forfeit.

The trouble with this was that the Pitmungo miners, not being a corporate body, were probably not entitled to sue. But in the event they were allowed to sue, and they lost—which Mr. Carnegie was certain they would do—they were liable to be fined for bringing false suit, to be ordered to pay all legal and court costs incurred and, finally, to bring the wrath of Lord Fyffe down on their heads.

The only thing Mr. Carnegie could finally suggest would be some sort of act, some sort of collective demonstration, that might draw the attention of the outside world and force the Tosh-Mungos to surrender their claim to the land and their rights to it by way of default.

"What kind of act do you suggest, sir?" Walter Bone asked. The law agent looked at them with amused surprise.

"Do you expect me to give you advice for rebellion?" he said, and charged them two pounds for the value of his judgment.

They had intended to go down to the little house at No. 4 Moodie Street, where another Carnegie had been born and raised—the great Andrew himself—but that little excursion was forgotten. They turned around and began the fourteen-mile walk back to Pitmungo. For miles no one had the heart to say anything.

"They would use justice to perpetuate injustice," Walter Bone said at last.

"And there's not a goddamn thing we can do about it."

"Watch your mouth, it's the Sabbath, man."

"Excuse me," the miner said.

The lawyer's last sentence kept running through all of their minds because it was the last course open to them. *Advice for rebellion.* Some act, some strong dramatic steps never contemplated by the men of Pitmungo before. It was a daring thought and Mr. Bone was aware of where it led. To achieve simple justice, he would be driven into the ranks of the revolutionaries. He put it best, as he was often capable of doing.

"If acting to save our moor makes me a revolutionary, then I am one."

No man would have believed that three weeks before.

At the meeting held up behind Tosh-Mungo Terrace in the White Coo plantation, out of sight of the town and Company men, Walter Bone made his report to those who had given money to the fund. When he finished it was clear what had to be done.

"What it means then," a miner shouted, "is tear down that fewkin fence."

"What it means is occupy our moor the first day they try to do anything with it. We have picks and we can dig. Let them try and drive *us* out."

It went on after that. Let them send down the Royal Scots Guard, let them order out the Black Watch; they would stand fast and take their message to the world. Even if they lost, no one was going to take their moor away without a fight for it. That much they could promise.

What they hadn't learned then was something Mr. Selkirk could have told them had they asked. When revolt is cooking on the stove, make certain to have a revolutionary for a chef. Mr. Bone was not the proper cook. And then there was the question of time. Nothing happened once the fence was built.

Nothing.

The fence stood as it was, blackly there, and then as it does every five or six years, winter came early, a rush of cold from the north that couldn't get dislodged from the valley. Winter was almost two months ahead of time and wouldn't go away, warming just enough to give hope that the mistake was being righted only to be followed by another driving storm from the north. Soon the moor grass froze, the long slender green blades becoming stiff from frost and cold winds, and as early as October the snows came, burying the moor beneath them. The loss was less keen then because when the wind was rushing across it, the moor became only a breath-taking ordeal to be endured in order to get to Uppietoon.

The problem that winter was that the people learned to live with their fence. It came to be accepted in their lives. People in the houses in the Doonie rows found that the fence broke the force of the wind below the Sportin Moor. And there was the question of the future. What if, as the older miners often said, some of the other pits were being mined out. A new shaft would mean new coal and new jobs. Giving up football and rugby wasn't too high a price to pay to keep salt and bread on the table.

A strange complacency began to push out thoughts of rebellion. The emphasis was on the grass itself. The grass came, in time, to lend an almost mystical reassurance to the people in Pitmungo. As long as the grass remained inviolate, the moor was inviolate. Rebellion slumbered under a cover of snow and green grass.

Only Sam couldn't seem to find some way to make his peace with the fence. He had sunk into a kind of numbness that worried the family. He came home from the pit and had his tub and his tea but when someone talked to him he didn't seem to hear and if he heard he had no interest in answering. After a time people made no effort to reach him and that seemed to please him just as well. He sat in his room and stared at the wall, and said odd things at times—little warning signals, Andrew told his father, that something was to come. Then he began to read, too, all of Rob Roy's books and then ones Mr. Selkirk recommended to his father.

"I want to know what happened to your family," he said one day to Gillon. "I want to know exactly how they were thrown off their land."

Gillon told him what he remembered, driven off what they had believed was their ancestral land to make room for grouse and pheasant and red deer and, sometimes, sheep; of their going to the edge of the sea and building the stone house and dying of cold and hunger along the shore. The story of Gillon's mother going for the mussels at night and having her creel cut off her back made Sam angry, the first sign of life they had seen in him for months.

"Did they fight it? Did they band together and resist?" Gillon knew where his mind was going, but he went on with it because it was better to see him this way than dead, the way he had been before.

"Some. Not many."

"Why not, why *not*?"

"I don't know. I never knew."

"What did they have to lose? They died anyway."

"I don't know."

"What happened to the ones who fought?"

"Oh, what you would think. They beat them and they jailed them. They fired houses and knocked them down. They killed a few."

Sam was nodding, his eyes bright.

"Did they fight well? The ones who died?"

"Some did, some didn't," Gillon said. "Like men. What man ever knows how he will react?"

"*I* know," Sam said. It sent a chill over the room. Sam never used words when he didn't mean them. Gillon was frightened for his son. He had seen how far he was capable of going, and no man wants to look at his son and see in him the makings of a martyr.

"Is there a book about it? I want to read all about it. Can you get me a book, Daddie?"

It was a risk Gillon decided to take. He asked Mr. Selkirk to get him a copy of Alexander Mackenzie's *The History of the Highland Clearances*, over Maggie's objections because of the cost of the book, and then prayed—the little short prayers that he made to whatever gods there might be—that this might not prove to be the spark that would set Sam's mind afire.

Ian came up with word that Rob Roy wanted to meet with his father, not in the house, but in the empty schoolhouse his mother had once taught in. They met the next afternoon after work and after a moment's hesitation they embraced one another, which was not like the Camerons at all.

"A long time not to speak, a father to his son," Gillon said.

"Aye. Of course, you ordered me away and so I went."

"I ordered you to come and you didn't."

They both were students enough of H. Selkirk to recognize a futile philosophical stand-off when they ran into one. Gillon smiled and then Rob smiled.

"You were always stubborn in your easy way," he said.

"And you're not stubborn in your quiet way?" Rob Roy said. They smiled again; the sparring was over.

With the most elaborate care, as if he were uncovering the Holy Grail, Rob Roy unfolded a letter he took from a little tin miner's matchbox.

"You won't believe this," he said. His voice trembled with pride and excitement. "Easy with the paper now." The handwriting was unschooled and hard to read at first.

Dear Brother Cameron:

The injustice you describe seems ample reason to me to bring people together. The righteousness of your cause should be strong enough to lead to the forming of an organization to right a wrong and the existence of an organization is the seed we need to make our movement grow. First steps lead to second steps.

Were I to come, which I wish to do, I would need safe lodging away from the eyes of police and Company officials. I am on probation and am prohibited from doing organization work and must conduct myself as any fugitive does because of my ideas. I would also need a place to conduct a meeting away from the ears of the above. If you satisfy those particulars, you have my word.

Please give my respects to H.S. He was a fighter once. Send details by ordinary post to Mr. Kyle Brine c/o Postmaster, Main Post Office, Edinburgh.

P.S. Have an arrival plan prepared for me. I expect I should arrive at Cowdenbeath in the evening and be walked to Pitmungo under cover of night.

"You know who it is, of course, Daddie?" He was so excited.

"By the way you handle the paper, I would say at least an apostle of Christ."

"I want you to be serious, Daddie." It was true; they communicated too much through banter. "It's no occasion for jokes."

"No, you're right."

"Keir Hardie. The great labor leader. Writing to your son." Gillon was happy for him, and disturbed. It seemed out of his depth. Rob was a dreamer and so little of a doer.

"You must have written a fine letter."

"I did, Dad. I would be lying to say otherwise. I wrote it twenty times until I got it down perfect. Even Mr. Selkirk couldn't make a change."

Gillon felt a moment of jealousy at the idea of his son carrying draft after draft of his letter to the librarian.

"I'll be the one to meet him at Cowdenbeath. Can you see that,

Daddie? Walking the great Keir Hardie through the night? What will I say to him?"

"I wouldn't worry. He'll do all the talking when he wants to talk."

"Aye, you're right. And the meeting can be held up in the plantation where the old house used to stand. Go straight out back from the house and never be seen at all."

"What house?"

Rob Roy looked confused. He opened his mouth to say something and closed it again and finally, in an irritated way, as if the question had been answered many times and long before, said, "Why, our house. Where else?"

It was Gillon's turn to be confused. He wasn't ready for it: Keir Hardie in his house, a wanted man, a fugitive perhaps, a Communist leader almost certainly.

But that wasn't all there was to it. Rob Roy should have known; he'd spent his youth in this family too.

"Your mother won't allow it. It's her house, too. She'll never have it."

"Won't allow it? Make her allow it!"

Gillon blamed it on Maggie but it was Sam he was frightened about, Sam some days seeming to be walking on the very edge of something dark and violent and dangerous. Gillon shook his head.

"I can't do it."

Rob would not believe what he heard. He had counted on it far too long. "You have got to do it," he shouted, his voice echoing back to them from the dark blackboarded walls. Gillon didn't like the look in his son's face. He turned away and stared into the cold bland blue eyes of Queen Victoria looking disapprovingly down on him.

"I crawled to you and you let me down," Rob said.

"There are things you don't understand now and . . ."

"You let me down. I came back to you and you let me *down*." He had put his hands on his father's coal-stained jacket, but now he took them away and went across the room away from him, as if he couldn't stand to be near him.

"You know what they call you, don't you? I hear it because they forget I'm your son sometimes. A John Thomson's man. Someone who's given up being a man in his own house. I should have known better."

He began collecting his things to leave, his tin piece bucket and his box of black powder tamps. Rob Roy always made more tamps than he needed, always thinking he was going to blow more coal off the face than he finally did in the day.

"So I'll write a letter and I'll say 'I'm sorry Mr. Hardie but I can't let you have the use of my father's house because his woman won't permit it. So the great work you wanted to start here will have to start some other time or way.' . . ." He dropped his head until his chin touched his chest.

"Och, my great chance, my one great chance," Rob said. Gillon wanted to go to him and put an arm around him, but he knew he couldn't do that now. He did move a few steps toward him and Rob spun around on his father.

"They say I'm the big dreamer around here, but you listen to me. Sometime in my lifetime we will have smashed *them*, we will have crushed them." Gillon made a move and Rob Roy headed him off. "No, you keep listening to me, John."

It was the cruelest thing he had ever said to his father and both of them knew it.

"There will be a society yet where Lord Fyffe's fat-assed grandsons will be down some pit with picks in their hand and some of us will be up on Brumbie Hill."

He was through then and Gillon let him stand there, trying to control himself. He wanted to tell Rob Roy about his brother Sam and he knew he couldn't. He tried to find a reason that would make it easier for both of them to accept.

"Sooner or later they were bound to find out Hardie stayed in our house."

"A risk."

"And Lord Fyffe and Brothcock would have our jobs for that. You had no right to run that risk for us."

There was a bad, long silence after that.

"Do you remember when I said that sometimes the men forgot I was your son?" Gillon refused to nod. "Well, sometimes I wish it was so. Sometimes I wish I could be Rob Roy Nothing—anything but what I am."

He pushed by his father, knocking children's chairs and desks awry as he went, and stumbled down the stairs and out into Colliers Walk—away, Gillon was happy to see, from the College. But he would be back, Gillon knew, and he would get drunk, sweeping-out drunk, fou, bitch fou, and there was nothing he could do about it. He waited in the doorway and after a time Rob came back up the Walk, headed for the College.

"Rob?" he said from the shadows. He prayed his son would stop, and he did. "I'll write that letter for you."

"Which letter?"

"The one you'll have to write Mr. Hardie telling him not to come," and then the enormity of his loss truly settled on Rob Roy, and although he intended to hate him, he found himself falling into his father's arms and sobbing as hard as any woman in Pitmungo sobbed when a husband or son was brought home from the pit and stretched out on the floor of the but. They had lost a man, Gillon thought, which is hard enough to understand, but Rob had lost his dream, which can never really be understood. The dead man goes to the grave, but where does a young man's dream go?

When Gillon got to the fence it was locked because it was late and he didn't want to go back down and find the keeper. He decided to walk out around the moor where the Gypsies had lived. They were gone, a few scraps of broken bottles and rags and pieces from earthenware jars around little stone fireplaces, all that was left of several hundred years of life. They had been driven out, but they hadn't died, he was certain of that. Somehow they had made a go of it. Then what was he afraid of? He thought of running back down to Rob and telling him to send his letter and set a date. A man can say no so many times, for so long, and after that he ceases to be a man.

But all the while he was seeing those eyes of Sam, eyes of a fox trapped in the back of its den, dangerous there. If Keir Hardie organized a movement, when he left—Gillon knew it in the depth of his being—Sam would be the one to lead it.

And Sam would be the one to pay for it. If he led it well enough, led it the way he would want to lead it, Sam would be the one to die. Could he risk the life of one son to mend the dream of another? Perhaps in the end he would only succeed in destroying them both. He went home to his tub and sitting in the good hot water he felt a coldness around his heart.

19

IN THE SPRING OF THE NEXT YEAR, AS SOON AS the snow melted and islands of green began to emerge on the moor, a steam shovel was dragged up from Cowdenbeath, eight heavy-footed Clydesdales pulling it the hard way across the High Moor because the shovel was too wide to get through parts of Colliers Walk. The workers knew how the people felt about what they were going to do because they built a head of steam in the boiler even while the horses were pulling it, a dangerous piece of business on roads like those that lead to Pitmungo, and the big shovel was ripping into the Sportin Moor an hour after its arrival, long before the men came up out of the mines.

The women stood outside their houses and saw it, big soft carpets of spring green grass flung into the air, and dripping clumps of black wet earth dumped into a line of waiting wagons below the mouth of the shovel. When the men came out, the area where the shaft was to be sunk was already cleared, all the ancient green cover stripped from the skin of the moor. The Clydesdales were on their way back to bring up the heavy drilling equipment and the tons of planking that would be needed, and the drillers had left in a wagon for Wester Mungo to bed down for the night. What was done was done, and there was nothing to be done about it.

So the ultimate sin had been committed. It had happened, what the people had begun to believe would never happen. They had violated the trust of the moor, they had violated the old sanctity of the grass, they had stolen and then raped the people's moor, and the people stood along the fence not knowing what to do about it, ashamed to look at one another and read their own ineffectiveness in their neighbors' eyes.

Someone should go see Lady Jane, they said, that would do it; she couldn't have known about it, they agreed, or it never would have happened. The Tosh-Mungos took too much money from the miners but they never went back on their word.

But it was nonsense and they knew it. Lady Jane was married to Lord Fyffe now and no one was going to go down to Brumbie Hall to petition his grace to put the grass back on their moor. Many men had worked for Lord Fyffe a good part of their lives and had never even seen the man they toiled for.

Gillon was ashamed to face his sons that night, but he found Sam smiling.

"Well, they've done it, haven't they?" Sam said. "You never believe they'll do these things, and they do, don't they?" He tapped his *Highland Clearances* book. "It's all in here, you have to admire them, you know. They know how to make up their minds. When *they* want something, they go out and get it. They go out and *do* it."

It was as if, now that it had finally happened, some spring that had been wound so tightly in Sam, containing him, had been unsprung and he was freed to be himself. He was positively cheery at tea, eating his sausages and cakes with a genuine appetite.

"Never forget they were bastards, Sam," Gillon said over tea. "Just because they got things done, don't forget they got done some terrible things, disgraceful things."

"Oh, no," Sam said, "that's what I never forget. It's just that they know how to get what they want. We don't; they do. That's why we're down here where we are and they're up there where they are."

"What I'm always trying to teach you," Maggie said. "Get your share."

The drilling crews were good. The men never saw them. They came to work when the day shift was begun and they were gone before the men came out in the evening. It was what they call a day level mine, one where water flowed out of the pit by gravity, not pumped out, and streams of orange acidy mine water ran over the moor and down through the streets and drains of Pitmungo. But beyond that the drilling and shaft-building caused little strain on the town. It was numb to the fact of the mine itself.

"I can tell you one thing," a miner called Beatty vowed. "I shall never set foot down that pit. I shall never mine coal underneath our Sportin Moor. And if they dare bring in any blacklegs, God alone can guess what will happen to them."

He got up a Vow Sheet, he called it, and passed it around the houses and down the rows and almost every miner, except for a few of the very old men, signed the paper.

In summer they shut down the Little Crafty mine, the mine down below the big Lady Jane No. 2 mine, because it was drawing too much water. For every ton of coal mined they used half a ton to keep the pumps and ventilators going. The mine provided work for a hundred and fifty miners but it made very little money, and on the Sunday before Lord Fyffe No. 1 was due to open on the Sportin Moor they stopped the pumps and let Little Crafty drown. On Monday morning, a hundred and forty-eight of the hundred and fifty miners from the Little Crafty had signed on to howk coal in the Lord Fyffe. When they came up that night they were apologetic, remembering the Vow Sheet, and ecstatic at the same time. The coal was six feet high in the Lord Fyffe seam and a man could load his tubs and make a good day's wage without even bending his back. One of the two men who didn't sign on was Wattie Chisholm, the parade marshal and after seventy years in the pits too old to go down a new mine, and the other was Walter Bone. Bone was too old to go back on principle.

It was a good mine. Long before winter three shifts were working the pit around the clock. The coal was high and good—Six Foot Pitmungo Parrot, rich in oil and low in ash. By the end of summer a slag pile rose where the cricket pitch had stood—all the refuse, the slate and gob from the new mine, climbing at a startling rate. In a few months the top of the slag pile had blocked the view of lower Pitmungo from the people on Moncrieff Lane. Where the sun had once shone from early morning it was now shadow until afternoon when it moved around behind the houses. A film of rock and coal dust came in the windows and under the doors of Moncrieff and by autumn it had moved up to Tosh-Mungo Terrace. But a little taste of coal dust in the food was acceptable as long as there was food on the table. The Pitmungo miners were eating meat three times a week.

Along with the slag pile, a second mountain rose, this one the coal bing. They were bringing coal out faster than they could prepare it and ship it, and so they piled it on the old quoiting grounds. The mine shaft was in the heart of the football field and the breaker room now buried Sam's beloved rugby field.

Gillon was mortified when Sam shifted from the Lady Jane pit to the Lord Fyffe when a miner got hurt.

"It's not my business, I know, but I never thought it of you," Gillon said.

"Wait until you see the pay packet he brings home," Maggie said, "and you won't feel so bad about it."

The men in the other pits were on a waiting list to get into the Lord Fyffe.

"The coal's there, the job's there, the mine's working with or without me, why the hell shouldn't I go down and get something out of it?"

His brothers studied their soup. They were embarrassed for Sam. Walter Bone was furious with him. He came all the way down the Terrace to say so. "Don't bother to come down to my house ever again," Mr. Bone said. "Turncoats the likes of you we can do without."

It had become a habit of Sam's to visit with his sister Sarah and Sandy Bone.

"When they offer me six feet of Parrot coal to mine, I'll take six feet," Sam said.

"Aye," Ian said. "Lucky devil."

"Lord Fyffe is a fact of life, Daddie," Andy said.

"You, too?" his father said.

"Oh, no, I wouldn't go down," Andrew said. "I was merely stating a fact. The moor is dead and the mine is alive."

Gillon left the table and went outside and looked down at the black fence and the new tipple. All that greenness gone. Was the pull of the pay packet that strong, to turn even a person like Sam around? Ian would go down. Andy would finally find an excuse to go down. A new blackness seemed to have come into their lives ever since the fence was built and the moor breached. Coal corrupts, Gillon thought; the very nature of the act, ripping open the earth, disemboweling it, stripping its black veins. Coal corrupts and mining coal corrupts absolutely.

I am sick to death I ever came to this place, Gillon thought.

20

SEVERAL MONTHS BEFORE CHRISTMAS, WHEN
the price of coal traditionally began to rise, the price of coal
began to drop. No one knew why.

"It's nothing to worry about," Walter Bone told them. "I'm not
defending the Company, I'm stating fact. It used to go that way
all the time—the teeter-totter, we've seen it all before."

But this time it didn't come up. The first snow flurries in late
October and early November came and the price of coal kept
falling.

"When the price goes down far enough, the sales begin to go
up. People who don't even need it buy it because the price is so low.
It means less gold for the masters and more work for the men."

But no one bought and no one knew why. Mr. Brothcock went
down to Edinburgh to find the reason why and no one knew.
It was the same all over West Fife. Coal was falling into the sea
off St. Andrew's wharf.

It was ironic, Gillon thought, just when the Pitmungo Coal
and Iron was mining more good coal than ever before, it was
selling less.

"It makes one almost believe in God," Gillon said, "in a sense
of justice."

"Whatever it is, it serves the bastards right," Jem said.

"It may serve them right," Andrew said, "but we're the ones
who are going to hurt."

The winter came on hard. The winds from the north as steady
and cold as ever, the High Moor bleak, clouds dark, houses wind-
whipped and chill, snows deep. Every hard storm was warming
for the Pitmungo miners.

"Now the bastards *have* to buy," the men would say, and wait.

"I have no brief for the Company, as you know," Mr. Bone said, "but there is a balance to things. No one still has last year's coal and there is cheap coal available. People either buy it or they freeze. I'm talking God's sense and order now. If there is coal in the ground and people need coal, God will see to it that men will mine it."

When no one bought it, Lord Fyffe finally went down to Cowdenbeath and go the Flying Scotsman at Edinburgh and went to London to find the reason why. The men felt better then. Old Fyffe would find out.

"He may be a bastard, and he is one, but he's a smart old bastard, man."

He found out nothing.

When he came back he told Mr. Brothcock to cut back on production until the laggard buyers began to buy, and then he cut the price of his coal two pennies the ton just to get the buyers to come through the door.

When a coal company lowers its prices there are several things it can do. It can increase efficiency to bring out more coal at the same cost. It can invest money in new equipment to mine more coal at the same cost. It can cut the profit it takes from its coal. Or it can cut the money it pays its miners to mine the coal. The easiest of these is the last. Sometime in November the men began being paid two pennies less for each ton of coal they mined.

"Think of it this way," Mr. Brothcock shouted to them from the tipple, when he announced the new pay scale. "Business is sick but the Company must go on or we are nothing. The Company has given us work, now we must give back our due. Think of it this way. If a man is sick, well, that is sad but we all go on. But if the Company is sick, then we all are sick. If the Company goes hungry, then we all go hungry. If the Company dies . . . well, I would rather not go into that."

He let that soak in, while the wind whistled through their wet work clothes.

"The Company has stood by you, now this is your chance to stick by your Company. Lord Fyffe expects every man to do his duty. Thank you. Good luck. God bless."

A few of the very old miners said, "Amen."

"And what about Lord Fyffe? Did they cut his pay packet, too?" a young voice shouted.

"Get that man's name," Mr. Brothcock said.

Two pennies a ton. It wasn't much when you got down to it. A few pints less here and there, no beef in the beef broth, no jelly with the scones, no butter with the tatties, just shift things around a bit.

But it was much in the Cameron house; the cut would go deeper, because nothing must be allowed to touch the flow of siller to the kist. The Cameron Pot came first, the Camerons' welfare second, and the stomach third, and almost everything else was out. Because now there was not only the obligation to the kist; there were the quarterly payments to Mr. Ogilvie to be met.

Sixteen pennies a day—and the loss would be more than that, Maggie knew—meant four fewer pounds of bread on the table. If they cut the children workers, the putters and fillers and pit-head girls like Emily, which Maggie knew they would do, the real loss of income would be, at the least, close to eighteen pence a day, nine shillings a week, four hundred and sixty-eight shillings a year if they worked steadily.

Over twenty pounds a year.

None of them had seen it that way, but there it was for them, the breaking point, the safety margin that made it possible for them to live on Tosh-Mungo Terrace, the margin that made the difference between being a Doonie and an Uppie, the difference between getting out of Pitmungo and being buried there in the coal for eternity. They went back to tatties and dab at the stool and then to tatties and point, a trick Maggie had learned from her parents in hard times. Bowls of spuds were placed in the middle of the table next to a piece of meat or fish. With each bite of the potato you looked at the meat and it was amazing, just as her father had told her, how after a time you came to believe you ate the meat along with the potatoes. So despite the cuts, the kist was served. And despite the cuts, the quarterly option payment was sent down to Cowdenbeath to Mr. Ogilvie. He never knew what denial and what privation, what hunger, went to him with those worn, coal-blackened pound notes. Mr. Ogilvie always had to wash his hands after getting the Cameron payment.

It was the mountain of coal outside Lord Fyffe No. 1 that finally forced the first major break. When the top of the coal bing reached the foot of Tosh-Mungo Terrace, they began letting miners go, the old miners first, no matter how long their service or how loyal they had been. After them went the known heavy drinkers, the ones who from time to time on Monday mornings, when a storm was hammering the side of their homes, discovered they were sick and couldn't make it to the pit. After them went the malcontents and complainers, who were not among the most productive miners. Rob Roy was one of them. But although the Camerons were on the "victimization" list, they also were among the best miners in Pitmungo. The efficiency program would begin with men. Fewer men would produce the same amount of coal, or even more, than the larger number of miners had before them.

The days of the squeeze began. Sometime in November, the men were ordered to load their coal tubs to the hilt, up to the top of the sideboards, to the point of overflowing. When the tubs arrived at the weigh station a heavy iron rod was swept across the top of the tub and all the coal that fell down, all the coal that had been piled up above the sideboards, was to belong to the Coal and Iron Company. It was, Mr. Brothcock said, a

voluntary gift from the men to the master. None of the sur-
vivors said a word. They filled their tubs to the brim and made
their daily gifts. They called it "Lord Fyffe's hump."

After the "hump" came "Lord Fyffe's clock." A new cut in
the payment for coal was required, Brothcock announced, to
keep the Company healthy, but so no man's take-home pay would
be cut, the Company had—generously, he said; those were the
superintendent's words—agreed to extend the hours of the shift
from ten hours a day to twelve. On the way out of the pit in the
evening, in the dark—it was entirely voluntary—those men who
wanted to could stop on the way home and help, for an hour
or so, to move the coal they had mined that day a little further
up the bing or to load it in the last of the available coal hutches. It
was heartwarming, Mr. Brothcock was able to report, how many
of the men, tired as they were, volunteered for work on the
bing.

Every one of them, in fact.

Which must have been gratifying to the people in Brumbie
Hall, Mr. Selkirk said. All those barrels of ale being paid for at
last. It was a gratifying example of how the classes could work
together when they had respect for one another. It was enough,
Mr. Selkirk said, to make you want to cry.

Gillon was the first in the family to show the effects
of the work and the diet. They were making their own soap
again, as they had years before, to save a few pennies. It was
not very good soap but it was strong and it worked and it
was cheap. They made it a hundred pounds at a time, six
pounds of potash and a quarter of a pound of resin bought at
the Pluck Me, and four pounds of lard bought from one of the
nearby pig farms. They stirred it all together and let the mess
react on itself for five or six days and then the mixture was
poured into a ten-gallon cask of warm water and stirred twice

a day. It was brutal work, the stirring, but after only ten days of it you had a hundred pounds of soap. The trouble with the soap was that it tended to stick and when Gillon stood up in his tub after work one day, the soap clinging to his bones gave him the look of a Halloween skeleton. He was afraid to look down at himself.

"Christ almighty, look at me," he said. "I can't go on this way. They're killing me."

"Och, hard-time ribs," Maggie said. "You're getting old; you can't expect to go along like the lads."

Getting old! It wasn't that. It was the diet: porridge and water, potatoes and salt, thin tea with no sugar; who could expect a man to work thirteen hours a day on that and look sonsie? But even granting that, when Gillon looked in the glass after the tub, he saw how deeply his eyes had sunk into the hollows of his cheeks and how the muscles in his neck were standing out like rawhide. He looked, he thought, sixty-five years old, and here he was only one or two over forty, he wasn't exactly sure how many.

That was the terrible irony about it; the harder he worked the closer it brought him to collapse or some form of starvation.

"You're a Highland man and a Highland man always goes on," Maggie said.

Gillon was no longer sure. He wasn't sure he might not end up like the men Henry Selkirk had described, the ones who put down their picks for a wee rest and never got up again, dead from hunger while at work.

That was the thing that hurt most of all if there was any justice left anywhere in the world. To work all week long, six long days a week, and at the end of it to be hungrier than at the start of the week, to be flirting with the outer edge of starvation.

But there was nothing they could do about it then; there was no way to stop the onward rush of the work, because the winter was settling in and Mr. Brothcock had them where he wanted them. His theory of commerce and labor relations was simplicity itself; it was embroidered on a sampler over his roll-top desk in the pay office.

A man must eat, musn't he not?
And a man's children must eat, musn't they didn't?

He had them where he wanted them. Others must have read what Gillon saw in his own face. On Saturday night, when the men crawled up out of the pit to be paid, Mr. Brothcock laid Gillon off.

21

GILLON LAY IN BED AND WATCHED THE OTHERS dress for work. It was getting to them, too, he could see. There was no zest to their movements, everything they did was designed to save energy. He thought it would be good to lie in bed and watch the others go off to work but it wasn't any good. He got up and had breakfast with the boys.

"You should have stayed in bed, Daddie," Sam said; "there's no point in getting up."

"There's no point in lying there either."

That was it, he thought, the thing that frightened him. There was no point.

As for food, there was oatmeal, at least, good and hot, with water and a pish of sugar.

"Can you spare that?" Sam said. "Can you really?"

"No," his mother said.

"Do you know what I'd like, right now? Three big thick blubbering slabs of bacon on my plate. That would see me through the morn," Sam said. "Not too well done, you see. A lot of fat oozing and drooling on the plate."

"Aye, with bread to slop it up," Emily said.. She was a thin little girl with a mine rat's appetite. After an afternoon working around the pit, she could come home and eat a pound of bread.

"Do you know what I would like right now?" Jemmie said. No one bothered to ask. They all knew.

"Be on a boat to America; that's what I'd like."

Silence. They wouldn't encourage him.

"You wouldn't see an American miner hoping to have three slabs of bacon on his plate. He'd *have* six for breakfast and six for his piece in the pit."

"Is there any more oatmeal?" Sam said. "Just a smick."

"None. The trouble with you is you gobble your food. You want to smushle it, nurse it along a bit, make it go further."

"It is, I am here to say," Sam said, getting up from the table, "a very sad day for Scotland when a working lad can't get a second bowl of oatmeal."

"I suppose you saw the pitprops they brought in Saturday morning?" Andrew said.

"No," Gillon answered.

"Pine. All green pine. Pine to save a penny."

"That's no good. They won't last a year," his father said. "There must be a safety law about that."

Andrew shook his head. He knew the book; he knew the laws.

"No law. Only the coal master's good faith."

"Oh, aye, that's good. That's very good. It isn't his head the goddamn roof is going to fall on," Sam said.

"Language," his mother warned. They were getting out of hand in the hard times; their language was falling apart; they were losing their style and becoming Pitmungo. She saw it in herself.

"The theory being that he is no more interested in seeing his mine cave in than the miner is," Andrew said.

"It's a very nice theory, especially when you're not under the roof."

"Mr. Brothcock says they'll replace them with ash when the coal begins to sell again," Andrew said.

"Yes. I will believe that exactly at the moment I see the new props come in and the old props go out," Sam said. "As of that moment I will become a true believer." He turned to his mother. "I will even begin to believe in God, how does that strike you?"

"If we live that long," Ian said.

"Aye, of course. In the faint chance we live that long."

There were doors closing on the lane and hobnails scraping against cobblestones.

"Let's go," Sam said. "Let's go the now. Mr. Brothcock does not choose to wait."

"Mr. Brothcock is in bed."

"Fool. You think he'd miss the looks on the faces of the men seeing the pine props being carried in? Worth an admission price."

They strapped on their pit gear, and without saying goodbye to their father, most likely forgetting that he wouldn't be coming with them this day, his having gone with them every day of their working lives, they jostled their black way through the door and out into the lane heading down for Colliers Walk and the Lord Fyffe No. 1 pit on the moor. Gillon could not remember feeling so alone.

"Where are you going?" Maggie said.

"I don't know."

"I thought you would stay here and fix some things around the house."

"No."

He wouldn't descend to that. Not yet, not the way the old men did, daundering around the house, trying to make someone believe they were needed.

"The least you can do then is go up the slag pile and cull out some small coal for us."

She was in the doorway with a creel in her hand.

"No."

He felt good saying no to her. Picking coals off the slag pile alongside the old rheumatic women with the out-of-work alcoholic husbands. He hadn't come to that yet.

He went down the lane in the direction the boys had gone, the only way he could think of going, the way he had gone almost every morning, six days a week, fifty-two weeks a year, for more years than he could quickly add up. He never tried to count them. Someone was cooking an egg in butter, and the smell of it made his stomach turn over with the richness of it. He was hungry, he realized, deeply hungry, bone-marrow hungry, but when he had been working he wouldn't allow himself to feel it. Now, with nothing to do, the hunger was out in the open, naked and unashamed. If he knew the person cooking the egg he would ask them for a minch of it, he thought, and knew he was lying. It hadn't come down to that, either.

There were other men his age in the doorways, sitting in the sun out of the wind. He didn't want to join them but he felt a little less alone. All in the same stall together. He was, after all, the last of the men his age to be laid off. That said something. Some of the men he passed and nodded to had been out of work for weeks now, some for months. They lived on church shillings and they didn't starve because they barely moved and they slept hunger away.

There was a strange smell to the town that he couldn't place. He wondered if he only smelled it now because he wasn't dressed in his pit duds, with the breath of the mine all through them.

He went down the Walk and through the gate that led to the mine's work area. There they were, as Andrew said, the new pitprops, white and clean and smelling green in the morning. Pine. Unmistakably pine. He lifted one of the props. The wood was still wet, resin running sticky from the knots, and it was light. On the cold dry days, when the barometer was high and the atmosphere sat heavily on the surface, you would be certain to hear them groaning and even breaking under the pressure. A splinter from one of them might pierce you like a wooden lance. He sensed someone standing behind him.

"Pine." It was Mr. Brothcock.

"Aye."

"Good, sturdy Scotch pine."

He wanted to say something to the superintendent, something subtle but pointed; nothing came to him. It had to be correctly said because he had no right to get the boys in trouble.

"Pine makes fine pitprops."

"Aye," Gillon heard himself say. Why had that come out of his mouth? He pitched the pitprop back on the pile and it thudded there, wet and green. *That* was comment.

"Some of the men don't like them," Brothcock said.

"Ah? Well, maybe . . ."

"But then some of the men will gurnn if you give them a roast beef for dinner."

He waited and finally Gillon said aye, and the super walked on down to the pay office.

He couldn't move from the pile of props for several minutes, ashamed of himself, those "aye's" leaping to his tongue like a dog's tail before his food bowl. He might just as well have crawled across the work area on his hands and knees. At last he found courage to move, and he went on through the work area, past the winding room by the down-shaft, where cages were already bringing coal steaming up from underground even before the last of the men had been taken down. He missed the smell of the mine and the wet coal. He went down past the tipple and the breaker shed, where Emily would be sorting the slate and gob from the clean coal and where the breaker itself, shifting and shaking the coals like rocks in a bucket until they found their right sizes, was working with a deafening roar. Please don't let her smash a hand in there, he thought, and walked on, forgetting her—out of sight, out of mind. She was too quick and clever to lose a hand.

He would go down, now that he was a man with time, and discuss Henry George, who he was finding more intelligent and readable than Karl Marx, with Mr. Selkirk. The Reading Room was closed; Mr. Selkirk was nowhere in sight. That would mean Mr. Selkirk had carried on a long dialogue between himself and his bottle. It was Selkirk's fate to find society's salvation in the bottom of a bottle at night only to find that it had slipped away in the morning.

He went back up then, for the first time in his life, and sat with the old men and the injured and out-of-work. It was depressing to be there. Someone was telling the story of how Jemmie Mowat had snuck over to Easter Mungo the night before the Easter Mungo vegetable show, got drunk, stole a giant cabbage, and then had the nerve to enter it in the Pitmungo fair. He won the blue ribbon, but then the owner of the cabbage called the police. When they arrived at Mowat's there was a blue ribbon over the mantel and a green odor of cabbage in the house.

"Nothing I can do," the constable said. "No cabbage, no case."

"How is that?" the man from Easter Mungo asked.

"No body, no crime," the constable said. "The writ of habeas cabbage."

What got Gillon was the way the gaffers each added a line in rote, as if it were liturgy or some reading from *The Book of Common Prayer*. It was depressing. Maybe you got to like it after a while. Gillon had heard the story twenty times before. He left the old men when they started on the story of how Alex Chisholm came home from America with a bagful of siller and drank himself to death the first night in Pitmungo.

He went back up Colliers Walk. Eight o'clock in the morning, the rest of the day stretching out ahead of him like a glimpse of eternity. There wouldn't even be an excuse to take a tub since he hadn't been down pit. He had to stop then and let out a laugh, the explosive laugh that erupts when one discovers a truth.

He missed the mine. He found he loved the deep black mine; he missed the sounds, the drills biting into the coal face, the squeak and rattle of the wheels of the coal tubs, the steady chunking of some good miner's pick in a nearby stall winning the coal; the noises and sometimes the silence, the lonely lights like another boat at sea bobbing along a roadway, the wink, the nod as he passed. He missed the sweat, and he missed the smell of the mine, that indescribable stink of life persisting even when mingled with death. He missed the darkness and the depth: three thousand feet down into the earth, four miles into the backside of a mountain; that *was* something. He missed the sense of danger, of stopping—wait, now, some new sound down the roadway, rumbling perhaps, the pitprops crying from some new pressure, a shift in the earth above. He realized, oddly, that he missed the danger because of the way it brought the men together:

"Did you hear something?"

"Aye, it's nothing. We're all right."

"Aye, we're all right the now," and then the eyes locking on each other, each man telling the other it was going to be all right because they were there with each other and so nothing too bad could happen.

So he laughed out loud on Colliers Walk and made heads turn. The unthinkable had been thought and he felt better then.

He passed the Pluck Me and then went back. He almost never went into the Company store. Their prices angered him and he made the children do the buying.

"Gillon Cameron," the clerk, a boy, said. They would never call a miner mister. "I will be damned."

He reached for the Grab Me book, the ledger in which the miner's purchases were put down, the total of which was extracted at the end of every fortnight, and put the book back.

"You're the only family in Pitmungo without an account, did you know that?"

"Aye, of course."

"Only one. How do you do it?"

Gillon shrugged. "We don't like to pay the interest on the unpaid bills."

"You buy things in other towns and other stores is how you do it. You go up and buy things on the farms, don't tell me other." He wagged a finger and winked. "I don't care. It's all tushloch to me. I only work here. But Mr. Brothcock knows all about it. What do you want?"

"An egg. One egg."

"*One* egg? One. You came all the way down *here* from Uppietoon for one egg?" He ran into a back room to tell his mother, who came out to look at Gillon. The boy was what they call a bullfart in Pitmungo, a fat and prissy person not fit for the pit but bright enough to avoid it.

"How would you like your egg, Cameron? A large egg, a medium egg, a small egg? A pullet egg, a pigeon egg, a duck egg? Brown, Cameron, or white—"

Gillon grabbed the boy by his shirt front.

"Give me one egg, now, or there will be egg all over your round pink grunzie."

He wasn't given to things like that; it was a long time since he had done anything like it, and it left him feeling pleased with himself, the way he had felt when he had said no to Maggie earlier that morning. The boy gave him a large brown egg for a ha'penny.

It was nice to feel it in his pocket, cold at first and then warm, and nice to think what was hidden inside it for him.

He crossed what once was the Sportin Moor, keeping away from the new mine, and came up to Tosh-Mungo Terrace thinking about the ideal way to eat his egg. There was the smell again, fishy, briny, something he knew and couldn't place. He didn't like the smell but it made him aware of his hunger again, such was the deepness of it.

Boiled brought out the very essence of an egg, but an omelet, with a touch of milk and a smidge of cheese, while obscuring the ultimate egginess of an egg, could seem like three eggs. It was no easy decision to reach. Walter Bone was sitting on the overlook at the lip of the Terrace. He had aged since they had laid him off; he knew he was never going back. They hadn't laid him off; they had let him go.

"So they got to you too, at last," Walter said. He couldn't help smiling a very little bit. Having a man as old as Gillon continue to work was an affront to all of them. "Well, you lasted a long time, Gillon, and that's a credit to you."

Generous man, Walter Bone, Gillon thought; a big man. They looked down on Moncrieff Lane below and the mine, down on the Doonie rows and the old mines beyond them. Something was wrong about Pitmungo, something beyond the smell.

"No smoke," Gillon said. "There's hardly no smoke."

"There's hardly no work."

"No smoke from the houses."

"No cooking in them."

"They could be keeping warm. More warmth, less food."

"They have no coal."

"But they could scrounge it off the slag pile."

"They don't have the energy for it. Lie in bed all day, you don't need much at night. Sleep your hunger away."

"Aye."

"Like the bears in winter."

"Aye."

The bullwheel over the tipple spun, winding up a few tubs of coal. Very few men in the pit now, just pit crews keeping corporal's guard. His boys down there, among the last. His heart went out to them. Good boys down there, good hard-working boys, not getting paid what they were earning. Turning into men when they still should be boys. He felt the solid, reassuring warmth of the large brown egg in his pocket and experienced a moment of guilt. His boys should have an egg, some sick child down the hill could use the egg right now.

"Do you notice the smell? What is the smell?" Gillon asked.

"Are you joking me? Are you blind then? Have you miner's eye?"

"That I have, but blind I'm not."

The old miner was pointing down to the roofs on Moncrieff Lane.

"There," he said, "there and there. There."

Gillon could not see it.

"The codfish," Walter Bone said. "Dammit, man, can't you see them? Codfish and skate?"

Then he saw them everywhere, once he saw the first one, white boned codfish stretched out on the slate roofs of the row houses, held flat by a stone on the head and a stone on the tail.

Almost every house had a fish or two on the roof. Now that Gillon saw them, the smell was stronger than before. The entire valley stank of drying fish.

"But what is it? What's it all about?"

Walter Bone studied Gillon. After all the years, there was still the Pitmungo fear that someone from the outside might be mocking them. He finally was satisfied.

"Och, you don't know, then?" Gillon shook his head.

"Codfish Christmas."

It meant nothing to Gillon.

"Salt-cod Christmas. When the mines are closed and everyone knows there'll be no geese or kidney pies or ham, the fish men come. Because you've got to have *something* for Christmas, don't you?"

"Aye, *something*."

It was different from when the Camerons used to bring the fish. The fish weren't fresh, they were lightly salted down and the fish men ran the risk of selling their catch on credit. A man with geese, for example, who had paid for feed to bring the geese to maturity, couldn't run that risk, and furthermore his geese would still be alive for sale when the mines reopened. But the fish were grabbed out of the sea and the seamen set aside a certain part of their catch and risked them on the miners. It only paid if you caught the fish yourself. To buy barrels of fish, as the Camerons had done, and then sell them on a handshake and a promise, was a recipe for ruin.

The two men went down the lane to look at the fish. They were good-sized cod, and somewhat fresh, some running three or four feet in length, enough for a family Christmas feast. They had been rubbed with sea salt and now were put out on the roofs, away from the rats and cats, to be rizzared and blawn—dried in the sun and the wind. The great debate was whether to bring the fish in at night or let them freeze and thaw by day. Mr. Bone was for freezing and thawing because it activated the juices in the tissues.

"But what difference?" he said. "When you have salt-cod Christmas, everyone is so hungry that everything tastes fine. Hunger is the best recipe; hunger is the best sauce."

There was nothing to say to that but aye, and rub the egg in his pocket. He had never felt more hungry in his life. There was a madness of hunger on him.

In his house he put his egg on the table.

"I want this egg cooked four minutes in boiling water. I want a pinch of salt and a smidge of butter and I want two fresh shaves of bread."

"Oh, aye, sir." Maggie wasn't used to being ordered. "Where did you get the egg?"

"Bought it."

"Waste. Where?"

"Pluck Me."

"Pure waste. I suppose they charged ha'penny for it?" She put the water on to boil. "One egg. They must have laughed at you."

"They didn't laugh long, I'll tell you that," Gillon said. She was being very casual with that egg, he thought, plopping it into the water like a common spud.

"That's an egg there," he called to her. He had his heart set on this one egg being perfect. The glands along his jaw were sharp for it. It was going to sting on the first bite. "Do you have a timer?"

"I know four minutes when four minutes have passed," Maggie said. "Who did you cow down there, the little fat one?"

Gillon nodded.

"Good Lord, *I* could ding him," she said. There went the little triumph of the morning.

"I wish you had a timer."

"Well, tell us. How did it feel being out of pit, stravaigin around the town like a toff?"

"Fine. Fine, indeed. Fitting for a man of my age."

She laughed at him. "Planning to retire, is it?"

"Thinking of it."

"I'd say another twenty years would about see you through. There are men here with sixty years in the mines." The thought of it, the twenty years, the sixty years, depressed him. It was no way for an entire life to be spent, no matter how desperate the circumstances.

"Four minutes *surely* is up, Miss."

She paid no attention to him.

"And how did you waste your time? Down with Selkirk cracking about Communism I would guess."

"'Spend your time,' is the expression. Speaking of time . . ."

"Camerons don't spend anything. We don't waste, either."

"And we don't talk about Communism, we talk about the social order. The redistribution of the wealth."

"You talk about the overthrow of the order, is that right?"

"Exactly right."

"Then that's Communism."

"Four minutes," Gillon said sharply. "Four is up." She tapped the egg and let it boil on.

"The way to beat the order is to beat it at its own game," Maggie said. "The way we're doing."

Gillon looked at her.

"We are?" he said sarcastically. "Me sitting here making a fool over myself for one egg and you tell me we're winning."

"Aye. We're winning."

She took the egg out of the boiling water with her bare hand. He had always admired the way she could shift coals around in the fire with her bare hand. "Doesn't it hurt?" he had asked her once. "Of course it hurts. What does that matter?" He never asked about it again.

She sliced off the tip and scooped out the egg so that it was almost intact. She buttered the quivering white sides and spreckled them with salt and then stood by the table waiting, as was the way in Pitmungo. The egg was perfect.

"Why do you deserve an egg when the others have none?"

His spoon, which had been about to penetrate into the sun of the egg, the core of its eggy universe, stopped.

"Because I am hungry," Gillon said. "Because I am a terribly hungry man. Because I *need* this egg."

"And you think they're not?"

I am not going to let her spoil this treat, he promised himself.

The spoon split the egg, and the golden protein spilled across the bottom of the bowl as if it couldn't contain itself. She had warmed the bowl and slavered the bread with pit butter and he joined the two together, hot egg and good bread, and ate. He licked the bowl like a dog. The last of the yolk with a few crumbs was best.

"Feel better?"

"Yes, much better. I had to have that." He turned on her. "No I don't and you know it. My gut feels good but I feel rotten, like I stole something."

Maggie put a hand on his shoulder.

"All right, I understand," she said. "I'm glad you had that egg."

"Why couldn't you say so then and make it easy for me?"

She shrugged her shoulders and picked up his plate and turned away from him.

"I don't know. We just don't seem to do that."

"And you never taught the children."

"How could I if I didn't know how?" It was his turn to put a hand around her shoulder but something wouldn't let him do it. He wasn't any better than she was, Gillon thought, he just masked it better. He watched her wash the plate and was glad for that—he wanted no traces of his feast left when the boys came up from the pit. They would be having their shaves of bread and cold tea down in the pit right then. He stood in the doorway.

"How are we winning?"

"We are winning."

"How, goddamn it!" he shouted. "You say we mine coal but we're not miners, and we keep on mining coal; that's all I know, we keep mining coal. When does *that* stop?"

"I don't know."

"You say we have this marvelous plan, this great plan that's going to put us ahead of all the rest. When does that start?"

"Close the door. Come in here and move the bed."

Together they moved the bed and lifted up the stone and took up the kist from where it lay buried. With the key on the chain around her neck she opened the strongbox. It was three-quarters filled with shillings and crowns and notes and pounds.

"It is a lot of money," Gillon finally said.

"It is a very lot of money."

"Why didn't you let us know?"

"Because I was afraid you might slack off."

"The boys are hungry."

"But no more so than the other boys still mining. I have an option to buy a business and it's going to take all the money we have. We can't quit now, we can't go back."

They buried the kist in its hole. It was ironic, Gillon thought; by now the major part of his life spent—lost, wasted underground —to become a property owner, a man of capital, and all he wanted to do was go down—now that he felt sure Selkirk was up and sober—go down and discuss Henry George on the dissolution of property. How deeply fraudulent can a man finally be?

"And now, to make up for the egg, why don't you go up to the slag pile and cull us a creel of coal?"

Gillon picked up the basket and slung it over one shoulder, feeling like a child. Once outside, the smell of the fish reached him and he came back in.

"Why don't we have a fish on the roof like everyone else?"

"Because we don't want one; we don't need one."

"Everyone else seems to need a codfish."

"We don't."

"So we'll have nothing for our Christmas, then." It was a challenge.

"Aye. Camerons don't need things other people need."

22 THE SLOPES OF THE SLAG PILE WERE DOTTED with children and a few laid-off pithead girls and old men and women. Down along the rows it was still but up on the pile wind blew the coal dust back and forth so that at times people were hidden in it. He would need his tub after all. Some of the children and women were barefooted because the ragged chunks of gob ripped leather, and feet that time of year were cheaper. One woman carried a stick which she used to balance herself on the hill and also to strike at anyone invading her territory. When she swung it she snarled like a wild dog. Every time Gillon found a chunk of coal hidden among the mine debris he felt a surge of satisfaction at wresting it out of the slate and dropping it over his shoulder into the creel. When the basket was half filled it got to be hard work and he put the basket down. They all looked like animals of some sort, he thought. Across from the slag pile was the mountain of coal, unguarded, and no one took a piece of it. It was amazing how good people were, he thought, or how afraid. When he picked up the creel it pained him but he thought of those women who carried the hundredweight creels up five and six

long ladders twenty times a day and kept going. They became true beasts, Mr. Selkirk said, some of them growing so lopsided, their legs so enormous, their hair so matted from sweat and coal dust, that it was hard to tell they were people.

He was hungry again. Maybe Maggie was right about it, it was better to deny and keep on denying oneself than give in and start the whole process of going without again. An old woman came sliding and slipping down the slag pile, trying to control a wooden sled filled with coal. It was threatening to run away from her or drag her down the pile with it.

"Oh, God. Give me that thing," Gillon said, and he realized from the look on her face that she thought he meant to steal it.

"Get away from me!" she shouted. "Get away."

"I want to help you," Gillon said, but saw the look in her eyes and stopped. He wanted to hit her. "Go on, get out of here before I do take it, get out of my sight, you make me sick."

He made himself sick. He stopped his culling, ashamed of shouting at the old woman, ashamed at finding himself on the slag pile like a gull outside a fish-packing plant, waiting to live on what was thrown out. It was the level he had come down to. He looked down on the town. Fish were drying on the roofs all over Pitmungo, and the whole town smelled of death and coal dust. To the north he could see Loch Leven and beyond the Loch the Leven Hills, still greened with patches of pines or brown with clusters of ash or oak, all the rest of it white, the moorlands under snow.

There would be deer in there, Gillon knew, in the deer preserves, the deer parks, nesting in the dark silent pines, stripping the bark off the aspens and ash, browsing beneath the oaks and beeches, nuzzling in the snow for acorns and beechnuts, fattening themselves for the hard part of winter to come.

They would be fed; nature looked after its own. A swirl of wind blotted out the hills, and when he wet his lips he tasted the mine again. The balance of things, nature saw to that. When they were hungry, the deer would be fed.

Red meat and sinew, fiber of flesh and rich warm blood. Venison: something enticing about that word, Gillon thought. He wanted meat. That's what his egg had told him. That was what his body was demanding of him.

Every Scotchman worthy of the name of Scot had an inalienable right to meat when his system demanded it. It wasn't a luxury; it was a heritage, a craving bred in his bones. Every Scotchman, as long as the hillsides and moors were crowded with deer, was entitled to at least one roe deer for one dinner in his life. Otherwise, what was the sense for God having born him in Scotland; what was the justice in placing all that meat upon Scottish grass?

This is nothing for a man to be doing, Gillon thought. This is no work for a human being. He lifted his creel and dumped his coals onto the stone, the coal dust from the basket trailing in the wind like the black banner of death. They had seen it, of course, the coal gulls on the slag pile, and now they came toward him, scuttling over the rocks like crabs in a tide pool.

He began to run down the slag pile. He knew what he was going to do, and knowing it, having a purpose again, made him happy.

No salt-cod Christmas for the Camerons. Let all those poor bastards down there have their cod and their skate's wings; the Camerons were going to observe their Christmas the way a Scottish family observes the midwinter festival, from the dark beginning of time—with a haunch of Scottish deer hot and heavy and bloody on the board.

Ran down, and stopped, before getting halfway to the bottom, knowing he was lying. Stopped a few hundred feet from the bottom, away from the gleaners scrabbling for his coal and above the people he could see moiling about in the rows.

Liar. Exactly what his wife had called him. The great Highland romantic, a nice word for a person who can delude himself the way a child can when it wants to. He couldn't poach a deer; he couldn't stalk a deer, shoot a deer; he couldn't snare a deer.

He was sorry now he had dumped the coals. It was all part of the same pattern—the vainglorious act, the romantic gesture. Drop the coals, throw them to the winds, donate them to the little poor people. As if his own house weren't glazed with chill, as if his own family weren't going hungry.

The sun, which had been behind clouds most of the day, came through them suddenly, and Loch Leven to the north, which had been a leaden gray, turned bright blue against the whiteness of the snow that ran down to it. Looking at that water, Gillon realized what a fool he had been.

His heart in the Highlands a-chasing the deer, when all the while there it lay, stretched out before him, the one thing he really knew how to do—how to find and kill a salmon.

The King of Fish: another inalienable right of all Scotsmen— the right to one full-sized salmon on his table if only once before he dies. Let them have their salted cod and wind-blawn skate; the Camerons were going to have a salmon on their table, or he was going to go to jail or die in trying.

Gillon knew where the fish would be—the December fish, the late ones, the last of the big ones coming in from the open sea. The winter salmon.

Even this morning they would be swimming the brine of the Firth of Tay, and down the Tay into the fresh water of the Earn, and from the Earn up the little tributary whose name he didn't know, up its roiling snow-fed waters through the dark glens of the Leven Hills, through a hundred possible pools where they would rest along the way, and up into the lake he was looking at. Gillon's heart clenched at the daring of it.

No one in the family was going to know, that much he decided on. He would go and get his fish and, perhaps for the last time in his life, be the provider for the family. Let Maggie see about her option and Andrew about the leases on the property; let the other boys howk their coal, but this year, the black year, he was going to put the Christmas feast upon the table.

23

THE RITE GILLON WAS REQUIRED TO PERFORM IF he was ever going to have a chance of carrying it off was to de-miner himself, to unblacken himself, to drive the coal miner out of his mind and body, because a miner in salmon country is guilty of poaching merely by being there. Gillon went down the hill to borrow Mr. Selkirk's tub. The librarian was outraged.

"What do you mean, guilty until proved innocent," he said to Gillon, who was heating water.

"That's the way they do it."

"Oh, I wish Karl Marx had known about this. What a little chapter that would have made! Christ, even the people's fish are controlled by the gentry."

Gillon had bought a little brush at the Pluck Me, and a pumice stone to grind the grains of coal dust out of all the crevices and cavities of his body. It was going to take two or three tubs at the least. The top of the first tub became coated with a scum of coal dust that settled on the water like a film on cooling soup. While he scrubbed, Gillon explained the facts of life along the salmon streams.

The essential fact, as Marx would have appreciated, was money. In Scotland, and only there as far as Gillon knew, the rights to the salmon streams, and thus to the fish in them, are owned by the Crown and leased by the Crown to gentle and favored folk. Even people who own land along the streams aren't allowed to fish them.

The second fact was a little more subtle. It had to do with the nature of the fish. The moment the salmon comes in from the salt sea to cold fresh water he ceases to want to eat. This makes it very hard for an angler to kill a fish. Gentlemen with their flies and baits and twenty-foot-long bamboo poles sometimes went years on end without getting a fish, at a cost to them of several hundred pounds at least.

"It serves the silly bastards right," Selkirk said. "Think how many children had to go to work for them to get snubbed by a fish."

But the cold, fresh winter water also makes the big fish sluggish. Tired out from their exhausting and dangerous run from the sea, exhausted by their fight up the white water rushing down on them, they have a tendency to lie in the pools just below rough water and rest, storing up energy for the fight ahead. Some of them were so placid in the evening that Gillon had known a man who could lie by the pools and stroke the throat of his fish. A poacher with a gaff or a grapple or a large net could take one of them as easily as he could lift a wading boot out of the water.

Gillon began his hair wash breaking his second egg of the day, mixing the yolk with borax and warm water, and raising a foamy lather on his head.

"So they're jealous, you see," Gillon said. "They watch who come to their streams."

"Jealous. Christ, they have everything else in the country. Go up there and get a great one, Gillon, and save a good piece for me."

Aye, go up there, Gillon thought, but it wasn't that easy and Mr. Selkirk didn't know the price if a man were caught. Simply to be caught in salmon country with a gaff or a spear meant a fine of five pounds—enough to bring disaster down on a family— and a jail sentence of several months, not to mention a beating, sometimes a savage beating, by the water bailiffs hired by the sportsmen to take care of their fish and the likes of G. Cameron, coal miner. Men's lives had been ruined by going after a salmon sleeping in a pool.

"I don't really know why they do it," Gillon said, as if he weren't going to be doing it himself. "The risk is so great."

He rinsed his hair with vinegar and warm water so that it wouldn't stand up as though it had been plastered, the usual sign that a collier has just washed his hair with laundry soap. The brush and pumice had brought up the color in his face; he had lost the grayness of the morning, and his hair glistened with a soft sheen.

Mr. Selkirk knew why they did.

"Never underestimate the quantity and quality of hunger among the Scottish working class.

"Never underestimate the hunger to get something for nothing, especially from the rich."

It was decided, Selkirk's idea, that Gillon would go north as a bird watcher. That would be his cover, his excuse to be found wandering in salmon country, his passport into forbidden lands. The librarian got down a handbook on the birds of Scotland and while Gillon did his last rinses, the cleanest he had been since the first day he had gone underground twenty years before, Mr. Selkirk read aloud. It was decided that Gillon would be a specialist in the red grouse and the golden eagle, and the librarian read the two chapters over and over in his penetrating voice until Gillon thought he would go crazy. At last he was able to get dressed and go home. The transformation from miner to man had taken the afternoon to perform but it was remarkable.

"My God, look at you. What have you done with yourself?" Maggie said.

"A man wants to look clean."

"You must be in luve. Are you in luve?"

"I am not in love with anyone."

She smiled at him in that knowing manner.

"Remember, Gillon, you're the one who said that."

• • •

He waited until the boys had gone down to the pit and Maggie had gone up to the washhouse, and knew it was time to go. The time was ripe.

"Ripeness is all." Mr. Selkirk's line. A very good line. He put the grapple inside the crown of his hat and took the plaid that would serve as his coat off the bed. A little eccentric but not unheard of, especially among bird watchers, and then took the brass-knobbed walking stick he had borrowed from Walter Bone and stepped out onto Tosh-Mungo Terrace. The sky was clear and the day was cold and hard, a good day for the road. It would be a long day's walk to Loch Leven and he would find a place to stay the night there. If he didn't, he would have to stay in the Loch Leven Inn and the thought of it frightened him more than the thought of water bailiffs. In the morning he would be in the heart of salmon country.

By afternoon he reached the snow line. It was mysterious to Gillon how swiftly it came, a trace of snow here and there and all at once snow coming in over the sides of his shoes. He knew he had made a serious mistake, then, wearing the shoes. He couldn't wear his miner's boots, but he needed something better than shoes. By the time he saw the lights of the Inn down by Loch Leven, his feet were wet and beginning to freeze. The Inn was inviting and the bar was open but Gillon was afraid of it—filled with local people now that the summer people had gone, and they would know. He could hear the whisper go down the bar . . . coal miner . . . and he would be done for. In all probability, this was where the water bailiffs drank. He went on past the Inn and down by the lake's edge, the night wind bitter off it now, and he slipped in among the pines and went down to one of the little summerhouses. There were blankets there in a closet and Gillon ate his four shaves of bread and ate some snow and made a nest on a bed and fell asleep.

• • •

He could see the lake from his bed in the morning, steel gray and cold, like sheet metal. A front had come through from the north in the night and Gillon could hear the wind whumpfing in the pines outside the cottage. He had put his socks inside his shirt to dry, and they had. He put them on and watched the water being driven up onto the ice-coated stones on shore. The wind wouldn't hurt him. It would cover his tracks and keep the water bailiffs close to home and the big salmon in the pools. When the water went below forty degrees, they didn't like to move. He decided to eat an early breakfast at the Inn, but he didn't want to reveal himself by getting there too early. He read the two chapters in his bird book several times over, and then arranged the cottage the way he had found it and went out into the pines and up on the road to the Inn. It was five o'clock in the morning. He looked around the darkened foyer and was deciding it would be best to leave when an old woman standing not three feet away from him spoke to him. His miner's eye—he couldn't see her when he looked right at her.

"We don't expect no one down till seven or eight."

"Aye, well I'll go on then."

"Nay, don't go on. I'll bring you food."

She took him into the empty dining room and put him at a table where he could study the country to the north of him. The snow was blowing on the moor up above the lake. She brought him a sun-dried haddock and two eggs and a slab of bacon and shaves of toasted bread with strong tea and sugar and milk. He knew he shouldn't eat it all, no gentleman would eat that way, but he couldn't control himself. The more he ate the greater his hunger. He had been starving for two months now.

"Is this when you start your day then?" he said to her.

"Och, there is no start or stop. I'm just here when someone wants to eat."

"It's not fair," Gillon said.

"Maybe not but it's the lot of the old."

What was it Selkirk said? "The test of any nation was the way it treated its old." Scotland was failing.

"This isn't the normal breakfast now, is it? Why did you bring all this to me?"

She looked around the dining room and leaned down and whispered in his ear. Gillon turned as red as the sun touching the far edge of the lake.

"Does it show all that much?"

"Only to those that know. My daddie was, my son is down the now." She put her lips near his ear again. "Are you goin' after one?" Gillon nodded. "For the family, for Christmas?" He nodded again. "A big one?"

"Aye, a big one."

"Good, go and get one." She didn't bother to whisper now. "Get a big one and take him hame with you."

"How do I pay for all this?"

"For all what?" she said, and their eyes met.

"God go with you and watch out for Mr. Maccallum."

"God go with you," Gillon said, as if he believed in God. When he got up to go he felt strong for the first time in weeks.

He walked the road, warm in his plaid, until he reached Path of Condie and at Condie he turned down the path to the salmon stream. There were anglers and their gillies coming and going, no one with a fish, a good sign, and no one paid Gillon any attention. His plan was to follow the stream down to where the glens got deeper, the water faster, and the pools more filled with promise.

After that it would be "Setterday's slop," the dangerous time then, the time from Saturday noon until Monday at dawn when it was forbidden to fish for salmon. The streams would be swept clear of anglers and anyone along the water could be considered a potential poacher. God's time they called it, in honor of the upcoming Sabbath, but everyone knew it was designed to control poachers. By the time the laboring men had finished work and gotten out to the salmon streams, there would be no excuse for being there. That was the risk Gillon was going to have to run.

He waited until two o'clock because his plan was not to hide but be conspicuous. The way along the water was well trod and in the steep places gillies had cut steps in the slopes so that the gentlemen in their waders wouldn't slip into the stream. The water grew rougher and at the base of boulders, where dark, sandy-bottomed pools were formed, he knew that fish were resting, their silvery scales almost black in the dark deep water, their tails waving back and forth arrogantly, the assurance of size and self-control. Nothing in these waters could best them, nothing could test them or tempt them. They were beyond their environment.

Gillon knew they were there, he could sense them there, he could smell them there, but he knew he couldn't go down and look for them in the pools; he was going to have to be shown. He found a pool that he felt was perfect and then he waited, pretending that he was strolling, walking up the path and coming down it again, which was where the water bailiff caught him. Gillon never heard him coming.

"Looking for something?" The bailiff touched him on the shoulder with a gaff. Gillon was pleased with himself that he didn't jump, that he didn't even turn and apologize for being there.

"Yes, I'm looking for one of the big ones. They say they're all through here but I've never seen one."

"There's no fishing here. The streams are closed."

Gillon continued to study the stream, and then turned to look at the man and was sorry when he showed surprise. The man was the image of Mr. Drysdale, the water bailiff from Strathnairn. A breed, Gillon thought. A breed created by God for this one purpose in life.

"I don't want to catch one; I want to see one."

"You don't catch a salmon, you kill a salmon."

"But you don't have to kill one to see one, do you? They tell me they sometimes run to thirty pounds."

"Thirty?" He was scoffing at Gillon. "Forty. *Fifty*, man." He was proud of his fish, proud of his stream.

"No?"

"That's fact."

"Have you ever seen one that size? With your own eyes?"

"Seen? I've killed them that size. Fifty-three."

"Fifty-three *pounds*?"

"Fifty-three."

The bailiff was studying Gillon closely. Flint-gray eyes, not conditioned to belief.

"But I don't know where to look for them."

"I told you, the stream is closed."

"Aye, that's why I'm here. They told me to come out when all the anglers are gone. Where do you see them, then, in the quiet pools or in the rapids? I suspect the rapids."

"Who told you?" His voice was as cold as any bailiff's heart.

"The people at Loch Leven Inn. Is it true what they told me, that the female builds a nest for her eggs in the sand? A *nest*?" The bailiff couldn't take his eyes off Gillon's hands.

"You're a workingman."

Gillon felt numb. It was a terrible thrust but he managed to keep talking.

"Aye, like you I suppose. Not like some of these toffs. I have to earn my way."

"And a workingman along a salmon stream is a poacher."

"Poacher?" Gillon forced himself to sound amused. "How can you poach a fish when you can't find one?"

"There are ways, there are ways," the bailiff said, and as soon as he said it Gillon knew that he must have concluded he wasn't one.

"You don't have the broad accent," the bailiff said, telling Gillon the reason for his trust.

"Broad accent? I wouldn't know about that. I'm from the

Highlands, you see. Cromarty Hills. We run a bull farm there. Shorthorns crossed with Galloways. When we work, we *work*. When we're off, we're *off*. That's what I like about it."

He studied Gillon a last time and turned back in the direction he had been coming from.

"I'm Maccallum. Come on, then. You might as well see one properly," the bailiff said, and Gillon followed him down the stream at a rapid pace.

"I'm here studying the birds," Gillon said.

"That's fine, but if you want to see fish you had better close your mouth. Fish have ears."

He had him now, teaching him, investing in him. Two Scotchmen, that was the point; not Sassenach gentlemen with gillies doing their fishing for them.

"Now I'll show you what a Scottish salmon stream is all about."

He showed Gillon hens in a gin-clear pool nudging stones and sand and gravel into a redd where they would lay their eggs, and long, haggard kelts, spent from spawning and spilling their milt all over the redds, and then he came to pools, all of them too deep, where the cocks were at rest, sluggish in the cold water, saving their energy for the rapids ahead of them. They went downstream, always closer to the point where the fish came in from the salt water, down to the pools where the clean fish, the ones that hadn't spawned yet, would be. Before the bailiff pointed it out, Gillon saw the pool.

"Quiet now. Move slow," Maccallum said, and went slowly down to the side of the stream, and there it was, as he knew it would be, lying close to the bottom of the shallow pool, the shadow of its body enormous on the water.

His fish—Gillon's fish. The pool shallow enough, the water clear enough, away from the roiling water just above it.

"Look at him," the bailiff said. Now there wasn't a shadow but the salmon itself, so big in the water that Gillon was startled by it, almost frightened by it.

"A bull," Maccallum said. "A bull salmon. You can go a month and not see one, a year. You can go a lifetime and never kill one."

"He's too beautiful to kill."

"He was born to be killed."

Gillon asked how long he thought the fish would stay there and the bailiff told him that if the weather stayed cold he'd hold there for a day or two at the least. Gillon felt his heart racing. There was his fish, asleep in the pool, waiting. The bailiff suddenly clapped his hands, causing Gillon to jump, but the salmon didn't move.

"This one will stay for days," Maccallum said. "Do you know what I'm going to do? I'm going to come back here Monday morning and kill him before the toffs get on the water."

"I thought the water bailiff wasn't supposed to take a fish." That was an error but the bailiff didn't notice. They were brothers in crime now.

"Once a winter, every once in a while when you see a cock salmon like that cock salmon, we bend a little rule."

He winked at Gillon and so Gillon winked back and said it would be a shame but he would be gone by then.

24 THE WAITING WAS THE HARD PART. A FIRE WAS too dangerous and it was cold, but Gillon made a little shelter of pine boughs up above the pool and waited for darkness and, after darkness, for the water bailiff's last sweep of the stream to make sure no one was trying to take fish by torchlight. At eight o'clock, Gillon estimated, he passed, Maccallum or one of his men, trotting upstream in the dark, and Gillon got up from

his pine bed, stiff from the cold but excited. He had to know if his fish was still in the pool. He began working his way down the steep side of the glen.

He was hungry, he was starving again. It had all begun with giving in to the egg the day before and the big breakfast in the morning. He had broken the chain of denial and was paying for it. There was no doubt it was better to go without than to have and then have not.

He studied the pool for any movement. At times the wind riffled the water and he thought his fish was moving, but then it passed and he waited again until the water stirred—that would be the fish moving in its sleep to balance itself—he waited for the large silver shadow to rise to the surface and break water, but it didn't. He was beginning to be able to see in the darkness again. And then it came up, the silver of its healthiness and cleanliness glinting arrogantly from its curved sides before sinking back down again.

"You're mine," Gillon whispered to it. "Now you belong to me."

He opened his coat and finally managed to make his numb fingers undo the buttons of his shirt. He wanted to move fast now, but his feet, partially frozen, made moving slow and clumsy. He uncoiled the oiled line he had wrapped around his waist and took the grappling hook out of the crown of his hat. By then, he was so cold he couldn't feel the wind on his body. He seemed to have passed through to the other side of coldness and it worried him. When he couldn't thread the grappling hook to the line he went back upstream and did it under water. The line slid through the eye.

He didn't worry about the fish any longer. He had complete confidence in his fish; he knew where it was and what it was doing. It wouldn't help him but it would wait for him. He dragged out the pine pole he had found earlier in the afternoon and worked it over the pool, having to stand in the water to do it—the water burned his feet—and finally he got one end on a boulder on the other side of the pool. Straddling the pole, he edged his way out over the salmon pool, knowing that if he fell from it he would probably drown in the cold black water. His fish was waiting for him. There was a moon now, nearing the full, and stars, and Gillon thought he could see the battered back of the fish, bruised and scarred from its beatings against the stones and weirs and rapids on the way up. This was almost certainly its second spawning, one of the rare salmon to make the journey twice, and that made Gillon feel better. He wouldn't deny his fish its function in life.

"I'll make this quick," Gillon said. "I'll make this as painless as possible."

Stupid to talk to a fish, he thought, but he wanted to, and if he understood the fish the way he felt he did, it would be a calming thing to do. He dropped in the line and the grappling hook hung before the salmon's eyes. Gillon knew the fish wouldn't take the hook, the hook must take the fish, and he eased the hook along the silvery head of the fish, a barb almost touching the salmon's eye at one time, until the grapple was actually resting on the gill cover of the fish. Although he was trembling now with cold and excitement, he let it slide down with enormous care until the hooks were under the gill flap; then he ripped.

He must have hurt it a great deal; the barbs must have raked the scales of the fish and even the tissue itself. The fish leaped and then went to the bottom of the pool and stayed there, a blackness of shadow to be seen moving back and forth in pain or anger, rubbing its head against the edge of a stone, trying, Gillon thought, to soothe the hurt or scrape off the lice it had accumulated on its gills in the ocean. When he put the grapple back in the water the fish flicked its tail and went to the far part of the pool. The grapple wasn't going to work. He tried it once more, giving it the Ballyshannon waggle, jiggling it in front of the fish's eyes in hopes it would finally get furious and snap at it, but salmon have more patience than men. A stream of bubbles rose to the surface. The fish, Gillon was certain, was spitting at him, and in a perverse way he was proud of it.

The fish was safe for him; that much he knew now. It wasn't going to accept his grapple, but it wasn't going to run—not a winter salmon in those icy waters. He had the fish but the fish had him, both of them trapped by desire, the fish's to continue upstream and spawn, Gillon's to kill. The question now was how. He thought of trying to drop something on it, to smash it with a heavy rock, but the fish had gone to a far part of his room, as Gillon had come to think of it, to sulk, and a rock would only waver its way down.

But then the word "room" seized him and he experienced a surge of exhilaration. Just as any good miner knew how to seal off one room from another room, or part of a room from another part, in case of fire or flood in the pit, Gillon could seal off part of the pool by making a brattice of rocks and clay, using stone the way he did when packing roof pillars to keep the mine roof from falling in.

It was all so clear that it made him laugh aloud at the rightness of things. Because he was a hungry miner he was here to steal a fish, and the reason he would steal his fish when others would fail was because he was a hungry miner. He would make his brattice and he would pen his salmon in it and he would do it in wet and darkness because for the better part of his life he had been working in wet and darkness this glen had never known.

It would be best, he reasoned, to work in all his clothes and dry them in front of a fire later. He would have to risk that, a fire at three or four in the morning, because he was never going to be able to carry his fish over the top of the glen and out of there in that snow and cold unless everything on him was dry. Neither he nor his fish would ever make it home.

He began building the first of his brattices, standing in water above his knees. He had hands for stone, an instinct for it, knowing even in the darkness where to reach for the next right one. At making a pack to support a mine roof, Gillon was considered the best in Lady Jane No. 2. And since the stones he found were mainly flat, the work of ages of water, the packing went swiftly. He could work that way for hours, bent over double, working from the waist and from the butt, and his little restraining dam rose and was finished without his having to stop. Only a pit jock could do that, Gillon thought. Now the salmon could no longer retreat to the deeper, darker part of the pool. The hemming in of his great fish was begun.

The salmon could, if it wanted, go forward, but Gillon had gambled that it wasn't ready to go that way yet. And it would not go back, that being against every natural pull in its migrating body. The pain in his feet had begun again and Gillon didn't know if that was a good sign or a bad one. He wanted to get out of the stream and start his fire but was afraid to. It would be the egg all over again. Better to learn to live with his pain. The water had not begun to turn to ice; it must be about forty degrees, Gillon thought, and his feet wouldn't freeze in forty degrees, not if the rest of his body was out of the water. As long as the water ran, his blood would flow and he began the second brattice.

He had no idea what time it was when he finished the second wall and came out of the water. Through the tops of the pines he could see stars and the moon, which would help swallow the glare of the fire he would need to start.

There were three walls now, the boulders in front of the fish and a wall on each side of him. He could try the fish now, assuming that it wouldn't go back, or he could build one more brattice, locking it in the pool. He went back into the water and began to build again. In perhaps an hour the pen was built, and the time for killing had come.

The water in the pool was three feet deep, too deep for Gillon to hurt the fish with rocks or to club it with his brass-knobbed walking stick. Now was the time to start his fire, a little one, a tempting one at the edge of the pool, because the salmon was like the Druid in its way, in love with the fire and the sun, helplessly drawn to them. He lit the fire and he waited, and when his fish's silvery head suddenly split the surface, he struck.

He thought he hit it, he was sure he had, but the head dipped under and the fish flicked away. He slashed at the water but it was no good. He dropped a heavy stone in the pool and the salmon let it brush its flank.

"Arrogant bastard!" Gillon shouted.

He was angry now, because he didn't want to face the reality of what he was going to have to do. The night was running out on him. If he wanted his salmon, he was going to have to go in after it.

He had heard of it when he was young, the wrestling of the fish. The initiation to manhood in the west of Scotland along the Highland shores, the boys being sent into the tide pools to kill their first salmon with their hands or a knife. But the water would be warm then and the pool shallow and the fish not as savage as a salmon on its drive to reproduce itself. He felt sorry for what he was going to do—for himself, but as much for his fish. He knew what it had endured to come this far—the years in the North Atlantic on the never-ending run from the porpoises and seals, sea lions and sharks, and finally the run for home, hundreds of ocean miles, then up the rushing rivers and snow-fed streams to here, to this pool, waiting its fate at the hands of Gillon Cameron, miner and poacher.

He climbed over a brattice and stood in the back of the pool. The fish made no move at all. He took a step and moved the fish forward, and then another, herding the fish against the boulders at the head of his pen, the fish finally touching the boulders, its lips touching stone, always facing upstream where its goal lay, and before giving himself a chance to think, Gillon leaped.

The strength of the fish, the force of its effort to get free, was shocking, as shocking as the iciness of the water on Gillon's body. He held the salmon in his arms, thrusting it up against the smooth stone, trying to crush it against the rock while the fish whipped in his arms, bending its body back and forth to spring itself free, and finally it did, with one powerful movement that Gillon couldn't control, and sank back to the bottom of the pool, stunned and possibly hurt.

"I'm sorry," Gillon said.

He leaned against the boulder and let the water run from his shirt and trousers into the pool. I must be mad, Gillon thought. He tried to see himself as he was—in a pool he had made, in a forest in the dead of night, in the dead of winter, in danger of being hurt, in danger of freezing to death, in danger of jail, trying to kill a forty-pound fish with his bare hands, hands that were bleeding, ripped by the fish's bony fins.

He found a stone, a small pointed one. He hadn't wanted to cut his fish or disfigure it but now he knew he would have to.

"I *am* sorry," Gillon said, and dropped again. He got his arms around the fish and tried to lift it up out of the pool, but the dorsal fin was cutting his chest and the fish's tail was beating his thighs. He drove the stone into the back of the fish's head and let it drop back into the water. The fish was at least five feet long.

His salmon was hurt, frantic now, coming out of its cold-induced coma to fight for its life and meet its obligation to create new life. It swam into one brattice, actually hitting the stones with its mouth, and then struck at it with its tail, trying to knock the wall down. It would jump now, Gillon knew.

There was no room to run in the pool and so the jump, when it came, was almost straight up and slow, barely arching, the body of the fish beautiful in that light, all gold and silver from the fire on the shore, and Gillon jammed it with his stone with such force that it fell back down into the pool with almost no resistance. Gillon looked at it lying a little on one side at the bottom.

"Die," he said. "For Christ's sake, die."

It surfaced again, very slowly, and Gillon, not wanting to pound it once more, not sure any longer what he wanted to do, seized the fish in his arms and slipped and went down into the pool, still holding the salmon when it thudded heavily against the stones. He tasted gravel and pebbles and something of salmon —its seed, he realized, the milt being poured out in the water to fertilize unknown eggs, the ritual being played to its end, life being served while death waited. Gillon felt the mouth and slid his hand along the head until he felt a gill and knew he had his fish then. His hand went into the gill until he felt it in the cavity of the mouth and he did have it then, his salmon, and rose, stumbling and trembling from the pool, clambering over the brattice, and carried it out of the stream, through the boulders by the edge and up the slippery bank onto the path. The fish barely moved. It lay in the snow and waited, one eye seeming to follow Gillon. It must know, he thought. He found the walking stick and with one neat quick blow to the back of the head, Gillon killed his salmon.

"I'm sorry," he said. "I am truly sorry."

He went back to the salmon stream and looked at the prison he had built. Without the fish it looked much larger than it had before, like a window naked of its curtains, and he was astounded at the work he had done. It had been his plan to break down the brattices so the water bailiff would never know what had taken place but now he wanted him to know. He wanted him to be astounded, too, and it occurred to him that the story of the miner—because sooner or later by the packing of the stone they would discover it was a miner who had done the work—would enter the legend of the stream and be told for all the years he would be alive, and after.

25

BEFORE THE FISH FROZE HE THREADED HIS twine through the gills and bent the fish in a bow, tying the tail to the head so that he could carry it on his stick, then fed the fire and crossed the stream and made a trail out of the glen in the way opposite to which he would eventually go. When he got back he took off his clothes and stood in his plaid and dried them, the way he dried his pit duds after working a wet stall. Now that he had his fish, the fire frightened him, the flames seemed enormous and the shadows from the fire danced down the glen for what seemed like miles. But he had no choice; the drying would be done or he would die.

They dried more quickly than he thought they would. The only problem was that his feet had begun to swell while he was standing by the fire, and that alarmed him. When he was dressed again he picked up his fish, amazed at its dead heaviness, and carried it up to the top of the glen, then came back down again with a pine bough and began backing up the path, brushing it as he went. With the help of the wind that would start up the glen in the morning, his footsteps would be covered. He let the fire burn itself out, he couldn't face the water again, and several hours before the sun was due to rise, Gillon turned his face south for Pitmungo.

When he reached the edge of the forest the sun was almost up and before going out onto the open moor he sat down in the last row of trees to study the land out ahead. Off to his left, a half mile away perhaps, a thatched farm lay open to the moor, smoke rising from the chimney, warm-looking and inviting. They would have bacon and eggs there, he knew that, but it was still too close to salmon country to trust, and then his father had once told him that any crofters who lived open like that to the moor winds were bleak, even dangerous people, made that way by the beating of the wind. So he sat then, his back to a pine, and waited to see if anything revealed itself to him and wondered what the dangers were in crossing the moor with the great fish on his back. Who would know it had been taken illegally and who would care, once away from the salmon streams?

He may have slept. He never heard the man come on him, only felt the tap of his boot on his swollen feet. The crofter carried a bundle of wood under one arm and an ax in the other hand.

"All right, let's go with it," he said.

"What do you mean, let's go with it?"

The man motioned toward the fish. A hard, ugly face, the kind, Gillon thought, you expect to find in jail.

"The saumont. I'll have my share the now."

Gillon was more amazed than angry.

"You're trespassing on my property. You stole the fish from Crown waters. Care to know what Maccallum would do to you if I told him where to find you?"

He kept swinging the blade of the ax in front of Gillon's eyes. An act, a bluff, Gillon thought. If his feet weren't so painful he'd call it.

"What do you want?"

"What's its weight? Forty, forty-five pounds. A bull you got. How'd you get him?"

"I went in and got him with my bare hands."

"Fewkin liar."

Which was the moment Gillon understood that no one was ever going to believe his story of the fish, that it would always belong to him alone.

"Ah, well, keep your fewkin secret; I wouldn't tell you how

I got it, either. Five pounds fish, that's your passport price."

"Five *pounds*?"

"Five pounds or I go to Maccallum now. Do you know what my reward would be?" Gillon shook his head. "If you did you'd know how cheap five pounds fish is."

Gillon untied the knot that held the fish. It was so beautiful lying there in the snow among the pines.

"What are you carrying the head for?" The man brought down his ax and the head was gone.

"Bastard," Gillon said. The man paid him no attention. He was right about the head, but wrong, too, because there was more to a fish than food.

"And the tail." The ax came down again. With the blade, he made a mark along the lower part of the fish.

"I would say about there is right," the man said, and before Gillon had a chance to examine it, a chunk of the lower part of the fish, perhaps an eighth of the whole, was gone.

"Goddamn good saumont, I'll say that for you. Clean. Just in from the sea. You can see by the sea lice on the gills. Next time you better come out by night."

"Thank you," Gillon said.

"Don't think a thing about it," the man said, and headed down the path to the moorland farm. Gillon's father had been right.

He didn't want to get up. He wanted to lie next to his fish on the snow and pine needles and rest, and with a spurt of fear he got up. If the man hadn't come, he would have sat there, his back to the tree, and frozen to death.

"Hey!" Gillon shouted. "You saved my life. Thank you."

Let that bewilder him for the rest of his wind-raddled life. He started across the moor as fast as he could force himself, because who was to say the man wouldn't go to Maccallum anyway? The wind was steady with a body to it and he remembered days at sea like that, but then the wind had always worked for him and now it only seemed to hurt. Miles of moorlands stretching ahead. He wondered if he could make it across, and then he thought of the women carrying the creels of coal up out of the mines. They did it every day; he could go on.

After a time, he didn't really know how long, he was aware that the snow on the moor had thinned and that there were islands of green out on the moor where the snow had melted. There were patches of pines, little pockets of green darkness out of the wind, but he was afraid of them. He needed a root cellar or cow byre or hayrick to crawl into. Finally he came out onto a rise that dipped down ahead of him and saw Loch Leven miles off to the east, deep blue and partly ice-covered. He had gone miles to the west, he, the old seafaring man who could dead-reckon on the water.

There was nothing to do but confess to the error, and he faced west and started down what they called the rough grazings, clumpy rutted moorland that Blackface sheep did their best to rip apart. He came upon a track heading east so he took it, because a track would mean a road and a road would mean the Cowdenbeath turnpike. He could see a few scattered crofts tucked away in creases on the moor and in late afternoon he came into a little clachan of five or six houses. A few people, very shyly, came out to nod at him but they really came out to look at his fish. They probably never saw anything larger than a one-pound trout from some moor stream.

"How far to the Cowdenbeath road?" Gillon asked. He could smell oatmeal cakes being cooked somewhere in the hamlet.

"I'll trade part of this fresh saumont for oatcakes." They looked at him. "It's all right, it's a legal saumont. Salmon for bannocks, what the hell do you want?" he shouted at them.

Some signal had been given. The people went inside their white little houses and shut their doors on him, and left him alone with the smell of hot bannocks stinging his nose.

"What's the matter with you people?" he shouted. He knew he

was making a spectacle of himself, but he had come too far now. He could see them looking at him through their leaded window-panes and suddenly realized that they were Gaelic speakers, a lost cultural island isolated on the moor, frightened by anything they couldn't understand, Gaelic innocents safe only in them-selves. He could see they lived with cows in the house in the old way, and he knew their fuel would be sharny peat, cow dung mixed with peat or coal dust, and the idea of cooking his fish over that disgusted him and he went on. A man came out of a byre with a muck rake in his hand and stopped and stared at him. The man was from another century entirely. He was wearing a dung-stained kilt.

He walked down and down until there was no snow. He couldn't remember going up so high. He would need a large farm with outbuildings, and somewhere near Loch Leven he found it, a large house with two floors and a bothy for the hired hands behind it, and all kinds of outbuildings beyond that, a byre for the cows, a cote for the sheep, and he knew this was the place. They had finished the milking, Gillon could hear them shouting something about feeding turnips to the cows, and then the door to the milkhouse clanged shut, men with a lan-tern went across the yard to the bothy, and the door opened and shut and it was still. The byre would be empty. He could go far around and come from behind or risk walking across the yard and going directly to it, and he did it that way, too tired to worry. A dog barked but he paid it no attention. There was a flood of light in the yard and Gillon kept walking. Border collie bark-ing, some footsteps, surprisingly close, running in the muck, a man shouting something about fox in the sheepcote, and then Gillon found the door, slid it open, and pulled it quietly closed behind him.

Safe.

The smells, the animal heat, the urine and dung and cowiness took his breath away. For a moment, in the dark, he couldn't find the hayloft and grew terrified that they didn't have one—

there must be hay or he would die, he thought—and found the ladder. He made a nest in the hay and covered himself with the plaid and lay down next to the fish to rest in the grassy warmth. He felt the fish. His hand slid down the silver flank. Still fresh, still frozen. He patted the fish as if it could feel his kinship to it.

26

IN THEIR WILDNESS, IN THEIR SAVAGE GREED, they woke him. Not the noises, the little squeaks of anger and excitement, but the scurrying feet, first over his chest and finally over his face, their stealth abandoned in their rage for fresh food. He couldn't see them but he could feel them, everywhere, all around him. Rats. They had smelled it out, come scurrying from every part of the farm, twenty of them, thirty of them now, tugging at his fish, nibbling at the rock-hard flesh, tearing, clawing at his fish.

"Get away," Gillon screamed. "Get *away*! Get *away*!" but they only darted to some other part of the salmon's body and began their assault all over again. He found his walking stick and struck at the rats. He heard them scream and squeal as the staff thudded on their furry bodies, but it didn't stop the others from coming. He was swinging wildly, at anything moving, any shadow, any noise, shouting at them, when he became conscious or light and of men in the doorway below.

"What in name of God is this?" one of the men called up.

"They're eating my fish!" Gillon shouted. "The fucking rats are eating my fish."

Two men ran to the ladder and came up into the loft.

"Oh, Christ almighty, that beautiful fish. Give me the stick."

With the aid of the light, without panicking, the farm hands began the destruction of the rats with a systematic savage joy.

"Never seen them *this* way before," he shouted.

"Aye, and they never seen a saumont before," the other said, putting the bodies in a tub. When the man with the brass-headed staff was finished, the turnip tub was filled with rats' bodies. Gillon was trembling with the horror of it, which made the farm workers genuinely curious.

"What's the matter, mon? You can't be cold in here. It's warm, mon."

They couldn't understand the feeling he got from rats running all over the body of his beautiful fish.

"This is my family's Christmas dinner."

"Ah, give me that." One of the men picked up the fish, and a little later Gillon heard a pump working and the man came back with the fish, cleansed of its blood and rats' blood, only little claw marks and teeth marks to be seen. No one would notice.

"Poacher, are you?" Gillon nodded. "Good man. Not easy to get one like that. Workingman, are you?"

"Coal miner."

"Where?"

"Pitmungo."

"Could you get us work down there? I hear they pay a man." Gillon shook his head.

"That's why I'm here. There's no work. Had to get food for the table. They have only salt cod for Christmas down there."

"Och, that's mean, man, that's crude. Stay here and we'll sneak you out with half a goose. Man doesn't have goose for Christmas, he's no a man and has no Christmas."

"Aye, might as well put a stake through your heart, man without a goose on table."

Gillon was a touch annoyed.

"A saumont will do very well."

"Oh, aye, don't know, never had one. We don't get that here, that belongs to *them*." They looked at his fish. Gillon pointed to the man's knife and cut two steaks from the salmon.

"Broil it with butter on it, do you understand? Don't boil it." The men nodded and thanked Gillon. One of them was at work looping a rope around the fish and soon they had it hanging from a beam, the way they did with their hams.

"Sleep in peace, man. But you got to be up and gone by day-sky. You hear the cocks and be gone, man, aye?" Gillon nodded. "Master see a man with a saumont, he won't understand. Man who'll steal a saumont will steal a sheep, aye, quick as you can say Jock Hector."

"No, no," Gillon said. They thought it was an act.

"Just don't steal one here, man."

They all thought he was a thief. It was, Gillon thought, a nation of thieves.

He had a deep warm sleep, sunk in the hay, feeling secure about his salmon for the first time since he had killed it. He woke from time to time listening for cockcrow, liking the waking because he could appreciate his nest. There was a window in the loft and he could see the stars; clean sky, the weather was holding. No sounds, no wind, no movement except the bumping of the cattle down below. When he woke again it was dawn and the cocks were at it all out. He arranged himself—his feet, he thought, felt better—and went down the ladder.

One half, almost exactly one half of his salmon was gone, as neatly trimmed as if a fishmonger had been at work.

The bastards, Gillon thought, the dirty filthy sons of bitches, coming back in the night to steal my fish. He thought of doing something terrible, setting fire to the byre, dry-mouthed with rage and impotence, looking at his beautiful fish dangling from the beam; and then a Galloway came across the floor and, as if she had been doing it all her life, rose up on her hind legs like a circus animal so that her nose and tongue just tipped what was left of the fish. The salmon had been trimmed to the exact height of the tallest and longest-necked cow in the byre.

Twenty pounds of salmon left. Who, looking at it, could

ever tell that this had once been a great salmon, a bull in the river, a cock among cocks?

Still, it *was* worth it, he told himself, no matter what had happened. Two pounds of salmon for each person, salmon just in from the sea. That was living, that was eating. Salmon wasn't salt cod for Christmas. He found the Cowdenbeath road where the farm hands told him he would, and he started down it. If everything went right, he would be in Pitmungo before the stars came out again.

There was no warning about the blister. He was walking well with no apparent pain, and then there was pain, a great deal of it, almost as suddenly as if he had been hit by something. When he took off his shoe and his sock, he was frightened by the mess he found. The swelling of the foot had given birth to the blister and the freezing of it had masked the pain. The entire heel was swollen, a dangerous-looking red and purple circle on the back of the foot that burned in the icy wind. He would never make it on that. There was nothing to do but sit by the road and hope some merchant or farmer on his way to Cowdenbeath would give him a ride. The cold air was good on the foot and the burning had subsided when the cart came trundling down with tatties for the tables of lower Fife.

"Can you take a man down to Cowdenbeath?" He saw the farmer look at his foot. "I'm trying to make it home for Christmas."

"I don't know, it's a weak horse carrying a heavy load. Perhaps if you made it worth his while?"

"His while?"

"His or mine." The man kept looking at Gillon's inflamed foot.

"Maybe he'd like a salmon steak," Gillon said.

"Aye, he would. Fresh, is it? He's gey fickle."

"Stolen last night in the Firth of Tay."

"Aye, then his master would like one too." Gillon looked at the man and at his fish and at his foot.

"Give me your knife," he said.

They didn't talk all the way down until they were near the town, when the farmer told Gillon what miserable bastards coal miners were and how they never should have been released from bondage and then when they got to Cowdenbeath he carried Gillon down from the wagon.

"Look, you now," he said. "Wrap that in beech leaves; that will drain it and poultice it. Well," he held out his hand, "God bless you and have a joyful Christmas."

How can you ever really judge people, Gillon thought.

He knew where he had to go, to the widow on Fordell Street who made knitted underwear and socks for miners who didn't have anyone to knit for them. He was overjoyed he had hung on to his money. She didn't want fish, she wanted cash. He bought two pairs of good knitted socks and made a spectacle of himself going out to the Pitmungo Road, a shoeless man with a mutilated fish over his shoulder. The road out was pitted with half-frozen potholes, but he made good time and the socks felt good and warm on his feet. When he reached the stand of beech where he had made love to Maggie in front of the sheep so many years before, he took the socks off, afraid to look at his foot, and went barefoot across the plashie part of the moor to the copse and came back with a handful of brown and burnished leaves which he put on the blister and covered with his socks. Because the sun was at his back, the sky ahead seemed clear and until he started up the High Moor and looked around he had no idea how low the sun was on the horizon. Very quickly after that there was the moon, pale and cold, first star and then the stars, and it was night.

They would be starting the cooking now in Pitmungo, making the sauces to disguise the cod, boiling the bony fish in water to make its leathery hide acceptable. It was still all right. Over a good flame, his fish would cook in thirty or forty minutes and he was only an hour from home.

At the top of the High Moor, he stopped to rest. There were stars in the water down below, bobbing and shifting in the harbor and out in the firth, coal bottoms being loaded on Christmas Eve. There must be work again in the mines, and Gillon didn't know whether he was happy or sad about it.

The first cat picked Gillon up just before the path went down through the White Coo plantation. At first, it seemed to be interested in his foot and the wet wool he was dragging, but then, giving no sign it was prepared to leap, it sprang and went halfway up his back in an effort to reach the fish.

"Get off me!" Gillon shouted. The cat dropped back and kept its distance but when Gillon turned away from it, it leaped again. He felt its claws through the plaid this time and it infuriated him. He knew he would have to leave his shoes and his clumsy plaid behind and, holding the fish under one arm, fight off the starving cats, for there were four of them now.

Baudrons, they called them in Pitmungo, too nice a name for wild cats. By the time he got down through the orchard, there were six or eight of them, keeping just out of range of his brass-knobbed stick, waiting, patient even in their hunger, for some misstep on his part, eying the fish as if they knew they were bound to get their part of it when the time was right.

He came down on the Terrace. There were lights in all the windows of all the houses on Tosh-Mungo Terrace, there were lights as far as he could see in every house in Pitmungo. So salt-cod Christmas wasn't as gray as they had told him it was, the people huddling in darkened rooms to save on fuel and light. In several of the houses there was singing, the old Scots carols that always made Gillon sad.

There was ale in the Japps' house. He saw a quarter-barrel in a corner of the front room. That he could use now, Gillon thought, a glass of warm ale and a few dollops of good whisky, and limped on down the lane, swinging his stick at the increasingly bold cats. They were making a noise now, a caterwauling, and when someone came to a window and looked out into the darkness Gillon suddenly could see what a fantastic, what an absurd sight he must be, the shoeless man with the band of wailing cats, his fish held high upon his shoulder, half frozen to death now, his shirt ripped by rats and cats and fish, unshaven, his hair wild from the wind, starvation and frostbite etched on the gaunt cheekbones of his face.

He could smell Pitmungo again, the wet coal dust as always, the faintly sulfurous smell from the workings in the valley, but, more than that, the heavy fishy stink of second-rate fish, salted cod and wind-dried skate, pounded with mallets to beat the toughness out of them.

It wasn't much for all he had been through, sixteen or seventeen pounds of cock salmon. He might have been jailed and he might have died. He wasn't foolish enough not to know that if the wrong infection set in, there was a good chance of losing his leg. But the thing was, he had done it. He had gone out to do it—it seemed so long ago now—and he was back and he had done it, the poacher home from his stream, the salmon in his hands. Christ knew it was foolish, but he had done it when none of the rest of them, all up and down the rows of Pitmungo, had done it. There would be a Christmas in his home worthy of a Christmas.

When he got to the house he stood outside and tried to adjust to the light. He didn't want to be blinded as usual when he went in. Through the window he could see them seated around the table, but they hadn't eaten yet and that was good. He couldn't stay outside too long, because they would hear the cats and come and find him and he didn't want it that way. Andrew was saying something, a toast or a grace before eating, and that was the time to go in. He pushed open his door and stood in the brightness of the room, uncertain where to go and what to say. He knew what a sight he must be.

"What the hell happened, Daddie?" Sam said. "What did they do to you?"

"They didn't do anything to me," Gillon said. "I did it to *them* for once."

He crossed the room, seeing better, and dropped his fish onto the table. He was pleased by the thump it made and to see how big it looked, resting on the wood. They had never had anything that size in the house before.

"It's beautiful, Daddie," Andrew said, and the others crowded around it but Maggie was looking at her husband.

"You've lost your hat," she said. "You've lost your beautiful hat."

His hand went up to his head, slowly, as if he were having trouble finding it, and he was surprised to feel his hair. When could it have happened, his beautiful hat? Did he dive in the pool with his hat on? From the water it had come, to the water it had gone.

"Who cares about a hat?" Sam said. He was excited. "We're having a Christmas fit for a man." He went to the dresser and got out the whisky and came back and poured out drinks in teacups and tassies. There would be a celebration after all. They looked at their father, waiting.

"No salt cod for the Camerons," Gillon said, and they lifted their whisky and drank—to their father and his fish.

27 A FEW DAYS AFTER HOGMANAY, MR. SELKIRK forced himself up the hill from the Reading Room to visit Gillon at home in his bed.

"I don't want to hear about it; I don't want to know what you did or where you went, some childish goose chase"—that made Gillon laugh—"but I knew you would want to study this."

He took an envelope from his pocket and took a clipping from it as if it were a splinter from the True Cross. It was from the financial section of *The Scotsman*.

LONDON—Jan. 3—Lord Fyffe of Fife and Brumbie Hall, Pitmungo, chairman of Pitmungo Coal and Iron, Ltd., was pleased to announce today at the annual meeting of the company's stockholders a net profit after all expenses of 54%. With the approval of the board of directors 14% of the net has been set aside for future development and contingency funds and a dividend of 40% declared for all shareholders on their investment.

This compares favorably with last year's dividend of 45%, Lord Fyffe declared, when the bleak picture of autumn's coal situation is considered. By stringent and imaginative economies practised by the company during this period, the company was able to maintain a stable earning position.

An ovation and a unanimous vote of approval for his policies was rendered Lord Fyffe and the board of directors at the conclusion of the meeting.

Gillon read the clipping several times in order to grasp the essence of it, to feel the full hurt of it. This was the bottom and there was no lower stage to descend to.

"Now are you ready to join us?" Selkirk said. Gillon nodded that he was ready.

"And if Keir Hardie comes, are you ready to have him?"

"Aye."

"And if the police or soldiers come, are you ready to stand up to them?"

"If I can stand by then."

"And when they try to break you, the Company, will you let them break you?"

"I'll bend, I think, but I won't break. I'm beyond that now. Look at these legs."

He pulled the sheet back and Mr. Selkirk wouldn't look at them, the smell was enough to warn him.

"Christ, man, what did they do to you?" the librarian asked.

And that was the truth of it in its way, Gillon understood then. He had done it, but they had driven him to it.

"I just got tired of saying no to myself," Gillon said.

He didn't know if Mr. Selkirk understood him or not and he didn't especially care. The important thing was that he understood himself.

"The time has come to say yes for a change," Gillon said.

"To what?"

"Yes to something, I'll know it when it comes."

Mr. Selkirk was impressed by the tone of Gillon's voice and by the look he saw on his face.

"Very well put," he said, "for a semi-literate man," and took his clipping and went back down the hill.

In the end Sarah saved him. She walked up each morning from the far end of Tosh-Mungo, at her mother's request—Walter Bone was correct after all—and bathed and drained the sore on her father's foot. When after a week the wound was no better, Dr. Gowrie was called in.

"In some stupid way you've managed to get yourself a good frostbite here and after you did it you went on and humiliated the flesh. If you want my opinion . . ."

"It's why we're paying you money," Maggie said.

". . . the leg wants taking off either here"—Gillon leaped; Dr. Gowrie didn't think miners really hurt—"or, better, here."

"I won't have it," Gillon said.

"We've lost two legs in this family," Sarah said, "and three won't do."

"When it turns black you'll have it off. You'll come crawling to me then, Cameron. Just don't crawl too late or you'll not only have no leg left, you'll have no life left."

Sarah drained and drained it after that, her patience was unending. She was determined to save for her father what her husband had lost. She mixed a poultice of oatmeal which seemed to draw the infection out. The smell was very bad and so they burned pulverized coffee beans in a shovel over the fire and that cleansed the room. Gillon's feet burned in the heat of the house when they covered them at night, and so Maggie moved into the but and they opened the window to his room and after that it became bearable, the frozen flesh reacting with less pain to the cold nights.

There was no single day when Gillon got better. A time came when he got no worse but stayed the same for so long that the condition came to be understood as being better. In February, Gillon decided he could walk, and he could—as long as he didn't put his foot down hard. When he did, the foot swelled like a frog's throat, ugly and greenish white. In March he was able to get his work boots on and he practiced wearing them a few hours each day. The rest of the time he sat in the window well and read, or sat in the doorway in the early spring sun and looked down at the black mountain growing again on the Sportin Moor and thought about the forty-percent dividend the Pitmungo Coal and Iron Company had issued through their imaginative economies. It became a fixation with him; Gillon was aware of that. He sometimes said the number aloud, to himself or when others were about, barely conscious that he had done it. He was much the way Sam had been when he found that the moor was going to be stolen from them.

He read a book or two a day at times; he read the Industrial Workers' Reading Room dry and began over again, starting with *The Tragedy of Macbeth*, although he still liked *King Lear* better. But he couldn't understand *Hamlet* and why the young man could never make up his mind, even when the evidence was right there in front of his eyes. Yet he secretly felt, though he never said it to Mr. Selkirk, that there was a lot of Hamlet in himself. He didn't care to be reminded of it.

Even those who lived with him from day to day could see the change taking place in him, the fullness returning to his face, the years falling away with the disappearance of the gaunt, hard lines of his neck and face. And it was revealed again what had been forgotten in the hard times—that he was the most handsome member of his family, that all of them, springing from the Cameron side or the Drum side, had absorbed something of Pitmungo in their blood, of the mines and the darkness and their being nourished on coal dust from the day of their entrance into the world. Gillon alone was free of it. After years of working at becoming one of the Pitmungo people, the Highlander in him was coming out and he was an outsider again.

He was reading Henry George on "The Effect of Material Progress Upon the Distribution of Wealth" for the third time, trying to get the points down so that when he used them they would seem to come from him, muttering "True, true" from time to time and underlining in the book, which Selkirk had begged him not to do, when Maggie looked up from a quilt she was sewing and stared at him in the soft light from the window. They never talked when he read, and he had long ago given up trying to read to her.

"You're the man I married in Strathnairn again," she said.

He looked up but couldn't see her. He still had trouble focusing from something near to something farther away. Miner's eye didn't go away just because you weren't in the mine.

"What was that?"

"It doesn't bear repeating," Maggie said, but he had heard her. He went back to his book but he didn't read. She was saying that she had seen him again. Occasionally he would look at her, her head bent over some commonplace chore, kneeling down to blow the coals of the fire, and he would truly see her. Then he wanted to reach out and touch her or say something that belonged just to the two of them. But something always held him back, some control that kept his hands where they were and his mouth silent. The seeing and touching always seemed to lead to confusion and a strange feeling of anger mixed with regret. It was better, he decided, to live the invisible way.

On the first day in May, when all over Scotland people were washing their faces in the May dew up on the moors and in the parks, Gillon went the other way. There was work for all again and he got dressed in his pit duds and put his books away and went down the hill to get work in Lord Fyffe No. 1.

He had forgotten how it was to go down into the pit. It was strange at first, and fearful, and yet by the afternoon, howking coal three thousand feet below the earth's surface was as natural to him as wiping the black sweat on his brow.

THREE

THE CAMERONS

1 IN THE MIDDLE OF THAT MONTH, AN ACCIDENT HAP-
pened to Gillon. He was finishing a room, on the verge of
breaking through the wall into the next room—he could tell
almost to the inch the thickness of a wall of coal by the sound
of his pick against it. He had gotten down on his knees to *tap,
tap* his way into the empty next room when through the wall
he was working on came flashing metal—he always remembered that later, the glitter of his lamp on new steel, of his hand
flying up to fend off whatever was coming at him, too late, too
late—and then the overwhelming thud of the metal entering
his body. He was knocked backward, off his knees, and he lay
still, afraid to move. A coal pick was buried in his shoulder.

"Oh, I say," someone shouted. "Good God, I say, oh dear,"
and the wall came down all around Gillon. He heard them
running from the next room around into the roadway and
into his room, and someone pulled him out by his feet from
under the coal, which hurt then as much as the pick in his
body. Gillon recognized Mr. Brothcock, but his being there
meant nothing to him. He had never seen the other faces.

"I'm sorry, oh dear God, believe me, I am so sorry," an English
voice was saying. "Will you tell him that I'm sorry?"

"Shouldn't have been in there in the first place," Brothcock said. He leaned down over Gillon. "What were you doing coming through the wall into the other stall?"

Gillon could only lie there and stare at him. He was too stunned to speak properly, but he could hear and reason clearly.

"Not supposed to go through walls that way, Cameron," the superintendent said.

Gillon thought, very controlled, Liar, the man is lying, why is he lying that way? But the insult his flesh had suffered made itself felt, a delayed-action fuse igniting in his nervous system, and his body recoiled, all of it, the way the salmon had done, and he let out one terrible cry beyond his control, until the spasm passed and he lay there silently again, looking up at them.

"Oh God, I am sorry, you know," the young voice said.

"Shouldn't we do something about the *pick*?" another voice said, very cool and almost unconcerned. The pain of the pick lodged in bone was becoming unbearable.

"Pick stops bleeding," Brothcock said.

"But it must be very painful." The voices were English.

"They don't feel the pain. Go and get some men," Brothcock said to someone, "to haul this man out."

"Take the pick *out*," Gillon heard himself saying, as if he were talking from a great, hollow distance away, "you fucking fool."

Brothcock came back and stood over him.

"Fewkin fool, is it?" He was enraged. "These are stockholders here. There are gentlemen here."

"Would one of you gentlemen have the courage to take the pick out?" Gillon said. He was conscious of being brave about it, of holding himself together with a tightness not expected or required of men hurt the way he was.

One of the Englishmen, a boy, really, knelt by Gillon's side.

"I'll give it a try," he said. "Do you think you can bear up?"

Gillon nodded. The boy seized the pick at the head where it was mounted on the handle and made a first, and painful, test of how deeply the steel was lodged in the miner's body. It had lodged in bone.

"When you do it, do it *quick*."

"Yes."

"All right, then do it!"

"Yes."

And the boy pulled and it wasn't enough. Gillon didn't want to but he screamed aloud; it *was* too much to bear, and the boy was shaking.

"Brothcock," Gillon said.

"I won't do it."

Gillon seized the boy by the wrist.

"Go down the roadway there, you see, and shout for Sam Cameron. *Shout*."

"You don't have to take no mouth from a—"

But the boy pushed by the superintendent and began, with his high clear voice, shouting his way down the road. Gillon heard him come running back down the roadway. He had found Rob Roy. Rob looked down on his father.

"Oh, God, what have they done to you?" He turned on Mr. Brothcock. "What have you done to my dad?"

"Please, quick now Rob."

Rob knelt next to his father and felt the steel of the pick. He put both hands on the pick, one on the steel and one on the wood, and there was no give at all. He had the feeling that if he pulled, he would take his father's rib cage with him, and his hands fell away from the pick.

"Now I fail you," he said.

Sam pushed his way into the room.

"Get the hell out of the way," he shouted, and flung the gentlemen aside. "Why is he lying there like that?" he shouted in Mr. Brothcock's face.

"Quick now, Sam," Gillon said.

"Aye, Daddie."

He put his knee against his father's ribs and in the same motion, before his father was aware that it was happening to him, and with a terrible shout, as loud and filled with pain as his father's cry, he pulled the pick point from his father's body.

Someone on the way out, in the old miner's way, put a handful of fresh-cut coal dust in the wound to clot the flow of blood. Gillon wouldn't have allowed it but Gillon didn't know.

"You have your feet and you have your arm, and by rights you should have neither," the doctor at Cowdenbeath was saying. Gillon was being discharged. "You should be a thankful man."

"I thank you."

"You should have thanked your God, not me."

"I don't have one."

"Then you're a fool. A lucky one but a fool."

"Luckier than him." Gillon pointed out the window where his son-in-law waited for him in the wagon.

"Should I know him?" the doctor asked. Gillon was surprised.

"Bone? Sandy Bone." The doctor shook his head. "The roof fell on the boy and he lost both legs," Gillon said.

The doctor shook his head again. He didn't remember. "We get so many you see," he said.

It was time to go. Gillon didn't know if a patient, a coal-miner patient, shook a doctor's hand or not. He held it out but the doctor didn't see it.

"I'll tell you this much. You have your arm but you'll never mine coal again."

"Will I be able to move it?" The doctor nodded, but said there would be no strength to the limb.

"Then I'll mine coal."

"When you do, bring a bag to me," he said, with no conviction at all.

It was a painful ride back home, the jarring of the wagon

wheels in the ruts of the road disturbing the balance between bone and muscle that had been so delicately established. It was a beautiful day, warm and with little wind, and Gillon was grateful for that. He wanted to go home by way of the High Moor. He could not remember coming to Cowdenbeath, only the pick coming through the wall, and pain, and darkness. And now here was the sun again, the little farms, and up ahead the open moor.

"How are you?" Sandy asked. "You look good."

"I'm like a bird with a broken wing. I look all right but I can't fly."

"You'll fly. You'll come out of this good. Mr. Selkirk heard you'll get a good croo."

"What the hell would he know about it?"

"I don't know. He said he heard the young gentleman asked to see that you did."

Croo was the "satisfaction" the Company deemed that it owed to a man accidentally maimed or killed in the mine. There was no set amount in Pitmungo the way there was in some mines, so much for certain injuries, so much for a leg lost or a hand mashed, for example. No one ever knew the amount in advance; no one ever knew who set the amount. It was a caprice, a kind of lottery in which the amount of the payoff depended on the extent to which the Company felt that the accident was the fault of the miner or the fault of the Company or a simple act of God.

For example, when Ian Benn, working in a gassy room, stood up suddenly and blew his head off, the croo was small. The croo-givers decided that Mr. Benn should have put his hat and open light on his coal pick and raised it slowly to the roof, letting his lamp burn the gas off the roof, especially since he had forty years' experience in the pit.

"What did you get?" Gillon asked Sandy. He could see the boats down in St. Andrew's. Coal was selling well; that should be a good omen for his croo.

"Twenty-five pounds," Sandy said. "Twelve and a half pounds per leg."

"Shylock would have paid more." Sandy didn't understand the allusion.

"I'd pay a good deal more than that to get them back," he said. Gillon marveled at Sandy's ability to stand away from and even laugh at his misfortune.

"It was very generous of them," Gillon said.

"Aye, you see they said it was really an act of God. If I had left on time and not stayed behind to do a little extra work the roof would have missed me, so it couldn't be the Company's fault. God was at His tricks." One had to admire the subtlety of the reasoning.

And then, suddenly, there was Pitmungo. It always came as a surprise to Gillon, no matter how many times he had seen it, how dark and deep Pitmungo valley was, how dark the houses and how dark the lanes, and now how dark the Sportin Moor.

"You might call mine an act of the Lord," Gillon said. It was a play on words and the Bone boy wasn't good at those. The young man who had pierced him was Sir Compton Elphinstone, Lord of Something-or-Other, a stockholder and director of the Company, although he wasn't yet out of whatever school it was he went to.

2   THE CROO DIDN'T COME, ALTHOUGH TRADITIONALLY it was paid the first payday after the miner returned home from the hospital.

"Nothing to do but wait," Andrew said. "You can't force them."

"We could go down and ask, at least," Jemmie said. "There might be a mix-up."

"*You* can't go down," Andrew said.

"Let them know we're expecting something very good," Ian said.

"You can't *force* it," Andrew said. "It's in their hands now."

"That's not fair," Sarah said.

344

"Whoever expected anything fair?" Emily said.

"Fair doesn't matter, it's the way it is," Ian said.

"Maybe I could go down and speak to Mr. Brothcock," Maggie said. "The man can't work. They owe him his croo."

But they decided to wait. It was, everyone agreed, a very unusual accident. People said—no one ever found out where they got the information—that Sir Compton himself, or his family, was deciding on a satisfactory settlement and probably didn't understand the way of the Pitmungo ritual. That must be it, everyone agreed.

They brought Gillon's bed out of the ben into the but so he could be with people, and he spent the time learning about the nature of investment from Andrew, and sometimes Maggie and sometimes Mr. Selkirk. He could not quite understand the fact that if people like Elphinstone's parents put up a thousand pounds, and a dividend of forty percent for the year was declared, the young man would receive four hundred pounds for doing nothing.

"What do you mean, *nothing*? He put a pick through your bloody arm, didn't he?" Sam said. "That's something. You don't see that very often, man."

Gillon didn't like the sound to Sam's voice these days. No matter what he said, even when he was joking, there was a dangerous edge to it.

"Nothing?" Jemmie said. "Christ almighty, he goes to school, man. That's something, too."

And Gillon found it just as hard to understand that even after the investor made his four hundred pounds on the risk of his money, that that wasn't the end, that he could go on getting money, three or four or five hundred pounds a year, and still own his original thousand pounds; that it was still all his, even though it had been paid for over and over.

"But the money has to come from somewhere," Gillon said. "You just can't keep paying out."

"You can if you keep mining coal. Coal *is* the money."

"But I dug that coal," Gillon said. "It was me that went underground. I sweat the sweat that produced the coal. I took the real risk."

"Correct," Andrew said.

"Then tell me one thing."

"Aye, I'll try," his son said.

"How did we ever let this happen to us?"

He brooded about it that night and over the next days. Every time the throb began in his arm, like an abscessed tooth in his bone, he thought about it. The number forty was obsessing Gillon's mind. Forty percent. And four hundred pounds. It never occurred to him—not then—that the number could just as well be four thousand pounds. Four hundred was enough for a miner to brood about. As the week became the next week it grew to be such an obsession with Gillon, the idea that four hundred pounds would be the proper croo for the nature of his wound, that he came to believe that it not only would be coming to him but that it was his right. The check had already been written, only the formality of picking it up remained. If there was any justice left in the world, and Gillon was certain there was, four hundred pounds would see it served.

The fortnight passed, and the men were in the semicircle for their pay. It was a cold night for May, raw and dark, flurries of snow and lashing of rain. The miners, still in their pit gear and pit sweat, huddled under the white light of Brothcock's guttering gas lamp. Because they were never paid in any order—pay-packet potluck, they called it—the semicircle had long been Pitmungo custom. Since the one command was that you had better be there quick when your name was called, the circle was invented so a man could bolt for the door of the pay shed without having to shove his way through a mob of men before the door was closed on him.

"Japp, Ranald." The voice from the door, a glob of light flood-

346

ing out onto the wet gray snow, and a man, sixty years old, fifty of those spent underground, bolting for the door like a mine pony belted with a pitprop.

"Japp coming, sir."

The younger miners wouldn't do it, but the old ones, from custom and from being slower, shouted to make certain the paymaster knew they were coming. Mr. Brothcock was in charge now and liked to see them run. It showed spirit, he said.

Andrew came out of the door.

"You got it? Did he give it to you?" Even non-Camerons crowded around. It had become an affair of the town. Andrew opened his envelope but there was only the usual pay.

"He'll give it to one of you, that's certain," someone said, and everyone agreed, but none of the other Camerons got Gillon's croo and Jemmie was the last.

"If you don't get it, you'll have to ask," Sam said.

"Aye, I'll ask," Jem said.

He knew the moment he felt his pay packet that it was the usual amount but he opened it in the office anyway—something not generally done; one took one's pay on trust in Pitmungo—and tried to get Mr. Brothcock's eye.

"*And* my Daddie's croo."

"Croo?"

"Gillon Cameron's croo."

"Gillon Cameron's croo?"

"Aye. The man the gentleman put the pick through."

"*That* one?"

"He can't work the now and wants his croo."

"*His* croo? The croo's a gift, not a right."

"When a man gets hurt he gets his croo."

Mr. Brothcock turned away from Jemmie and began an exaggerated search through the pay-packet box.

"There's an envelope here." He turned around and showed Gillon's packet to Jemmie. "But it's empty." He turned it upside down. "There is no croo."

"There must be croo. The pick went through his arm, sir."

"There is no croo."

"The point come oot in his wind works."

"Look, you, I've been very patient with you and your gob. Do you ken the English tongue? *There is no croo.*" Brothcock couldn't resist it. "Croo don't go to incomers. Croo don't go to people who call other people fewkin idiots, you might tell that to your father. Croo don't go to colliers in the wrong. Your father shouldn't have been where he was."

"*That's* a fewkin lie."

"Which one are you?"

"James Drum Cameron."

"That's a five-shilling fine for bad language in the Company offices."

"He was where he ought to a been and you fewkin well know it."

"Five more." He smiled. "That's not what I wrote in my report to Lord Fyffe."

Jemmie's hands were trembling on his pick. He wanted to sink the tip of it right where the tip had gone into his father. Brothcock knew it.

"Thinking of something?" He was still smiling. Whatever one said of Brothcock, he knew how to control himself.

"I was remembering something," Jemmie said. He was going too far now, and he knew it but he wanted to go on. "Do you remember the stone, Mr. Brothcock, sir? I would if I were you."

"Aye," the superintendent said, and came up with his foot, so suddenly that Jemmie was never able to make a move of any kind before being sent sprawling backward through the pay-shed door and then backward down the wooden steps, groping for the railing, and landing on the back of his head in the coal-flecked mud.

"Caught the filthy little thief with his hand in your pay packets," Mr. Brothcock said. "If I was one of you I'd want to do something about it."

"The man who touches my brother," Sam said very evenly, "will never work another day in his life when I'm through with him."

"You wouldn't do that in America, you bastart you," Jem shouted. He never knew if the superintendent heard him.

"Hope, Wullie," Mr. Brothcock called out, and little Willie Hope went hopping.

The news that Gillon Cameron had been denied his croo stunned the town and, when the shock wore off, frightened it. They had learned one thing out of it: that the croo was the whim of Lord Fyffe. He could be mean at times, that was a risk they had always run, but mostly he had been generous, and his croo had stood between them and disaster during the time a family was trying to re-establish itself after some maiming in the pit. So the word went up and down the rows in whispers, as though it might somehow disappear if it just wasn't said aloud.

"Did you hear about it? Cameron didn't get his croo."

Because after what had happened to Gillon Cameron, somebody sticking a pick through you, and you unable to work and not a penny to see you through, could any man in Pitmungo consider himself safe?

All that evening they trooped up to Tosh-Mungo Terrace to tell Gillon what a dirty hand he had been dealt—they're crying for themselves, Maggie said—and then Mr. Selkirk came up after ten, red in the face from the climb and from drink, but very cool about it all.

"You understand what you are, don't you?" Gillon said that he didn't. "You've entered history. You're a monument to stupidity and simple ignorance."

"I don't understand."

" 'I don't understand,' " Selkirk mimicked him. "Of course you don't understand. That's why I weakened my heart climbing up here; to make you understand."

Gillon had expected sympathy, even from Mr. Selkirk.

"Because you don't know your own rights. You don't know the simple laws of your own land."

"All right," Gillon said. "Tell me."

"You lie there like a wounded lamb waiting for people to come by and smooth your wool. Don't know your simple rights."

"What rights? What the hell are you talking about?" Gillon was shouting even though it hurt him.

"Waiting for a handout from on high." The sarcasm was so heavy in the voice that it sounded like a satire of sarcasm. "Waiting on the whim of his Lord. How ungodly sweet. How he must like that, to see his little miners looking up, waiting to see what flutters down on them."

"You don't have to talk to my husband that way," Maggie said. Little hot coals of eyes meeting little blue chips of ice.

"'My husband,'" is it? You talk about him like he was your coal scuttle." Mr. Selkirk smiled. "Instead of the beggar he is." Now Sam was in it; he stood up but Gillon motioned him down.

"Did I say anything wrong? Because any man that lies there with his hand stuck out praying someone will pop some money in it—do you have another word for it except *beggar*?"

Put that way, it was hard to deny. They were all beggars in the eyes of Lord Fyffe.

"And why do you have to hold your hand out?"

"Because it's the way," Andrew finally said.

"And do you like it?"

"It works. At times. Sometimes."

"Is that what I asked you? The whim of the coal master. Do you like it? You like to dance when he whistles his tunes? You like that?"

No one could answer him. He was making them feel disgraced for themselves.

"No, you're the family that could have had Keir Hardie here but you wouldn't dare that. You wouldn't even go down to Cowdenbeath to the union there and find out about your rights.

Sit up here, lost in your miserable valley, and wait for the coal master to bestow your own rights on you."

When the diatribe was over, the edge of his bitterness dulled, the librarian began to tell them about a law that had been passed in Parliament, in London, that mysterious place of power which none of them ever dreamed of seeing, yet which controlled their lives, even the food that was put on their table. The law was the Workmen's Compensation Act, Mr. Selkirk told them, proposed by a bunch of frauds so they could face their ministers on Sunday and passed in a conspiracy of silence. The law stated that all workmen were entitled to proper redress and compensation if injured at work by faulty equipment or negligence on the part of the company.

"It isn't a whim," Mr. Selkirk said; "it's a law of the land. It is your native right."

There were others in the room, people from the Terrace, and they were moved by what they learned; that they could be freed from the grip of the hand that held the croo. But, like the Camerons, they were afraid. To use the law meant confrontation, and confrontation in Pitmungo meant catastrophe.

Too many were still too close to slavery to forget the way the last great law had worked. The law had said a man was free and all he had to do to get his freedom was to go to the sheriff and announce that he was unsatisfied with his conditions and that he wanted to be freed from his coal master. If he was persuasive enough, he got his freedom: the freedom to scrounge along the sides of the roads looking for roots and grubs to eat. The freedom to starve to death.

"What do I have to do?" Gillon asked.

"Sue."

There was a desire not to understand. It was too dangerous a thought. The resistance to going ahead rubbing against the desire to keep going generated a current of electricity in the room.

"Sue who?" Gillon finally dared ask, swiftly. "Sue what?"

"Do I have to say it for you?" Selkirk said. Gillon nodded.

"Lord Fyffe."

It was too outrageous a concept to be understood at once. The room had fallen silent. There was a sensation of danger in the silence and yet there was something delicious about it. One of them was going to be taking a step into forbidden territory.

Somewhere inside him, Gillon was beginning to form the word "Yes." It was there, wanting to come out, waiting for the right moment when, once said, it could not be withdrawn.

"Do it, Daddie," Sam said, in a low, awed voice. "Sue the son of a bitch."

Gillon waited. To say it by suing Lord Fyffe? Was this the right time and right way to finally do it? A simple man sue a lord? A miner, a coal jock sue Lord Fyffe? It needed time, it needed saying over and over, to become believable. Gillon felt people looking at him in a new way. He knew what they were thinking: That this man, living on their lane, would have the ultimate gall to try and take Lord Fyffe, who some of them had never even seen, into common court!

"Aye, Daddie," Jem said, "go on and sue him. Sue him for what he done to you."

"Sue him for what he done to me!" Sandy Bone shouted.

Walter Bone was standing and pointing dramatically down the Terrace, down to where the Sportin Moor once stood.

"Sue him for what he did to all of us. We'll stand like a rock behind you."

The rage was out. Men began shouting the names of brothers and fathers who had been maimed in the mines, men who had crawled to collect Lord Fyffe's croo, some seeming literally to have hung on to life to get their croo and then die on getting it. The noise in the house was loud and contagious. It spread down the Terrace and down onto Moncrieff Lane as rapidly as the news that Gillon Cameron would get no croo had come up it.

Gillon Cameron was going to sue Lord Fyffe.

Gillon Cameron was going to have him hauled into court like a common thief, like a snatch-purse on the streets.

They came running up from Moncrieff and the end of the Terrace until the house wouldn't hold them, and then Mr. Selkirk was pounding them to order by smashing Mr. Bone's brass-knobbed walking stick on the table, leaving dents in the wood with every blow.

"Now you've all had a good uproar and feel very valiant about it," Mr. Selkirk said. "What I want to know now, which of you is going to be the first to run down to the College and spill it all over the tavern floor with his ale?"

He studied them as if he truly expected the one who would do it to hold up his hand and admit it.

"Which one of you is the next Judas Iscariot of Pitmungo?"

They were beginning to get angry with him.

"He's here! Because you're conditioned to be Judases here. *They*—they have played you off against one another for so long you no longer know what it is to stand together for *anything*."

He was getting to them, and they were starting to shout back, no sentences but guttural cries of outrage, which Gillon realized was what Selkirk had wanted from them all along: to make them commit themselves in front of each other. He slammed the walking stick down hard. It had a thump of finality about it.

"Because when we serve that summons, when the paper is served to Lord Fyffe himself—*himself*—it must come as a total surprise."

The thought of it: that quick little inoffensive act, the passing of the paper from one hand to another, and the most meaningful moment in Pitmungo since slavery was abolished would have taken place.

"I don't believe a common workingman can bring an earl into common court."

It was Andrew, sensible Andrew, cautious and unhappy about his blushing. "And if he can, he can't win."

Gillon was forced to admire his son's stubbornness. It was a legitimate question but the men were angry with him for it. He was chilling the spirit of revolt.

"If he does dare, the peer must be tried by a jury of his peers and they *never* find for the common man."

They saw it as disloyal, but Gillon knew better: by his refusal to go along Andrew was only trying to protect the family. It was strange how lying in bed made a man better able to see things.

"That is in criminal cases and under common law," Selkirk said. "This is a civil case and under civil law, and Scotland is ruled by civil law, that's *one* thing the bastards down there never were able to take away from us. Scotland is ruled by civil law."

They applauded it, not knowing what they were applauding.

"A common man can't sue a corporation because he isn't himself a corporation, do you see that?"

They all claimed they could.

"But he can sue the man—the *man*—who runs the corporation. And Lord Fyffe *is* a man. Did any of you know that?" They didn't, really. "That when he gets up in the morning he puts his hurdies on the pot even like yourself, and that when he gets off it stinks as much as yours. Can you believe that?"

"And worse," someone called out. "All that fine food and French wine."

"And what are we going to do, then?" Walter Bone asked.

"We're going to haul his—and you must excuse the expression, Mr. Bone—haul his ass into Court of Session like the common law violator he is."

The Court of Session.

They loved the sound of that, and the thought of it. Their Laird standing in the same dock where wife beaters and habitual drunks and sheep stealers had stood.

"Brought there by a summons from the people, delivered by a messenger-at-arms as an agent of the Crown's court."

A gasp then, because this was taking them places where they had never expected to go.

"A summons no man can refuse without becoming a fugitive from the justice of the Crown and all of Scotland."

A cheer after that.

"It could only be done if one man dared come forward, and now we have that man."

Gillon tried to find Maggie in the room, to see what was in her eyes and face.

"Up here is a man; down there is a man," Selkirk said, pointing in the direction of Brumbie Hall. "And we shall see justice done between them."

He wouldn't allow the applause then; it was too serious a moment for that. He's using me, Gillon thought, he's taking me and running away with me and I don't care.

"For the first time in Pitmungo. In all the five hundred years of blackness, for the first time."

Mr. Selkirk had been right about it. There was no applause now but a general, awestruck silence. The librarian had his hand in the air.

> "*What though on hamely fare we dine*
> *Wear pit duds, an' a' that?*
> *Gie fools their silks, and knaves their wine—*
> *A man's a man for a' that.*
> *For a' that, an' a' that,*
> *Their tinsel show, an' a' that,*
> *The honest man, tho' e'er sae poor,*
> *Is king of men for a' that.*"

Mr. Selkirk pointed at Gillon.

"Are you ready to go down to Edinburgh and file papers with me?"

Mr. Selkirk had set his stage well. There was no going back now.

"Aye, I'll go," Gillon said. "I'll get out of my bed and go."

They would have carried him out onto the Terrace in his bed if it would have made any sense.

"Nooo," Gillon heard her shout. "Nooooo, I won't let him go. I won't let him do that to us."

They were cheering then and paid no attention to her, but her children heard. Sam came up behind his mother and clapped a hand over her mouth, and then picked her up and carried her out of the room. He sat her on a stool in the ben of the house.

"My father is going to do what my father has to do, and no one is going to stop him," Sam said, and then took his hand away. She hit him full in the face, which didn't surprise him, and then went to the larder to get a flannel towel to stop the flow of blood from his hand, which she had bitten almost to the bone.

3 BUT THEY DID TALK, IN THE COLLEGE AND AT PIECE time in the pits, down the rows and the lanes, because no one could keep a secret like the one they were trying to keep. The question was whether the talk had gotten to Brumbie Hall. When Gillon and Mr. Selkirk left for Edinburgh that night, intending to walk through the night and arrive at Edinburgh in the morning, starting down Colliers Walk after tea, there were lamps in windows all the way down and the doorways were open, lighting the way for them, people in the Walk all the way down to send them off, no one saying anything, just a nod of the head, a movement of the hand, the little knowing communications of the underclass, and then the doors would close and the way would be engulfed in blackness behind them. It was a moving sight.

"They're with me now," Gillon said; "do you think they'll stay?"

"They don't have to stay. This is a matter of law," Selkirk said.

They reached the Low Road to Cowdenbeath, no more houses, and it was just walking then. It had been a wet and snowy spring and the river was running high, making it impossible to talk over the roar of rushing water, which suited Gillon. He wanted to think about the day: law agents and solicitors, matters of litigation and judges of the land. The courts, the Crown, justice, and the LAW.

The law, above which no man could live for long, not even a Lord Fyffe. He felt a tingling of excitement in the place near his buttocks where he used to think his soul resided.

"Christ, I'm thirsty," Selkirk suddenly shouted. "Can you drink this stuff?"

"Mine rats won't drink it," Gillon told him. "And when they do, they curl up and die."

That was another thing, only a little one. For fifty years the men had petitioned the Company to provide some form of fresh water in the pits, just a barrel brought down in the morning on the cage. But the Company had never deigned to do it. Gillon went back to his thoughts.

If he lost, there would be damages and court costs, he had found out—one deterrent that helped make a man think twice about suing for his rights. And the pursuer, which Gillon would be called, could be sued in turn by the defender for false suit. But the men had agreed, through a committee formed by Walter Bone—the Cameron Defense Fund—to pay the costs and the damages if he lost and to contribute a penny each a week to keep the Cameron family going until it found some other acceptable way to exist. The Defense Fund took a lot of the fear out, and Gillon was thankful for it. But Mr. Selkirk saw it as something else. Here was the framework, the nucleus to form a organization of some kind. The miners were together on one thing at last.

Although it was painful for Gillon, they walked the night through to Dunfermline rather than spend it in Cowdenbeath and pay for a room, and in Dunfermline they caught the first morning train to Edinburgh.

• • •

They were early and walked in the gray morning through Princes Street and down George Street and up Frederick, all the while watched over by the castle looming over them. It was overwhelming for Gillon.

"What am I doing here? I don't belong here," he suddenly said. Even the schoolchildren seemed more mature than he did. He had never felt more like a coal miner and a member of a race apart than in these stern gray streets.

"You're here to see that justice is done," Selkirk said. "That's what those buildings have been constructed for."

Everyone in the streets seemed so determined, so clean and well dressed, so assured of what his role in life was. There was still an hour before the law agents' offices were open and they climbed up the road to Edinburgh Castle where they looked at Mons Meg, the enormous cannon that for some reason meant so much to Scotland, Gillon never learned why, and then he turned around toward where Fife lay.

"That's where I belong and you know it," Gillon suddenly said. "You glib-mouthed me into this." He was trembling, from the long night and the lack of breakfast, from the early morning chill seeming to breathe from the stones of the castle and from fear.

"Look, you. You belong in the courts of law and you're going to go in them or I will tell you this. You'll never lift your head up as a man again, not in Pitmungo, you won't."

Gillon noticed when they went back down on Princes Street and passed the little tea shoppes and hotels, that Mr. Selkirk, as hungry as he was, didn't volunteer to go into any of them; he was no more sure how a person was supposed to handle himself in one than Gillon was.

They waited in the anteroom to be announced. It was all dark wood and heavy leather and the names of the two advocates were in gold on dark wood.

Angus MacGreusich MacDonald
Alisdair Calder

Who needed two "Mac's" in a name? Gillon thought. He was trying to be at his ease. The other people waiting in the room— all of whom seemed to know one another, but not well enough to talk to one another; that was the way of the upper class, Gillon noted—were gentry. Gillon kept twirling his cap in his hand. He wished he still had his hat; that would have helped.

Who was it who had said, "When you need a martyr, make sure you send a martyr"? Gillon wanted to ask Selkirk but he wasn't certain it was allowed to talk in the anteroom.

"Stop it," Selkirk whispered in his ear.

"Stop what?"

Selkirk wouldn't look at him or the cap. "The cap," he said from the side of his mouth. "Put the cap in your lap. Just because you're a miner you don't have to act like one."

"I understand."

"You don't see these men twirling their hats. Sign of weakness. We can't show that." Gillon nodded.

"No."

"Just relax. You might as well get set for a wait. They're not going to take us ahead of them."

"We were first," Gillon said.

"Oh, Christ, Cameron, there are realities. Just because they help the workingman doesn't mean they cater to him. We're charity here. We're begging help."

"Aye," Gillon said, although it did occur to him that the reason they were there was that they were sick to death of begging. "But still . . ."

Selkirk was furious with him.

"I picked the wrong man," he said aloud. "It doesn't take a genius to see that."

Everyone in the room, in a slow, disinterested way, turned to look at them, and both Gillon and Selkirk stared at the floor and then the secretary was at the door with a card in her hand.

"Mr. Selkirk and Cameron," she said. "This way." She had added "please" to the others, Gillon noticed, when she had offered them a seat. He also resented the absence of a "mister" before his name, but he couldn't help, at the same moment, admiring what a beautiful young woman she was, crisp in high-collared starch shirt, her hair piled high with an affected carelessness and when he looked up from her skirt, there she was, studying him.

"Yes, she is," Mr. MacDonald said.

"Is what?" Gillon said, and turned scarlet.

"Very pretty."

He was tall, immensely tall, and lean in the way of people who choose to be lean and not have it forced on them by hard work or hunger. Selkirk had seemed to disappear into the leather and heavy walnut wood, leaving Gillon alone in the middle of the room.

"Calder . . . he's here."

The other law agent, an aristocratic fawn of a man, thin and young and alert, came into the room. They circled Gillon, studying him, as if he were something they were thinking of putting money on. Gillon found himself feeling ashamed of his suit, feeling the shine on the shoulder blades of the jacket and the seat of his pants. He was especially conscious of the girl.

"So this is the one who's going to do it."

"Going to try it," Mr. MacDonald said.

Calder went up very close to Gillon.

"But this isn't a miner," he finally said.

"I'm considered the best collier on my shift," Gillon said.

"He doesn't even talk like a miner."

"All the better," MacDonald said, ignoring Gillon. "This is someone *they* can understand. He looks like one of our . . . *their* kind. Extraordinary luck. All right," he said to Gillon, "let's see it."

"See what?"

"The wound, man. Come on." With the help of Calder, who

touched Gillon's shirt with the very ends of his fingers, as if he might get less contaminated that way, they began undoing Gillon's buttons.

"But, ah . . . but . . ." Gillon, turning red again, began nodding at the girl.

"Oh, good God, man," Mr. MacDonald said. "Miss Tweed's seen many a man, I assure you. Haven't you, Miss Tweed?" She smiled ever so mildly. It was strange, Gillon thought; that kind of thing would not be allowed in a coal town and here it was all right. He didn't understand these people.

The cast was intact, covering a good part of the right side of Gillon's chest, but part of it was stained a dull red from seepage. Underneath the cast something in the wound had opened, and blood had worked through the gauze and plaster. It embarrassed Gillon because it seemed so personal and vile.

"I'm sorry," he said.

"Sorry? This is a blessing," Calder said.

"Unless, of course, he dies of it."

It struck them as amusing, and Selkirk roared with laughter. They asked him to turn around several times.

"If you dressed him up properly he could pass for a toff," Mr. MacDonald said. "Selkirk?"

Selkirk seemed to materialize from the drapes on the window overlooking Princes Street.

"He's as good as you wrote. I think we have our find."

They stood and looked at him. MacDonald had his hands folded before him, the tips of his fingers touching.

"But what are those two lumps on his back?" Miss Tweed asked.

"These, Miss?" Selkirk said. She nodded. "Muscles, Miss, they're called muscles."

There was that laughter again, so light and airy, not the way miners laughed, and the lawyer asked him where he was educated, because he spoke so well.

"Nowhere," Gillon said.

"Remarkable. Did you know you were a remarkable man?"
Gillon shook his head.

"So far," Calder said. "The pressure hasn't come yet."

"Once the summons is cleared through the court, it doesn't matter about pressure, it's out of what's-his-name—Cameron's hands. If he can go that far, we can go the rest. Now, tell us how it happened."

He told it as clearly as he could and was angry to see the two lawyers begin to laugh and finally begin to roar with laughter. Tears were actually running down Calder's face.

"I'm sorry," MacDonald said, "I truly am sorry. It's just Elphinstone. You'd have to know him. Such a *fool*. Such a complete *idiot*. It's what makes the case so perfect, you see."

Gillon was given his instructions then. Under the rules of the Compensation Act the workman first had to make formal application to the company for compensation for injuries received.

"How much are you asking for?" Miss Tweed asked. Gillon knew the demand was exaggerated; for a moment he considered cutting it in half but didn't.

"Four hundred pounds."

It was met with silence. Even to the law agents it seemed a large sum.

"For a workingman," Calder said.

"It's all right, it doesn't matter," MacDonald said. "The judge will set the final sum. We just want the case in court."

When the application was rejected, as they knew it would be, Angus MacDonald, on behalf of his client, Mr. G. Cameron, Esq., would then ask the Writer to the Signet to draw up a summons ordering one C. P. S. Farquhar, better known as the Earl of Fyffe, to appear in the Sheriff's Court in Cowdenbeath on such-and-such a date and answer to the judge why he didn't choose to pay Mr. Cameron ample money for injuries received in his employ.

When approved by the court the summons would be impressed with the signet of the Keeper of the Signet and then delivered to a messenger-at-arms for personal service on Lord Fyffe at Brumbie Hall.

And following that, Mr. MacDonald said, all hell was going to break loose.

For the first time Gillon felt his stomach flutter.

"How much is all this going to cost us?"

"Oh, a few pounds."

How easily the words came out. A few pounds, and how much sweat lay behind them. Yet the Cameron Defense Fund could cover the costs without anyone feeling any hurt at all and for the first time Gillon sensed what it meant to be organized. A dark, strong-looking young man put his head inside the door to the office.

"Is this the man then?"

He came in and took Gillon's hand, not noticing Gillon wince.

"It's not going to be easy. I want to warn you of that." Gillon said that he knew.

"They're not going to like it. You know what you're up against? You know who's stacked against you?"

"I have most of my life." The handsome, dark man laughed. He looked at Gillon in a different way from the way the lawyers had.

"You're going to do, you know that?" He turned to the others. "He's going to do, by God," and opened a side door and stepped into the hallway.

"Just don't let us doon," Gillon heard him say down the hall. The "doon" was hollow and had the sound of death about it. "No matter what they do, don't you let us *doon*."

It was time to go. Gillon could see the little tea cart standing in the doorway, a signal for the miners to be on their way.

"Would you care to take some tea?" MacDonald said in a weak way.

"I'm sorry, we can't," Gillon said, and saw the look of relief pass over their eyes as swiftly as shadows at sea. He didn't understand them but he understood this much: it was one thing to help a man in trouble and quite another to take tea with him.

"Why do you do this for us?" Gillon suddenly asked. It surprised them.

"Why, for the cause," Calder said.

"What cause?"

They looked at one another. It was very bad manners—Gillon sensed that—like asking someone the price of the gift he had given you.

"The . . . ah, cause. Justice, rights, all *that*."

The serving girl was making discreet little tinkling sounds in a teacup with her spoon, warning them that their tea was getting cold.

"I do it from guilt if you want to know," Mr. MacDonald suddenly said. "I saw what my father did to get me here. I'm not about to give it up but I want to pay part of the price for it."

It was an embarrassing moment, but Gillon could sense that MacDonald was happy to have said it.

"Since we're all being so honest, I'll tell you why I do it. I do it for love," Calder said.

"Oh, come, now," Miss Tweed said.

"No, it's true. I want to say it. Do you know the poem that goes, 'For a' that, an' a' that'?"

> *"For a' that, an' a' that,*
> *It's comin' yet for a' that,*
> *That man to man the world o'er*
> *Shall brithers be for a' that."*

"We're all brothers, all on the same little boat, all traveling to the same end. Not all equal, of course, but we *are* brothers. Just try a flood or a fire sometime. When a hand reaches out you don't look at the hand, you grab for it."

It was hard to imagine Mr. Calder in a fire or a flood, somehow, but even so Gillon was inspired by his concept of brotherhood. He wanted to tell them of the feeling he had sometimes coming out of the pit, all the backs ahead of him bent, hunching their way to the shaft head, all black with sweat and coal dust and the wonderful sense of love that would suddenly possess him for these men, asking for so little out of the world, asking for a little bread and salt to put on their tables, asking only for a little respect and to be treated like the men they were. But he decided against it, and the tea cart was pushed into the room. Mr. MacDonald, with a sudden enthusiasm, took Gillon by the hand.

"Oh, you're going to do fine. How I wish I had had you to throw up against my father."

As hungry as they were, they decided not to eat in Edinburgh, where they felt out of place, and to take the train back out to Cowdenbeath, where, they assured each other, the food would be better and cheaper. Selkirk was himself again.

"Love, for Christ's sake. Did you hear him? 'Love is what it's all about,'" he said, imitating Calder, although, as Gillon tried to point out, Calder had never said it. "Ah, well, at least we have them working for us."

"Us?"

"The movement. As soon as we win, they go. The price of victory. New problems, new tools, as simple as that." He made a sign with his finger over his throat. Gillon was glad the compartment was empty. Mr. Selkirk always made Gillon ill at ease in public.

"Love," the librarian said sarcastically. "Organization is what it's all about. Organization is the only thing that sticks. Love doesn't last. And love doesn't win battles, my friend; battalions do. Love, my wounded miner, is bourgeois bullshit and should be dumped back in the cow barn where it was invented. Do you want me to go on?"

The librarian could see that he was turning a good trip into something sour for Gillon, and to his credit he stopped.

"No, no, Gillon, love has its place. Even Marx admits that, in case you didn't know."

"No, I didn't know."

"It's just that hunger is the dominant fact in life, and the fear of hunger is what drives men, my friend, and not love."

" 'Hunger is a good master,' my wife always says."

"And since Mr. Calder has never been hungry an afternoon in his life, he doesn't know what in hell he's talking about."

They were coming to the Forth Bridge, and the gigantic reach of the cantilevered towers across the firth commanded their attention. It had been dark when they had come over it. Gillon had never seen anything as remarkable before.

"Think of the number of men who must have died building it," Selkirk said.

"Yes, but maybe it was worth it?"

"Nothing can justify the taking of a workingman's life."

"I don't know." Gillon smiled rather sadly. "I think I'm about to give mine for a hell of a lot less than this."

Even Selkirk was obliged to smile.

"But think of the plaque we'll be putting up on the wall of Number One Tosh-Mungo Terrace," he said.

The firth was rough and Gillon could see a little fishing boat trying to beat its way to the shelter of Inchgarvie. The wind was very hard and the current strong. The seaman was in serious trouble. It was strange to sit up there, far above the sea, head propped on hand, and casually watch a man struggling for his life down below you. It occurred to Gillon that that was what they were doing to him in Edinburgh. They would be in the position of being in the train, and he would be alone in the sea.

All right, Gillon thought, if that was the way it was going to have to be, so be it.

The boat had overturned. The seaman had failed to make his turn and now he was in the water, holding on to a rope tied to the gunwale.

"They don't understand that down there, you see. Hunger," Selkirk said. "No man who has a full stomach can ever quite understand hunger and the things it can make men do."

He wouldn't last long in that water: the roughness, the current, and the cold. He was in over his depth, beyond his abilities. Out there alone and foundering. It made Gillon shiver.

A whaleboat was starting out from Inchgarvie. There were people on the shore, women helping the men get the boat in the water. He could see the white spume flying as the water slapped the prow; touch and go and then he saw the oars flashing. Good brave men. That's it, what I mean by love, Gillon thought. What reason had they to take that little boat into that rough sea, what right, even, to chance their own lives, but they were doing it, oars digging in and lifting out, going to the help of some man they might never have seen in their lives.

"The thing of hunger," Selkirk said, "is that when it's around you don't have an appetite for love."

Gillon hoped the man could see the whaleboat, because it would fire him, in that freezing water, with the will to hang on.

"Love, in everyday life, is a luxury."

"What you are saying then," Gillon said, "is that hunger is a good master but a poor lover."

"Aye." He smiled.

"Or love is too good for the poor. Who was that man who came into the office?"

"Who was that man?"

A man in the bow of the whaleship was on his feet and had a line in his hand. It was a good sign. The smaller boat had washed up against a great black stone off the island and the rush of surf against it was handing man and boat a terrible beating.

"That was Keir Hardie, man."

"Keir Hardie? That man? Why didn't anyone tell me?" Gillon

turned back to the window. They were across the bridge. The boat was gone, the stone was gone, the island was gone.

"Now I'll never know."

"Never know what?"

"Nothing," Gillon said. "It's nothing at all."

He couldn't account for it but it made him feel better about the thing he was doing. Life was like what he had just seen when you were able to see it from afar, one life, one little boat in a broiling sea, and in the end, if you made it through the gap in the firth, who really knew and who really cared, and if you didn't, what did it really matter? The trip was what mattered and you did that as well as you could and no one could ask for more of you. So Gillon felt better, despite knowing that a fellow man very possibly had just died for his bread beneath his eyes.

But he wondered if the man had made it after all, because it was an omen, of that he was sure. If the man made it, Gillon felt certain, *he* was going to make it, and if the man went under, Gillon was going to go under also.

"Do you know one thing?" Gillon said, surprised at his own discovery. "You're the real romantic. I just want a little better world while I'm alive and a little better world for my children but you want a workingman's paradise. No wonder you're bitter, it's so hard to see paradise in Pitmungo."

Mr. Selkirk sulked. He didn't like being criticized by coal miners and, worse, he recognized a certain amount of truth in what Gillon said. "The final goal, that's what counts, and all the rest is nothing," he said when they got off the train in Cowdenbeath, and it occurred to Gillon that in the most improbable of ways, Selkirk was much like Maggie. They just arrived at the same final belief by two different roads.

They stopped in the Miners' Arms for late breakfast. It was dark there and quiet. They had baps and tea and, on second thought, a rasher of bacon—it *was* an outing; they had been to Edinburgh and seen their capital and the castle, had met their law agents and Keir Hardie—and then Mr. Selkirk allowed as he would have just one or two Newhaven gills of whisky to see him the final jog home. It was a nice way to put it, Gillon thought. Since a gill was four ounces and a Newhaven gill was double that and since when Mr. Selkirk said one or two he meant two or three, Gillon left him after the first Newhaven gill went down and began the long walk home. Mr. Selkirk was searching for paradise in the bottom of a bottle again. When the shift was over that afternoon Gillon sent Sandy Bone and Sam to Cowdenbeath to bring Mr. Selkirk home in the wagon.

4   THEY WENT DOWN THE NEXT MORNING—GILLON and Walter Bone as witness—to see Mr. Brothcock. Gillon knocked on the pay-shed door and when there was no answer went quietly along one side of the building, trying not to crunch the slate and coal, until he was able to see the superintendent at his desk. He came back and knocked again, and when there still was no answer Gillon pushed the door open and stood in the doorway. Brothcock didn't look up.

"Sir? I have come to file . . ." The superintendent looked up.

"Who asked you to push my door open?"

"I knocked and when there was no answer—"

"You *knocked!* If I knocked on the door of your house . . . You're Cameron, aren't you?"

"Aye."

"Christ, you'd know, wouldn't you? Would you expect me to walk in your house?"

"I thought, sir . . ."

"Answer that!"

Gillon stood and tried to keep looking him in the face.

"You can't, can you?"

". . . this being a place of business, a public place . . ."

"All right, enough of the shit." Brothcock swung his chair

369

around so that Gillon would be talking to the back of his head. "What do you want?"

Gillon read from his paper, swiftly but clearly.

"Having been gravely injured while about my duties in Lord Fyffe Number One of the Pitmungo Coal and Iron Company—"

"Get on with it."

"I hereby make formal request for ample and fair compensation by the Company for the injury received, expenses incurred, the loss of past and future wages because of the aforementioned injury—to wit, a coal pick stuck into claimant's shoulder by a visitor to the mine, namely one Elphinstone. Under the rules of the Crown governing the operation of mines . . ."

"Rules?" The back of Brothcock's neck was red. "We make the rules here." He was beginning to swivel his chair around.

". . . and the matter of compensation for men injured in the mines through negligence on the part of the owners of said mine, complainant asks fair and just recompense of four hundred pounds."

The superintendent had fully turned around by then and as he did Gillon put the paper he had read to him in his hand. Brothcock pretended not to notice it.

"One hundred pounds I might have laughed at, do you understand that? Something to bargain with, something to fool with. But four hundred pounds." He got up from his chair and it wasn't until he was up and angry that one realized how powerful a man Brothcock was. He was fat, but beneath the fat the residue of a violent body still lurked, waiting to be summoned. "Four hundred pounds annoys me. Four hundred pounds makes me angry. Now, I am going to tell you what I plan to do. Since you entered my office unlawfully I'm going to throw you out of it and when I do I want to know if you want to go with a kick in the doup or a kick in the gowls—which one do you want, Mr. Cameron, take your choice," he said and began to move toward Gillon. Gillon backed away.

"You have my paper, it's in your hand."

Brothcock rolled the paper into a ball, opened the lid to his coal stove, and threw the paper in and watched it burn.

"No, I never had any paper."

"This gentleman saw you accept the paper. Heard you, saw you."

Walter Bone nodded.

"Then the gentleman is a liar. His word against my word. Whose do you think they'll believe?" He turned on Gillon suddenly then. "I kicked your thick-headed son down the steps a few days ago; it's your turn now."

"If you lay hand on that man," Walter Bone said, in a voice as hard-edged as broken ice, "this pick goes into your arm where the boy's pick went into his."

"Why, son of a bitch. Walter Bone," Brothcock said and wheeled, and in the same wheeling motion smashed Walter Bone in the ribs and sent him backward through the door the way Jem had gone before.

He was hurt and it wasn't an easy thing for Gillon, with the use of only one arm, to get him to his feet. He motioned to some pithead girls across the way, loading pitprops on the cage, to come and help, but they had seen what happened and didn't want to help Mr. Brothcock's victim, not where he could see them.

"How are you, Walter? Are you all right, then?"

"Och, Christ." Gillon had never heard him use profanity. "I can get up, if that's what you mean. The bastard broke my rib."

"It was a terrible blow."

"Aye, but this isn't the end of it."

"No, this is the start. You should sue him too, Walter."

"No, no." Bone was very excited. "Your suit first, man. One at a time. Keep our eye on the main chance."

He was right, Gillon knew that. Mr. Bone would have to live with his damaged rib and pride.

"Will you help me write the letter to Mr. MacDonald? I can't write yet."

"Aye, if I can. Right now."

They started up what was left of the Sportin Moor. It was slow going because each breath caused Mr. Bone sharp pain.

"Do one thing," he said. "Don't tell my sons. There are some of them who would do something about it and I don't want that now." Gillon agreed on that, and then, despite everything, found himself laughing at the sight the two of them must be making, two battered men barely able to climb over the potholes on the moor, preparing to mount a revolution.

"Would you really have hit him with the pick?"

"I didn't have one."

"Well, would you though?"

"No, I don't hit men with picks." He was such an honest man, Gillon thought.

"Well, I'm sorry for you anyway," Gillon said.

"Sorry? I wouldn't have it any other way."

Once in the house, Mrs. Bone wrapped him in an old sheet as if he were a mummy, immobilizing the rib, and the pain was better. Miners understand broken ribs, as Mrs. Bone said. If you stopped work for every broken rib, a man would starve to death. He got out his quill pen and honed the point and thinned out his thick ink with water.

"How do you address a lawyer?" Mr. Bone said.

"They don't like to be called lawyers, I know that. They're advocates, I think. Or solicitors. Or law agents . . ."

"Barristers, aren't they?" Mrs. Bone said. In the end they settled for "Angus MacDonald, Esq." and opened the letter "Dear Sir." They told him what had happened, that their request for compensation had been made and rejected, and that they wished him to file suit in the Sheriff's Court at Cowdenbeath against the Honorable C. P. S. Farquhar, the Earl of Fyffe.

Although it was evening when they finished the letter, Gillon asked Sam to trot the five miles down to Easter Mungo and post it because it was understood that all the mail in and out of Pitmungo enjoyed the scrutiny of the Company, and after that Gillon went home and waited for the mill of justice to begin grinding the kernel of his complaint.

It happened sooner than they were prepared for. No one in Pitmungo saw the Messenger-at-Arms come or go, so that moment when the summons was served on Lord Fyffe was never established. When the reaction to the summons was considered, many felt the messenger fortunate to get out of Brumbie Hall alive.

Perhaps the paper had been handed over at the weak time, the drowsy time after lunch when the port had been put away and the Earl's sheets were being turned down for his nap. Whenever it was, the impact of the summons was unexpected, sudden, and severe.

That same afternoon, when the shift was over and the men were coming out of the pits, Lord Fyffe shut down his mines and locked out his miners.

Lord Fyffe No. 1 and Lady Jane No. 2 and all the older, smaller pits in the valley were closed. By nightfall, thirteen hundred men, women, and children were out of work. By morning, the following notice was posted at the mouth of each of the mines:

TO ALL MY COLLIERS

One among you has seen fit to have a summons served upon your coal master, the effect of which would be to have him taken to court like a common criminal, thus risking the erosion for all time of the relationship that has existed through so much and for so long between his Lordship and his men.

As all of you know, Pitmungo Coal and Iron Company, almost alone among coal owners in the area, has been generous in the extreme in compensating those among you unfortunate enough to suffer injury while at work. Let this much be known by all of you:

No collier is hurt in any of his mines where that hurt is not felt in Brumbie Hall. Prayers for a successful recovery are said at grace and plans for an equitable compensation made at once.

This relationship, his Lordship would wish to believe, has been not unlike that of a father to his sons, each contributing in his own way to the happiness of the family whole. Now that relationship has been soiled. One of his sons has been disloyal to his family and the hurt to his Lordship has been a true one, and cruel.

As in any family, when one is hurt all must suffer, and that is even more true when the head of the family is the one hurt. Until the time when this contemptible suit is withdrawn and stricken from the Court calendar, this pit—these mines—will be shut for good.

In the spirit of trust between us, in the knowledge that God will see that our ordained family will continue to exist, father with son, one with the other, in the old old way, I close:

God Bless You, God Bring You Back Your Work Again:

Fyffe

5 THERE HAD NEVER BEEN ANYTHING LIKE IT IN PIT-mungo before. Partly it was the lockout and the exhilaration of the men being together. But partly it was June and the sun coming out again. The men hadn't experienced a June since they were small children.

Once more winter had been defeated just when there was the feeling that perhaps this was the year God would forget and there would be no spring after all. The low smothering clouds that had been drifting down from the north since March, so heavy with wet snow they seemed to scrape along the High Moor, were beginning to break apart, and there were whole minutes of such a clear, bright blueness before the banks closed in again that it made a person light-headed and even giddy. The sun splayed down into dark corners of the town where black snow still hid, melting the snow to blackish water. Water was running, everywhere, down between the cobbles on the lanes and rows, taking the frozen coal scud with it, and then the town began drying, from Tosh-Mungo Terrace on down. Windows were opened, and all the accumulated sourness and smells of a miner's winter began fading in the soft, sun-warmed winds drifting down the moors.

No one minded the lockout then. Each time the sun broke through the people poured out of the but-and-bens and bathed in it, faces to it, barely moving in it, performing without knowing it some old Druidic rite, seized by the sun the same way the salmon were. It was something in the blood and it had been denied them too long. There was a feeling of festival in the air those first weeks, of carnival and carelessness.

All those days the men filed up to Tosh-Mungo—there were no Uppies and Doonies any longer—to give Gillon their hand and assure him they were behind him and what he was doing. Clerks from the Company were writing down the names of the men coming and going from Tosh-Mungo Terrace and then one of the miners masked his face with coal dust and that ended the name taking. He became what a miner so often is—an invisible man. After that the others blacked their faces, and then a "committee" of men went down to the walk, caps low, faces black, and took the notebooks away. It all added to it, days plashy with sunshine and the feeling of all being together. As much as the compensation, Gillon soon found, it was the Sportin Moor that still inflamed the men.

"*Now* he'll pay for that, the son of a bitch. Be sure you bring that up," they would say, pointing down at the moor.

But the compensation loomed as large. Hardly a family hadn't waited for days and weeks to see what the Laird would lavish on them, if he wished to lavish anything at all.

"Och, how I wish my daddie was here to see this day, to see what you have done," a young miner said. "Rob Hope, remember him? He lost a hand and starved to death because he wouldn't take a crumb from us. It makes me cry the now. Five pounds croo he got, and had to crawl to Brumbie Hall and put a please note on a plate at the door to get it."

The stories were endless, there was one for every house in Pitmungo it seemed. Even Maggie was touched. She knew what she was hearing was true, and she knew that it was only by luck that it hadn't happened to the Camerons. Of course, for the Camerons there was always siller in the kist to fall back on. None of the others had that.

As the days passed, the real issue became focused. It wasn't the money Gillon wanted that disturbed Lord Fyffe, but the fact that he was demanding it. It was the threat to his fatherly right to decide how much to give and if to give at all. In the end it was the struggle to hold on to the past against the desire to bury it and find new ways. The pick in Gillon's arm and the pain it caused him came to mean nothing at all.

The solution rested in the Courts, but in other places as well— mainly in money. No one had counted on that at first. Every day the men didn't work cost them a few shillings, but every day the mines stayed closed, the people at Brumbie Hall—Mr. C. P. S. Farquhar, as the people had begun calling him, and his tall dry wife, Lady Jane Tosh-Mungo—lost hundreds of pounds. It was a question of how long pride could come before profit.

"Now, listen, I wouldna worry too much if I was you," Archie Japp came and said. Japp, who for so many years had been so hard on Gillon. "I wouldna' fash mysel.' I know these people better than you. When the people down in London don't get their dividend checks there'll be strange letters coming to Pitmungo. They have their habits to attend to, do you understand what I mean? If Mrs. Cameron wasn't in the room I'd tell you about a few of them."

"Such as?" Maggie said. "It isn't a child sitting over here."

He thought about it for a time. If he wasn't such a dark man, such a true Pict, as Maggie would have described him, a person might have imagined that he blushed.

"Would it surprise you to know that one of them keeps a house —an entire mansion, mind you—for young—young . . ."

"Bosh, do you think I can't imagine a world like that?"

"*Boys?*"

"Oh."

"Beautiful young boys. All dressed in silks and satins and some of them dressed like young ladies?"

The room was very still after that.

"I mean to say, you asked and all. It wasn't that I . . . scandalmonger and all. Oh, well."

"And that is where our money goes," Gillon said.

"It makes you want to fight the harder," Mr. Japp said. The two old enemies shook hands.

"What would he do with them?" Maggie said, when Mr. Japp was gone.

"Who?"

"The man with the boys in the house."

Gillon thought about it. The question annoyed him because it took his mind away from the speech he was writing in his head. Sometime he was going to be asked to make a speech rallying the people to him and he wanted to be ready for the challenge.

"I don't know what he would do. Whatever it is it couldn't be healthy."

"Maybe you are doing the right thing, Gillon. Perhaps."

"Oh, my God, that *is* big. Every important man in town comes up here to lend his support and his own wife allows there might be something to it. Och! I should summon the family."

Surprisingly, the one person pessimistic about the outcome of the struggle was Henry Selkirk.

"Do you remember what I said about those well-meaning people down in Edinburgh, that they didn't understand about hunger? They never should have thrown the challenge down at this time. The people are feeling the pinch already, and the battle barely begun."

It was startling to Gillon. He walked up and down the Terrace and Moncrieff Lane. The timing had not been right. The kail yards behind the homes were all planted with the root crops, potatoes and turnips and beets, and the greens and beans and salads were in the ground, still vulnerable to a killing frost, but it would be months before any of them would be ready to eat or be canned and stored and pickled. Had the lockout begun in August or September the people could have lived off their gardens for months, with the heavy coal-buying and mining time coming on.

But nothing was up now but a few radishes, and even miners couldn't live on radishes alone. Then Lord Fyffe closed down the Pluck Me and the bakery and for the first time in Pitmungo there was no credit, which had always been encouraged before as a way of making the men beholden to the Company. For the first time Gillon had his doubts, but then a letter was delivered by hand from Cowdenbeath.

Dear Cameron:

Don't think that we don't know what you are going through. This is not the first time this has been done in Scotland. But this is the first time it will succeed.

Great victories such as yours demand great courage and endurance. Nothing worth earning is easy. You have much to lose; they have more. It is a comfort in hard times to remember that. You have much to lose in character by giving in; they have little. It is a comfort also to consider that.

Together, to all of us here, these two factors spell success. Do not think that you fight alone. The eyes of Scotland's miners are on you. The hopes of Scotland's workingmen go with you and the men of Pitmungo.

Your comrade,

Keir Hardie

Copies of the letter were made and passed down through the rows and lanes.

"They'll help us, you'll see," Walter Bone said. "The Scotch Miners' Union will see us through the pinch."

It was so strange to Gillon, this turning about of ideas in Pitmungo, how what was dark and unseeable, what was even disagreeable and dangerous, was suddenly seen in its new light. A few months ago the word "union" had frightened them and now they all knew that in their unity was their hope and they spoke about it not as revelation or some new concept but as an ancient truth a man would have to be a sumph not to go along with. The tyranny of rightness. Here was Archie Japp wanting to know how a chapter of a union could be established and Andy Begg, once the strong arm for the Company, wheezing up the hill, the black lung had him now, asking that when the collieshangie began in earnest he be given Mr. Brothcock to handle—or manhandle—all by himself.

Gillon could still smile in those days.

"There are others in line ahead of you, my son Jem for one, but you have waited the longest. Aye, I give you Brothcock for your own."

What worried Gillon about himself was the sense of power he felt when he said it.

6 THE PINCHING, THE CUTTING BACK, BEGAN IN earnest after the first weeks in June. There were still turnips and barrels of oats left over from the winter before and so there was still life. Neep brose, oatmeal mixed with turnips, was the big meal of the day. Piss-a-beds were popping up on the moor, which the world beyond Pitmungo knew as dandelions, and they were good as field salad and boiled and in stew, if anyone had anything to put in stew. There was cockcrow'n' kail, chicken soup without any chicken, just boiled moor grass, but it was acidy and made a man's stomach sour.

"And now it's time for the women," Selkirk said. "I've seen it before in other towns. You can't blame them. When the children start to cry themselves to sleep from hunger you would be amazed how small a principle can suddenly appear."

"Oh, these are good women," Sam said. "We've known hunger here. They'll stand fast behind our dad."

"Only those who haven't gone without are afraid of hunger," Andrew said. "We all know hunger here."

"Hunger by choice?" Mr. Selkirk said.

It bothered them when it was put that way. What was he trying to do, anyway? Why did Selkirk have to come up here and damp every fire they lit?

"But what the hell, the people *have* no choice," Sam said. "The decision lies with Daddie. It's up to him to withdraw the suit and he's not about to do it."

"No, the women will stand fast behind the men," Gillon said, and looked at Maggie and knew she didn't believe it. But then she had always had a very low estimate of Pitmungo women when it came to denial and doing without.

On Sunday, in kirk, he saw the first of the looks, felt them as much as saw them, the questioning looks, the faintly hostile and accusing looks of some of the older women, who didn't understand why Gillon was doing such a thing to the Laird or to them, upsetting the reliable balance of their lives.

The sermon for the day was an old and tested one with Mr. MacCurry—knowing one's position in the order of things. There was a ladder in this world stretching all the way to eternity, as it were—not literally, he spelled out—and on that ladder there was a rung for every man and woman. In his infinite wisdom God placed each person on his proper rung and every man knew when he had reached it because he found himself happy there and experienced a feeling of contentment and satisfaction with his life and his duties in it. Knowing one's place on the ladder was the font of true happiness, Mr. MacCurry said.

One great sin in the world was backsliding, because when the Lord placed a person on His ladder, He put him there at the peak of his powers and responsibilities and one owed a duty to live up to them.

But another, greater sin was that of false aspirations. Avarice of position. Aspiring for a higher place on the ladder by climbing over the people God had placed on the ladder above you. In the end it could only lead to failure, because it became the source of anxiety and dissatisfaction and threw one out of step with the ordained rhythm of the world. Sooner or later life would shake the false aspirers to pieces. People were beginning to turn and look at Gillon.

Jemmie got up and walked out. Mr. MacCurry quit his preaching and stared at Jemmie's back, as if imploring God to bear him out by sending a providential thunderbolt to strike the young man dead. Sam got up after that and from the other side of the kirk Sarah Cameron Bone.

"Don't worry, I would be up if I could make it," Sandy Bone said. Everyone heard it. "Where do I stand on the ladder, with no legs to stand on?"

Gillon sat in the pew and felt his face redden at the public scene, and then to his surprise Andrew, sitting next to his mother, got up and walked out, his face as red as his father's. Others got up after that, but only a few. The protest was made but the message was also taken. On the way out of the kirk, an old woman Gillon barely knew stopped him.

"Who in God's name do you think you are and what are you aspiring to?" she said. "Why can't you leave well enough alone?" Gillon was struck by the hostility in her eyes, and hurt by it, old pale blue eyes, like saucers that had been washed too often.

"Do you ken the suffering you've brought down on us to satisfy your pride and fill your pocket?"

He couldn't fail to see those other heads, mostly older ones then, nodding in agreement, or fail to see the anger poorly hidden in their eyes.

They began by asking when the case was going to be brought to trial. There was a general belief that once the case was in court the lockout would be over, because there would be no more point to it. But Gillon didn't know about the progress of his case. Mr. MacDonald didn't write with any news. The miners' duty was to stand and wait. And none of them had any experience with how long it took a case to come to court.

"All the proper papers filed, I suppose?" someone would ask.

"Aye, I suppose they are."

"But you don't know?"

"Well, I have a famous law agent and he must be doing the right thing."

"Aye, I suppose he must. Because we're getting a wee bit hungry the now down at our place."

"Yes, the same is true in our house."

They were used to the sun by then and the joy of being out of work was fading. The problem with the movement was that there was none. The struggle was taking place in courts and law offices far beyond them. In Pitmungo there was only sitting in doorways and waiting. Some of the men went up poaching into the Lomond Hills at night and brought back moor stream trout and grouse and a few snared rabbits, and the daring ones—desperate was more accurate—stole lambkins from the sleeping flocks at night. But most of the men sat in the sun in the doorways and smoked their dwindling supplies of tobacco and listened to the cheerful cry of the work whistles and the steady rumble of the breaker coming across the valley from Wester Mungo. They had never had more work there, Pitmungo heard.

"All right. I come to you. What do you think I should do?" Gillon said to Maggie. It was the first time they had really spoken about what was taking place in Pitmungo since the night Maggie had bitten Sam's hand.

"I don't know." She refused to look at him. "You got yourself into it. Get yourself out of it."

"I don't want to get out of it. I don't intend to get out of it. But I want to get *them* out of it."

"You can't have it both ways, can you, Gillon? You're always trying to have it both ways."

"I came to you for help."

He went to the window of the ben and looked down into the great dark swaying boughs of the Scotch pine. There had been nights with the wind soughing in the boughs when Gillon had thought of himself hanging from a limb of the tree.

"I can't stand to walk down the lane and have them staring at me. I can't stand hearing the children begging for food. I can't stand them crying. I hear them at night."

"All you have to do is walk down to Brumbie Hall and ask for your summons back."

"I can't go down there and come back as Gillon Cameron and you know it."

"Is your neck that stiff? Is your pride worth that much?"

"It's gone beyond pride, and you know that, too. It's us against them now, out in the open. The right of a man to come down and steal our moor away from us without so much as a single *word*— not one word—being raised against it? Do you understand what that means? Our heritage stolen in front of our eyes and we stand there pretending to smile? I've told you this and I mean it, Meg. I will not deny myself any longer. I will no longer live in a place where I'm forced to smile while I'm being beaten. It's the smiling I object to."

She got up from her work and came over to him. She didn't touch him but she was close to him, he sensed that.

"All right. You both have your pride, but he's got a million-pound business to run. Have you checked the boats, man?"

"What do the boats matter now?"

"You don't think he would have called a lockout if there were coal bottoms at the wharf, do you?"

There are times when a man hears the truth and at that moment he knows he has been a fool. He needn't admit it to anyone, it simply burns of its own accord inside one. He had been a fool, in his heart, in his mind, in his essence a fool.

In the wrong season, when the men were in their weakest position, Gillon had let them go ahead. When all the advantages rested with Lord Fyffe, he had let the summons be served. He had chosen to wage war with Fyffe and then allowed the Earl to choose the battleground and take his pick of weapons. There was no point in blaming Angus MacDonald; a city lawyer couldn't be expected to know the facts of daily life in a coal town such as Pitmungo; and Gillon, because he wanted to, had shut his eyes to them. He was sick with himself. They had suffered a month now for nothing.

"When enough coal bottoms are standing off St. Andrew's, Fyffe will find some excuse to have Brothcock open the pits and the men will go down, Gillon, because the women and the children will make them go down. Nothing will have changed."

"But the case. You forget the case. We will have won that; he'll never be able to get around that again."

"Do you believe that?" Maggie said. She shook her head a little sadly and somewhat fondly. "How many other Gillon Camerons do you think can be found in Pitmungo?"

He came away from the window.

"What do I do now?"

"Oh, God, Gillon, get going, man. Get someone up on the High Moor tonight and take the count of the boats in the harbor so you know where you stand."

He felt like a fool once more.

It was rainy and cold, an unseasonably raw night on the moor.

"He won't be able to count them in this weather," Gillon said.

"Then he'll have to go down and count them at the dock. Good God, Gillon, you have babies crying the night through for food and you don't want to ask someone to get a little soaking on the moor?"

What seemed like generosity was only weakness, he knew. Jemmie was lying near the remains of the fire, curled in a ball next to it.

"I don't want to go up there, Daddie," Jem said.

"Why not?" He was very stern. Maggie was right about it. There had been all too much softhearted, softheaded nonsense. The carnival part of it, the sun festival, was over.

"I'm not feeling so good."

"Not feeling so good. And how do you think the children of Pitmungo are feeling right now? Do you know they found a boy eating clay, handfuls of clay, up behind Moncrieff Lane at the claybank yesterday?"

Jemmie admitted he hadn't known that.

"The boy said he'd been eating it for a week or more just to have something to fill up his baggie. Sit up." Jem did it. "You look all right to me."

"That may be, Dad, but I don't feel all right."

His mother came back into the but then and put a hand to his cheek and then to his brow.

"You feel all right. Go look into the glass."

Jemmie got up and dragged himself across the room.

"Now, answer me this," his mother said. "If there was a match in Cowdenbeath this afternoon, a championship match, and you could go to it, would you go to it? Look in the glass. Honest now."

Jem finally smiled at himself.

"Aye," he said, "I'd try."

"Then . . ."

"All right, all right."

He came across the room, putting on his pit vest, and although he never wore it except at work, he went upstairs for his cap. When he looked at Gillon, his face was drawn and his breathing labored.

"But I don't feel good," he said at the door. "Good night." Gillon felt the chill all the way across the room when the door opened and closed.

"Maybe he shouldn't . . ."

"Maybe he should," Maggie said. "If he's really sick he'll be back."

"He's terribly stubborn. He's like you."

"Och."

"Once he's started he doesn't stop."

"Look who's talking the now."

"No, it's true, though. He's your boy, Meg. The very things that keep you apart are what you have in common. He's a Drum to his soul."

"Soul, soul. Why do you keep saying soul when you don't believe in a God or a soul?"

. . .

They were eating oatmeal cakes and drinking cups of hot water for the filling effect when Walter Bone tapped on the door.

"I want you to know this before you hear it elsewhere," he said. "Jean Wallace died this afternoon in her chair in her house. Dr. Gowrie has put down malnutrition leading to starvation as cause of death." The spoon fell out of Gillon's hand.

"It's my fault then. I killed her," he said.

"Now don't get dramatic on us," Mr. Bone said. His voice was hard.

"I killed her."

"Stop it." He came close to clapping Gillon's mouth shut. "Everyone in Pitmungo knows Jean Wallace had a tumor the size of a melon in her head. Dr. Gowrie is paid by the Company and I expect you to understand that. No one is starving to death in Pitmungo yet."

Gillon picked his spoon up off the floor and put it on the table. There would be no more eating for him.

"I expect better of you. It's the first of their moves. If you don't stand fast who will stand fast?"

"Aye." He got up and took Mr. Bone's hand. "I'm sorry."

"Don't be sorry, man; be determined."

Because it was rainy and cold and dark the lane was deserted. The doors were closed and the curtains were drawn against the wind to keep the night out and the warmth in, so there was no one at all on Tosh-Mungo Terrace to see the men who came and threw the cobblestones against the door and the front window, smashing the diamond panes of glass and the wood and lead of the frames. They heard shouts and the sound of feet going back down the Terrace, hobnails against the cobblestones. Miners. A note was tied to one of the stones.

Your no Jesus Christ. We don't want to die for your sins and siller. Withdraw!

Gillon put boards across the windows and tried to go back to sleep but the wind moaned through the boards and it was cold. Poor Jem on the moor, Gillon thought. I should never have sent him out. It was all starting to go bad.

"Oh, God, what am I going to do?" he said aloud.

"I'll tell you one thing you're not going to do," Maggie said. "You're not going to go down the hill for people like that. When you go down you'll go down because you want to go down, not for those bastards. Now go to sleep like a good man."

When he woke, because no light came from the boarded windows he had no idea of the time. He got out of bed and went upstairs at once to the boys' room: no Jem. He went back down and opened the door onto the Terrace. The rain had stopped but the wind was still high. There was a touch of gray in the east, a suggestion of sun.

Glintin', they called it. False dawn. A hint, a glisk of day to come. No Jem. It gripped like ice around his heart. Chips of ice were on the floor, and then he remembered the stones and the glass. It was strange he would forget that so soon.

"Get up," he whispered in the boys' ears, "Jemmie's somewhere on the moor."

They took a shutter from the front window. Those should have been closed last night, Gillon thought. They would be from now on.

Should. Everything was *should* with him, it seemed. They went through the plantation and then spread out on the moor, as far apart from each other as they could go and still be sure of covering the ground. Sam found his brother just short of the crest of the High Moor, in a grass pocket out of the wind, huddled in a ball. He was shaking. When Sam turned him over, he barely could recognize Jem. One hand was at his throat as if trying to force it open. He said something but it came out as a croak and finally he held up six fingers and made the sound again.

"What is it?" Sam said.

"Six boats," Gillon said; "he went down and counted them," and felt tears start up. Stubborn, sick like that and still go on. They took off their coats and sweaters and wrapped them around Jem and tied him to the shutter and started back down the High Moor as swiftly as they could go without upsetting him.

"I think this is serious," Andrew said. "I think it's very serious."

They brought him down through the orchard. He opened his eyes and with one finger pointed at the green buds. The apples and cherries were in full bloom. When they brought him into the house, Maggie was up and a fire had been started. She looked at her son and then at Gillon.

"He must have been really sick," she said.

There was a small group of men at the door when they came through and Gillon thought they had come to look at the damage, but they had come for him instead.

"Where were you?" Walter Bone said.

"Jem was lost on the High Moor."

"Mr. Brothcock came calling on you."

It didn't seem to matter much then.

"Lord Fyffe wants to see you at Brumbie Hall on Saturday afternoon at tea."

7 "GET COAL," MAGGIE SAID. "GET ALL THE COAL YOU can get."

Sam and Andrew went out of the house and down the lane with their coal creels.

"You," to Emily. "Down the Terrace for your sister Sarah."

They carried the good bed from the ben into the but near the fireplace and put on all the coal they had left. She removed his wet clothing and began rubbing his body with a rough dry towel until his skin began to glow. Bricks had been placed by the fire, and when they were hot enough she wrapped them in flannel and lined his body and his feet with the hot bricks and covered him up. After he was covered she gave him a mug of hot tea that he had trouble getting down but that seemed to help.

"You keep the bricks hot, one by one," she told Gillon, "until he begins to sweat."

"Now, you," she said to Ian. "I know you've been stealing from the Pluck Me . . ."

"Mother!"

"Shut up! Did you think I didn't know, boy?" It was the nearest they had ever come to seeing Ian look uncomfortable. "I don't know how you'll get in and get out but you're going down now and get in and out for your brother. Bring back a bottle or two of lemon juice, the extract, you understand that?"

"Aye."

"A bag of brown sugar. A bottle of glycerine. One bottle of good whisky."

"They have no whisky."

"Then run down to the College and have your no-good brother get you a bottle. I don't care how he gets that either. Do you have that straight?"

"I never forget a shopping order from the Pluck Me," Ian said. He was his old self again.

Little weasel, she thought. Going to have to go to work on him. But even a weasel has his uses. She knew one thing about him, at least. He would get what was asked. There was that much Cameron in him.

From the larder Maggie produced a chunk of salt pork she had been saving for harder times, animal fat for when their bodies were depleted. She cut two strips and simmered them in a skillet in hot vinegar and when they were bubbling let them cool for just a moment and applied the strips of hot fat to Jemmie's throat, one slab on each side.

Sarah came up the Terrace.

"He's had a terrible chill. He suffered exposure on the moor.

If we can get him sweating, he'll be all right," her mother told her.

"What was he doing on the moor last night?"

"Your father sent him up," Maggie said. She went out of the front door, through the knot of people gathered there, and down to the pump for water. When she came back, as she was pouring the water in the kettle over the fire, she said, "I sent him."

Sarah knew better than to ask more. It was the great virtue of patience, she had discovered, that if you didn't ask or fret about a question, sooner or later it would be answered. Sooner or later people would demand to tell you what you wanted to know. They dressed him in knitted underwear and covered him up again.

"And what do you think of our father and Lord Fyffe?"

"I think six empty boats will talk louder than our father," Maggie said. "We can thank our Jemmie for that, at least."

Sarah didn't understand but she didn't ask. It would be revealed in time.

Rob Roy was at the door with the whisky.

"Can I come in?"

His mother looked at him the way she used to look at certain of her pupils in school.

"Of course you can come in. This is your home."

"I've never been in it."

"Well, it's your home. You shouldn't ask dumb questions at a time like this."

Rob Roy looked at Sarah.

"Things come and go in Pitmungo but some things never change," Rob said. "How's my brother?"

Sarah pointed to the bed and the huddled mass of Jem.

"Shouldn't we get the doctor?" Rob said.

"We've done all Gowrie could do," Maggie said, and Sarah nodded yes and so Rob accepted it as true.

"I came as quick as I could. They don't hand out good whisky when there's no money about to pay for it."

"What do we owe you?" Maggie said. He gave his mother the same kind of look she had given him.

"That's my brother lying under there, lady," Rob Roy said.

Sam and Andrew came back with the creels of coal and shook hands with Rob. There was no need for words among them, they saw each other in the pit, and after that Gillon came into the house. Jem was his main concern, but the full meaning of the meeting with Lord Fyffe was beginning to make itself felt. He stood over his son, wanting to touch him but afraid to, listening to the hard breathing of the boy, and then went over to the table, where for the first time he saw Rob Roy.

"I'm glad you came. Welcome to your house."

"I'm glad to be in it."

They shook hands and embraced one another. Some of the neighbors' children were in the doorway. The house, once so clannish, had become an open house in recent weeks. People came and went where once they weren't wanted or didn't want to go.

"I'd keep them out of here," Rob said. "Send them home. This is when they're most vulnerable to it, four to eight years or so."

"To what?" Maggie said. Rob Roy seemed puzzled by the question.

"Diphtheria. That's what he has, isn't it?"

The word put a chill on the house.

"What is diphtheria?" Emily asked and no one would answer.

"What makes you say that?" Gillon said. He was angry with his son.

"The way he looks, the way he sounds. I've seen them down at the barracks." His voice could barely be heard above the shuffling of his feet against the floor.

"When he begins to sweat, when he begins to soak those blankets, he'll be on his way," Maggie said, coming in from the ben.

"What's diph . . ." Emily began before Sam got a hand on her mouth.

"Aye, sweat's the thing," Rob said, happy for a chance to turn the talk another way. "Look," he said, seizing his father by the arms, not knowing the pain he was causing him, "before I'm in the house another minute. Here I am, the big talker and here you are, the one who's gone and done it."

"Och, who wouldn't do the same?"

"Here I am in my red bandanna, all ready for the barricades, revolution running from my mouth like a river of blood, and, Jesus, *here's* the man who goes out and does it."

Jem groaned. "Rob," Sarah said, but he didn't hear her.

"No, people don't say these things enough. Here's the man who has the Earl of Fyffe have to ask *him* down to Brumbie Hall to discuss the collapse of the capitalist society." He clapped his father on the back and it hurt almost as much as the arm. Jem groaned again.

"Do you remember when I said I wanted to change my name from Cameron? What did I say then?"

"Nothing," said Gillon. Rob was puzzled for a moment and then recalled.

"Aye, that was it. Rob Roy Nothing. Brilliant thought, wasn't it? Now I wouldn't change my name from Cameron for anything in the world." He was expansive and shouted the word "world," and Jemmie made his first intelligible sounds.

"I love you, Rab, but for Christ's sake, shut up," Jem said.

They propped him up after that and spoon-fed him a half gallon of strong tea and lemon juice, glycerine and whisky, as hot as a man could get down. In early afternoon, Jem began to sweat as if he were in the middle of a shift working a low, tough seam. He erupted in sweat; he poured out sweat until the knitted blankets seemed to steam. Maggie reheated the slices of salt pork and put them back on his throat and they fed him brown sugar and hot water to keep up his strength and sweating at the same time while Sarah bathed his hot head with cold water and witch hazel so that he didn't lose his senses from the heat. Sometime in the evening the sweating began to stop and Jemmie's voice began to come back. They changed his sopping underwear and washed out the blankets and put dry ones on. The worst was over, and they could get back to the real business of the day.

8 "IT's THIS WAY," GILLON SAID. "I DON'T KNOW WHAT to *call* him. I don't even know his *name*. What do I *say*?"

They looked at him. Not being faced with having to go down to Brumbie Hall, they hadn't thought through the personal part of it.

"I mean, do I take his hand? Kiss his ring? Do I bob to him? What do I *do*?"

"You act like a man. You go in there a man and you come out a man, as simple as that," someone said. "That's why we chose you."

Chosen him, Andrew thought. No one chose his father.

"That's easy to say, not so easy to do," Gillon said.

There was a murmur of "aye's" in the house. In deference to Jemmie and the Camerons' broken windows, the policy meeting was being held in Walter Bone's house. Thirty men in all, from every walk of Pitmungo. Uppies and Doonies crammed together in one room for the first time.

The mood of the town had shifted back again. The Laird had been forced to ask the miner to the manse!

"And Lady Jane, pouring the tea. I presume she pours the tea. What do I say to *her*? How do I call *her*?"

"Countess," someone said. "She's Lady Jane to us, see, that's the way we've always known her, but as the wife of an earl she's a countess."

"How would *you* know that?" Mr. Bone asked.

"A man gets around," the miner said.

There was silence in the Bone house. It sounded right, but that

394

only went to prove that none of them had any idea of what was really proper.

"One thing is plain. The formalities of it don't matter. If the Laird asked you down to his palace"—that was a mistake—"his house, his hame . . ."

"Some house!"

"Some hame!"

Gillon felt a sinking feeling again, an empty feeling in his stomach—nerves, he knew—as if he wanted to vomit, although he hadn't eaten anything since he heard the news.

"It doesn't matter," Archie Japp said. "If the master asks Cameron down for a cup of tea, he's not asking *Cameron* down for a cup of tea, he's looking for some kind of settlement. So I say, a settlement for Cameron here is a victory for all of us."

That rated applause and Gillon felt better. What did it matter if he dropped a cup of tea in his lap, what did it matter if he broke the back of one of the little gilded chairs they sat on, when the welfare of thirteen hundred workers was involved? And he felt like vomiting again.

"But what do I say? What do I settle?"

"First, tell him what a shit he was about the Sportin Moor, tell him *that* to start with." A lot of applause.

"And what do I wear? I'm representing you. I'm not going down to Brumbie Hall blinding people with the shine on my suit. I won't do it, I won't be seen that way."

"The man is right," Andy Begg said. "That's what they want, you see. That's why they have you down there. Want to make you feel like a fewkin cripple—"

"Language in this house."

"Excuse my mouth. Like a—a—"

"Cripple," Mr. Bone said. "You can just say cripple and we can understand you." It came as a revelation to Begg and some of the other miners.

"Aye, then. So when it comes time to open your gob you're

like a little pit mouse in front of them, something to toss a crumb to and then shoo away when piece time is done."

"I'd loan you my new suit but you're too tall. You're too tall for anyone in Pitmungo."

"When the time comes to stand up and talk, Gillon Cameron will stand up and say what has to be said; you have my word on that," Walter Bone said.

But they went back to the suit. They did not want to be represented by a man who looked in need of a handout.

"We don't send a beggar down there, we send a man," a miner shouted out. "If he stands for me, I want him standing there like a man." They cheered that.

"Buy the man a suit, I say," Archie Japp said. "I'm close now and we're all close but if a thousand men can't buy one man a suit we better open these doors and walk out of here and never come back."

"A beautiful suit," a miner said, "a great suit. We got the man here to wear it. Here's a man can carry it. It's why we chose him."

There it was again, Andrew thought: chose him. It was an insult, really. His father taking the dare, the dangerous step, and all the others taking credit for it. His father was now the community's property, to be used as it saw fit.

And then, not for the first time since this crucial meeting began, his mind wandered away from things in a way it never had before. They were talking about his father's fate, his own fate, but his eye wasn't looking at the men who were talking; it was finding the eyes of Walter Bone's youngest daughter, standing in the shadow of the doorway of the ben.

"Edinburgh for a bolt of the finest worsted," Andrew heard someone shouting. They were always shouting and he could barely hear them.

"No, no way, man. Pitlochry's the place for our man. Mac-Naughton's mills, right at the foot of the Highlands where our man comes from."

"That's tweed, man, tweed, not . . ."

He didn't hear the rest of it. He could not take his eyes off Alyson Bone in the doorway.

"Tweed, aye, but beautiful tweed, soft tweed, beautiful to touch, fit for a laird, fit for a *lord*."

Beautiful to touch. She was so beautiful standing in the shadows there he couldn't understand why all the men weren't watching her. He tried to drag his mind back into the room with the men but he couldn't force it to come away from the doorway. He wished they would quit the shouting about the kind of vest a man should wear. Why were miners always shouting? His heart was acting in a strange way, tick tacking in his throat, and he wondered what the matter was with him. The diagnosis would have been simple if he had been more familiar with the signs, but Pitmungo people weren't trained to recognize the symptoms of being in love. Alyson went away from the door and disappeared into the other room and Andrew felt himself deserted. He wondered then if there was just some chance that he might have some kind of attachment for the girl.

"Moffat's and Son in Frederick Street is the place for our man. The earl gets his duds there himself." Andrew couldn't follow it.

Love had never been a common commodity in Pitmungo, he knew that. It wasn't expected in daily life and so it wasn't often asked for and not often given. Colliers "went" with pithead girls and when a house came open it meant it was time to marry, the word love never mentioned, only the dimensions of the house. It wasn't that they were against love, only that the way of life there was ordered against it, and not opening itself to the risks of passion.

The girl came back out and Andrew felt the beating of his heart flutter up again and a feeling of gladness swarm over him and as little as he knew about love he was wise enough to know, to his astonishment, since he had never said a word to her in his life, that he was in love with Alyson Bone. It couldn't have come at a worse time, he realized, and was wise enough once more to know there was nothing to be done about it.

Her father was pounding the table, angry at something, and Andrew's mind, at rest now, came back into the room with the others.

"All of this is nonsense, all of it out of order. We can't get him a suit in that time, anyway."

Andrew got to his feet, something he wouldn't do ordinarily, getting the attention of the room. They were silent and still he hadn't said a word. "Go on with it," someone shouted at him.

"I know something my father can wear that no Scotsman can fault." He blushed a little, in the Cameron way, but spoke well. "He doesn't have to go down there as something he's not but he still can go down in something to be proud of." He paused again, looking for her and not finding her.

"Go on, go on," Mr. Bone said.

"Your kilt, Daddie. What do you call it—your filibeg."

There was a great deal of head-nodding. It was a cunning idea; the one dress that was out of class, beyond class. Lord Fyffe wore a kilt on certain national occasions. He liked to wear it potting rabbits on the moor and running down the fox.

"It's old and dirty," Gillon said.

"No, clean, Daddie," Andrew said. "Clean as a bone in a box of straw in the loft."

"True," Sam called. "We used to prance about in it when you weren't about."

"With the shoulder pin and the badge for the cap. They're in the box," Andrew said. "And that thing you wear in the front, the wallet there."

"The sporran," Gillon said.

"Never used, Daddie. Good as new."

They all turned to look at Gillon again, trying to dress him in his kilt.

"Is it your true kilt? Your true tartan?" Walter Bone asked.

"Yes. The Seventy-ninth Cameron Highlander's filibeg. The Queen's Own Cameron Highlanders now. But the Cameron kilt and tartan, oh, aye."

"So he couldn't call you false? It's your clan you'd be wearing, not only an army thing."

"No, my clan, whatever that means."

"It means a lot, man, it means a lot in Scotland, man."

The idea intrigued them—one of them, one of their own, marching down Colliers Walk to Brumbie Hall in his clan kilt. Nothing to bow and scrape about, a thousand years of history and valorous deeds swinging down the Walk with him.

"Do you have a sark? One of those ones with the wee ruffles on them?" Gillon didn't.

"That we can get in Dunfermline in the morning. There's that shop there for the Scottish gentry where all the Englishmen go. All those tartans and silver badges with the precious stones in them and all the velvet things."

"Velvet," a miner shouted out. "How about our man in velvet! Top that if you can."

"No, no, that's for nighttime. This is tea," Mr. Bone said. "A tweed jacket is the thing. Like when *they're* out stalking on the moor."

"Aye, tweed is correct," Gillon said. Now they had him. "No matter how you cut it, for rich or poor, tweed is tweed."

There were scores of acceptable tweed jackets to choose from in Pitmungo, but still they argued tweeds for several minutes and Gillon thought of Miss Tweed in the law agent's office, so languorous. What did they mean about her seeing so many men? He'd never know the answer. How could his mind roam away at times like this? He looked at his son and was surprised. Andrew's mind seemed as far away as his own.

"And then he'll wear his hat," someone said triumphantly. "The great wonderful hat." Gillon felt suddenly guilty in letting them down.

"I lost it," Gillon said. "My hat."

They could all appreciate the enormity of it. They had ridiculed the hat but only because it had posed such a challenge to them.

"You lost the beautiful hat?" The room had fallen silent.

They looked at him as if he had been found stealing from the Defense Fund.

"I can get a glengarry," Gillon said. "The caps with the red-and-white checks along the sides and the ribbons fluttering down? They're very handsome hats." It cheered them up again.

"Dunfermline in the morning."

"And I'll need a pair of knee-length hose that turn down at the top."

"With tassels on them, Cameron. Won't do without tassels."

"Dunfermline in the morning."

"And a little scabbard for your knife."

"No knife," Gillon said. "That's going too far." They all agreed. No knife.

"And then the shoes. You've got to have the shoes with the tongues flopping out," John Trotter said. He was a crafty little man who never had had to work underground, always in and out of places, always knowing a little more about what was happening than anyone else. "What size do you wear?" Gillon told him ten. "Can you squeeze into nine?" Gillon nodded aye.

"I can get a pair of them for you tonight, just don't ask me how."

They had him dressed. How did I get here? Gillon wondered. What set of circumstances down through his life had combined to place him, of all the people in this room, in the position he was in, selected now, whether he wanted it or not, to walk down the hill and join battle with the most powerful coal master in Fife? He felt sick again. Now they were deciding what he should say and what he should ask for and what, in their name, he could settle for and still preserve *their* pride.

"Sixty pounds should do it. It would set a record for Pitmungo."

"No, no. A man asks for four hundred pounds, that man cannot come down to sixty pounds and save our face; his face."

"Why the hell did he ask four hundred pounds?" someone demanded to know.

"What does it matter now? The fact is, he did."

The green on the moor outside the window, as it so often did, reminded Gillon of the sea, the wind in the high grass like wind over the waves, the good clean cold running sea; that was where he really belonged, and then his mind was back with the man in the boat beating his way to the island in the firth.

Did he ever make it? Gillon felt he had to know right then, that the success or failure of the mission to Lord Fyffe rested on it, and he wanted to get up and go right then to Dunfermline and rent a little boat to take him out to Inchgarvie and find the answer. But he didn't move.

"What are those things on his back?" she had said. It had embarrassed him then but it made him smile now.

"Muscles, Miss. They call them muscles."

"What are you smiling about?" Walter Bone said. "I see nothing to smile at."

"What?"

"Didn't you hear, man?" Mr. Bone said. "You don't exhibit much concentration for an affair of this order."

"What is it then?"

"They've decided you're to accept a hundred pounds if it's offered you."

"It's a little low," Gillon said. "I'll look the fool. I've asked four hundred." That sum always irritated the town. Part of the trouble, the town felt, stemmed from that. It was what they had shouted when the rocks struck the door and the windows. "My pride will take a strapping."

"But it's to be a *guarantee*, man, a response to a demand, not the Laird's whim. Think of that, Cameron. That's where *his* pride takes the strapping. Think of that, man, keep your eye on that."

I did, Gillon thought, I really did. What in the name of God did they think he was here for?

The meeting was over. They were all around him after that, offering advice and encouragement and suggestions.

"Now remember," a man was saying to him, "when the sarving girl asks what you want in your tea you say, 'A little dash of lemon, if you please.'" It was John Trotter. "Something loose and easy, to show you know your way around a tea service. 'I wouldn't care if I had a little slap of lemon, Miss.' Like that. Nooo milk, nooo sugar. Miners have milk."

"But I'm a miner."

"You're *our* representative. Lemon, got it?"

"Aye."

"*Lemon.*"

Gillon wondered what Karl Marx would take in his tea. Then they were all gone except for Gillon and Andrew and Walter Bone.

"Taking tea with the Earl and Countess of Fyffe at Brumbie Hall," Walter Bone said. "Who would ever have believed that the day you came through Gaffer's Gate? I know you'll stand us proud, Gillon."

"I know I'll try."

"Then that should be enough." Gillon felt shards of ice in his stomach.

"Luck go with you, Mr. Cameron," Alyson Bone said from the shadows of the doorway. "You're the best one to do it." Her voice, to Andrew, was like a soft wind running in dry reeds.

9 "WHAT TIME IS IT NOW?"

"Noon, Daddie," Sam said. "Few minutes after."

"It can't be."

"Do you want it to be sooner or later?"

"I don't know. Sometimes I wish it would be now and sometimes never come."

"It doesn't matter, anyway. Time is its own master."

Master. Everything was master in this place. Coal master, Earls and Countesses, Walter Bone, hunger: none of them any good.

"This is madness," Maggie said. She was resewing the lining of Gillon's borrowed tweed jacket so that it had a brisker look to it. "Wasting my morning making some other man's jacket look good."

"Your husband will be in it."

Ian came into the house. He had been making a polish for the shoes—a little of the salt pork that had been used on Jem boiled with a little vinegar and lampblack added to it.

"What time is it?"

No one answered him. Time was too unnerving now.

"The pot stinks. I hope the shoes won't stink that way," Sam said.

"I asked what time it was."

Sarah finally told him. "Five hours, that's all, five more hours. He'll have to leave here in four and a half."

Gillon felt his stomach tighten again. It was the word "have" that got him. He looked up suddenly with a fresh excitement in his face. *He* didn't have to go, he didn't *have* to go anywhere. He didn't get a summons, he got an invitation. There was no law in the world that said he, G. Cameron, free citizen, had to go down that hill and take tea with Lord Fyffe.

"I don't *have* to . . ." Gillon began, but the boys were fighting. He would wait.

"Jesus, the shoes are going to stink, man."

"The shoes will *not* stink," Ian said. "When I get through with them, they'll smell like heather and shine like a collier's nose."

"There's no law that says . . ." Gillon began again.

"I wonder what it's going to be like in there?" Andy Begg said. Well-wishers had begun dropping by the house, shoring up their representative.

"Hot as hell," Ian said, looking up from his shoes. "He keeps it hot to boast how much coal he's got."

"Nonsense. A man like that doesn't have to boast of having coal."

"That's what he does, though."

"Who says?"

"They," Ian said. "The people who know."

You could never win with Ian, Gillon thought. He always got it around to his own territory, where there was no answer. He suspected it would prove to be that way with the Earl and he felt the clench in his stomach. How many times could his stomach tighten and release that way before something gave, Gillon thought. Emily came in with the sporran. The leather had been washed with sweet saddle soap and lightly oiled and the fur of the wallet's cover dry-cleaned by the cobbler.

"He charged a bob for it," Emily said. "Can you imagine it?" No one could.

"Five hours to go," Ian said.

"Christ," Gillon suddenly shouted, "it's not an execution! I'm not going there to die."

The room fell silent. It was a reluctant, nervous silence. They wanted to talk but they respected what the man was going through; to speak would seem to be to invade his privacy and destroy the delicate balance he was working to achieve in his mind. At one moment he could see himself moving easily through the room, talking to the assembled guests, if there were any, and he felt elated, and not a minute later he could imagine the opposite, his tongue twisted in his mouth, stumbling, people not understanding him, people laughing at him, not being able to make out what he was trying to say.

The thing was that either one was possible. It all depended on his mood the moment the door was opened. That would set the pattern. If he caught the right attitude, the right mood now, he wanted to nurse it, to keep it alive in him until he reached that front door and tinkled the bell.

"Does anyone know about a man who might have drowned in the Firth of Forth a few weeks ago?"

He saw them looking at one another, as if the man who was going to represent *them* was taking leave of his senses.

"I'm all right," Gillon said. "I assure you, I'm all right."

The silence descended again, a sullen silence, hard to keep and hard to break.

"Strange they didn't invite me," Maggie finally said. "You don't invite the husband to tea and not invite the wife." It had never occurred to Gillon that the Countess could be in bad taste and it made him feel better, a little nugget to cherish.

"Maybe they found out you were a Drum," Sam said.

"That isn't nice," Sarah said.

"It isn't very funny," his mother said.

"Maybe Lady Jane has designs," Mr. Selkirk said.

"And that isn't nice."

"Strapping aristocratic-looking young specimen in full flower of life. They say that she and Lord Fyffe, well . . . best left unsaid."

"And *that* isn't very funny."

They ought to know about me and Mrs. Cameron, Gillon thought.

"The truth is never funny," Selkirk said.

"You really fancy yourself some kind of wit," Maggie said.

"No. But those I tell my jokes to, do."

And silence again, Sam's voice droning on, reading *Walden* to Jem, adding to the heaviness of the silence, and now wind was moaning in the pine outside. It was a gray day, a down day, but there had been no rain. That was good, Gillon thought. *Wind before rain, soon to your ale.* It was important that it not rain, that he not arrive at Brumbie Hall with his hair plastered down, his kilt dripping water on the polished wood floors, or whatever they would be made of.

"They say he has a *cruel* temper," Ian said. "They say Broth-cock is afraid to look him in the eyes."

"Aye, but Brothcock's a thief, that's why. Our dad is no thief. He's not trying to steal something; he's just trying to get what belongs to him," Andrew said.

Trying to make him feel good in a situation in which he could not feel good. He picked up his soft tweed tie and noticed that his hand was trembling. He put the tie around his neck to see what it would look like. Too much tweed, he thought, altogether too much, and realized he had forgotten how to knot a tie.

"I don't think they're still wearing ties like this," Gillon said. "Time has passed it by."

"They were wearing them last year at the matches," Sam said. "The toffs, the gents. There are ties and ties, and then there are ties."

"What the hell does *that* mean?" his father shouted. Sam wasn't alarmed.

"It means that there are some ties like there are kilts. You don't see a new fashion in kilts come along much more than every other century or so, do you?"

Then came the tub. Because he hadn't come from the pit the women felt it was indecent to be in the room and went into the ben. That strange blindness when it came to the pit and coal dirt—Gillon had never gotten over it although he had learned to live with it. Now he was sorry that he wasn't going to see Lord Fyffe after work, his face safely masked in coal dust, clothed in honest sweat, his credentials of good faith. The scar on his arm was ugly. Some of the coal dust had never been cleaned out and the jagged wound in his shoulder was an angry red rimmed with blue and blackness.

"You should go down without your shirt," Selkirk said. "Lady Jane would keel over. 'Pay him the money and get the bloody bastard out of here,' she'd say."

"Remember, Daddie, don't use your right hand for *anything*," Andrew said.

"I'll do exactly as much as I can with it. I'm not going down there to lie to the man."

"But you can't use your hand, not really. You can't work. It isn't lying to let the man see the arm is no good at all."

"It only dramatizes the truth, you might say," Sam said. Where did they get this, this using of truth as if it were a starting point,

not an end, a means to be used, not something to strive toward?
He didn't understand the people he had raised. He didn't understand anyone, he thought.

"Now, when they hand you the tea," Maggie called in from the
ben, "you take it in your left hand and you say, very loud, 'Excuse me, but I have no use of the proper limb.'"

On any other day, Gillon would have smiled. He didn't smile,
but he understood a little better.

Andrew got up then to go up on the High Moor to take the
last count of the ships in the harbor, to know how much pressure
Lord Fyffe would be working under. Jem had found six. If there
were eight or ten coal bottoms sitting there waiting to be loaded
with coal, the pressure on the Earl to end his lockout would be
enormous, and the knowledge of that could be Gillon's secret
wild card that he could win the pot with.

An hour and a half up to take the count, forty minutes
back down at the most. There would be plenty of time. Even
so, Andrew decided to jog part of the way, at least until it got
steep. It was good to be out of the house, filled with people coming
and going since the night before. Too much advice pouring in
on his father, everyone coming up with some smashing idea of
how to *handle* Lord Fyffe, not just stand with him as an equal, but
put the Earl of Fyffe in his place. He felt good running, the afternoon was clearing and there was a charge of excitement in him
and the house, the family and the town. When he reached the
end of the Terrace, before it runs up toward the White Coo plantation above it, Alyson Bone was standing where the Terrace and
Colliers Walk meet, as if she had been waiting for him. He
slowed down, imperceptibly he hoped, because he didn't want
to seem to be stopping just for her. They had something in common now: his father and he had been in her house; he had spoken
up in her house, he had seen the very bed she slept in. When he

neared her he stopped running altogether, as if he were tired, although he didn't look at her. It would give her a chance to say something if she wanted to.

"That was a good idea you had," Alyson said. He turned toward her in surprise, as if he hadn't seen her.

"Oh." He blinked. What a fraud, he thought, and said: "What idea?"

"The kilt. It makes all the difference."

"I hope it does." He still stood there, pointing himself upward toward the High Moor, and couldn't think of another thing to say. She was so beautiful, and so strange for Pitmungo. Pitmungo girls always chided the boys or insulted them; it was the style of the town. It grew boring after a while but it made talk easy.

"How is your father today?" Andrew could smile at that.

"Och, nervous. What you would expect."

"I can't blame him."

"Stravaigin up and down the house like a man possessed. In the but and then the ben, smiling and then angry, you know."

"Aye, I can imagine it."

He didn't know why he had used the Pitmungo word; to show he was like everyone else, he supposed. She was like his mother —she hardly used the dialect, as if it had passed her by without her ever hearing it. She was easy to talk to, *easy*, Andrew thought, and it filled him with confidence.

"Can you imagine going down to Brumbie Hall yourself?"

"No," Andrew said.

"My father says it's a very brave thing."

"Well, it is."

"I can't imagine doing it. I don't know what I'd do."

"Oh, you wouldn't have any trouble there." She looked surprised.

"Why do you say that?"

"Well, you're so . . . so. You wouldn't have to . . ." He stopped, furious with himself. What he wanted to say he couldn't say, that people as beautiful as she was didn't have to do anything, the way she didn't have to work like others, but just stand there and be beautiful. Her family wouldn't let her be soiled around the pithead and everyone accepted that. It was a fact of life: Alyson Bone was too pretty for the pithead.

"So *what*? Wouldn't have to *what*?"

"Beautiful," Andrew blurted out and started heading up toward the moor because he was blushing too strongly to face her. She was following him.

"What is that supposed to mean?"

Did she really not know, he wondered, and finally decided to face her. If his father could go down to Brumbie Hall he could look at a girl.

"Because you're so pretty, you just stand there and everyone is pleased, you see."

"Och, that means nothing."

"Oh, no. It does. People like pretty people, that's all. It's true. Pretty people are apart."

"Then he'd ask me something, Lord Fyffe or Lady Jane, and I'd stand there and not know what to say to them."

"And they wouldn't care."

He was still walking, it was the best way to talk, and she was still coming along with him. He was thrilled by it; he realized he must have wanted this to happen for two years, no, much more, five or six. He was a little dizzy about it all. As long as he had gone that far he decided to dare it all. It was a day for it.

"Would you care to go up to the High Moor with me? It's clearing."

He was afraid to look at her. He didn't want to seem to be asking and he didn't want to seem to be pressuring her and he didn't want to see her or her to see him in case he revealed something if she said no. She didn't answer for a long time.

"Aye, I'll go on the moor with you." His heart thumped.

"Aye, well. Come then," he said, and started up the path through the orchard ahead of her. Now that he had her with him he didn't know exactly what to do with her. She was slow, he usually walked up the moor all out to get it over with, and he couldn't have her be too slow. After a time the silence between them grew too heavy for him to bear, but she saved him.

"How's your brother Jem the now?"

"Oh. Jem." He turned to look at her. The climb had put color into her face. She was so beautiful that he was surprised every time he turned and saw her, and amazed that she was going up on the moor with him. Ordinarily only pithead girls and green gowns went up on the moor with boys they barely knew. They both were conscious of that.

"Jem is good now, I think. Over the worst. My sister's nursing him and she's the best there is."

"She's a wonderful woman. She's my sister too now."

That bothered him. He didn't want it to be just that way, sisterly and brotherly. When he got through the plantation he waited for her. There were little green apples on the trees, which meant the fruit pinchers, like Ian and Emily, couldn't be far behind. She had tried to keep up but she was forced to stop and rest.

"If I ask you something, will you tell me?"

"Oh, aye, I guess. I think so."

"Why are you Camerons always going up on the High Moor?"

He was stunned by the question because he knew he couldn't answer it honestly. Sam had a way to turn it aside and Jem had his way but Andrew had never been asked it. He always knew, before, when the question would be asked and managed to avoid it.

"To look for grouse eggs." It was the standard answer, the one the family always used, the one Sam got away with. "But you never find any," they always said to Sam and he would say, "But that's the fun of it, you see, imagine the day we *do*," and it was over with. But Andrew couldn't carry it off that way.

"I know that one," Alyson said. "I'm asking *you* why."

He began to walk upward again.

"I can't tell you," he said.

"Because you don't trust me."

"Oh, I do." He turned around to her. He would trust her with anything, he thought then.

"Then tell me."

He wanted to, more than anything he could remember.

"I can't," Andrew said.

"It's not a matter of can't. You can if you trust me." When she looked at him he didn't know how he could not tell her. But it was the secret of the family, it didn't belong to him. It was the Camerons' secret.

"It doesn't belong to me."

"What doesn't belong to you?"

"Oh, God. What we *do*." He held out his hands, knowing he looked pathetic. "Can you understand that I can't tell you?"

She looked at him with those eyes that were so knowing and yet so young, even innocent, unlike most knowing eyes.

"No."

He stood there, helpless to go on or go back and conscious of time passing. "It's clouding over. It's going to rain again."

"No, I don't understand that you can't trust me." She turned away and started back down the moor.

"Don't go," Andrew called to her. It was more like a call for help. "You can come with me." She stopped and he trotted down to her.

"You can come."

"Can I see what you do?"

"Yes."

"And will I understand?" It was astonishing to him how close she seemed to come to what it was they did. He had a feeling she knew and was testing him.

"No."

"But once I've seen it, will you tell me?" He wanted to say yes and found that he was shaking his head. She walked on down until she reached the edge of the orchard.

"Please, don't leave that way," he said, following her.

"You can come with me if you want, " the Bone girl said.

"No, I can't." It was a cry of pain. "I *have* to go up. They're counting on me." He held her arm, surprised at himself. "Look, the Bones are a proud family. If you had a family secret you were sworn to keep, you wouldn't tell me."

"Oh, aye, I would though." He hadn't expected that and he was thrown altogether off balance. "Because I would trust you."

And still the words wouldn't come, especially this day, his father waiting to go down to face Lord Fyffe, the family a rock behind him, he couldn't break the secret they had all kept so many years. She started down through the apple trees. He felt bound in some way, held by some tie much stronger than himself that kept him from doing what he wanted to do.

"Alyson? Come back. I'll tell you," but he didn't go down to her and he knew that if she came back up he wouldn't tell her. He started to run up the moor then, to punish himself, and because the pain of the running was good. The family came first, the family was always first, without the family there was nothing. Bones might tell their secrets but Camerons never would.

It sounded good, it always had, and it made him sick to think about. Why did he have to be born a Cameron, he said to himself, aloud now with each painful step up the moor, why me? why me? knowing he had possibly given up the only love of his life in order to hold on to another. It was too much to ask of a young man, Andrew thought.

10

IT SEEMED TO GILLON HE HAD BEEN IN THE tub for hours. Washings and rinsings, a hair soaping and then a vinegar wash to shine the hair and get rid of the alkali. If they wanted to make him look crippled, he thought, they were going about it in an odd way. In theory they should carry him down on a shutter and deposit him at the door and here they were, sending him down like a Highland warrior on parade.

"How much *time?*" he suddenly cried out. Hours must have slid away.

"Three hours until you walk," Maggie called in.

Until you walk. The hangman's words. They sent a chill through him.

When he dried himself he noticed his hands were trembling again.

"There ought to be a pill a man could take to settle his nerves," Gillon said.

"There is, only it's not a pill," Mr. Selkirk said. "You pour it out of a bottle."

She came out of the ben into the but then, although Gillon was standing there naked in the center of the room.

"What the hell's the matter with you?" she shouted at Henry Selkirk. "You'd have your friend pour a little courage from the bottle, is it, and go down there stinking of whisky? And you, get dressed. Standing there all white and shaking like a bush on the moor."

Maggie took the whisky off the dresser and into the ben. Rob Roy was at the door and the rush of air that followed him in was no help to Gillon. He could not stop trembling.

"Got them," Rob said, holding up the knee-length socks. They were good gray wool with a faint red pattern, just a suggestion of Argyle running through them and topped with little tassels.

"And look," he cried. "Can you see them?" He passed the stockings around. "Little snecks to hold your stalking knife." He was elated; he also had been drinking.

"I am taking no knife to no castle," Gillon said, and the silence fell on the house again.

"What's the matter here?" Rob said. "It's like a house of the dead in here."

Gillon began to get dressed, thoughtfully the way a man might dress knowing it would be his last time doing it.

"Well, you ought to get outside. The whole town is waiting. It's a festival out there. Andy Begg wants to send down to Cowdenbeath for a piper to pipe your way down."

The cold feeling came over Gillon again but he forced himself to keep moving. He put on his clean knitted underwear. If the mansion was overheated he would sweat but it was a risk he would have to run. There was no going down in a kilt without drawers, that much in all of Scotland was certain. Every movement seemed heavy to Gillon.

"Christ, what do they think this is?" Gillon said. "This is a serious day."

"The Miners' Second Freedom Day," Rob said. "The common man forcing his way into a world that was closed to him before. A simple workaday coal jock forcing himself before the mighty Earl of Fyffe. Think of *that*, now; before the powerful—"

"I won't do it!" Gillon cried out. "I will not! I won't go down there like this."

He had stepped into his kilt and hooked it closed and the transformation was total. That one movement of the arm, the snip of metal meeting and clicking shut and Gillon was transported out of their drab world into a world of his own, alien to theirs.

It was almost embarrassing. Here he was, in the center of the small dark room, brilliant against the grayness of smoke-smothered walls, a tropical bird come to rest for a moment with the sparrows in some working-class back alley.

The pleats of the kilt rippled when he moved, a subtle movement of the wool like a breath of wind across the moor, and the colors of the tartan, strong with blues and hunting greens, streaks of red and yellow flashing out at every movement, were startling in this world that knew only grays and blacks. The ruffled shirt above the kilt, softly white and as creamy as good linen can be, brought out the gaiety of the Erracht tartan.

"But Daddie," Emily said, "you're beautiful."

"Aye, it's true. You look like Scotland," Sam said. Everyone knew what he meant. In his kilt Gillon was the heart of the dream people have about themselves. Gillon had a sense of it. He knew that none of the others had the lean grace or the fine-boned face that would let them feel that the clothes belonged on them. There was an ancient rightness about it on Gillon that none of them possessed.

"Jemmie wants to see you, Daddie," Sarah said.

"No. He doesn't want to see me, because I'm not going down to Brumbie Hall."

"Please, Daddie. He wants it very much." Poor Jem, all right, little slope-shouldered Jem. He would just let him see the kilt and then he'd take it off for good.

"Let me get my hose on then, the filibeg's not right without it," Gillon said and they had the feeling that his resistance was failing. He went into the ben, where Jem was lying in his parents' bed.

Jem nodded and then he smiled. He tried to sit up and when he couldn't he made a small fist and motioned for Sam to come to him.

"What does he say?" Gillon asked.

"He says if you don't go down and act like the man you look like, he's going to get up and breathe in your face."

They laughed, their first real laugh, and it changed the house. Everyone wanted to talk then, to Scotch-up the Scotsman until perfection was approached.

"I want a drink of good whisky. . . ."

"No, no you don't," Maggie said.

"And I intend to have it."

Gillon brushed by his wife, no John Thomson's man now, and got the bottle.

"Any that want to share it with me can share it," Gillon said, and poured two thick fingers' worth into his tassie.

"To Jem, that he be well soon."

"To Jem."

"To our dad, that the words come right."

"To our dad."

"To our mother, who has taken us this far," Gillon said.

"To our mom."

"To the Earl of Fyffe," Gillon said.

"To the Earl of Fyffe!" they shouted. Gillon suddenly turned and clumsily threw his cup into the fireplace, where it shattered.

"Why did you do that?" Maggie said.

"I don't know, but it's what I intended to do."

It was all new after that. The glassers came to straighten the lead frames and replace the broken glass. They took down the wooden planking and light swarmed into the house as if the light itself were a sign sent for Gillon. He could see people in the lane outside waiting for him.

"I would like you to meet our uncle, Sir Lauriston Cameron," Sam said.

"A pleasure, I'm certain, sir," the glasser said, and took his cap off before recognizing Cameron. "Ah, Cameron, for Christ's sake. You're too loovely to look at."

The socks had performed the same little miracle that the kilt had for Gillon's too long, too work-wiry legs. The legs looked hard and compact underneath the taut new wool, deerstalker's legs, and the knees, somewhat long and suggesting too much bone, looked . . . *correct.* He put on his tweed tie, knowing how to tie it now, and then slid into his tweed jacket, which made his miner's shoulders look broader and less bunchy. The shoes were tight but he could bear that, and to his surprise they added more than an inch to his height. Whoever had owned them had had the insides built up to exaggerate his size. Everything was right; everything worked.

"Now I know why you went up there and got him," Sam said to his mother. "I never saw it before."

"Aye, that's what I went for and that's what I got. Too bad some of you didn't get more of him."

"Always bring it down to earth, Mither. Perhaps it was we got too much of you," Rob Roy said.

"Aye. Perhaps it was."

An hour to wait. It was too long. Gillon was ready to go right then. He forced himself to sit down and read in his Henry George to prepare his mind, to get it oiled for the arguments to come.

But the lawless license of early English rule has been long restrained. To all that vast population the strong hand of England has given a more than Roman peace; the just principles of English law have been extended by an elaborate system of codes and law officers designed to secure the humblest of these abject peoples the rights of Anglo-Saxon freemen. . . .

Wherever you turned, Gillon thought, there it was, something Pitmungo had never seemed to have learned. No man above the law, no man greater than another because of his station—not where the law and a man's rights were concerned. He saw the door in his mind again, the great door at Brumbie Hall, and this time he didn't feel the cold inside.

"What are you going to say to the bastard?" the glasser said to Gillon through the window.

"I don't know. I'll think of the right thing when the time comes," Gillon said, and was sure that he would.

"I know you will," the glasser said. "That's what we're counting on." It didn't bother Gillon any longer.

"I'm on fire again," Jemmie whispered. "Tell Sarah to come."

Sam put the book down and went to get his sister. They did it all quietly because this was no time to disturb their father.

She tried all of her tricks, the cold compresses and the soothing witch hazel, but the fever stayed up and Jemmie fought against delirium.

"As soon as Dad goes, I'm going to get the doctor," Sarah said.

Sam was angry. "I don't want that bastard to touch my brother."

"But I've done what I can do," Sarah said. "Aye, he's a dumph but there's a chance he can do something."

"A chance! You think they'd let that butcher inside Brumbie Hall if one of *them* got sick?"

Mr. Selkirk had been listening. "What about ice? You could pack him in ice to bring the fever down," the librarian said. "It's what they're doing these days."

They looked at one another. It was worth some sort of try.

"If we had ice," Sam finally said.

"I can make ice," Maggie said. While Gillon read she slipped into the ben and looked at her son. He barely recognized her.

"All right," she whispered to Sam. "Get Ian. Bring him in the back way. It means the loss of one of our stone bottles but we'll have to take the loss."

When Ian came up she sent him down to the Pluck Me to steal a few ounces of saltpeter.

"I know that I'm setting a bad precedent with this stealing," Maggie said. "You understand the word?" Ian nodded. "And when this thing is over I'm going to knock the stealing out of you, you understand that, too?" Ian nodded. "Knock it out of you so you'll never want to steal again. But I'm sending you down the now to steal."

It was the trait Sam admired most about his mother. When a thing had to be done she knew it had to be done, and when she knew it, she did it. When Ian got back the water was boiling and she poured it into the stone bottle, leaving room for the expansion of the water into ice, and added two or three ounces of the niter.

"Now, you," she said to Andrew. "You take this down to the well on the moor and dip it down as deep as it will go and let it stay there for three hours. Bring it up once in a while for the change in temperature and put it back down again."

They all saw his hurt. He would miss his father's walk, for which he had already lost his love. He had never felt so sorry for himself in his life.

"Have you seen your brother recently?" his mother said. Andrew shook his head. "Then I think you should."

He came out of the ben and went out the back way so no one would see him crying while he made his way to the moor with the stone water bottle.

"That was hard on Andrew," Sam said.

"Aye, hard, but who was there to rely on? Those you can rely on get relied on. That's a fact of life. If you catch them young enough they get so they won't have it any other way, even when they don't like it."

Rob Roy came bursting through the door, and it made Maggie and Sam laugh, because without his knowing it Rob Roy had made a statement. Rob Roy would never be sent to the moor to make ice.

"Time to go, Daddie. Mr. Bone says it's time to go down now."

Gillon shut his book and rose from his chair with elaborate calmness. The time had come for the setting of the cap. The hair to be brushed and then the glengarry seated just so, the hair brushed around the sides of the cap so it seemed natural and then the two black ribbons streaming down the nape of his neck and the crease of the hat just right, the angle jaunty but stopping short of being cocky. When he was ready he went into the ben to see Jem once more. Sam was sitting by the bed, a book open on his lap, and Jemmie slept, breathing heavily.

"What are you reading him?" Gillon said.

"*Highland Clearances.*"

"I thought you were reading him *Walden?*"

"Aye, I was. He got tired of it. He says it's not his idea of

America." Sam got up and shut the book and went over by the window. "I was reading him the time, Daddie, when the Duke of Sutherland went up to the Highlands to raise a regiment to fight in the Crimean War. The people were all hungry, Dad, and he made his touching little speech about how the Crown needed them and then he spread out his packages of crisp bank notes and his platefuls of gold and waited for the line to form."

"I don't remember."

"Not a man stood up, Daddie. Not one man, where fifteen hundred men had been raised on two days' notice a few years before. They had finally learned to say no, you see."

"Go on," Gillon said. He knew when Sam was making a point. He didn't make them often or easily any more.

"So then the Duke finally stood up and said, 'What's the meaning of this insult to your Laird, your clan chieftain, your Crown?' And no one would stand up, Daddie; that's a little more than anyone had the guts to do. But finally, one man, an old one, found the guts and got on his feet and told him.

"'You took our land and abused it and now you ask us to give you loyalty and go out and die for you. I'll tell you what to do, sir. You send your deer and your roes, and send your rams and dogs and shepherds to go fight your war for you. We'd rather stay home, sir, and starve.'"

Sam looked across the room at his father.

"One brave man."

His father understood.

"Do you want to walk with me? Or stay with Jem?"

"It doesn't matter. I think you should walk alone."

"And you?" He looked at Maggie. "Will you walk with me?" She shook her head.

"I don't belong there. This is your day, Gillon."

Walter Bone tapped and opened the door.

"Time, now."

Gillon spun around and the swirl of his kilt was almost an affront to the drabness of the others in the room. He shook hands with Rob Roy and Sam and Ian and then with the other men in the room, Walter Bone and Andy Begg, with Archie Japp and finally with Henry Selkirk. When he kissed Sarah he tasted salt on her cheeks and then he lifted Emily and she whispered something in his ear, one of Emily's incantations, an Emily oath, and then he crossed the room to kiss Maggie. He couldn't recall kissing her in front of the children before and not in front of people except the day of his wedding.

"When you talk to him look him square in the eye, Gillon," Maggie said. "Because you're a better man than he ever was. And when he offers a decent settlement, have the courage to take it."

Gillon went back into the ben. Jem was still asleep. He picked up Thoreau's book that Sam had been reading him and glanced at it, taking his sweet time about things, a defiant act of independence, and the line he read made him laugh. Sam had been so good, making his point, shoring up Gillon's courage, and now this.

"*Beware of all enterprises that require new clothes.*" Gillon himself had underlined it years before and Sam had done the same. He shut the book and leaned over toward Jem.

"Don't kiss him," Sarah said.

"Aye, I'll kiss my son," and he did, and then walked out of the ben through the but, seeing nothing really, and out into the crowd of men and women waiting for him there. Their cheer— a roar it was—on seeing him rattled the new glass in the front windows.

"What is it, what's happening?" Jemmie suddenly cried out.

"Easy. It's Daddie going down to see the Laird."

"Sam?" Jem whispered. "Did he look good?"

"Jesus, Jem, you would have been so proud. He looks like a Highland chief going to take charge of his regiment."

"Oh. And Sam?"

"Aye?"

"I think I'm going to die."

11 GILLON NEVER CLEARLY REMEMBERED THE WALK down Tosh-Mungo Terrace and Colliers Walk. Pieces of a dream he was playing a part in. He saw the faces but he couldn't make them out; he heard the people calling to him, but the words made no sense, and all the while the fliskie sensation of his kilt flinging left and right with each click of his almost new leather heels tacking against the stones of the walk. And then for a time he was alone, passing from Uppietoon across Sportin Moor and Lord Fyffe No. 1, the newly shined shoes picking up coal sludge on the way, and then Doonietoon and the uproar all over again. The children in Doonie ran along beside him, wanting to touch the kilt, trying to imitate the swirl of it. Down past Miners Row and Rotten and Wet, down past the College, where the few men who still had pennies to drink with gave him another rousing send along, and then alone again, except for a few children be-hind him, down past the Reading Room, and through the works, past Lady Jane No. 2, where he had first gone underground so long ago, and then onto the Low Road to Cowdenbeath, which would take him out to Brumbie Hall. His feet kept marching him along, the way the legs of soldiers must move, Gillon thought, when headed for the front. Something more powerful than his own desire was moving him ahead. He didn't want to go ahead, and there was no turning back.

A few drops of rain caused him to look up, but it was a mizzle of rain, nothing more. He was getting used to the feel of the kilt now. He liked the lift and fall of the streamers from his glengarry on his neck and then there it was, as suddenly as that, the great house among the oak trees, with the little houses huddled behind it as if they were kneeling at prayer. Gillon felt his heart muscle squeeze and release, a spasm of some sort.

Before the gate, which was not guarded, Gillon stepped into deep grass and, hoping he was out of sight of the main house, bent down and worked the pit glaur and wet coal dust off the sides and soles of his shoes. *"A man's a man for a' that an' a' that,"* he kept saying to himself, wiping the mine muck off him, shoring himself up with the words, wanting to believe in them the way a man in a small boat wants to believe in the seaworthiness of it, all the while knowing that Burns was a hopeless romantic and that some men, for all kinds of reasons, were superior to other men.

He went through the gate thinking he would be stopped before he reached the door, and crunched his way up the gravel drive. The door was enormous, studded with iron like an ancient shield, and Gillon stopped to settle himself. Did he walk in with the hat on or did you have it in hand and give it to the girl? What if there was no girl? What if Lady Jane herself answered the door? Did a collier hand a countess his hat? And that suddenly made him feel better. What was he but a miner and how else did they expect him to act? But then why was he here in this costume? He was at the door, looking for a bell to pull or something to push, a knocker or a place where people knocked, and he suddenly turned to run when the door opened.

"Yes?"

"Well ... I ... ah ..."

He felt his face redden. He didn't want any of that this day.

"What do you want?"

Irish by the sound of her. He saw her looking him up and down, a little Irish kind of smile, impudent, around the edge of her lips and nose.

"Want? I don't want ... I mean, I was, after all ..."

"Who shall I say is calling?"

"Why ... ah. Cameron. Yes. *Mister* Cameron. Mister G. Cameron."

"Which of the three d'ya want?"

There were other girls behind her, Irish too, sarcastic little smiles, dressed in crisp black full skirts and enormous starched white fronts like nuns in the Roman Catholic church.

"Mr. G. Cameron to see Lord Fyffe."

She left him at the door. He could hear the serving girls snickering out of sight behind it. They must have known he was coming. So typical of the Irish working class, Gillon thought, to snirtle at one of their own. No wonder they had never managed to organize a decent labor movement, always falling apart in the face of the masters and the English and their own priests. She was back, smiling openly now, a sly pawky smile all over her face, the kind of smile children in school give other children as they are on their way up to get whipped.

"Come in, Jock," she whispered. "It's not exactly the pit in here, is it?"

He turned to her, furious, and then saw by her eyes that she hadn't meant it that way at all.

"You'll go to the left and down to the Great Hall." She touched his arm and he winced. "They're not bad people. A little stiff and Scotchy . . ." She put her hand to her mouth. "Oh, what did *I* say?"

Gillon was forced to laugh.

"You be yourself and you'll get by down there," she said.

He turned down the long dim corridor, feeling better, feeling almost at ease. He may use a lot of coal, but he took it easy on the gas, Gillon was thinking when he heard her coming after him, clattering over the wooden parquet floor.

"Mister?" He stopped. "Your hat."

He didn't understand her.

"Give me your hat, in the name of God."

"I think I'll leave it on."

"I never saw a man wear a hat in this house before."

"You ever see a miner in this house before?" She shook her

head. She was young and pretty, too young to be sent so far away from home.

"Aye, well. Miners wear their hats in house and I'm a miner."

"Fine by me, Sandy," and she winked at him. Fresh, he thought, fresh as grass, but nice.

When he turned away from her he was sorry to see that several of the people from inside the Great Hall had been watching and he knew it took him down a few notches, as if he were on a par with the Irish serving girl, and one could hardly get lower than that in Scotland except by taking up with an African.

He came into the room and no one noticed him. There were eight or nine people there, moving about the room, clinking cups and talking to one another, and no one seemed to see him. The faces were as remote and blank to him as the faces along the Colliers Walk. It was brighter than in the corridor, and he had trouble adjusting to the change in light, as he always did now, his eyes blinking against his will.

"What have we here?" a voice said. He couldn't see the man. "I say, what have we *here*?"

Gillon turned toward the voice but the head was against a bank of guttering candles and he couldn't make it out.

"It's Cameron, my Lord." He recognized that voice: Brothcock. "The collier, sir."

He could see some of them and sense the others putting down their teacups and cakes and turning to see him better.

"Here," someone said. A lady. "Let me take your cap."

"Yes, my hat," Gillon said, and took off the glengarry, sorry now he hadn't left it behind.

"*Collier?*" The voice was not unkind. "He looks like he's come in from stalkin'."

"No, I . . ." Gillon started to speak, but he realized they didn't want to hear him.

"Here, now. Come around here so we can get a better look at you."

Gillon went around to the other side of a large, high-backed chair in which the Earl of Fyffe was slumped.

"Brothcock here assures me you're one of my colliers but I don't believe him. I say you've just come off the moor from a good long hunt and are about to present us with a brace or two of grouse." Gillon didn't know why people laughed. He was still blinded and that helped, the way a layer of coal dust helped, the way a mask will allow people to do things they wouldn't ordinarily do.

"I wouldn't like to say Mr. Brothcock was more correct than Lord Fyffe, but if you'd care to study my hands, sir."

It was rewarded by a nice little laugh.

"Well *put*," Lord Fyffe said. "The man has tact. Give the man some tea."

Someone put a teacup in his hand and said, "Cream and sugar?"

"Lemon, please. A little dash of lemon will do."

"*Lemon?*" the voice said. He guessed it was Lady Jane. "Did you hear him ask for *lemon?* What elaborate tastes. I'm afraid we have no *lemon.* I'm afraid we're a cream and sugar family." She spoke very slowly, accenting all kinds of odd words, and Gillon supposed that that was what made the young men in the room laugh so often.

"Tell me," Lord Fyffe said. "What *is* his name again?" he said to someone at his side. They told him. "Tell me, Cameron, what are you doing in that . . . that getup?"

The voice was more pointed now.

"It's my special-occasion suit, sir. Marriages and funerals and such," Gillon said. "I considered this a special occasion."

"I'd say that it was, I'd say that much," a young voice said. "You're the first collier ever to see the inside of this house."

Gillon wondered if he was supposed to say something. He didn't seem to know when to talk.

"And the kilt. The army, of course."

"My family. My clan." There was a laugh following that.

"Fancy," the same young voice said. "The collier has a clan."

Gillon flushed at that, but it passed and he wasn't blushing any longer.

"There have got to be those in a clan who aren't chiefs or there couldn't be any chieftains," Gillon said. He hadn't known he was going to say that.

"Got you, Warrick. Stung you," another young voice said. He sounded so much like Lord Fyffe that Gillon assumed it was his son.

"You're very agile with your mouth," Lord Fyffe said.

"You learn that down pit, sir. The give-and-take."

"That isn't *all* you learn there," the Earl said, and Gillon didn't know what he meant.

"You don't talk *Scotch*," a young voice said. "What's the matter you don't talk *Scotch*? I promised this young man some *Scotch*."

"I'm sorry, sir. I'm from the Highlands."

"And how did that come about?"

"I married a Pitmungo girl. She brought me here to be a miner."

"But how did you *meet* her?" Lady Jane asked.

"She came and got me, Ma'am."

"That was enterprising of her. What was her name?"

"Drum, Ma'am. Margaret Drum."

Lady Jane shook her head. The name meant nothing to her. Two hundred years of service to the family and she had never heard of the name. Tom Drum would have been hurt to know it. Someone had handed the Earl a card and he studied it. Gillon wondered if it would be forward of him to take a sip of his tea. He did and it tasted like no tea he had ever had before.

"Gillon Forbes Cameron," the Earl read. "*That's* a fine name for a collier."

There was an edge to the voice that made Gillon feel uncomfortable. He took the teacup from his lips and stood in the attitude of a soldier at attention.

"One of my grandmothers was a Forbes," Lord Fyffe said. "Did you know that?"

"No, sir."

"So you might say in some small way we're related. Kith and kin, you might say."

"In a way, yes, sir. Different levels."

"Kinsmen. Clansmen. What is the first virtue of a clan member, Cameron?" He said it very swiftly.

Gillon didn't have an answer.

"What does one member of a clan expect of another member of the clan above all else? You *know* the answer, Cameron. Make a try."

Gillon felt himself turning red, not too badly red, but they were all watching him. If only they all didn't watch.

"Help one another in hard times, sir?"

"Don't ask me the question. *Answer* the question."

"Loyalty, I suppose."

The Earl made a sudden move as if to get out of the chair. For a moment Gillon wondered if he should lean down and help the man up but he was only straightening in his chair. Everyone waited, watching Gillon, the way men watch a fish in clear water nudging about the hook.

"You hurt me," Lord Fyffe said. His voice was very loud and in that great, quiet room there was a quality to it that caused it to echo from the walls. Gillon could feel it inside him.

"You hurt me more than any man has *ever* hurt me."

Gillon was frozen, his cup halfway to the saucer, rigid in his stiff right hand.

"*Disloyalty!*" It was shouted. "Lack of faith. And you come down here looking like that, wearing the clothes of loyal men. You have no right to wear such a thing."

The last words were almost sobbed.

"You could have come to me, to your Laird, to someone who knows you and respects you, but you turned on me and went to *them.*"

He tapped the paper.

"I know who they are. I know who you went to. Crept to. Sold your *self* to."

"I—"

"Shut your mouth," Brothcock said, "when his Lordship is speaking."

"You would have me summoned into court like a common criminal. You couldn't come to me like a man, you had to sneak to Edinburgh and fall into strangers' arms for the sake of money. Then you come down here in the dress of a clansman and expect to get money from my purse."

Gillon was looking at his feet. It was odd to look down and see someone else's shoes on your feet, flopping black tongues against the grain of waxed wood.

"Do you take me for a common criminal?" Gillon said nothing. "I asked a question. *Answer* it."

"*Answer* your master," Brothcock said.

"No."

There was much doing with teacups then. They were passing the cakes. He looked up and found one of the serving girls pouring more tea in his cup.

"No, I won't . . ." But she filled it, and he was frightened he was going to spill it on the beautiful floor and on his shoes because his hand was trembling. He tried to drink but it was too dangerous, the trembling too pronounced to take the cup safely to his lips, and so he was condemned to stand where he was with the tea tipping at the lip of his cup.

"And what did you do in the Highlands before going down pit?" a young voice asked. "It must have been a bit of a jolt."

"Seaman." Pause. "Sir."

"You don't have to *sir* me, Mr. Cameron. You're old enough to be my father."

Someone fingered his kilt from behind. Gillon started to turn around but didn't.

"It's the genuine article, all right," the voice said.

"From top of the sea to bottom of the pit. An odyssey, wouldn't you say? It must have been horrible."

"A what?" Gillon asked.

"Odyssey. A *journey*. Do you follow me at all?"

"Aye, I follow."

"These bleeding liberals."

"It's not all *that* bad, is it?" someone asked.

"No picnic. Sir."

"Do you think any of us have a picnic in this world? It's all relative."

"Seriously now. How do you find it in the pit?"

"Good enough."

"Good enough," the young man said sarcastically. "Very rotten, you mean. Why did you ever go down?"

"I had no choice. Hunger is a good master, sir."

"Oh, very good that." He repeated it around Gillon's shoulder as if he weren't there. "You'd better get that one down, Teddy. Your authentic folk wisdom at work."

Gillon continued to stand at attention, tea cup poised as if ready for teacup inspection.

"I wasn't always a seaman. My family were driven from their croft during the Clearances, you see, and—"

"Yes, we know. Into the sna' at Christmastime. And they burned the roof over your head and put you out into the blast with three small bairn and a mither with pneumonia and fed your grain to the deer? That was it, wasn't it?"

"Easy, Warrick, just because he stung you."

"I just don't like their lies is all. I can't stand their proletariat *lies*."

The room was quiet. There was some signal, some movement that took place in the room which Gillon couldn't discover, that let them know Lord Fyffe wished to talk and that the clattering of the cups and the chattering should cease. They all watched Gillon again.

"Loyalty." His voice had changed. He was reasonable now, a man of the world talking to another from a lesser world, but a man for all that. "I don't think you have a deficiency in that virtue. I have a feeling that somewhere down in you lies a seam of decency waiting to be mined out."

"Very *good*, Father," a young voice said. It was sarcastic.

"I also feel you are a sensible man, as most men who care about money tend to be."

"But I . . . it's not the money . . ." He was silenced. They were getting him all wrong.

"What are the two main concerns of your miner?" He didn't wait for Gillon to answer.

"Protection from injury and protection of his job so that with the help of his coal masters he can maintain his family in simple decency. Now, I ask you this. Who do you seriously think can better offer you both, the labor agitators or the Christian gentlemen God has seen fit to put in control of property, upon the successful management of which so much depends for us both? Answer that."

Gillon couldn't.

"What do you throw your lot in with? God's sensible order, tested by time, or the anarchy of the have-nothings who will stop at nothing if it will get them what they want for themselves? Answer *that*."

Gillon stood, looking blankly around him, vaguely aware that his teacup was tilting and drops of tea were dripping on the floor and his shoes.

"I don't know any labor agitators," Gillon finally said.

Lord Fyffe began to laugh, not unwarmly Gillon thought, such an infectious laugh that Gillon found himself wanting to smile and, finally, smiling.

"You never met Keir Hardie?" "Hardie" was said in such a way that Gillon wanted to flinch from the name.

He felt tears of humiliation at the edges of his eyes. He had forgotten Hardie because he never felt he had really met him but as far as it went with them, Gillon Cameron had been caught lying. So he stood there until his hand began to tremble again.

"Now, I know why I've been put on earth. I've been put here to mine coal to make money, and I'm going to do it."

Gillon found himself nodding.

"If everyone felt he had a right to sue the company for everything that went wrong, do you know where we would be? Do you know?" Gillon shook his head.

"You know but you won't say it, so I'll say it for you. *Out of business.*" He allowed time for that to sink into Gillon's consciousness. "Your beloved butties out of work, their bairn in the workhouses, the pits flooded with water. All because of one man's self-righteous, self-serving selfishness."

One of the serving girls at the far end of the Great Hall dropped a teaspoon and it clattered on the floor. It was not enough to cause even the other serving girls to turn and look, a single teaspoon on the parquet floor, but Gillon looked up and as he did the enormity of the room made itself felt to him. He hadn't really seen it before, the looming portraits of ancestors looking down, sprawling tapestries of hunts and stalks and festive scenes on the walls. He felt unsure in the room's vastness, and without knowing it, angry.

"You've already caused enough misery in this town to last it a lifetime. Because of your arrogance thousands of people have gone hungry, thousands of pounds of wages will never be paid, thousands of tons of coal gone unmined and unsold."

My arrogance, Gillon thought. Mine! and then felt the reassuring warmth of anger.

"Because of you one woman is already dead of starvation."

"Mrs. Wallace died of—"

"Shut your gob when Lord Fyffe is *talking*," Brothcock said.

"Dead of starvation! We have the medical examiner's certificate to that effect."

The medical examiner? Dr. Gowrie!

"Now, I have a proposal for you. What are you asking from me?"

Gillon was hesitant to say it aloud, it sounded so unrealistic in his mind, but he said it, *four hundred pounds,* in a voice so low that it had to be repeated over again around the room, each time to be met with a laugh of incredulity or scorn and anger.

"But that's more than I spend in a year at university," one of them said. "Who does he think he is?"

"Put a kilt on a collier and he thinks he's a peer."

"That's absurd, isn't it?" Lord Fyffe said. "And you know it, Cameron. *Look* at him," he told the people in the room. Even the serving girls moved closer. "Look at the color of the man's face. If he had a sensible demand, would he have to stand there with the face of a man about to be hanged? Or, better, *whipped?*"

Against his will Gillon looked down. There had been too many eyes on him for too long.

"*That's* a tradition my father honored, and things were better then," Lady Jane said. "Ask any of the old miners. They preferred it that way. A good whipping and a man knew where he stood."

"Of course, we don't do that any longer," the Earl said in a cool voice, "but there *are* men in Pitmungo who just might do it for us, when they face starvation because of your efforts at robbery. What was that you said about hunger?"

"Hunger is a good master."

"Yes, well, hunger is a good flogger."

He let that stand in the silence of the room.

"We'll supply the whips and your neebors their good right arms. Cake."

A tray of frosted cakes and shortbread was wheeled into the circle of people in the room and Gillon noticed that they ate them with their fingers. The girl pushed the cart toward him but didn't stop.

"Now, this happening," Lord Fyffe said, but Gillon couldn't hear the words because of the cake in the Earl's mouth. The sides of his mustache were sprinkled with crumbs.

"The what, sir?"

433

"The happening—the happening in the mine."

There are little things that can change a man's mind and make him see in some new way. For Gillon it was the cake being wheeled past him by the working girl. He suddenly didn't care what happened to him or to his class. They wouldn't even give one of their own a piece of bread. And then there was the word "happening."

"It was a *pick*, sir. A *pick* through the shoulder into the bone." He said it quite loudly. One of the young men winced.

"Ah, yes, a pick. I notice you're doing quite well with your tea service . . . for a cripple."

"It's done with a good deal of pain, sir, which I didn't wish to show."

"I'm sure of that. A *very* heroic man." It was the same boy who had called Gillon a liar about the Clearances.

"The gentry don't think we hurt as much as they do, but we do, sir."

"That's romantic nonsense, Cameron." It was Mr. MacCurry. Gillon hadn't noticed him before. "That's more of your agitator gibberish and you know it. The working classes are conditioned from birth to endure certain hardships, just as other classes are trained to appreciate certain refinements. It's one of God's protections."

"If you had put your pick through Elphinstone's shoulder the poor ninny would have died from fright," the Earl said.

Brothcock handed the Earl a second card. "After all is done," Lord Fyffe said, looking over the card, "you can't really expect to retire for life at *my* expense."

"You already have at mine." Gillon was barely able to believe he had said it.

"What did you say?" Brothcock said. "What was that you said to master?"

He wasn't sorry that he had said it but he didn't feel ready to say it again. One of the girls took his cup away and he was grateful to her.

434

"Damned impudence, I'll tell you that much. The fellow does want a beating," one of the younger men said.

Lord Fyffe went on as if nothing had been said. "This is what I'm offering you. Forty pounds, largely because of a letter from Elphinstone asking that I be generous—that would be a record croo from the master; is that correct, Brothcock?"

"Aye, my Lord."

"That's forty more pounds than you were going to get. A withdrawal of your summons in return for the payment and your signature on this paper."

He held up a paper and Gillon found, when he started forward to reach for it, that he could barely force his body to move. There was the number forty again, coming back into his life.

"Can he read?" one of the young men said. "Maybe it should be read to him. A lot of them pretend from pride, you know."

"He can read," Brothcock said. "This one can read the fine print off the bottom of the contracts."

I, ——————, do solemnly swear that under no circum- stances whatever will I sue my Company or my masters for injuries sustained while working for the Company and my masters.

I understand that I will rely upon their generosity and their discretion, as has been the way before, with the understanding that that generosity will honestly reflect what is best for both the collier and his Company.

"Every miner who wants to work for me in the future will sign this paper before going down one of my pits. I will not be af- fronted in this fashion again, I assure you of that."

He was talking to the others more than to Gillon. All the paper asked was that a man surrender all his rights.

"Forty," Gillon said aloud. He didn't know if he had intended to say it out loud.

"Yes, forty."

It was the number that was aggravating a sore in his mind,

throbbing there like the nerves around the bones in his shoulder. The *forty* after the ordeal of getting his salmon. The forty percent of cod-fish Christmas.

"That will keep your family nicely until you're ready to go back down."

"I may never be able to go back down," Gillon said. Forty percent dividends in the bad year, the year they had put grass and stones in the soup. He felt the anger rising in him again and was glad of it, and afraid of it.

"Nonsense. You'll go back down. They always do."

"You really don't think we bleed when we're cut. Would you care to *see* the wound, sir?"

"What kind of blether is this to master?" Brothcock said.

"This isn't my master. This is my employer." Gillon felt his face burning but not from embarrassment.

"What is he talking about?" Lady Jane said. "What is he trying to say? We have always been masters here."

"Forty percent is what I am talking about, Ma'am," Gillon said. "Forty percent dividends when the children ate boiled grass, when we were driven to putting stones in the soup for taste. My God, I have to ask, what did you people take in the good years?"

It was followed by silence because they weren't prepared for the outburst.

"Where did you get that nonsense?" the Earl said. "Who fed you that pack of lies? I want to know so I can deal with it. Speak up!"

"I *can* read, sir. Lots of us can read. I read it in *The Scotsman*, sir. I can recite it for you if you wish, sir; I read it so often, you see, sir."

"What is it he wants?" Lady Jane asked. It was all incomprehensible to her. "What is he after? Is he a collier or not?"

"Yes, Mother."

"Then what is he talking back for? Colliers don't talk back to master."

"I think he's a little daft," someone said.

"All we ask is that when we finish a week of work that we be not hungry for it. Is that asking too much? And that when we're hungry and the Company is fat, we might have a little of the fat to see us through."

"When my father was still alive," Lady Jane said, "colliers were flogged for acting this way. We used to beat them."

"And we want to see that we are subject to the laws, and not to the whims of any master, sir. There is no master and no slave in this country any more, sir, and the men are learning that."

"Is that it?" Lord Fyffe said. "Are you quite through . . .?"

He couldn't remember what it was he had said; it had all poured out in such a rush that he had no sense of the words he had used. All he was conscious of was that for once in his life he had said what he wanted to say to the man he wanted to hear it, and he wasn't sorry. He knew that it was all over for him in Pitmungo, and he wasn't sorry. He was as dazed now as he was when he had come into the room.

"When I came down here, I came down to accept your offer—" Gillon started to say.

"Silence," Brothcock ordered. His face was almost touching Gillon's but Gillon barely saw him. "I'm going to shut your mouth by breaking it."

"There *is* no offer now," Fyffe said. "You're going to be crushed and your family crushed with you." He sounded amiable about it.

"But he needs his beating first," someone said.

"He needs a good whipping. His kilt down and flogged like a schoolboy."

"He needs," a young man said, "another pick inside his arm."

They were silent again, the signal that Gillon could never see.

"This is a civilized house and we are a civilized people," Lord Fyffe said. "When the time comes for a flogging, he will get one because his own kind are going to give it to him for the misery he is going to cause them. Now get out. Go!"

He didn't know which way to go. People were all about him.

He was afraid of someone hitting him on his bad arm and when someone touched the arm he almost cried out. It was a serving girl leading him out. He passed through them, conscious of the sway of his kilt against his knees but not of any faces.

"And Cameron, one other thing." The serving girl stopped him and turned him around to face the Earl.

"Why are you wearing my shoes?"

"Your shoes?"

"My shoes."

He stood as he had turned, halfway around, his mouth open, not understanding.

"My *shoes*, Cameron."

Gillon knelt down and clumsily, barely able to manage his fingers, untied the laces and slid off a shoe. In the back, near the heel, were the Earl of Fyffe's initials. Gillon looked up, still not comprehending, and they began to laugh. It was the kind of laugh that grows upon itself and it continued to grow for as long as he knelt on the floor of the Great Hall looking inside the shoe and up at them. He untied the second shoe and placed it next to the first one. Just the sight of the shoes in the middle of the room made them laugh. Even Lady Jane could see the humor now and was laughing. A man in a kilt in the middle of the room with no *shoes* on. Gillon got up and for a reason he never understood began backing across the room, backing his way to the corridor, and once in the corridor he turned and began to run. He ran down the hallway to the door and turned the heavy knob one way and pulled and it wouldn't open and the other way and pulled and pushed, it was the last of their tricks, he felt, they had locked him in where he would be forced to listen to the sound of their laughter—when the girl opened the door and he was outside, running on the gravel walk. The gravel cut his feet but he didn't mind; he liked the humiliation of the stones' hurt.

"Sir," the girl was calling from the door. "Jock. Your hat," she called. "You've left your hat." But she didn't offer to bring it out to him and he would never take a step back toward her and so he continued on his way, running once more, out to the Low Road. All that he could get straight in his mind was that he had lost another hat. Maggie would never forgive him for a second hat.

12 "No settlement."

That's all they learned at first, but the words went up the rows and lanes ahead of Gillon, leaping from house to house, through stone walls and across the Sportin Moor in the mysterious way news is spread in small towns where all the interests are one.

Gillon met Walter Bone and the other leaders on the Low Road and told as well as he could—the parts he could remember—what had taken place in Brumbie Hall, and then he handed them the paper and started down along the river to be alone. Mr. Bone and the rest of them went back to town to tell Pitmungo what they knew.

For many of them it was sad and for some frightening. They were set for settlement. They had had enough of hunger and living on nerves and marrow. But still, as far as they could learn, one of their own had done what no one had ever dared before; he had talked back to the coal master. For most that was enough to keep supporting the cause. And then there was the "yellow-dog agreement," the paper that asked the men to give up their rights before going down in the mines. The agreement solidified them. Before Gillon came back up the hill, the words "Dogs Sign, Men Don't" was the rallying cry of a new resistance.

He remembered later as little of the coming up as he did of the going down. He heard the questions being called to him and he tried to answer a few, but mostly he kept walking upward, asking himself over and over if he had done the right thing and not being able to remember exactly what it was he had done or said.

"Where are your shoes?" people would ask. "What did they

do to them, man?" and his mind would go back to some other aspect of the afternoon. How had it gotten to the point where neither of them could find a way to back down? When had the turning point come, the time of no turning back? He couldn't recall, he could only see himself kneeling on Lord Fyffe's floor taking off the Earl's own shoes.

"What happened to the beautiful hat we bought you, man?"

"I don't know."

Dr. Gowrie came down the Walk toward Gillon and Gillon had difficulty recognizing him and hearing him.

"Looked in on that lad of yours. He's going to be all right. Can't keep a mine boy down."

"No."

"If the pits were open tomorrow, which I gather thanks to you they won't be, I'd send the lad down."

"Thank you."

"Little inflammation in the throat but we took care of that. A little fluid in the lungs but we'll dry that out. What we might prescribe for your hard head is another matter."

"Thank you," Gillon said, and started back up.

"I don't know, I'm sorry, I forget, I forget," he said all the way up through Doonietoon and past Lord Fyffe No. 1 and up to Tosh-Mungo Terrace.

They were arguing about something, Sam and Sarah and Maggie and Andrew, in tight, hushed voices, when Gillon came through the door.

"We heard, Dad, we heard all about it. There was nothing else for you to do," Andrew said.

"We heard. You really told the son of a bitch the facts of life down there, Daddie. Oh, we're proud of you," Sam said.

Maggie wouldn't look at him. "What have you done, Gillon? What have you done this day?"

"I don't know what I've done."

"Then you shouldn't have begun," she said bitterly.

"He did a brave thing," Sam said.

"Brashness without wisdom isn't valor, boy. A dumb horse with blinders will run into a cannon. Call that *brave*?"

Gillon pushed his way through them and went into the ben. He had to be away from them. He lay down on the cot they had fixed for him since Jemmie had the bed and studied the patterns on the smoked ceiling. They were arguing again in those controlled hushed voices, low but filled with tension. If only, Gillon thought, he could convince himself that what he had said had not been the vainglorious mouthings of a fool. But he couldn't remember what he had said, things about slaves and masters and the rule of law. If only he could feel proud of himself, if only he had been able to walk out of the Great Hall in dignity instead of fleeing from it, the sound of laughter in his ears. He could hear Jem, from the bed in the corner, shift his body and groan once and then begin to breathe in a terribly labored way, gasping for air like a man coming up from a long immersion. He got up.

"Dr. Gowrie says Jem is better."

"Dr. Gowrie is a fool," Sarah said. "I don't believe he's even a doctor."

"What are you arguing about?"

They turned their backs away from Jemmie.

"We want to send for Dr. Doomsday," Sam said.

"He's seen the doctor once and the doctor says he's all right," Maggie said.

"Dr. Gowrie is what Sarah says he is. My brother is dying. I know someone who's dying," Andrew said.

No one knew his real name, not in Pitmungo. They called him Dr. Doomsday because he was never summoned until the case was almost hopeless, because he came a long way and he cost money. Many of the people he saw in the mine towns were dead by the time Doomsday got there, or died after he saw them no matter what he did, but his arrival made the families feel better. They could hold up their heads; they had done all they could do, they had made the ultimate sacrifice; they had put up the money to call the specialist from Cowdenbeath for the final extravagance of all.

Through all the business at Brumbie Hall Gillon hadn't thought of death and now there was this terrible new thing to get through to him. Jem, the toughest of them all, dying? He couldn't accept it.

"How long has this been happening? In front of my eyes and I don't notice. My son dying and I don't see it!"

"He is not dying," Maggie said. "You give up too easy."

"Dying all around me and I never even notice," Gillon said. "Maybe Lord Fyffe is right. Self-serving, selfish man."

"You *noticed*. You just didn't think he could be dying," Andrew said.

"Aye, that's it. Say it louder so he's sure to hear it," Maggie said. "Mrs. Bone doesn't think he's dying, Mrs. Hodges doesn't think he is, Dr. Gowrie says he's going to be fine and you want to bury him."

"If he's not dying, all the better, then," Gillon said. "Then it makes sense to go for Dr. Doomsday." He turned to Sam. "Take the horse and wagon and go alone; it will be lighter that way."

"I'll run," Sam said. "I can outrun the pony. The doctor can bring me back in his trap. Give me money." Dr. Doomsday made no move from his surgery without money in hand ahead. Those who died were very poor payers.

The bed was moved and the stone lifted. Gillon looked up and saw Maggie's face when he took the kist from the hole.

"If he's well, he's well," she said. "If he's dying, he'll die, there's nothing the doctor can do. Two pounds for nothing."

"What if there was just one chance?" Sam said. "Just one little chance in the world. Would you spend the two pounds?"

Maggie looked at the kist and said nothing. She, alone among them, had already figured out what was waiting for them ahead.

There was nothing to do but wait then.

The way the news from Brumbie Hall went up the hill, the

news of Jem went down. The men who had planned to come for a hearing on what had taken place in their names stayed home and waited. They waited for God to make the disposition of Jemmie Cameron final, and for the Lord of Fyffe to make his disposition known.

Pitmungo waited.

The sun had gone down and they sat in the house in darkness, listening to Jemmie's thick breathing, not realizing that darkness had taken possession of the room.

"It's dark," Sarah said, as if it were some kind of astonishing discovery, but no one got up to light a lamp.

"It's hard to be running in the dark. He should have taken the horse, the horse can see in the dark."

"Sam can see in the dark. He knows the road in the dark. He's run it before," and the memory of the night when Jemmie caught Sam fell on them as thickly as the darkness, and Sarah, for the first time, began to cry. It was the day she had run away, it was her happiness and Jem's terrible effort all mixed together.

"Hush," Maggie said, "get hold of yourself, you don't want him to hear you doing that," and Sarah stopped.

"Eight miles to Cowdenbeath. He should be there by now."

"Twelve," Ian said. He had just come home, bringing some stolen coal from the bing outside Lord Fyffe No. 1. There were two guards on the bing to keep the people from getting coal, but Ian had his way.

"That will stop when this is over, too," his mother said.

"Aye, Mother, it all will stop," Ian said.

Gillon didn't know how far it was, eight miles or ten or twelve, but it struck him as just another sign of the way they were kept in bondage by ignorance. They didn't even know how far they were from medical help and from the courts, or from police protection in case Lord Fyffe did try to crush them in some way.

Jean Bone, Sarah's mother-in-law, came up the Terrace to see if she could help. She stood over Jemmie and knelt down near him. Through the doorway they saw her shake her head, but when she came out there was a kind of smile on her face.

"Weel, there's no question he's no very weel, but I've seen cases like it before and I think he'll come through it a' richt."

"We've sent for Dr. Doomsday."

The smile melted from her face. There was no need for pretense any more.

"Dr. Doomsday." She looked back toward Jemmie. "You done the right thing, I think," she whispered.

And that went down through the village. The preparation sign, the beginning of the end: Dr. Doomsday on his way. Gillon sat down to write Mr. MacDonald everything that had happened this day. That should help him get it clear in his mind, he thought, and make the evening pass. Gillon heard Mrs. Bone through the window.

"He's no richt at all," she said. "I doubt he'll no come through it." Mrs. Bone needed lessons in tact.

He wrote without stopping, telling his law agent of the plight of Pitmungo since the lockout began and then of his visit to Brumbie Hall. The scratch of the pen helped drown out the rasping sounds of Jem, and the work drove out thoughts of his son. The others sat and waited.

"I think you should give him some water," Maggie said.

"He won't take it," Sarah said.

"He will if you spoon it down."

But when she lifted up Jem's head he cried out, and when she slipped the spoon of water between his lips he rejected it and beads of water dribbled down his chin.

"He should be there by now."

"Long time ago," Andrew said. "He can run ten miles in an hour."

"No one can run ten miles in an hour," Emily said.

"Your *brother* can!"

It had been a quiet evening, but a wind was coming up and

there was a sudden splash of rain against the windows, almost as if someone had thrown a pail of water against the panes.

"Oh, this rotten country," Gillon said. He got up from the table. "Can't there be one day without rain or snow or something smashing people down?"

He thought of Sam in the doctor's trap. The doctor would have foul-weather gear and there Sam would be, in his singlet, sweating from the ten-mile run, getting his own chill of death in the cold rain. He turned on Maggie with a sudden, savage anger.

"We never should have sent him up on the moor."

Maggie got up and went across to her husband.

"Listen to me now, Gillon, and don't ever forget or abuse it. I am not going to have that ripping us apart for the rest of our lives. The boy was sick before he ever went up."

"Aye, before we sent him up. Before we *drove* him up."

"He went up because he was Jem."

Sarah was crying again. "You talk about him as if . . ." She couldn't say it.

"Don't you forget that, don't you ever forget that again," Maggie said, and went across the room to her daughter and put her arm around her. "That's doing no good at all if he hears you," she whispered, "no good at all."

"Aye, aye."

"Hush-a-baa, now."

"Aye. Aye, Mother."

"Dinna greet no more."

"No, it's over now," Sarah said, and they all heard it at the same time, quick clip-clop of hoofs on cobbles, Dr. Doomsday's famous little trotter that could outrun any horse in the shire. Maggie lit a second and a third lamp and then the doctor was at the door with Sam behind him, shivering.

"Good evening," he said. He had come to Pitmungo many times but this was the first time they had ever seen him, a tall, somber man who looked his name, who looked as if he carried all the sadness of West Fife in his black bag. "Good lad you have here," he said, pointing to Sam. "Dry him off, rub him down, a little whisky and he'll do. He's chattering now but he's still warm from the run. Now let's see the other one. Ladies back, please."

"It doesn't matter, sir," Maggie said, "we're miners' women."

"Aye, it doesn't matter to me if it doesn't matter to you."

They stripped Jem to the waist, and the doctor knew he needn't go any further. The light was brought as close as it could be without its burning Jemmie's face. He was fighting against the doctor but the doctor was expert at holding his patients down and going on with his examination. After the throat he tested the swollen glands and took a rectal fever reading and then began tapping down the length of Jemmie's lungs. He looked at Jem for a moment and Jem suddenly opened his eyes and looked back at the doctor and they thought they saw him try to smile, a smile of recognition, perhaps, or of understanding or pain. Then the doctor covered him up again and Sarah began to cry, and they went out into the but, where Sam was changing into dry underwear.

"Do you want to hear the truth or to hear what most families want to hear? I think from the lad who brought me out, I know."

Gillon liked the man. He could see now that the reason he was feared and resented in Pitmungo was that he represented the truth, which in most cases was unbearable.

"Your boy is suffering from diphtheria with bronchial complications. There is a membrane growing across the throat which is making breathing difficult and very painful. I have heard people cry out through the night and none any worse than this lad. He is in pain."

The whir of the wind and rain in the Scotch pine outside the ben window caused the doctor to look up.

"That can't be of any help," he said.

"I'll cut it down the now," Sam said.

"This is a fever disease and it kills by dehydrating, wasting, and debilitating, do you understand me?" They nodded. "The membrane over the throat is highly serious and it could be bypassed

446

by a tracheotomy, that is, by cutting a hole here in the neck and inserting a little pipe and getting air directly to the lungs, but that would only prolong the agony. The lungs are so filled with fluid, which I have no way of draining, that the boy is, in a manner of saying it, drowning in his own bed."

He began to pack up the few things he had needed in Jemmie's examination. He looked at them for a long moment.

"I have a medicine that is somewhat effective against the further development of the membrane, which will make breathing that much easier, at least, and allow the lad to talk a little if he has any wish to do so. Or strength to do so. He may just want to slip awa', as we say."

He gave a bottle of the medicine to Maggie.

"A teaspoon every several hours will do. If he has a choking fit, and they are bound to come, this will help for a while and then there will be no further help."

He was standing up. A tall man, the tallest man ever to enter their house. Dr. Doomsday in their house. How fast it had all seemed to come to pass.

"Why do I tell you all this? Do I tell it to you to cause you suffering? No, I tell it for the sake of my patient." He spoke as if no one was in the same room with him. "I have another medicine here that I have found works well for certain cases in towns like this one, far removed from hospital. I am going to leave it by the patient's bedside and when the choking gets too severe, I suggest that one of you be decent enough to give the poor lad his . . . treatment."

They went back into the ben. None of them except the doctor could bring themselves to look at Jem, not right then. The doctor opened his bag and took out a small bottle and put it on the table by Jem's head.

"Good evening," he said when he came out, and put on his black slicker at the door. "There is one other thing I try in Scotch houses, with little success, I find. Do not be afraid to cry. The patient doesn't really mind, the patient always knows, and it's very good medicine indeed for those who stay behind. Dry eyes and death don't go well together."

They heard the pony whinny, impatient at having been left in the rain, and then the rapid *tick tick* down the cobbles and Dr. Doomsday was gone. Until he was gone, all sounds of him gone, no one made a move of any kind until finally Maggie went to find a teaspoon and Sam went into the ben to look at the other bottle of medicine the doctor had left by the bed. It was difficult to read the label in the dim light, but Sam was reluctant to take the bottle out of the room. Eventually he got the letters down, and when he did he made a little sound that he hoped no one else heard. The letters spelled out "Chloroform."

The medicine worked well in offsetting the effects of the membrane in Jem's throat. It let him talk a little, something he hadn't been able to do, and to swallow some water which put life back in his burning, dry body. He asked to be left in the ben, where he could be alone, and then he asked that Sam be sent to sit with him.

"Don't cut down the tree," he said, and the hair rose on the back of Sam's neck.

"You heard then?" Sam finally said.

"Aye, I heard."

"All of it?"

"People think because you can't talk you can't hear, but your voices are like drums in my head."

The effort exhausted him and he lay looking at the ceiling and then closed his eyes, and woke again later as if time had not passed at all. He could see enough to know that Sam had been crying.

"Och, man," Jem said. "Do you think I didn't know, then?"

Sam got up. He couldn't bring himself to look at his brother.

"It's cold in here. I'm going to get a bucket of hot coals and put them by the bed."

"Not for me it's cold," Jem said. "Sit down."

Sam held his brother's hand but sensed it hurt him and he let it go. He sat by the bed, relieved that the heaviness of the breathing had softened, listening to the wind in the branches at the window.

"I don't mind that sound," Jem said. "I've come to like it."

"You used to hate it."

"I've grown up, man. It used to scare me. Made me think of . . . of doomsday." He tried to smile. "I've seen that now and it's not so bad." He did smile.

Sam wanted to change the subject. "You know the thing I'm sorry for?" he said. Jemmie watched him. "The day I won the Marathon."

"Och, you *won* it, man."

"I cheated you, you know that. Laying off all those weeks."

"What's that matter? You won the race."

"You ran my goddamn legs off, man. You beat the hell out of me. You ran my heart out."

"How could I beat you if you won the race?"

Sam didn't answer and Jem drifted into sleep. He woke a little later and asked for more of the medicine. Sam came back with the spoon and the syrup.

"Och, I've thought of that a hundred times, Jem. A thousand times. Why couldn't I let you go by when you deserved it so much? Of all the things I've done it's the one I regret the most."

"But what would you do? *Let* me win?"

"Oh, I was so proud of you when you caught me. You couldn't do it but you did it. I was so proud I could have died of pride for you. Why? Why did I do that to you?"

Don't let me begin to cry again now, Sam told himself. Hold on now. He put his nails into the wound his mother had made in his hand and hoped the sting of it would work.

"You won it all, Sam. No one will ever do that again."

"Aye, I stole it from you. You're the one who won that race by rights. Oh, why?"

Then he did cry.

"But that's just it, Sam. You had to win. Don't you see that much? That's you. That's me. That's us, Sam. There's nothing we can do about it. There was nothing else you could do."

Sometime in the night his mother tiptoed into the room. "How is he the now?"

"Well, he's sleeping now you know. The doctor gave him something good."

"It won't last too long."

"Aye, I know, Mother," Sam said.

He was awake. They never knew when he was awake or asleep, then.

"Well, I'm never going to get there, am I?" he said later, after Maggie had left.

"Get where, Jem?"

"Where do you think, man—America. Never even going to get to see it."

Sam found that he was crying again, but so lightly and so silently that Jemmie didn't seem to notice.

"That was Dr. Doomsday, wasn't it?"

Sam decided not to answer him. He thought he had known.

"Wasn't it?" He tried to lift himself from the bed. "Wasn't it?"

So Sam nodded.

"Don't ever lie to me, Sam."

"No. No more, ever."

A long pause then. Sam slept. He had run the ten miles and it was late and like everyone else in Pitmungo he was weak from a lack of decent food.

"Tell me about my daddie."

The voice made Sam sit up in his chair. He had forgotten where he was. He told the story as well as he could, as much as he knew, in a low quiet voice because he knew even the sound of his words

450

hurt Jem. His brother lay back and listened with his eyes closed, because the light hurt them; but there was a smile at the edge of his lips.

"Oh, I would have given my life to be there and see it. My daddie telling that son of a bitch off to his *face*. Oh, what a day for Pitmungo, eh, Sam?"

"Aye, what a day."

He got more medicine, but whatever it did it was no longer doing as well. The heavy breathing came back and there was a ragged quality to it that had not been there before. Jem kept trying to clear his throat, to get something out, but each effort ended in pain and failure. Sam was afraid of coughing. He had the feeling that once the coughing began it wouldn't stop until something terrible happened. But Jem didn't cough.

"He really went down there and did it. Will you tell him later how proud I am of him?"

"You tell him."

"I can't tell my daddie that. Straight out like *that*."

"No, I'll tell him for you."

"Sam?"

"Yes, I'm here."

"I want a slip coffin."

"Och, Jem. Jemmie!"

"Do you know the cost of a coffin can buy a ticket to America?"

13

IT WAS DAWN. SHRIEK O'DAY, BUT YOU COULDN'T tell it in the ben because of the shadows of the tree and because there wasn't a cock or a hen left in the town. They had gone into the pot weeks before. So dawn was silent in Pitmungo.

"I made it through. That's the bad time they say."

"You made it through. I don't know, Jem." Sam was suddenly excited. "I can't say, but you look better. I mean that." He got up to call the others, if they were awake, to come in and look at Jem.

"Liar. I told you not to do that to me."

"But it's true."

"My fever's going up again, you fool. Sam?"

He sat down.

"You're going to do something about the Sportin Moor, aren't you?"

He nodded.

"What? Tell me what?"

"I don't know. I never have known. But I'm going to do it."

"It's fire, isn't it? You're going to set fire to the mine."

"I don't know."

"Blow it up, then? Isn't that it? I ken you've been saving black powder."

"Where'd you see that?"

"You think you can hide a thing like that from your brother, man?"

"If you know, who else knows?"

"Who else is your brother? Your sneaky brother?"

"Andrew know?"

"No, he doesn't think in those terms."

"Ian?"

"No. If he did, he would have come to me and sold the information."

"Aye, that's true. What are we going to do about him?"

"He'll be all right, he'll come around. You'll see. He's a Cameron too." They went back to business.

"Which is it, Sam? Tell me. I'll carry your secret to the grave, man."

How could he joke that way? It brought tears to Sam's eyes. Dr. Doomsday was wrong about that, Sam thought. What was needed in Sam's case were a few less tears.

"I don't know. I never have known. It has to be done right when it's done."

"But you're going to do it?"

"Aye, I'm going to do it. I'll do it for you, Jem."

"Aye, well, I'd like that. Och, Jesus, man, I wish I could be going along with you."

He wasn't better. The medicine brought him back for short periods during the day and then Jem asked members of the family to come see him in his room. It was very formal for Jem, nursing his supply of life long enough for them to come so he could say good-bye to them, but he managed to say what he wanted to say. Gillon went in in the afternoon.

"You made me proud, Dad."

"Och, Jem, what any man would have done given the chance."

"What no man ever did. Promise me one thing, Daddie. Don't ever sign the yellow-dog paper."

"Och. *Jem!*"

"Nor Andy. Nor none of you."

"None. *Ever!*"

"You were a good father to me. You tried to teach me; I couldn't learn."

"You knew things we didn't."

"No, it wasn't that. I was different than you, Daddie, from the start. I was the brown guy. I couldn't get my head in the book, Daddie. I could not do it."

"But you weren't an ignorant boy, Jem. That you never were."

It was hard for them to talk that way, but a recognition of death has its virtues.

"No, you're going to lose the best barber and best cobbler on Tosh-Mungo. Who's going to take it up after me?"

"Emily," Gillon said and then could have bitten his tongue off. It was the final admission. They were already counting Jemmie out. Gillon sat in humiliated silence, for long minutes, but finally he decided he would have to ask because he had to know.

"Did you throw the stone at Brothcock?"

"No."

"Then Sam did."

"No, Sam didn't. I don't know who did."

"But Sam is planning something with Lord Fyffe Number One, isn't he?"

"No, he's not."

"I have to know."

"He's not. He came to me and said he couldn't take the jobs of other men away."

"Is that true?"

"I swear to God, Daddie."

Gillon tapped himself in the head. "We hadn't thought of that."

"Of what?"

"God. Do you want Mr. MacCurry to come?"

"Oh, man."

"Do you believe in God?"

"I try, Daddie, I try all the time, and I can't make myself believe, even now."

Then your swearing isn't worth very much, Gillon wanted to say, but kept his mouth closed.

"Go away from this place, Daddie. There's no more life left here for us. And never come back no more."

"After the trial, Jem. We'll go after that."

"Ooh, Daddie, how I would have loved to see that trial and then how I would have loved to have gone."

He began coughing after that and it was as bad as Sam had feared. He had to strangle for air then, and steel himself, with almost no energy left at all, as if something were rupturing in his throat. There was nothing to do but hold him and bathe his head and for those waiting outside to grip their chair or stool until their knuckles were white.

In the evening, after he slept, he asked to see his mother.

"Don't make Daddie sign the yellow-dog paper. He'll die like me if he does."

"You're not going to die, Jem. You've held on too long for that."

"That isn't what I asked."

"Aye, then."

"That's not much of a promise."

"I won't ask him. I promise that."

"Then I'm satisfied."

She was a good nurse. She knew how to handle him to get done what had to be done. The others, except for Sarah at times, worked too gingerly and they hurt him that way. She changed his wet shirt and it hurt him but at least it was done.

"Do you know what you never did?"

"Lots of things."

"One thing you never did to me." He lay back and looked at her. He wasn't in any hurry. "You think."

Maggie finally shook her head.

"You never kissed me in my life."

A prickle of needles ran up her back and neck.

"Oh, Jem," she finally said.

"No, Mither, not once in my life. Do you think I wouldn't remember?"

She turned quickly around to see if anyone else was in the ben or standing at the door and was relieved to find herself alone. It was too terrible an admission to have anyone hear. She made a move to reach out for him but Jemmie shook his head.

"It's too late the now. I wouldn't have it the now."

"I loved you as much as I knew how," she said. She talked low and swiftly, she didn't want the others to hear, but she did desperately want to make him hear. "I tried, but we never learned how in our family. Can you understand?"

He gave her no sign at all.

"It's Pitmungo that does it to you, it knocks it out of you. I wanted to but I didn't know how, can you believe me, Jemmie? I didn't know *how* to kiss my own son."

"It's too late now."

"Yes, too late."

"Too late, Mom."

"I can't even cry when the time comes for it," Maggie said, but Jem was asleep. She waited until his breathing, as labored and anguished as it was, had some kind of rhythm to it, and then she leaned over the bed and kissed him on his burning forehead and on his strong bony cheeks. It was amazing how strong he still seemed, this close to death. He was the strongest of them all. It wasn't fair. So much like her father. Her father had never kissed her, either, or had he, that day she went away to get her Gael? She couldn't remember. She thought of kissing Jem on the lips but decided against it. She snuffed out the wick with her fingers and left him in the darkness of the room.

He began coughing again and after each cough there was a terrible struggle to get enough air through the closing membrane of his throat. When it stopped he called for Sam.

"Don't let me drown in my bed," he whispered. "You know, in all the years in the pit I was only afraid of drowning there." Coughing again. Sam held his hand although it hurt him. "Don't let me drown now. Promise."

"Yes, promise."

"And a promise is a promise, eh?"

"Aye."

"You know one good thing about this disease?"

"What?"

"You're anxious to go." Sam couldn't talk for a while after. It was up to Jem to make the effort, then.

"We had good times. It was worth it."

"Oh, yes."

"Sam?"

"I'm here, Jem."

"I'm glad you won the race."

"Och, Jem, don't bring that up again. Don't leave me with that."

"Aye, I see, I understand. All right, I don't care then. I don't give a damn who won or lost the race. It doesn't matter."

"No, it doesn't matter."

"Still, you done something no one else will ever do."

Oh, God, what a Cameron, Sam thought, to the very end, and felt Jemmie's hand slip away from his.

"Good-bye the now. Brother."

"Good-bye."

Others came in after that, Sarah and Andrew, Gillon and Maggie again, so Sam was not the last to see him or, perhaps, to be asked about the drowning. At midnight or some time after it, Maggie gave him a large dose of the medicine and it reacted better than it had done all day and when the terrible breathing lessened there was an overwhelming sense of relief in the house and a deep tiredness settled over the people in it. The tension had been broken for the time, and they all found themselves in the web of sleep. Gillon crawled onto his cot and tried to put the pieces of time back in place but he fell asleep. All over the house, people were asleep on their beds or on the floor. Rob Roy had come up from the College, a little drunk, and had looked in on Jem and curled up on the upstairs floor. The whole house was asleep.

It was the suddenness of the movement that woke Gillon. Someone moving swiftly through the but toward the ben.

"Yes?" he said, and waited. For the moment the sound ceased and he thought of sleep again and then they came once more, the sounds, someone moving very quickly, too quiet to be ordinary night sounds. There was a voice and some kind of answer; he couldn't hear at all, and all at once he knew he didn't want to hear and never would want to hear or know. Some kind of struggle in the other room, very brief, the bed moving an inch or so along the floor, the faint sound of glass falling against stone and not breaking and silence, a minute, two minutes, no sound of any kind from the room and then that same quickness again, coming back, someone who by now could see in the dark, cutting across the room, bumping his wife's cot, silence then—and footsteps from out back, from the larder, or from the stairwell going up, he couldn't tell, he couldn't place them, a sound of bumping upstairs, or steps, he thought, coming down.

"Maggie?"

When she didn't answer he got out of the cot and crossed to hers. She wasn't in it. The door to the back of the but was left open. The wind had died down, which was one reason the noises had waked him, and there was a moon and all at once she came in the door.

"What are you doing here?" he said.

"And you?" She held a wet sheet in her hand. "I washed his sheet. He'll need a fresh sheet in the morning."

"But it's wet. It's sopping."

"I'll dry it."

So she *was* there, but what had been the noise on the stairs? Up and down, swift and sure, the movement in the but across the floor like animals that scurry in the darkness, and the noise from the ben. He went back to bed because he didn't want to go into Jemmie's room then and after a while he felt his pillow wet with his tears. When he woke before dawn, she was still asleep, as completely asleep as any child would sleep after a long day. The sheet was hanging near the cold fire still dripping wet. He didn't want to go in then, and so he went upstairs as quietly as he could, and they were all asleep in the two rooms there: Sarah and Emily asleep in their cots and Rob Roy, in the wrong room, on the floor. He studied all their faces. There was nothing to be read in them.

"Daddie?" It was Sarah. "How's Jem?"

"He's fine. He's fine, I think."

"Oh, good."

"Go back to sleep now. He's asleep."

"Aye."

He went back downstairs and started for the ben but decided that he wanted to breathe some of the morning before going in to see his son. When he opened the door the step was covered with little bottles of water. Those would be the bottles of unspoken water he had heard about, water taken from beneath a bridge over which the living walk and the dead are carried, brought to the house at twilight or dawn without the bringer ever saying a word on the way coming or going. All at once he became convinced, for one joyful passing moment while looking down at all those little bottles, that what he had heard in the night was nothing, and that the silence from the ben was the work of the magic water. Jemmie was only sleeping.

There *must* be something to it, the magic of the water, or the people wouldn't do it, getting up before dawn and walking in darkness down to the pool below town and coming all the way back up the hill before the sun was up. They didn't do that because there was nothing at all to it, Gillon told himself. He closed the door and ran back across the room and into the ben knowing that the worst was over, that he would see that firm brown face at rest now, the crisis broken sometime in the night. He fully expected to see his son awake, lying in bed, even smiling up at him. But the bed was in disarray, he saw that, the sheet and plaid not even covering the upper part of his son's body. On the floor beside the bed lay the empty bottle and the stopper.

He pulled the plaid over Jem, making it straight and neat, but not over the face—he had never liked that—and Jem looked very good lying there, much the way he always looked, as if he might wake and be ready to get up and go down the pit again. After that Gillon picked up the bottle and stopper and found the flannel that had been used and put those in his pocket, and then looked down on his son. Who was it that had had such courage; who was it that had had such love? And then he left the room to wake the family and tell them Jemmie was dead.

14 THE DAY AFTER JEMMIE WAS BURIED, DROPPED naked to the earth to save siller on a suit and box, Lord Fyffe announced the mines were open again and the Company was taking on every loyal miner who would agree to sign what the Company called the Mutual Trust Agreement. It was a victory for the Camerons and for the men and it was a shame that Jem couldn't have hung on to enjoy it. It was the first crack, the first backing down in the history of the Pitmungo Coal and Iron Company.

The Camerons stood fast on Tosh-Mungo Terrace, the suit for compensation was still in the courts and Lord Fyffe had reopened the mines. It wasn't a total victory, since the men were still required to sign the yellow-dog agreement in order to work, but the point remained, which the men knew only too well, that because of their solidarity the option to work had shifted to them. They could work if they chose to work.

They didn't choose to work. When the whistle blew on Monday morning, a great many men went down to the mine mouths but not a man in Pitmungo went down in the mines.

"We go down when he takes that paper and shoves it wherever a lord shoves it," Archie Japp said. He was becoming a leader on the side of the men with as much force as he had once driven them. It was the kind of thing that was happening in Pitmungo. No matter what the outcome of Gillon's battle, things would never be the same there again.

"Look, man," Mr. Powell said at the College. His tavern was feeling the pinch very badly. "This town lives on coal. How are we going to get the coal out?"

"Let the coal walk out, man. Send Mr. C. P. S. Farquhar and his fat sons down, man."

Everyone knew about the forty-percent dividend, which united the men, and the yellow-dog paper, which insulted them, but the issue remained personal. "Stand fast with the Camerons," still stood as a rallying cry and the death of Jemmie added to the fervor of it. People came to feel that Jem had died for the cause.

"They gave their son to the fight; the least you can do is tighten your belt a notch."

For a week the whistle blew and the men went down to see who would be the first bastard to give in and sign Lord Fyffe's agreement and not a man did. They heard about it in Easter Mungo and in Wester Mungo and down in Cowdenbeath. They heard it in Edinburgh and they were watching all over West Fife. The men were sticking together.

A message was sent up from Edinburgh:

We don't know how you did it but keep it up. This is the first time there has been 100% solidarity in any mining village in West Fife. What you have done is make history and pass a miracle.

I hope your wound is better but not too much better. Our case is on the calendar for the new session. The mills of justice grind slow but fine. We shall have our Lord in court yet. Stand fast. Hold on. Hold out.

Angus MacDonald

Below it was scrawled:

We are watching you; we stand behind you.

KH

The letter was passed around to the men and it impressed them. They weren't alone; the world was looking into their black valley. It made their hunger easier. Only Selkirk continued to be unenthusiastic.

"Did you tell them how goddamn hungry the men are?" he asked. "You mustn't be too proud to let them know the men are beginning to starve. Tell them to get some food in here or it won't last another week. What is it you and your loovely wife are always spouting? 'Hunger is a good master.' Well, you're right. Emotion isn't enough, desire isn't enough. You've got your unity, now you have to build an organization out of it."

When you need a martyr, make sure you send a martyr.

When you need a leader, make sure you have a leader.

When you attack power, make sure you lead from power.

Gillon knew the sayings, backwards and forwards, but he couldn't apply them in an organizational sense; there was nothing to organize about. The issue, as Gillon saw it, was a man's pride and his obligation to it. It was as simple as that. They had been locked out of their work because a man asked for justice under the law and now they were being offered the privilege of sweating for the Earl at his whim if they were willing to crawl back in. It was no longer a question of Gillon Cameron or of an organization, but of the integrity of each man in Pitmungo who mined coal.

"The reason they call it a yellow-dog agreement," a miner explained to his son, "is that only a yellow dog would sign it."

As simple as that.

On Saturday night, on what would have been pay-packet night, the Pluck Me was reopened. The constable from Cowdenbeath came with four soldiers from the Edinburgh Fusiliers, armed and looking foolish and a little ashamed of themselves, and stood in the doorway in case any hungry colliers got ideas in their heads.

Unlimited credit, Mr. Brothcock announced from the steps of the store, would be advanced against future earnings for all those willing to sign the Mutual Trust Agreement and appear for work at the pits on Monday. Food would be sold at cost.

"Aye, at the cost of your manhood!" Japp shouted.

A rock sailed by Mr. Brothcock's head and crashed through the glass behind him. The four soldiers went down on their knees and pointed their rifles at the crowd of men in front of them, but Brothcock never moved.

"At least they can't blame that one on your Jem," someone said.

"My Jem wouldn't have missed," Gillon said.

"For those of you sensible enough to sign, there will be fresh pork on your table tonight and bacon for breakfast in the morning."

They stood fast but it wasn't easy for any one of them. In the end, as Selkirk said again, it would be the women and the hungry children that would decide the issue.

They weren't ready for the discipline of the Communists and the intricate arguments of the Socialists, they weren't ready, these people who had just ceased to fight among themselves, for outsiders such as the Miners' Union to come in and tell them what to do. It was their battle and they wanted to wage and win it themselves. Gillon wrote to the Scotch Miners' Union but Keir Hardie was in Wales, running for Parliament there because he couldn't get enough votes in Scotland, and the Miners' Union was under a court injunction to cease its organizing activities. That was all right with the men from Pitmungo. They went down each day and stood around the mine mouth, and then, as if drawn there by magnetic force, they gathered in front of the Pluck Me, seemingly to monitor those who might try to slip in through the door, but actually drawn there by the sight of food. It seemed to reassure them to know that food still existed in the world.

"That store is going to kill you," Selkirk told Gillon. "If you want to win you'd better burn it down."

There was talk of rushing the store and taking what they needed, what they had been cheated out of in the past, but there was no one to lead them. There was no tradition of that kind of lawlessness in Pitmungo. And so they stood and waited outside and smelled the smells from the store, and the women began to faint. It became a kind of craze, a rage. The women, who hadn't eaten a decent meal in over a month, began simply slipping to the stones, one following the one beside her, dropping to the ground and being carried home and put into bed to save her energy. And then the mood of the crowd, as Selkirk had warned, began to change. "You watch," he had warned, "if there's no structure to shelter them in, the crowd can be as moody as the flocks on the moor."

"Where are they now when we need them?" a man suddenly shouted out one afternoon. "Where's your great Keir Hardie? Why should we have to starve for him?"

There was all too loud a grumble of "aye's," but Walter Bone silenced it.

"It's not for them, it's for ourselves!" he shouted. "It's for the moor they stole from us. It's for the manhood he wants to steal from us. We've pushed him this far, we can push him farther. Do we have to be cowards just because we're treated like slaves?"

It held them, but a crowd has a short memory, and a starving crowd, in the end, no memory at all of anything but food. In their hunger, Bone realized, they were searching for somewhere to place their blame in order to free them from the burden of themselves.

"I ask you one thing," a man called out. "Why should we starve to save Cameron's pride?"

The "aye's" could be heard again above the crying of children in the doorways at the back of the crowd.

"It's not Cameron any longer, it's us!" Bone shouted, but they didn't hear him.

"It's all for Cameron's gain. He's using us to get his siller."

"To get his gowd."

"He's not going to get his siller at the cost of my bairns' lives, I'll tell you that."

They began to move, to shift, as if some force was moving them against their will, a reluctant step, but one step after another, toward Colliers Walk.

"You know it's not so!" Andy Begg shouted. "He's suffered as much as us and worse. There'll be no work for the Camerons in this valley and you know that. No work in all of Scotland and you know that."

But they were moving, not with any great energy, not with any true desire, just a massive shifting of people without a leader and without a cause it believed in, but with a need to move, to do something, to go somewhere. It had been too long and asking too much for them to stand still any longer.

"The Camerons always make out, don't worry about them!" a man shouted. "They got a kist of siller in their hoose would sink a boat."

The house, more than the silver, was what stirred them, because it offered their aimlessness a direction.

"The hoose, the hoose," they began to chant, and as they did, they started milling their way up the hill toward Tosh-Mungo, and then "Tosh-Mungo, Tosh-Mungo" became their cry because it excited them more. They had no idea what they would do when they got there except that with the certainty of mobs they knew some answer would be waiting for them.

"Mobs and cowards believe such easy things," Walter Bone said to Andy Begg, watching the people push their way up the hill, and when he turned back to Begg, Andy Begg was gone with the rest.

Maggie was the first to hear them, sewing in the front window seat, and she knew at once what it meant. She was calm about it.

"They're coming for you," she turned and said to Gillon. "I knew they would sooner or later."

"Why should they come for me?"

"Because you're holier than they are and they can't stand it."

"I don't believe you."

"If you don't, you'll soon find it out."

Even with the windows closed and the door shut, they could hear the cries through the foot-thick walls. If only they didn't come with fire in mind, she thought. She never considered they might have come for the kist.

"I don't understand," Gillon said, "I don't understand."

They came up the Terrace and the shouting became more of a roar. There was not much anger to the shouting, or much direction, but still it was frightening; who can ever tell about a mob? Five hundred people were shouting five hundred different things, but gradually they came to settle on one that gave them the most satisfaction. "Cameron, come oot, Cameron, come oot!" they chanted, and things shook and trembled in the house. A tassie fell from the dresser.

"What am I going to do?" Gillon asked. He had to shout to be heard.

"This is your mess; you made it, you get out of it."

The anger in his face when he turned to her frightened her.

"And this is your family. You made it. You want to get out of it?" He was right, she knew: the family was in it now and they had to stay together.

"Then you'd better go out, Gillon, or they're going to come in. I don't think they'll hurt you; I don't think they know what they want."

Gillon stood by the door and waited. They were growing more violent.

"The family will only excite them," Maggie said. Gillon nodded. "You'll have to go it alone."

He still stood behind the door and she came over to him and put a hand on his shoulder.

"Come on, Gillon. You'll know what to do." She reached around him and put her hand on the latch. "Waiting's no good now," she said, and worked the latch and the door began to open and there was nothing for Gillon to do then but go out and face them.

When they saw him, the men nearest to the door fell silent and some seemed a little ashamed. Then others saw him in the doorway and began to grow silent, and soon the only sound was the shifting of people's feet on the cobblestones as they scuffed about for a better look.

"What do you think you've come for?" Gillon called out.

Sooner or later, a true mob, if it comes without a leader, invents one, but this mob didn't have the leader or the will. Gillon sensed that in them and began to feel the way he had in Brumbie Hall when the words ran away with him. He asked them why they had come, and what they thought they would find or could get, and they were silent. In the protection of the little square by the Pluck Me their collective voice had thundered back at them from the walls, but up on the Terrace the wind sweeping down from the High Moor swallowed what sound they had.

"Sign the paper, Cameron," someone finally managed.

"The pits are open. Any man who wants to sign the paper is free to do it. Just don't come up here and ask me to do it for you. Don't ask me to forgive you."

Some of the men began studying the stones and cobbles on the Terrace. Some at the back of the crowd broke away from it and drifted back down the hill.

"The children are hungry, man, the children are crying."

"Do you think I don't hear them crying at night? It makes me cry, too, but understand this much. I'm not going to do your quitting for you. The question is, do you want to live under law or under the whim of the master for the rest of your lives?"

The other Camerons had come out by then. Whatever mob strength had resided in that collection of people, it was gone from them now. They were weaker, if only because of their size—a massive, collective weakness—than one strong man.

"If you want to sign the yellow-dog agreement and get food for your children, you know where to go to do it. Just know this, too. My son Jem will never sign. The rest of the Cameron family will never sign. I will never sign."

They broke up after that. Fushionless they called it in Pitmungo, a withering away of the spirit, and not one of them on leaving ever looked back. Gillon and the rest of the family watched them go, and when most were on their way, straggling alone or in little groups back down the hill, they opened the door and went inside.

"Is that the way you sounded in Brumbie Hall, Daddie?" Sam asked.

"No, it's the way I wanted to sound."

"Och, Jem would have been proud of you today, Dad," Rob Roy said. "That would have been his true eulogy."

"Aye, he would have been satisfied with that," Andrew said.

Maggie went over to Gillon.

"You were right, I was wrong," she said. "And you did it almost as well as it could be done."

They thought Mr. Selkirk had come up the hill to congratulate Gillon for what he had done but he hadn't. A few days after the march up the hill a group of men, no longer able to face the eyes of their children staring at them from their beds, too weak to play, sleeping their hunger away, formed a Hardship Committee, a group of citizens before whom a man could appear and prove that his family had gone over to the far side of starvation. If the Committee agreed, with no prejudice to be held against him, with no loss of respect in the eyes of the town, a man could go down to the Pluck Me and sign the yellow-dog paper and take a creel of food home to his house.

"So there it is, Gillon," Henry Selkirk said. "The crack in the dam, the leak in the dike. It's a fact of life, Gillon. No starving man can smell the stink of melting fat coming from his neebor's house without killing him or joining him. It is my humble opinion . . ."

"I didn't know you had any of those, Mr. Selkirk," Maggie said.

". . . that they will join him. Unless you have a finger for the dike?"

Gillon shook his head. He had reached, he thought, a point in life when he could recognize the truth when he heard it.

"It is my humble opinion, Mr. Selkirk, that you are full of shit," Sam said.

"Aye," Andrew said, with great vehemence, "aye." They thought he would be angry and they waited for the explosion to come but it never came. Mr. Selkirk merely stood in the doorway and smiled.

Over a hundred heads of families appeared before the Hardship Committee the first week alone, and on Monday morning over three hundred men—every one of them staring hard at the ground, the collar of his work jacket pulled high up around his face—appeared at the mine mouths and pitheads and waited for the cages to take them down. No one said anything to them going down or coming back covered with their pit dirt. Most of the women made an effort to cook as covertly as possible, trying to keep the smell of cooking food from wafting over neighboring houses, but nothing can keep the smell of food from hungry men. Each day there were more of them ready to sign and go back down to work, each day more and more coal came steaming up the shafts, and the hutches of coal began to roll once more toward St. Andrew's dock. By the end of the second week it was over, although not completely over. Twenty-one men, most of them heads of families, still refused to sign and go down and Gillon knew what that meant. Like it or not he had become the father to twenty-two families.

"How are they going to live? How are they going to survive?" Sam said.

"We'll see that they do," Gillon said.

Maggie understood at once. "Not with my siller they won't," she cried.

"Aye, with *our* siller they will."

She was staring at Gillon with an anger so deep and so dangerous that it touched on madness, they all saw that.

"There is the price of coal and we've paid that," Gillon finally said. He was very calm about it, and quiet. "There is a price for Jem and we're paying that. There is a price for pride and we'll start paying that."

"*Pride!*" she shouted. Her voice cut through all of them. "God, look what you've done with your pride, your great romantic pride. You've lost our work and you've lost our home and now you'd steal our future. For what? What? All for your stupid dignity, your Cameron pride."

Maggie spat.

"But you're the one who taught me," Gillon said. "I never knew about pride before."

She ran into the other room and when she came back out the key to the kist was on the chain around her neck.

"If you touch the kist, God will have to account for what happens to you," she said, and to their amazement and horror, since they had never seen it before, she fell to the floor and wept with no tears.

15

PITMUNGO WAS AS DEAD AS JEM IN HIS DEAD-hole, as dead as the inside of a dead-kist. No man wanted to drink in the College because it was an admission that he had dogged, as they came to call it, and so they hid in their blackness and sent their bairn to the tavern for their pints and drank them in darkness and silence at home.

The men sneaked off to work, muffled silence in the morning, no more the raucous Japp-like shouts down the rows and lanes,

all that gone, because they couldn't stand the eyes of the Twenty-
One, the righteous men, the men with hollows for eyes who
stared at them from the doorways so that some men would stop
and go back up the Walk and climb over fences and come sneaking around those eyes until they reached the mine mouth and
were lost underground in the privacy of coal and blackness, safe
from everyone but themselves.

Some of the Twenty-One had begun going down to the shaft
heads and watching the men line up, waiting to go down.

"Have a good day doon pit with Lord Fyffe, Tam," they would
say to old friends, and Tam would wish he could fall down the
shaft. But no man who signed quit, because once the chain of
hunger was broken it was impossible to go back to hunger.
Gillon finally had to go down to the shaft heads and restrain the
Twenty-One.

"This is their right; their choice. Ours is our right and our
choice."

"Oh, aye, some choice. Theirs to get fat and ours to become
bones. Their children to blossom and ours to become weeds."

"Why don't you go back down then?" Gillon would ask.

"I don't know. Quit preaching to me, Cameron. I can't go down
and you know it. It's all right for you; you're the big hero here,
the saint of Pitmungo. I just can't go down. It destroys my dignity
as a man, if you must know." The men were embarrassed by the
idealism and still they couldn't find a way to get around it.

"All right, that's it then," Gillon said. "No man is going to die
of hunger or lose his dignity as long as I have siller in my house."

That night Gillon took the key from around Maggie's neck.
She didn't say a word.

Which was the start of it.

Until the trial—when, Mr. MacDonald assured Gillon, the men
would have to be given their jobs back because the judge, like
it or not, would be forced under law to find the yellow-dog

agreement an illegal document—the men would need to be given money in some way that wasn't charity. At a meeting in Walter Bone's house, away from the eyes of Maggie, they founded the Sportin Moor Society, the organization that in the future would speak for the people of Pitmungo to the masters of the Company. The Twenty-One, as they came to be known, were to be the recruiters and organizers for the Society and no bones were made about the fact that they were chosen because the flame of their resistance had burned a little longer than the ordinary man's with the purifying flame of hunger and denial.

The motto of the Society, although she was never told it, was supplied by Maggie Cameron.

The beaten are not always defeated.

The men who had signed the yellow-dog agreement could redeem their spirit and salvage some of their pride by joining the Sportin Moor Society, which would take some courage and some risk because it would put them in open opposition to the Company.

They began to sign. The wages of the recruiters, which Maggie didn't know at first, were to be supplied by Gillon Cameron as an advance to be paid back by the Sportin Moor Society when it became a solvent organization. In the meantime, as the Society grew, the siller went out.

The siller went out. It became the overriding fact of life in the Cameron house. There was no regular system of payment for the men: when they were strapped and down to bone, they came up to Tosh-Mungo Terrace, the kist was opened in the other room and siller was put in the hand. It wasn't much, just enough to keep a man's family short of starvation, but it was twenty-one families and they had to eat and it wouldn't stop.

So the siller went out. Instead of the old weekly *chink, chink, chink,* the lovely solid sound of siller meeting siller in the kist, now it was the muffled sound of siller slipping into waiting hands. She tried to be good about it. She listened and saw and said nothing, holding her tongue, feeling the blood pound in her

head and her heart race as the siller went, as their treasure dwin-
dled, day after day, week after week. Once she had dreamed of
the clink of siller and chests so heavy men couldn't lift them, and
now she had dreams of kists that turned out to be coffins, kists
that were black and rusted, kists gaping and open and empty.
Several times, she was so certain it was gone that she had to get
up in the middle of the night and move the bed and lift up the
stone to reassure herself that the kist was still there.

Twice the case of Cameron v. Farquhar, the Earl of Fyffe, was
dropped back on the calendar, and Mr. MacDonald suspected
political pressure from high places. And each week the kist grew
lighter, the men coming up with their bony hands held out—
the troublemakers, the hardheads, the red bandanna wearers, the
overprideful, the dreamers with their talk of human dignity and
human rights—and all the while the siller running out, a stream
of siller, steady run, steady drain; and all her hopes and dreams
draining away with it. The payments to Mr. Ogilvie would fall
due.

What no one in the Cameron family saw—what they should
have known and should have understood—was that it was driving
their mother to the point of breakdown.

Lord Fyffe knew nothing about the men who worked
for him because there had never been any need to know. Superin-
tendents did that for coal masters. But he learned of the Twenty-
One and was wise enough to recognize that a cancer which can
kill could be started by one little wild erratic cell, no larger than
a pinhead. He determined to eradicate the disease before it could
spread, and at some risk to his personal pride he sent a second
invitation to G. Cameron to come to Brumbie Hall for tea and
discuss cancer in a civilized way. The invitation was written on
thick stationery, with the crest of Fyffe embossed over the top
quarter of the page and delivered by Mr. Brothcock himself,

which the Earl didn't understand was immensely demeaning to his superintendent.

Cameron:

Come to tea tomorrow. I think we will be able to understand each other better than before.

Until then:

Fyffe

Informal dress.

It was a bribe, it smelled of a bribe, it was crisp with bribery, all neat and packaged for him. There would be a secret settlement he couldn't resist, there would be payments and special little privileges for simply being sensible and Gillon knew he would never be able to live with himself again.

"Half past four," Brothcock said.

"Half past four what?" Gillon said.

"The tea, man, the tea." He was close, Gillon sensed, to saying something in the nature of "idiot." The superintendent was showing restraint these days.

"It's what I thought you meant," Gillon said. "I'm afraid you'll have to tell the Earl I can't be there."

Brothcock had begun to walk away from the house, throwing words over his shoulder, but he stopped. "People are always there when Lord Fyffe summons them to tea." He came back to the doorway. Mr. Brothcock had no intention of being the man to tell Lord Fyffe that one of his colliers didn't choose to have a cup of tea with him. "When Lord Fyffe calls, you come."

"Not in this country I don't. You must be thinking of somewhere else." Gillon wished that the superintendent still didn't frighten him, that he was beyond it, but he wasn't. It still took all of his courage to talk the way he did.

"When I tell the Earl what you said, there's going to be serious trouble."

"I thought we'd had enough."

"You haven't seen anything." He brought his face very close to Gillon's. "Now, are you coming?"

"No."

Brothcock turned his back on the Cameron house. "You have just made your life impossible here," Gillon heard him say.

Maggie was wild with rage.

"You fool!" she shouted at her husband. "You arrogant fool. Who do you think you are? You're mad. Something's gone in your mind. You're destroying us."

She was looking at him in a crazy fashion, and it worried him.

"Don't you know what they'll do to us? They'll turn us out of our house, they'll burn us out, they'll come and burn us alive in here. I know them."

"You're acting hysterical," Gillon said sharply. "Control yourself."

"They'll come and burn us, you'll see. It's the way they do. All you had to do was go down and now you've destroyed us." Gillon tried to seize her, but his arm hurt him too much. She pulled away from him.

"Who *do* you think you are? Who in the name of Christ do you think you are?" she said, and went into the ben and closed the door. He was afraid she was crying in the sobbing, dry-eyed way again.

He didn't know who he was any more or how he had gotten to the point he was at. All he knew was that he couldn't stop now. The people of Pitmungo found it hard to believe, that one of them had refused a summons to go down to the Laird's hall. Even Mr. Selkirk felt Gillon had pushed his situation to the breaking point.

"You should have gone down. There was no sense in what you did. There was no pride involved. The loss of pride was all on his side."

"I couldn't go."

"'Couldn't go,'" Mr. Selkirk said. "You're a romantic, man. You *had* to go."

Gillon shook his head.

"All I seem to know is that the time has come to say no, and I can't stop it now."

Mr. Selkirk shook his head.

"And all I know is that you haven't seen what they can do to you. All I know is that no earl was put on this earth to be snubbed by a one-armed collier."

Mr. Selkirk was right and Maggie Cameron was right. They came up the hill the next afternoon with Brothcock at their head, a gang of laborers from Easter Mungo and a wagon-load of demolition tools.

"All right in there," Brothcock shouted. "You have one hour to clear this house. This house is to be taken down. This house is a possession of the Earl of Fyffe and he's ordered it pulled down the day."

But Sam was ready. The Twenty-One were waiting in and around the house with tools of their own: miner's picks and screw augers, six-foot-long iron dynamite tamps, a few creels of stones picked from the river that morning, and the regular tools a workingman might have around his house—lengths of chain and cable, crowbars and sledge hammers, and a few whittled-down pitprops here and there. And then there were not only the Twenty-One. They had done their recruiting job well on Gillon's pay. Of the eight hundred miners in Pitmungo valley, only fifty or so—old men too frightened to sign their names to anything—had not joined the Sportin Moor Society. It had been foolish for Mr. Brothcock to come up after the day shift was over. Of all people, he should have known better. More than a hundred of the men, anonymous in their masks of coal dust from the mines, were waiting for him.

Gillon went out to face Mr. Brothcock.

"I'm warning you this," Gillon said. "This is my home. I have paid for it in advance. I have a legal lease on it for two years. In this country a man's home is his castle, and it can't be entered without a search warrant from the court."

The men began to tap their tools, little metallic rattling noises, on the walls and the cobblestones, steel and iron clanging against stone, a hundred men all rattling steel and iron, perhaps two hundred of them. The laboring gang, with a smell for trouble and no stake in what was happening, began making themselves inconspicuous, drifting away, until Brothcock was alone.

"We don't need no warrant," Brothcock said. "Lord Fyffe's orders are the law here."

"Sir?" Sam said. He had to talk in a loud voice now because of the rattling of the tools. "I'm sorry to bother you, sir, but your tool wagon just rolled away."

Because of the noise from the men and their tools, it was difficult to hear the cart thundering its way down from the Terrace, but as it picked up speed it wasn't hard to hear, down over the Terrace, through Moncrieff Lane and down, running amuck, the tools flying from it in every direction whenever it hit a bump, and finally, with a thunderous sound, a satisfying sound, slamming its way into and through the fence around the Sportin Moor and coming to halt halfway through the wall of the breaker house at Lord Fyffe No. 1.

"Cameron!" Brothcock shouted at him. "You are a son of a bitch and you're going to suffer for this."

There never had been doubts about Mr. Brothcock's courage but there was some question about his good sense. Eight or ten miners, indistinguishable in their blackness, picked the superintendent up and carried him down the Terrace and then down Colliers Walk. It was, those who saw him said, a comical sight. They carried him down through the gaping cut in the fence around the moor and on down to Lord Fyffe No. 1, where they put him on a cage and dropped him three thousand feet, all stops out, to the bottom of the pit. Mr. Brothcock never came up to Tosh-Mungo Terrace again.

16

IT DIDN'T MATTER ABOUT MR. OGILVIE ANY more, Maggie realized one day, because even if he died and they took title to the business, no mineowner in West Fife was ever going to buy a piece of mining equipment from the Camerons or would even accept a piece of equipment from them if they gave it away.

All gone, she thought, gone—the money, the business, the way out, the dream. To save his pride he had killed her dream. As she brooded on it, more painful than the loss of the siller was what it represented. All the work that had gone into getting it, all the wit. All the saving and all the petty scrimping. The doing without, the going without when others around them ate. The denying—pretend they didn't like sweets so they didn't miss them when the others were eating; pretend they didn't need sugar in their tea like others did, or butter on their bread, because they were Camerons. She hardly came out of her room at all any longer. She sat in the dark and brooded about her loss.

There had been times when she had thought of killing Mr. Ogilvie, times when she spent entire afternoons plotting out the perfect murder, and that had alarmed her. Now, when she woke in sweat from the dreams of empty black kists, she thought of Gillon dead and that alarmed her too. She didn't want to kill, she knew that, yet her mind kept coming back to it over and over again. She saw him dead everywhere she turned, dead sitting in chairs, dead with his head down over his bowl of soup, dead—especially—in his bed. She knew that something had to be done, or something horrible could happen. She had to act or lose her mind; she was still enough in control to know that.

478

. . .

It had been easy for her to leave the house. She could move through it without making a sound of any kind, as softly as any cat in Pitmungo. She managed to dress and get out the door and into the lane without anyone stirring in the house. There was no moon or any stars and at first it was hard going down the Terrace, but she was thankful for the darkness and her eyes were getting used to the night.

On the Sportin Moor it was difficult, the piles of equipment strewn about in the careless way of mines and miners, but there were lights farther down where the winding room was operating. It was strange to think that men were down there now, blackness into blackness, the backshift preparing the pits for the men to come down after dawn.

"Who's there? Hold there the noo," a voice said. She wasn't alarmed.

"A mother. My bairn is sick and I'm going for the doctor."

He couldn't make out her face in her shawl, the beautiful Paisley the Bones had given her, but he was only interested in seeing if she carried a creel to steal some coals away, as the very old and very poor women did.

How easily she lied, she thought. That had always been one of her assets.

She went on down through the works, startled once when a huge bull wheel above her began spinning, but regaining control of herself. She had been right to move, to act. She felt like her old self again, all the madness draining from her as she walked through the darkness.

Down through the lower rows then, the pitiful rows, Rotten and Wet below their old house on Miners Row. How long ago that was, how far they had come and now how far they had gone. But they would work before they left, she was determined on that, and the flow of siller, which had been driving her mad —she understood that—would stop this night.

The College was closed and she was grateful for that, but there was a light in the Workers' Reading Room. Selkirk would be reading his Communist books or be stretched out in a drunken stupor while his lamp burned down. Flame would be his end, Maggie thought, and his destiny, too. Perhaps that was the moment it had all started, the moment he had come into their lives with his ideas and books and doctrines that he gave to others to live out for him. Why couldn't they ever see it, that they were only his dupes to live out his own cowardly life?

When she reached the Low Road leading out to Brumbie, the moon swifted through the clouds, there were patches of light and darkness and up ahead the blackness of trees. She was grateful. God watched out for lonely women on the road.

Lonely women on the road. Her mother was crazy and her father never knew. Never *knew*. Perhaps that was why she, Maggie, didn't like the night. Her mother would leave the house at night and not come back until dawn, and Maggie never wanted to know where she had been. But she came back smelling of oil and smoke and some of the stains on her clothes were blood, of that she was certain. There were wounds all over her body when they washed her down before her burial, and no one could explain them.

There were lights in Brumbie Hall. *They* could afford to burn them through the night, and there were dogs out there somewhere, chained and trained to bark. She would be their fox for the night.

Little fox teeth. She had always liked it when he said it. There was nothing wrong with him as a man, she thought, just that he had promised to go one way and now had gone the other, and for that he would have to pay. She had given her life for them and now they had chosen to throw it in the glaur and trample on it. For that they would have to pay.

There were patches of fog along the way, strips of fog floating up from the black river, fog shifting in the sporadic light from the moon and the darkness of shadows from the trees along the road, and then she was at Brothcock's house. She didn't hesitate at the door. She found the knocker and pounded it hard. She could hear it boom inside the house and the sound go down the road and cause the dogs to bark. When no one answered quickly enough, she pounded the knocker again, and finally a woman's head appeared at the window.

"What do you want? What are you doing?"

"I have got to see Mr. Brothcock at once."

"Mr. Brothcock is fast asleep. You must be crazy to come like this. Go home and come back in the morning."

"Go tell him Mrs. Cameron has come and it is an emergency. Tell him, or I'll pound the door until he does."

He came to the window as she had her hand on the knocker again.

"What in Christ do you want?"

"I want to sign the yellow-dog papers."

She could see even from below that he was confused, dazed by sleep, but interested, as she knew he would be.

"How do you mean, sign? What kind of pliskie is this?"

"There's no trick. I want to sign. I'm their mother and legal guardian. They can't legally sign a contract or an agreement of any kind until they're twenty-one. But I can sign for them."

"We don't want them. We don't want the sons of bitches in our mines."

"Oh, but you do, you see. Of all the names in Pitmungo, those are the names you want."

"Wait a minute," Brothcock said, and she heard him mumbling something and movements in the room and then there was a light and after a while the door opened and he told her to come in.

"Now, go over that again," he said, and she did. It made sense. What would happen to the morale of the Twenty-One when it was learned that Rob Roy Cameron, that Sam Cameron, that all the Camerons except Gillon had signed the yellow-dog agreement?

Had *been* signed, of course, a technicality that a great many people wouldn't grasp or want to grasp. The fact would be that the Cameron names were on the Mutual Trust Agreement and "the cause" was all fraud and deceit and sellout, which many people were anxious to believe it was if only to relieve the pressure of their own guilt.

The house smelled of fat. The fireplace seemed to be coated with it and there were grease stains all over the oily dressing gown Brothcock was wearing. He was wearing nothing underneath it, the bristles from the hair on his chest showed through an opening at the top and below it she could see part of his male organs.

"I want them to work," Maggie said. "I won't have them lying around my house while other men are in the pit. They're stealing the siller from my kist and stealing my life awa'."

He didn't understand what she was talking about, but he went into the next room with the light, leaving her in darkness. There were mice in the house, or rats. She could hear them licking the fat on the bricks by the fireplace. The people who live here are swine, she thought, and waited. Something ran over her foot and she leaped the least bit.

And I am dealing with swine, she thought, and it didn't bother her. That was the way it was. Brothcock was a swine but it didn't matter, he was merely the agent for the papers. He came back and the rats scuttered off as quickly as they had come.

"We call it, Mrs. Cameron, the Mutual Trust Agreement, not the yellow-dog papers."

When he plumped down again he exposed himself more than before and she realized what an ironic name he possessed.

"It is a crazy time to be doing business like this," the superintendent said, "but the ways of God are strange."

For some reason that struck him as immensely funny and he began to laugh, a rumbling hearty man's laugh.

"Do you know how to write?"

"Aye, I know how to write."

"Most of them don't," and he laughed again, remembering the tea at Brumbie Hall.

"What does your husband think of *this*?"

"He doesn't know. Why else do you think I came in the night?" Like your rats in the dark, she thought, and put it out of her mind.

"A fine man in his kilt," he said sarcastically. "Oh, he cut a figure there and made quite a wonderful fool of himself. You heard about the shoes, of course. All right, then. Let's have the names."

"Rob Roy Cameron."

He wrote it down, very laboriously. "Isn't *that* a fine name for a miner? You were thinking high, Mrs. Cameron, thinking high."

"Andrew Drum Cameron."

The scratch of the pen. The rats were darting out again, the fat too tempting.

"Samuel Sutherland Cameron."

"There's one who's going to get *his* handed to him one day, if I may say so. He's what we call a smairt-ass, like his younger brother."

One of the rats was standing in the ashes of the cold fireplace, on its hind legs, licking the bottom of an unwashed skillet. It was very clever the way the rat did it, Maggie thought, balancing himself by his tongue even while he was using it to lick the fats.

"He's dead, you understand," she said.

He didn't understand her.

"Jemmie Cameron's dead."

"The next one, now. Give me the name of the next one."

"Jemmie."

"That's not a name. I need the full Christian name." The superintendent was growing impatient.

"James Drum Cameron." She had gotten to her feet and was walking around the shadowy room in a distracted way that annoyed Mr. Brothcock.

"He's dead, you see. I can't sign the paper for him because he's dead," Maggie said. Mrs. Brothcock had come down the stairs and was standing on the landing.

"Something's wrong with her," she called to her husband. "Watch out for her; keep away from her. She's crazy."

"What am I doing here in all this fat?" She stood in front of Brothcock. "Do you remember when one of my sons told you to look out for your head?" She began to look carefully around the room for a poker or a coal shovel to strike him in the head but when she found her weapon, it was too late to do anything with it. Mr. Brothcock took her arm and twisted it until she felt it was breaking and she dropped the iron poker on the stone floor. The pain from her arm and the clatter of the iron on stone broke the trance she was in, the spell that held her, and the room began to come into focus again.

"Did I try to hit you?"

"You never had the chance."

"I didn't really want to hit you. I wanted to thank you. You taught me something." Mrs. Brothcock had come down from the landing and, staying away from Maggie, had edged around the room to the door and opened it.

"The door," she said. "Here's the door."

"Aye, I see it. Do you know what an unnatural mother is?" she said to Mrs. Brothcock. "Did you ever have any bairn of your own?"

Mrs. Brothcock didn't answer. Everyone in Pitmungo knew her children.

"Aye, well I'll tell you this much now. You were a better mother to them than I was to mine and you living down here with rats and fat and a swine like your husband."

"You're crazy, can you understand that?" Mr. Brothcock said. He wasn't hostile, it was stated as a fact. Maggie could appreciate that. "You're a very sick person, you're a danger. I'm going to tell Dr. Gowrie about you and he'll have to put you someplace."

"No, it will pass," Maggie said. "It will all pass now."

She knew she had been somewhere—her mind or her spirit, whatever it was—and that she wasn't all the way back yet. She hadn't wanted to use the word "swine," because it wasn't correct, but it had come of its own accord. She had wanted to break his head open like cracking the shell of an egg; it was what she had wanted, but the urge was gone now. The visions had come and gone; the room had come in and out of focus, and that was going now too.

"I wanted to crack your head like an egg and I'm ashamed for that and ask your pardon."

He didn't speak, and Mrs. Brothcock was still afraid of her, and that meant she must have been looking the wild way again. Mr. Brothcock rattled the papers in his hand.

"Aye, I'm going."

She could hear her father's voice as plainly as if he were in the room with her, the last words he had said to her before she left for Strathnairn and Gillon. That had never happened to her before.

"Never deny your own. In the end it's all you got."

As simple and clear as that and she could see that now.

"You'll want to sign these," Brothcock said.

Maggie looked at the papers as if she had never seen them before and it took an effort to remember what they were. It struck her then as singularly dumb of Mr. Brothcock that he would think she still would want to sign them.

"Have you been in this room with me? I've been here and I've not been here but you've been here. What in the name of God would make you think I'd want to sign any papers like these? No, we don't want to sign any papers like these."

"She's crazy," Mrs. Brothcock said. "Watch out for her, Hamish."

"You are crazy," he said.

"Was," Maggie said. "I was."

She wasn't all the way back from where she had been and even in the state she was in she knew that. But while it worried her, she didn't care how she was now because she sensed the worst was over with her and she was on her way back. Gillon would no longer have to be worried in his bed. That much of it was over. Mrs. Brothcock had wedged the door so that it stayed open without her having to be near it. People in Pitmungo thought madness was catching.

"You're a mother," Maggie said. "Think of a mother like me. I almost signed away the dignity of my dead boy to save a little siller. No, that's not true. To get even with him because he hurt me once. Now, that *would* be crazy, wouldn't you say?"

She went out the door and as Mrs. Brothcock ran to close it Maggie came back again, causing her to get behind the hulk of her husband.

"My shawl. Some people forget hats but I don't forget shawls."

"You also don't make any sense, do you know that?"

"That may be, but I will. And Mr. Brothcock. For such a very big man, you have a very tiny thing. I see much better than that at home."

And then he was angry.

They were all out searching for her, the way they had done for Jemmie the few weeks before. It was odd how the thinking went. They didn't go up on the moor but by instinct down to the river. If she did anything violent to herself, they knew it would be the water. It was Rob Roy who found her because he had moved back down to Doonietown and was farthest out along the Low Road when she came back from Brumbie.

"Och, Mother, we were worried about you."

"Aye, well, you had reason to be. I'm better, I think."

"You look better."

"I am better. I think I was sick for a while."

"Well, sick, yes. Something else."

"Gone awa'?"

"Yes, like that. Gone away for a while."

She wanted to tell him one thing, to tell just one person, in the hope that in telling it some of the pressure of it would be freed from her mind or spirit, this terrible pressing on her. "I never kissed Jemmie once, I never held him to me once." But she couldn't bring herself to say the words. There should be someone, she thought, a stranger you could go to and tell things like that to and the awful pressure would go away.

"It's why I left the house," Rob said. "I was afraid something might happen there."

"Yes, I understand. All that is gone now."

"The death of Jem and all. It was too much."

And so he had touched on the second of her shames. Jem's death had affected her more deeply than she had known it would, and it satisfied her to find she could feel, despite what was happening around her. But still she knew it was the loss of the siller that had driven her to the edge of her despair; not Jem, but the kist.

She wanted to say that, too. He would understand. Of all her sons Rob Roy was the one who always seemed to know, standing there at the edge of it all, watching. It was what had made her so angry with him at times. He *knew*.

They were making their way up by the Lady Jane mine and she had forgotten how black and filthy it all was. The sun was barely up, false dawn, and everything was gray and clarty and wet and black. For over twenty years she had sent her man down into this to fill up the box he was now emptying. It *was* his siller, after all.

"I want you to come home," she said to Rob Roy. "It's not right for you to live down here alone."

"I have my things."

"We'll send the wagon down."

He thought about it. He looked at her. There was a change, he knew that. Nothing terrible was going to happen now.

"All right, then. I'll do that."

"Yes, you come this afternoon. Will you do that, Rab?"

"Aye, this afternoon. You must be cold," he said, because she was shivering. She wasn't cold and she didn't know why she was shivering.

"I've lost one and now I want one back. Can you understand that? Is that selfish, Rab?"

He smiled at her.

"Aye, sure. All mothers should be selfish." He didn't know if she heard him.

"Because we have to stick together now."

"Yes to that."

"Because it's all we have. We're all we have left." She took his hand. She had never done that before.

They walked back up Colliers Walk. The mist was rising from the rows, and the town was beginning to stir itself to life again. He felt close to her, closer than he ever had. She was still a little bit away—he knew that—but not beyond recall. All he knew was that something had happened and it was probably for the better. He looked sideways at her and her face was at rest for the first time in a very long while. He had a feeling that she would be able to sleep, which she had not been doing, sleep for a long time, and when she got up she would be better still. They were picking up the others one by one on the way, and none of them said anything at all about the night to their mother. Her mind was somewhere else, and yet they knew it wasn't bad now, that the worst of it was passing, or had passed.

She had made up her mind that she wasn't going to tell about Jem and about the kist, those would be her medals of humility to wear in secret, to consult when she found herself getting out of hand, to wear in place of the key she used to wear until Gillon snapped it off her neck that night, nearly snapping her mind;

nearly breaking her heart. It was all right, they both would heal, her heart and head, she knew that, and maybe in the long run it would all be for the best. Time would have to tell.

It was a little embarrassing going up, all the Camerons together, because the men were coming down to go to work and they were ashamed to look the Camerons in the face.

"Say hello to them, nod to them, let them off the hook," their mother said. "They're good men even though they signed the papers. Everyone can't be Camerons."

17

THE TRIAL OF CAMERON V. FARQUHAR WAS not what the Camerons and the people of Pitmungo dreamed it would be.

The Earl of Fyffe wasn't hauled into Sheriff's Court like any common criminal. Instead he was represented there by a small clerk of a man named James Riddell, law agent for the Company's sales office in Cowdenbeath, who didn't even study the brief until the morning of the trial.

"Would you care to settle out of court and spare us all this boredom?" Mr. Riddell said. "We'll pay you fifty pounds and costs and I will assure you it is more than Sheriff Finletter will award you."

"I want my day in court," Gillon said. "I want to see justice done and precedent set."

"You should have studied law instead of being a collier," Mr. Riddell said.

Sheriff Finletter had been drinking. The smell of alcohol filled the Court, and he went on drinking. The water tumbler was dark glass and the pitcher was dark glass, so what was drunk could not be seen, only surmised. But the courtroom smelled like the College on pay night. Gillon was depressed and then Mr. MacDonald failed to appear.

"My law agent. Oh, my God, where is Mr. MacDonald? He wouldn't let me down." Gillon said in the hallway outside the court. He asked the court attendant and then Mr. Riddell, who merely smiled, and then he and the others ran out into the streets of Cowdenbeath searching for Mr. MacDonald.

"You didn't really expect him to come, did you?" Mr. Selkirk said.

"Aye, yes, yes."

"He doesn't care about *your* compensation. You have to grow up about things like that," Mr. Selkirk said. Gillon was amazed. "Once the solidarity was broken they had no need for you any more." When Gillon came back inside the court his case was being called.

"Sir, I have no law agent for my case."

"You can speak the Queen's English, can't you?"

"Yes, sir."

"Then you're a law agent. Get on with it. How did it happen?"

"Well, I was in my room in the—" Gillon began.

"I thought you were a coal miner?"

"We call the place where we work a room, sir, or a stall."

"Use stall. Less confusion. Water."

Gillon described, in good and solid detail, how the pick came through the wall and was embedded in his shoulder.

"Rather ghastly, I would say," the sheriff said, showing some interest in the case. It was, he noted, a little different from the roof falling on one's head.

Mr. Brothcock was called, and attempted to prove that Gillon should not have been in that particular room at all.

"Why not? Got any evidence to prove it?"

"No, sir, not in the strictest sense. As superintendent of the mine I would simply *know* it."

There was an outburst of laughter in the court, from all of the Camerons and Mr. Selkirk and some of the Twenty-One who

had come down to Cowdenbeath to see their Laird take his drub-
bing. There is a telling truth in laughter, spontaneous laughter,
that can't be imitated or denied.

"When is the last time you were down pit besides this day?"
Sheriff Finletter asked. How brilliant, Gillon thought, how right
to the point the man had gone. He felt heartened by the display
of justice in a land of laws.

"Well," Brothcock said. "Well, now."

"Remember, sir, and remember it well, the penalty for perjury
before the court. If you're not familiar with it, the clerk will read
it to you."

They read it to him. Five years in jail and/or five hundred
pounds sterling.

"It is not in the nature of my duties to go down pit every day,
Your Honor—"

The laugh once more.

"I should tell them not to laugh," the sheriff said, to no one in
particular, "but it has a certain value. *When?*"

Brothcock flushed in that angry way. He put a finger to his
temple and stared up at the ceiling of the courtroom.

"You are a little hefty for the pit, I would observe," Finletter
said.

"Your Honor," Mr. Riddell said, "because a man is built like
a—like a—"

"Grumphie," Selkirk said.

"I object to that, Your Honor."

"Sustained. Built like a what? Can you think of a *better* word?"

They settled on heavy.

"Oh, twenty years ago," Brothcock said.

"And how many colliers do you have?"

"About eight hundred, sir."

"And you know where all of them are all the time underground?"

"Yes, sir."

"More water," the sheriff ordered the clerk.

They went through, in a minute or two, the procedure for clearing a room and breaking through the wall into the next stall. One went into the next room, saw it was empty, left some kind of marker by the wall that was to be broken through, and went back and chipped into the next stall.

"And did you check the other stall?" Elphinstone was now on the stand.

"Oh no, sir, not at all, sir, we never checked, sir—in no manner."

"A 'no' will do. And did you *chip*?"

"We did *not*. We were *encouraged* to *smash* away at the wall —oh, God, it was awful—and *I* had to be the one smashing when my pick flew through the wall and embedded itself in this poor chap's shoulder. Well, I, of course, immediately—"

"Do you want to hear the rest of the story?" Finletter asked Gillon.

"No, sir. I would prefer to forget it."

"You, sir, can step down."

"Step down? Me? Is that it, then? All the way up from Edinburgh for . . . for *this*?"

"You've done enough, have you not?"

"Awfully sorry," Elphinstone said to Gillon as he passed down the aisle on his way out. "Can't begin to tell you how sorry I am. I'll certainly never go down a pit again. Dreadful."

"What are you asking for?" the sheriff asked.

"Four hundred pounds damages, sir."

"Ridiculous!" Riddell said.

"What did they want to settle for?"

"Forty pounds, sir."

"Ridiculous!" the sheriff said.

"We offered fifty just this morning, Your Honor," Riddell said.

"Oh, so you admit you're guilty? Into the chambers."

They made Gillon take off his shirt and they looked at the wound and the atrophied arm.

"The money is important, sir, but what I want to accomplish

is the right of a man to sue for damages, to get his compensation not at the whim of the master but through the rule of law."

"Humph. You *are* a law agent. Awful-looking thing. What is all that black?"

"They stuff coal dust in the wound to stop the flow of blood, sir."

"Ugh, ugh, ugh. Water! Why *do* men insist upon going into pits?"

"Hunger, Your Honor, is a good master," Gillon said. It pleased the sheriff and they went back into the courtroom.

"Now, that was well stated," Finletter said. "You state well for a collier, most of them come in here and grunt. Don't know what's the matter with 'em. Well, you've made your point."

"And then there is the matter of the yellow-dog contracts, sir." The sheriff looked tired and sad. He called Brothcock to the bench and they could see the superintendent nodding and saying yes, sir, and then Brothcock turned and left the court.

"That's the end of *that*. End of your yellow-dog thing. Where are you from again?" the sheriff said.

"Pitmungo, sir."

"I've never gone there. It must be the black hole of Scotland. One hundred and forty pounds damages."

There was a sucking in of air in the court. It was better than any of them had hoped for.

"I must warn you, Your Honor, that I intend to appeal that judgment," Riddell said.

"Appeal? Appeal to what? Don't you want to bring another case into this court and win it?"

"Yes, Your Honor."

"Then if I were you I would have a check made out and forget about appeal. I don't like appeals." He smiled very sweetly for a florid-faced man. "I like water. Water!" The clerk came running.

They began filing out of the court.

"Pitmungo. I don't like the name," he said, to no one. "Good God, it must be a dreadful place. Next."

18 THERE WAS NOTHING LEFT TO DO AFTER THE trial but go. That was understood. The precedent had been established and they had to pay for the establishing of it. The law might guarantee the return of the miner to his pit but not the quality of his life in it afterward. It might not be worth the living. It was time to go.

Andrew was sent down to Glasgow to buy their passage. That was the kind of thing Andrew did, solid and reliable work; he'd get the best berths on the best ship for the best price, everyone knew that, and then it would be good-bye to Scotland; there was no future there for the Camerons any more.

Time to go. They still had their wagon and their horse; those Andrew would sell in Glasgow when they got there, and when they put all their things in the wagon it would be astonishing how little all the years had left them. What better reason than that to go? What was there, really, to lose now?

And what, really, to leave behind? A table and a dresser, some beds that were never very good. A house they couldn't buy and a piece of land up in the cemetery where Jemmie lay naked in the clay, fast becoming earth himself. And almost nothing else after a combined family total of almost a hundred years underground, after cutting enough coal to make a tunnel from Pitmungo to Calcutta, Andrew figured, or to light the city of London for three days and nights.

Nothing to be sorry for, nothing to cry about, unless you included one's lost youth and one's lost life. Or one's lost love.

Sam was the one they worried about, and watched. He had

promises to keep and the old wild darkness seemed to have come on him again. But while Sam was planning, it was Andrew who was brooding. Ever since his return from Glasgow with the bookings for America, the loss that he was about to experience was growing unbearable. It was stronger in him, the sense of leaving, because he had been on the wooden decks of the ship that would take them away from Scotland forever. To the others, no matter how realistic they tried to be, the leaving was still a piece of a dream they only imagined; but to Andrew it was real and final. The Sunday before they were due to pack the wagon, after their kail soup and bread—knowing that he could be making a fool of himself and for once in his life not caring—he went down Tosh-Mungo Terrace to ask Walter Bone for permission to talk to his daughter.

"That you have," Mr. Bone said, "and always will have, but I don't know if she wants to talk with you."

But she did, and they walked along the Terrace and up to the edge of the orchard, where they could be in the trees and still look down on all of Pitmungo. They didn't talk on the way up and when they stopped Andrew still didn't know how to begin. She was patient. There was no pressure on him to say anything and at last he found the way to get around to it. He pointed down at the dark hillsides and drab rows of Pitmungo.

"Is that enough for you?" Andrew said. How often his mother had said the same thing.

"Aye, yes, that's enough for me." But she was puzzled by what he meant.

"To grow up and live and die here? Never to know anything better than this?"

"I'd like something better, I think, I don't know, I've never tried it. What do you want? What are you trying to say?"

"What I'm trying to say is . . . what I am getting around to. Och." He opened his jacket pocket and took out one of the steamship tickets, exciting-looking official-feeling pieces of cardboard, with the picture of a gigantic oceangoing vessel underneath the words on the ticket and at the top, in red letters: "NEW YORK." Alyson studied the ticket.

"It's very heady." She handed the ticket back to Andrew but he put it back in her hand.

"It's yours," he said. And then he felt he had to add: "If you want it."

"What do you mean, it's mine if I want it?"

"What I said."

"But what *did* you say?"

"I said you could have the ticket. It's yours if you want it."

"Why?" She was genuinely bewildered. "Why would anyone do that?"

Andrew thought about it and the best way of saying it.

"Because he wanted you to go to America with him."

"Who?"

"Och, Alyson. *Me.*"

She began to laugh. She was a gentle person and didn't mean to laugh that way but it couldn't be helped. He stood there frozen, red in the face, unable to respond in any way.

"Why would you do that?"

He tried to say the words but they sounded absurd in his mouth. *Because I love you.* He finally did say them and as he said them they sounded the way he feared they would. The terrible part was that she heard it, the absurdity of them, and it caused her, against her will, to laugh again.

"Oh, Andrew, you don't love me. Not really love me. You wouldn't tell me the secret—no, your family came first. If you loved me you would have told me, Andrew, but you didn't love me enough, you know that. And you wouldn't ask my father for permission to tell me you love me if you really loved me. You'd just *tell* me."

I do though, you don't know, I do, Andrew told himself, it was just a style he had, a way.

"And you wouldn't bribe me with a ticket to come to America,

496

Andrew. You could have me with your love but not with a ticket to New York."

"It wasn't a bribe!" Andrew said. He shouted it at her and she waited a moment until he was calmer. The lights were going on all down the valley. Sometimes they looked warm and cheery but now they looked like oily orange smudges in the smoky valley.

The winding wheel at Lord Fyffe No. 1 was turning, sending a cage down. That shouldn't be, Andrew thought; not on Sunday night. Someone was going down into the pit illegally. The wheel was turning very slowly, almost silently; the cage was almost drifting down the shaft. Unless you looked very closely, you wouldn't see that it was turning at all. Andrew felt a sense of fear but he was helpless to do anything about it.

They walked a little way into the orchard, and Andrew was afraid that he was going to start crying, from fear of what Sam was doing or for the loss of Alyson, but no tears came.

"I do, you know," he said, when it was dark beneath the thick-leaved apple trees and the shadows guarded his face.

"Do what?"

"Love you."

"Oh, but you see, Andrew? You can barely bring yourself to *say* it. I don't say you can't love. Your parents, yes, and Sarah. And Jemmie, oh, yes. Do you know what I think?" She let go of his hand. "I think you can only really love a Cameron." They had been sitting but Alyson got up.

"No, I couldn't marry a boy like you," he heard her say, because he couldn't see her in those shadows, not meaning the hurt in the words, only stating a truth. "I'm going down now. Would you care to kiss me?"

"Do you know that's one thing Jemmie said when he was dying? He never kissed a girl and wondered what it was like."

"It's all right if you don't want to."

"No, I guess I don't want to. It doesn't seem fair now."

She stood outside the cover of the trees and he could see again how beautiful she was. Maybe, he thought, she was right, that was why he wanted her, the most beautiful thing in Pitmungo.

"Well, good-bye, Andrew, then. Good luck to you in America," she said and started down the path.

"I'll never forget you, Alyson."

"No. Nor me you," she said, and he sat there not moving until she was gone. For a long time he sat in the orchard thinking that what he wanted most in the world would be to trade places with Jemmie in the earth, and finally he got to his feet and suddenly patted his pocket and was relieved to feel the stiffness of the pasteboard. It would have been humiliating to have to go down to the Bone house and ask her to give it back.

It was long after midnight when he came out of the orchard and went down to the Terrace. He went very quietly into the house and straight up to the room, and he felt his stomach tighten. Sam was not at home. On his bed was the book, the *Highland Clearances* book, Sam's dangerous book. Sam's madness book. It was open and he took it downstairs where he could read in it without waking the others.

The section was outlined in red and black ink, scrawled on, tortured over. He read:

> We are not unacquainted with the Celtic character as developed in the Highlands of Scotland. Highlanders, up to a certain point, are the most docile, patient, enduring men; but that point once passed, endurance ceases and the all too gentle lamb starts up an angry lion. The spirit is stirred and maddens at the sight of the naked weapon, and that, in its headlong rush upon the enemy, discipline can neither check nor control. Let the oppressors of our Highlands beware.

Below that, in the margin of the book, in a handwriting so strong that the pen had gone through the page, Sam had scrawled: *Do what the blood commands.*

.   .   .

It was almost dawn when Sam came in, in his pit clothes, covered with pit dirt from head to toe.

"Where have you been?" Andrew said.

He seemed at ease, but Andrew couldn't tell. His teeth glittered in his black face.

"Saying good-bye to the mine."

"And what did you do to it?"

"Nothing."

"We have a right to know. If you did what I think you did, it could be the destruction of some of us."

He didn't seem bothered. He seemed to be his old self, cocky Sam, a little arrogant, a little playful, and yet Andrew sensed it was all designed to hide some other, more private feelings.

Sam moved swiftly around the but getting water for his tub and to wash his pit clothes.

"Now," he said, "I'm going to tell you something and I expect you to believe me. No one is going to be stopped leaving this town, no one is going to be waiting for us in Glasgow to take us off our boat. Now I don't know what's happened to you but you look sick to me and I suggest you crawl into your own little trundle bed and get some sleep."

There was nothing to do about it anyway, Andrew thought, he might as well sleep, and he was starting up the stairs to his room when Sam touched him on the back.

"Andrew?"

"Yes."

"Would you like a good book to read before falling asleep?"

The old Sam. Or was it? Andrew couldn't tell. He thought, when he got into bed, that now would be a good time to cry, and he tried. He tried for Sam and what the life here had turned him into and what it had forced him to do and then he tried for Jem and for leaving Pitmungo, which, as black as it had all turned out, was his birthplace. And then he tried to cry for himself and for Alyson Bone; he tried until the sun came up and he heard the men gathering out on the Terrace preparing to start down the hill to the mines. The Twenty-One would be going back to work this morning, Andrew thought, their battle over and won, and now only the Camerons were left. It was sad, all of it, he thought, and almost managed a tear or two before he fell asleep.

It took them less than an hour to pack the wagon and they were ready to go. One of the unhappy things—or one of the blessings, depending on how you saw it—in leaving a coal town is that there is almost no one to see you go, the men thousands of feet underground and the women in the back of their houses at work. Before eight o'clock in the morning they shut the door on No. 1 Tosh-Mungo Terrace and prodded Brothcock, the pony, and the wagon, with the Camerons stretched out behind, started down Tosh-Mungo Terrace. A few people were out to see them go but not many of them had much to say beyond the standard "Good luck's" and "Good trip's." The truth was that Pitmungo was pleased to see them leave. They had become a wound in the collective memory and now there would be time to heal.

No one seemed envious of their going because none of them had ever considered going anywhere. They were *there*, locked to Pitmungo as tight as the coal below it. Whatever it was that Sam had done, there was no sign that anyone had found it or that he had, in fact, done anything at all. But at Colliers Walk there was a surprise for them. Sarah was there with Sandy Bone.

"We want to come with you," Sandy said. "We don't want to stay here forevermore. Do you have the money to take us? I know we can pay you back."

Andrew fingered the extra ticket in his jacket. The irony of it, that it would be used by another Bone in the end, his sister's love and not his own.

"Can we do it?" Maggie asked him, and he pondered a moment,

adding money in his mind, seeing Alyson in Sandy's face, and nodded that they could.

"Help the man onto the cart," Maggie said, and they knew then for certain that whatever had happened to Maggie that night, the change in her was more than mere talk. They were buying a ticket to America for Walter Bone's boy.

"Why didn't you ask sooner?" Sam said.

"I don't know. Afraid, I guess," Sandy said, and glanced at his mother-in-law.

"I don't think you need to be any more, not the old way," Andrew said to him, and they started down Colliers Walk. Almost no one was in the Walk and almost no one came out of the rows. They should have been happy, getting out, the dream of so many men who have spent too much of their lives underground.

Going to America!

But an unaccountable sadness held them. So much of themselves had been left behind in this dark place.

"I thought we might go out by way of the graveyard," Gillon said, "but I don't think the wagon would hold." They had planted a slip of the Scotch pine at the foot of his grave and that would have to say it for them. Jem would have liked that. So they went down the regular way, down across the Sportin Moor, where the tipple now stood, down through the old rows below it, down Miners Row from where Maggie had started north toward Strathnairn so long before, and where they had lived with the Drums and the children had been born and spent their childhoods, what little there is to them in mine towns.

"A little different from the way we came in," Gillon said to Maggie. "There's no one at the gate to hold us in."

"Do you remember you took my hand coming down from the moor that day?"

"Oh, aye."

"You could do that again."

"Are you afraid like we were then?"

"Yes, aye. Afraid."

"So am I," Gillon said. No one held hands in Pitmungo, but they did, down through Rotten Row and Wet Row, and past the Coaledge Tavern where some men on the backshift were drinking in the morning, nodding to them; still holding hands down past the Industrial Workers' Reading Room while Mr. Selkirk slept, his best pupils on their way to the new land, and then on past Lady Jane No. 2, where Gillon was first dropped down into the darkness of the pit a generation before.

"Well, was it a waste, all of it?" Maggie said.

"How can a man answer that? It was a life. Is life a waste?"

"I don't know yet," Maggie said.

There was Brumbie Hall off to the right when they reached the Low Road by the river, but Gillon didn't want to look up that way any more than Maggie wanted to look beyond the hall to the Brothcock house behind it. For all of it, good things had happened in those houses to both of them, but the experiences that had brought them about were still too painful to be thought about. They went on, not turning around, and when Gillon finally did turn for his last look at Pitmungo, Pitmungo was gone.

"You know what that marker stands for, don't you?" Sandy Bone called down. "We're legally in Cowdenbeath country now. And you know what that means, man? We're free. We are *free*." He was the happiest of them all.

19

THE TRIP TO GLASGOW WAS A HARD ONE, RAIN part of every day, their clothes constantly wet, and once they were forced to crawl under the wagon to hide from the stinging ice shot of a savage hailstorm that left them chilled. But they made it to the city, looking more like a band of Gypsies every day, and out to Clydebank two days ahead of sailing time, and were allowed to go on board if they didn't ask to eat. It was a large ship, the *Clunie Castle*, a grain hauler that fit in a few passengers as if they were extra sacks of barley.

Gillon felt re-born being on water again; it was, he thought, where he was meant to be. All the months before he had felt like a stranger, but now he was back in the world. And he was in command of his family once more because this world was his world and he knew his way around in it.

"America, is it?" a sailor said. "I wouldn't be doing any dances about it if I was you. Why do you think I'm here? They got as much hunger over there as we got over here."

But they wouldn't let it discourage them. A new feeling of excitement was beginning to seize them. All that was holding it in check was the knowledge that the only one of them who had yearned to make the journey was lying in the coal and clay of Pitmungo.

It wasn't fair, Andrew thought. God wasn't fair. He didn't know if he wanted to go on believing in Him. And he kept watching Sam, and streets leading to the wharf and the harbor area, for police. But even with that fear always with him, he began to feel the excitement, too. He had gotten good money for the horse and the wagon, enough to pay the extra two passages, and that made it easier for his mother to take, although she was taking it well as it was.

By the rising of the tide and the movement of the currents in the harbor Gillon knew when they would go.

"They'll be hauling anchor in an hour, we'll be going then," he told the family and when they did, the great anchor crawling up from the muck of the harbor on schedule, they were impressed with their father. The anchor up, and then the *Clunie Castle* backing out of her berth, deep-throated horn bellowing the news to the city, sliding out into the oily Clyde, slipping slowly down past Clydeside headed toward the sea.

They all were excited then, even Maggie, out on the deck, waving to strangers they would never meet, crowded on a small deck behind the seamen's work area, watching the river towns approach and fade from view. The ship was burning cheap coal and sulfurous fumes drifted down on them from the stack overhead.

"How do you stand it out there?" a seaman asked. "No one comes out here until we hit the open sea."

"We mined the crap, man. We ate it for breakfast," Sam told him.

"It's our fate," Rob Roy said. "We're taking Pitmungo with us."

By midday they were out in the Firth of Clyde and they had their first intimations of the open seas to come. That excited them too, and put a little fear in them. There were moments when they couldn't see the shore. The wind was stronger in the firth and the fumes spewed backward over their heads and it was better after that.

"You'd better start looking hard now," Gillon warned the family, "because this is the last look you're ever going to have of old Scotland."

It still hadn't reached them, the completeness of the cutting off. As long as there was Scotland out there, little towns with people in them that they could understand and be understood by, the cord had not been cut. For a time there was no land in sight and they thought it was the end of it all and they were sad about it because it had come too fast. But then in the afternoon the Island of Arran rose on their right, all moorland and timber, enormous sweeps of green grazing lands and clabbers of clouds bumping their way along the sides like pregnant cows and they let up a cheer because they had their Scotland again.

"You'll never see country like that again," Gillon told them. They heard the pride in it. "That's Highland country."

"Is that what it's like where you came from?" Sandy Bone asked and Gillon nodded.

"Whatever made you leave?" Rob Roy said. "How could you ever leave that for Pitmungo?"

Gillon waited until they were looking toward land and looked down at Maggie. She was smiling. For a time the clouds covered the sun and turned the sea a dark jade green the way the sea around Strathnairn had so often been.

"That's about the last of Scotland," Gillon said to Emily.

"I don't care," she said.

"You're not sad?" Emily troubled him.

"I just hope it's better where we go. I want to go to school. Can I go to school in America?"

Gillon wasn't sure what the children did in America. But he said, "Aye, Emily, you can go to school."

When they came on deck after eating their lamb stew, the worst lamb stew ever served at sea according to Rob Roy, an expert at matters like that, Arran was gone and there was only the sea.

"All right, Scotland's behind us," Andrew said to Sam. "What did you do down in Lord Fyffe?"

"I told you."

"I don't believe you. I saw you come home. It was fire, wasn't it. Some device you left in the mine."

Sam didn't answer him.

"One of those acid things that eats through the container and touches off some black powder. The mine's on fire now, isn't it?" Still he said nothing. "Christ, man, I saw the books you had."

Sam finally turned on Andrew.

"Aye, it *was* fire. That's what I wanted but I couldn't do it, you see that? I failed us. I failed Jem. Oh, Christ, what a mess of it I made."

Andrew was excited then.

"You didn't leave the box then?" Sam shook his head. Andrew had never seen his brother look sadder, not even after the death of Jem.

"I wanted to leave it. Something wouldn't let me."

"Yes, but that's just it, don't you see it, Sam? A Cameron couldn't do that. Set fire to the mine. You could have killed men down there, Sam. Hundreds of men out of work. Families broken apart. You couldn't do that, Sam."

"Jem would have done it," Sam said. "He would have gone down and seen justice done," but Andrew kept shaking his head and gradually Sam became quiet because he began to understand that Andrew was right.

"Do you know what I am? I'm sick to death of being a Cameron. Can you understand that?"

"Aye. And you know another thing? There's not a thing in the world you can do about it."

If the weather held Gillon knew they would see the shores of Scotland a last time, and in the gloaming, the late evening sun touching its steep walls, the foot of Kintyre came out of the sea like an enormous ship bearing down on them.

"Last call for Scotland," Gillon called down into the sleeping quarters and all the family came back up on deck. There wasn't much to see but it was the last of it, the very last, and so it was important. A fishing village huddled under high cliffs and the captain loosed a blast from his steam horn. It probably was a ritual, a salute to the last of Scotland before heading out beyond. It sent a shiver down his back.

"Did you know your family has a slogan," Gillon told the family. They kept looking at Scotland dropping away from them but they were listening.

He said it in Gaelic first, pleased with himself for still being able to say it, remembering the fight with his father when he had made him memorize it. They never told him what each word meant, only that he had to say the slogan by rote the way a parrot might.

Chlanna nan con thigibh a so's gheibh sibh féoil

They were impressed with their father again.

"Sons of the hounds, come here and get flesh."

It meant nothing to them and yet something at the same time. They had had their flesh and lost it and now they were on their way, trying to win it again.

"Why didn't you ever say that before?" Maggie asked him.

"I never saw any reason to."

But she seemed moved by it and said the words several times and Sandy Bone seemed the most moved.

"I want to become a Cameron," he said. They didn't understand him. "I want to change my name. My children will be half Cameron anyway."

It was embarrassing and flattering at the same time. How can a man go about denying another man the use of his name?

"You want to be a son of the hounds then?" Sam said.

"Aye, that's what I want."

"Then you are one," Gillon said.

Kintyre was all but lost to them then, a black shadow to the east but still there. They were leaving the North Channel, entering open sea, and the water off the Mull of Kintyre was rough. Gillon could feel the sweep of open water under the hull and the cargo of grain was shifting lightly with it, causing the ship to roll.

"So you're not going to be sick?" Gillon said to Maggie. "This is as rough as it ever was at Strathnairn."

The boys and girls had all taken their turns at being sick. Ian had been curled up like a little animal since the morning.

"Getting sick is for the young and spirited. When they're still alive inside for that. I'm too old for it. I've outgrown it."

At first he was sympathetic and said nothing and finally was surprised to find he was angry with her. He pulled her away from the rest of the family.

"You haven't outgrown anything," Gillon said to her. "You're dying too soon. Don't start dying on me before your time. You're only forty—you're not even forty. You have no *right* to say that. Now you owe *me* some years."

The lighthouse at the point of the mull had been lit and while they couldn't see Scotland they could still see a glimmer from it.

"Oh, I was frightened that night," Maggie suddenly said. "When Drysdale's light swept over us." Gillon was amazed.

"You were? Frightened then? You never told me."

"I thought I was going to drown."

"You never told me."

"No, I never told you."

They knew they were touching on something very deep to them that they would probably never find the words for.

"I should have told you," Maggie said. "I see that now. But I don't know if I knew."

"I was frightened too."

"I know."

"We could have helped each other."

"I know."

The light was more powerful than they first had suspected and during its sweep the beams passed over the ship like light through the wings of a moth, seeming to dust it with a soft eerie glow. It was deep into gloaming tide then.

"About that not being alive. You owe a lot more living than that," Gillon said.

"To who?" Gillon pointed to their children lined along the railing of the deck, all of them staring back at the light.

"They can fend for themselves now." He was angry with her again, for making himself reveal himself this way. He seized her wrist and hurt her.

"Ah, Maggie. To me. To *me*."

Some of the children turned to look at their father and turned back to the sea, but Rob Roy came across the deck toward them.

"Well, it's gone," Rob said. "Farewell to Scotland, land of poortith and porritch. It better be better beyond." He took a bottle from his jacket pocket. "And farewell to usquebaugh too." He dropped the bottle over the side into the sea and looked at his parents.

"It makes a nice gesture, Rob, it makes a beautiful act."

"It's no act."

"Time will tell," his mother said.

"Aye, time always tells."

The others came along the rail. The water ahead was black, it was true night now, and time to go down. It had been a long day. They said good night. Sarah had been crying but none of the others showed any special emotion at leaving their homeland behind them. They went down to the dining room to play cards before getting into their hammocks. He wanted to hold Maggie's hand and when he reached for it on the railing he didn't feel it, and when he turned he found she had left him and he felt a sadness that was touched with bitterness. He wouldn't go down to her then and so he stayed at the rail and watched the phosphorescent waves wash up against the sides of the ship and explode in stars. Then he heard her come back up the stairs, it was hard to see, there were no lanterns lit and he thought he saw the movement and then was certain he saw the splash in the sparkles of the wave and the swift creaming of the water before the sea closed over again.

"What was that you did?" Gillon said. "What was that you threw?"

"You know."

He tried to think but nothing came to his mind.

"Oh, God, Gillon. The kist, man. The kist."

The way it was the day he had met her, he had nothing at all to say. Her sacrifice had gone beyond any words he had.

"Now, this is what I think," Maggie finally said. Gillon looked out to sea. It was better, he had come to think, not to look at a person trying to tell you something.

"I've thought about it. I think I could be happy but I don't know," Maggie said. "I've never tried before."

Ahead of them, Gillon knew, the Hebrides lay but he would never see them now and that was a shame because he had always wanted to see them.

"Then you can try."

"Yes, that's what I can do." She made him, with the force of herself, look at her. "But, I can't change all that much, you know. Can you understand that, Gillon."

"Aye, I can understand."

They were out beyond the protection of Kintyre by then, nothing but the sweep of the Atlantic Ocean ahead of them, and America at the end of it. Scotland was over; Scotland was behind them.

"But I can try," Maggie said, and ran a finger along the back of Gillon's hand and went down the steps to sleep.

A NOTE ON THE TYPE

This book was set on the Linotype in Granjon, a type named in compliment to Robert Granjon, type cutter and printer—in Antwerp, Lyons, Rome, Paris—active from 1523 to 1590. Granjon, the boldest and most original designer of his time, was one of the first to practice the trade of type founder apart from that of printer.

Linotype Granjon was designed by George W. Jones, who based his drawings on a face used by Claude Garamond (1510–1561) in his beautiful French books. Granjon more closely resembles Garamond's own type than do any of the various modern faces that bear his name.

Composed, printed and bound by
The Haddon Craftsmen, Inc., Scranton, Pa.

Typography and binding design by
Virginia Tan